anet and Colin Bord have
3ritain's mysterious heritage,
Guide to Ancient Sites in Brit
nd – most recently – *Ancient*
    From their home in Wale
devoted to rural Britain, prehistoric sites and
nomena. They are now compiling a guide to *Modern Mysteries*
f the World.

C000281454

By the same authors

Mysterious Britain
Mazes and Labyrinths of the World
The Secret Country
A Guide to Ancient Sites in Britain
Alien Animals
Bigfoot Casebook
Earth Rites
The Evidence for Bigfoot and other Man-Beasts
Sacred Waters
Ancient Mysteries of Britain

JANET AND COLIN BORD

Modern Mysteries
of Britain

One Hundred Years of Strange Events

GRAFTON BOOKS

A Division of the Collins Publishing Group

LONDON GLASGOW
TORONTO SYDNEY AUCKLAND

Grafton Books
A Division of the Collins Publishing Group
8 Grafton Street, London W1X 3LA

Published by Grafton Books 1988

First published in Great Britain by
Grafton Books 1987

ISBN 0-586-06529-6

Printed and bound in Great Britain by
William Collins Sons & Co. Ltd, Glasgow

Photoset in Linotron Imprint by
Rowland Phototypesetting Ltd
Bury St Edmunds, Suffolk

Contents

Introducing Britain's mysteries

It was not until we began seriously researching this book that even *we* realized just how mysterious a place Britain is. In fact it threatened to be a book without end, because there is simply too much material, and we had finally to limit our coverage. We decided to omit those events that are essentially personal in nature, and to concentrate on those that are linked to a certain place. Therefore we have omitted reincarnation, metal-bending and other psycho-kinetic phenomena, possession and exorcism, out-of-the-body experiences, spiritualist phenomena and so on. We have also had to limit the number of UFOs and ghosts we could include, so we have in both cases concentrated on the most interesting reports available to us. The phenomena we have included cover a wide range of events, from encounters with phantom hitch-hikers to sightings of ball lightning, and we feel the book gives a taste of the mysterious happenings occurring in Britain today. If you wish to experience mysteries for yourself, the best county to be in is undoubtedly Devon, which for some unknown reason has a much higher number of strange events than any other county. If you want to find out whether anything strange has happened during the last century in any area well known to you, please consult the Gazetteer for the relevant county, where you will find in brief all the cases described in the main chapters, plus many others we could not find room for. There is also a Chronological List of Strange Events which shows what happened when, covering 1885 to 1985.

Of course, we have not been able to include every strange event that ever happened in Britain during that period, not only because there are too many, but because we do not know about all of them. So if you have personal knowledge of other similar events which are not described here, please send us the details for possible use in a subsequent edition of this book. We would also welcome the help of readers in correcting any inaccuracies that may have crept in. We have tried to give all the facts correctly, but inevitably errors will have been made, as so much diverse material from such a wide variety of sources has been included. We have not been able to check all the facts ourselves, and have had to rely on other people having the standard of accuracy that we would hope to maintain. Sometimes press reports have to be relied on, and we realize that they are not always dependable. However, material whose source we know to be unreliable has not been used.

We would also be interested to hear from anyone who has access to photographs of strange phenomena, since we run the Fortean Picture Library, supplying illustrations to researchers and the media. We will be glad to give our professional opinion of photographs sent to us, but please write in the first instance, giving brief details. All correspondence, whether about mysterious events or photographs, should be sent to us c/o Grafton Books, 8 Grafton Street, London W1X 3LA.

Because of space limitations, we have been unable to delve deeply into any one case, much as we would like to have done so, and readers wishing to know more should continue their reading in the source books and magazines indicated. For up-to-date coverage of mysteries around the world, *Fortean Times* (address in Bibliography) is essential reading. We have extracted many strange cases from its pages, and wish to thank editors Bob Rickard and Paul Sieveking for their tireless work in producing the magazine, and for making their material available to us. Also we thank the many researchers whose work is acknowledged in the Notes, and Ivan Bunn, Michael Goss, Paul Screeton, Doc Shiels, Bob Skinner, Nigel Watson and Dr K. J. Weston, who all answered our questions promptly and cheerfully. The following kindly allowed us to quote copyright material:

Dr G. T. Meaden (from *Journal of Meteorology*), Orbis Publishing Ltd (from *The Unexplained*), Dr Anne Ross, Mrs Nellie Thomas, Mike Williams.

Thanks also to the picture sources:

Picture credits

1. Celestial garbage

Can fish really fall from the sky? John Lewis of Aberdare (Mid Glamorgan) thought so:

> On Wednesday, February 9 [1859], I was getting out a piece of timber . . . when I was startled by something falling all over me – down my neck, on my head, and on my back. On

Ron Langton holds two of the six fishes found on the roof of his house in East Ham, London, on 28 May 1984. Other finds were reported from Canning Town, not far away. The fish were identified as flounders and smelts and may have fallen in a heavy rainstorm the previous night.

9

putting my hand down my neck I was surprised to find they were little fish. By this time I saw the whole ground covered with them. I took off my hat, the brim of which was full of them. They were jumping all about. They covered the ground in a long strip about 80 yards by 12, as we measured afterwards . . . My mates and I might have gathered bucketsful of them, scraping with our hands.[1]

Someone suggested that a hoaxer had thrown the fish as a practical joke, but who would go to the trouble of collecting thousands of young minnows (for this is what a British Museum scientist identified them as), and be able to throw them unseen over such a large area, in order to play a practical joke? This hypothetical hoaxer has kept busy since 1859, too, for there have been many reported fish-falls since that date.

It does not appear to have been raining during the Aberdare fish-fall, though it usually is raining during similar events. At Hendon, a suburb of Sunderland (Tyne and Wear), on 24 August 1918, a heavy shower caused a group of allotment-holders to take shelter in their sheds, from where they saw small fish falling in the rain. The fall lasted for about ten minutes and covered about a third of an acre, several hundred fish being found on the ground. They were identified as sand-eels and they were stiff, some breaking on hitting the ground, suggesting that they had been out of water for some time.[2] By comparison, the frogs that sometimes fall in the rain are always alive, and they have been seen hopping away into the gutters and ditches in their hundreds, apparently unaffected by their miraculous descent from the heavens. On very rare occasions have falls of frogspawn and tadpoles been recorded. One such case occurred in June 1979 in Bedford, where Vida McWilliam of Marten Road found frogspawn and also tiny frogs. She did not actually see them fall but found them during the week after a wet Sunday – there were tiny frogs all over the lawn, and frogspawn hanging in the bushes.[3] It has often been suggested that frogs seen after a rainstorm did not come down from the sky; they were already present on the ground, hiding under leaves and in crevices, and came out into the open when rain began to fall. But it is unlikely that so many

One of the tiny frogs found in a Bedford garden in June 1979, and presumed to have fallen from the sky.

frogs (hundreds in many reports) would be hidden in a small area – 'we couldn't walk about without treading on some of them', said one witness – and how did frogspawn come to be hanging on the bushes in Mrs McWilliam's garden?

Fish and frogs are the most frequently reported creatures seen to fall from the sky in Britain, though occasionally snail-falls have been reported. Elsewhere in the world other animals are said to have fallen – in 1894 a gopher turtle measuring 6 × 8 inches and entirely encased in ice fell during a hailstorm in Mississippi, USA.[4] Other unexpected falling objects are hazelnuts, coins, grass and earth, seeds, peas and beans, rocks and clinker, all reliably reported in Britain during the past hundred years. The hazelnuts fell on Mr and Mrs Alfred Wilson Osborne, who were returning from church in Westbury Park, Bristol (Avon), on 13 March 1977. Hearing a clicking noise, Mr Osborne thought he had lost a button, but to his surprise it was not a button but a hazelnut, followed by several hundred others, which fell out of a sky which was 'practically clear and blue with one cloud drifting over'. Mr Osborne described the fall: 'They were peppering down on the road and bouncing off the cars. They were coming from the sky and coming from what I should estimate was a considerable height. I collected half a dozen or so to take home. I tried one of the nuts later. It was sweet, fresh and quite delicious.' He learned that a friend, passing the same spot minutes later, had

11

also experienced a shower of hazelnuts. This well-documented case raises some intriguing questions, which are also pertinent to other sky-falls. Where did the nuts come from, how did they get into the sky, and, most strange of all, how could 'sweet, fresh and quite delicious' hazelnuts appear in March, when hazelnuts do not ripen until the autumn? Assuming they were the previous autumn's crop, where had they been since then?[5] This case is paralleled by an event in Dublin, Ireland, in May 1867, when a quantity of 'berries' fell during a heavy rainstorm. They were later discovered to be hazelnuts which had been partly fossilized in a peat bog, though no one could begin to explain how they came to fall from the sky.[6]

Equally puzzling are the eggs which fell on schoolchildren on several occasions at Wokingham (Berkshire) early in December 1974;[7] the clods of earth, roots and grass which fell on Poole (Dorset) in August 1977[8] and also on Ruislip (Greater London) in June 1942,[9] on both occasions the clods seeming to come from, or through, a cloud; the seeds of mustard and cress, millions of them, which fell on Roland Moody at Southampton (Hampshire) in February 1979, followed on later days by maize, peas and beans, the neighbours experiencing similar falls at different times.[10] We could continue indefinitely with this listing, but lack the space – brief details of other strange falls will be found in the Gazetteer.

One obvious similarity common to all the reports we have quoted is that when a startled witness reports a fall, he or she reports only one type of item falling at a time. Even Mr Moody's mustard and cress seeds fell separately, the cress seeds first, the mustard seeds following three-quarters of an hour later. If, as the sceptics would like us to believe, the falling objects have first been sucked up from somewhere on earth by whirlwinds, waterspouts or tornados, how have they managed to be so selective? Why are the fish-falls always of one species only, and even of the same size? Where are the other inhabitants of the pond, stream or river, where are the mud and stones and waterweed? We know of no report containing other items of the victim's environment, and have never heard of anyone actually seeing a whirlwind, waterspout or tornado scooping up hundreds of fish, or peas, or hazelnuts.

There is a possibility that some apparent falls are in fact paranormal events, though this in no way helps to explain the phenomenon. Reports of showers of stones being thrown at houses are described in Chapter 25, 'Poltergeists', though it is not easy to tell which cases of this kind are paranormal and which normal falls (if any falls can be judged 'normal'). For example, during the night of 21/22 June 1980 houses at Hampshire Place, Peterlee (Durham), were peppered with stone chippings found littering paths and lawns next day.[11] Did the stones simply fall from the sky, or were they directed by a paranormal agency, such as seems to have been at work in the stone-throwing case at Thornton Road, Ward End, Birmingham, described in Chapter 25? Other falls of a possible paranormal nature are the clods of earth already mentioned (those that fell at Ruislip were said to have floated down slowly and gracefully, which is a feature sometimes noted of missiles in poltergeist cases), the peas and beans that fell on Southampton in 1979 (one family afflicted by the deluges reported that if anyone opened the front door they were pelted by broad beans, though there was no one in sight and no apparent way a human agent could have precipitated the beans – again a feature of poltergeist cases), and several intriguing falls of coins from an empty sky. Into this category must also come the notecase which hit Lynne Connolly as she hung out her washing in her garden in Hull (Humberside) around 21 October

Some of the stones which fell on houses in Peterlee (Durham) on 21/22 June 1980.

This large ice-bomb crashed through the roof and ceiling of eighty-year-old Fred and Elsie Down's house in Exmouth (Devon) during the evening of 19 June 1984, and here Mrs Down surveys the damage. Mr Down said: 'When we opened the bedroom door I could not believe my eyes. There was a terrible mess. You could see the sky through the roof. It smashed clean through the slates and broke a rafter. There were also lumps of ice the size of two men's fists lying on the bed.'

1975. Feeling a tap on her head, she picked the notecase out of her hair. It was silver, measured 63 × 36.5 mm, and carried a scroll design with the letters JB or TB, SE, C8, a six-pointed star, and the name 'Klaipeda' which is a Baltic port. Inside were the remaining thirteen pages of a notepad.[12] Its origin remains a mystery, but it was possibly teleported (inexplicably carried from one location to another instantaneously; or dematerialized and later rematerialized somewhere else with any amount of time between the two events) into Mrs Connolly's presence. Teleportation is a convenient solution to this and possibly other cases of falls, but one which attempts to explain one mystery by producing another. We return to the subject of teleportation in Chapter 15.

We have left until last the most common type of sky-fall reported in Britain – chunks of ice. As will be seen in the Gazetteer, very large chunks of ice fall out of the sky surprisingly often, frequently smashing through the roofs of houses and then through bedroom ceilings, scattering fragments of ice all over bedrooms and greatly alarming the inhabitants. Fortunately, and surprisingly, no one has yet been injured by one of these 'ice-bombs', though there have been near-misses. The only victim we know of was a sheep, discovered dead in a field near North Molton (Devon) in November 1950, its neck cut through by a 14-pound chunk of ice which then embedded itself in the ground. Other fragments the size of dinner-plates littered the field.[13] Whenever aggrieved victims of ice-bombs report the events to the press, in an attempt to allocate responsibility and perhaps claim compensation, the authorities invariably blame a passing plane, which obviously became iced up and happened to discharge its load over a built-up area. This explanation is generally accepted, because what other explanation can there be? The melting ice sometimes leaves a coloured liquid which could conceivably be waste water from a plane, so no doubt some of these missiles have come from aircraft. But very often the witness to the fall was in the open air and saw no plane overhead; on 11 October 1980, Ray Wood and some friends were playing golf at Romford (Greater London):

> We had just played our second shot and there was a hissing noise, then an almighty thud. We turned around and there were lots of ice chunks, each about the size of a cricket ball. We stood in amazement for a few seconds. The ice block left an enormous hole in the ground. There wasn't an explanation. The sky was blue, without a cloud in sight, and there were no planes about.

The 2-foot-square ice block was 'explained' by the London Weather Centre: 'It could only be hail, or ice falling from aircraft.'[14] Despite the weather centre's certainty, there are other possible explanations, which we shall examine later; and, of course, ice-bombs were reported in the centuries before planes were flying.

In 1973 part of a 4½-pound block of ice was retrieved and later analysed for some clues to its origins. The near-victim of the ice-fall was Dr Richard Griffiths, walking home in

Manchester on the evening of 2 April. The ice block missed him by 10 feet, shattering on the road. He picked up the largest piece and took it home to store in his freezer. The tests he later performed showed that the block was made of fifty-one layers of ice separated by trapped air bubbles and had been formed from cloud water, but he could not determine how and where the block of ice had grown. It would also have needed a very strong updraft of wind to keep it aloft. Although two planes were in the area at the time of the event, one had landed just before, and neither suffered any icing problems. Nine minutes before the ice-fall, a single flash of lightning was noted by Dr Griffiths, but no connection between the two events has been established, and the origins of the block of ice remain unknown.[15]

Several possible explanations for falling ice blocks or 'hydro-meteors' are put forward by William R. Corliss in his book *Tornados, Dark Days, Anomalous Precipitation, and Related Weather Phenomena*,[16] including the possible aggregation of many hailstones to form one large hailstone; that hydrometeors may be formed as a result of electrostatic forces after severe lightning strokes (could this be the explanation of the Manchester ice block, just described?); and that some ice-falls could actually be meteors of ice from outer space. It is very likely that all three solutions could provide answers to such events, depending on the circumstances of each. However, we must look for different solutions for falls of organic and inorganic matter. Falls of lightweight objects such as hay and leaves can be easily explained by whirlwinds, though such lightweight items as the mustard and cress seeds which fell on Southampton in 1979 present an obvious difficulty: were the seeds piled up in the open, where they could be whisked into the air by a strong current of wind? It seems unlikely, but how else could they have found their way into the air? They were fresh seeds, which soon sprouted all over Mrs Stockley's garden, much to her annoyance. Her deluge had occurred a year before neighbouring Mr Moody's, but she had not told anyone about it. Mr Moody also noted that the cress seeds which fell on him were covered in a sticky jelly, which fact tends to confound the mystery rather than helping towards its solution. As mentioned earlier, whirlwinds, waterspouts and tornados may sometimes be responsible for falls of heavier objects, but we are still faced with the problem of selectivity. Perhaps we should seriously consider the theory put forward by Charles Fort (see Bibliography) of a Super-Sargasso Sea somewhere above the earth's surface, where refuse from sources terrestrial and interplanetary has collected, resting there in suspension until shaken down occasionally by storms, to cause wonder and amazement to simple mortals here on earth.

Waterspouts are sometimes thought to be responsible for falls of unexpected items; but they are rarely reported seen at the time of such falls.

2. A weeping Madonna and other religious phenomena

Our Lady comes wearing a white robe and blue cloak. She has a crown of golden stars: her feet are not visible. Her hands are slender with a scapular on her right wrist. The scapular is reddish. Her hair is long, wavy, and dark brown, parted in the middle. Her face is long, her nose is long and slender and her mouth is dainty and very lovely: her lips are just a little bit thick. Her complexion is quite dark but lighter than the angel's and it is a very beautiful voice, very unusual. I cannot explain it. There is no woman who is like Our Lady, either in voice or in any way at all. Our Lady seems to be about eighteen years old.[1]

This description of the Blessed Virgin Mary comes from Conchita, one of four children who saw a vision of the Virgin some 2,000 times at Garabandal in Spain during 1961–5. Similar visions have been experienced in various parts of the world over the past 900 years, almost exclusively in Catholic communities as might be expected, and they still occur. The most recent events have been taking place at Medjugorje in southern Yugoslavia, where in the early 1980s six young people were seeing the Virgin daily and individually, the events up to 1984 being described in a booklet entitled *Mary, Queen of Peace* and written by two eye-witnesses, Lucy Rooney SND and Robert Faricy SJ.[2] The most famous visions of the recent past include those at La Salette, France, in 1846, at Lourdes, France, in 1858, at Pontmain, France, in 1871, at Knock, Ireland, in 1879, and at Fatima, Portugal, in 1915–17.[3] These all occurred in devout Catholic communities where an underlying atmosphere of religious fervour was encouraged. The scarcity of similar events in Britain and other Protestant countries can be attributed to their small Catholic populations and a more phlegmatic public attitude to religious practice. We know of only three visions of the Blessed Virgin Mary in Britain, and only one of those took place in the last hundred years. The first happened as long ago as 1061, when Richeldis, lady of the manor, had three visions of the Virgin at Little Walsingham in Norfolk. She told Richeldis to build a house the same as the one at Nazareth where Jesus had lived as a boy, and she said (according to an account written 400 years later, so the words may not be totally accurate): 'And there at Walsingham in this little house shall be held in remembrance the great joy of my salutation when St Gabriel told me I should through humility be the mother of God's Son.' A house (in local style) was built at Walsingham and thus the first shrine to the Virgin Mary in Europe came into being. Walsingham is still a lively place of pilgrimage, nine hundred years later.

From eleventh-century Norfolk we move across Britain and on 800 years in time to the next documented visions. These took place in 1880 at Llanthony Monastery (founded 1870 and not to be confused with the ruined Llanthony Priory a little further down the valley). One of the Sisters saw a ghostly sacrament, and later the same day, 30 August, four boys living in the community saw a vision of the Virgin in the twilight. A 'bright, dazzling figure' glided across the meadow towards twelve-year-old John Stewart:

> . . . a halo of glory shone out from the figure all around in an oval form. The form was of a woman, a veil hung over the head and face, the hands were both raised as if in blessing. It approached very slowly . . . They saw the beautiful form enter the hedge, and after remaining there in the light for a few moments, passed through the bush and vanished.

Several days later, on 4 September, a light appeared in the same place and a veiled woman and a man wearing only a loincloth were seen. On 15 September four people singing an Ave Maria in honour of the Virgin witnessed a further vision:

> . . . the whole heavens and mountains broke forth in bulg-

ing circles of light, circles pushing out from circles – the light poured upon our faces and the buildings where we stood and in the central circle stood a most Majestic Heavenly Form, robed in flowing drapery. The Form was gigantic, but seemed to be reduced to human size as it approached. The Figure stood sideways, facing the Holy Bush. The Vision was most distinct and the details were very clear; but it was gone in the 'twinkling of an eye' . . . A few minutes after this Mr E. from Oxford and one of the boys, saw the shadowy form of the Blessed Virgin in light, by the enclosure gate with uplifted hands. This is the last of the visions vouchsafed by God's mercy to us.[4]

More recently, according to a press report, visions of the Virgin Mary were seen at Middleton near Sudbury in Suffolk, but we have only tantalizingly brief details of the events there. The visions were said to have been seen in February 1933 by the Rector, the Revd Clive Luget, and a Dr Thornber, the latter having seen a vision on the lawn. The parishioners were demonstrating against the closure of the church and grounds to the public, which had presumably been done to prevent the place being overrun by sightseers, but we have no further details of the original or subsequent events.[5]

The decorated egg from Doncaster (South Yorkshire) which was seen to weep.

Other strange phenomena occurring in a religious context include weeping and bleeding icons or religious images. Such events have been widely reported during this century; for example a picture of Christ at Mirebeau in France began bleeding in 1911 from the hands, head and heart, and though tests at the Lister Institute in London showed that the blood or serum was not human, its exact composition remained a mystery.[6] Such events can apparently happen anywhere if Catholics and their religious images are present: a portrait of the Madonna wept in Sicily in 1953; a plaster statue of Christ bled freely from the hands in Pennsylvania, USA, in 1975.[7] There have been a very few reported weepings and bleedings in Britain, four that we are aware of being the weeping Madonna at the home of Theresa Taylor in Walker, Newcastle upon Tyne (Tyne and Wear), which began to weep on 10 October 1955, an event witnessed by neighbours; a 16-inch crucifix owned by Alfred Bolton of Walthamstow (Greater London) which was seen to weep on at least thirty occasions between May and July 1966;[8] and a hard-boiled egg decorated at Easter 1984 with the face of Christ, which began to weep from the right eye. Hundreds of people saw the weeping egg at Doncaster Junior School (South Yorkshire) and it was examined through a magnifying glass, but no one could explain how so much water was oozing from a hard-boiled egg, and at exactly the place where the tear duct would be. Twenty-six-year-old Anne Schutterlin who had decorated the egg felt that 'divine intervention' was responsible, since she had prayed that 'someone would see Jesus through the egg'.[9]

The fourth case took place earlier, in 1920, and was investigated by Father Herbert Thurston SJ, who was extremely knowledgeable on all the physical phenomena of mysticism and wrote a book on the subject. The case was basically one of stigmatization, where the unnamed female subject, living in a town in northern England, experienced bleeding of the palms of the hands on Good Friday, and at other times. She also possessed a crucifix which sweated blood, beginning on 17 March 1920, the very day that the *Daily Herald* published a photograph of the bleeding picture of Christ at Mirebeau, mentioned earlier.[10] Thurston suspected that she might have faked the bleeding crucifix, having read of the events at Mirebeau, but it is also possible that she somehow caused the bleeding to happen subconsciously, as indeed may be the answer in all similar cases. Even if this is the correct solution we are still a long way away from understanding the mechanics of such events.

Subconscious forces are also likely to be at work in cases of so-called miracle cures. How the body marshals its healing powers is only vaguely understood, but in recent years it has become clear that a patient's state of mind can help to kill or cure, and also that many physical ailments are psychological in origin. According to the criteria announced in our introduction miracle cures should not be included in this book, but we will nevertheless describe one major example because of its religious overtones. The patient was John Fagan of Glasgow (Strathclyde Region) who by January 1967 was almost dead of cancer. A priest who administered the last rites left with Mrs Fagan a medal of the seventeenth-century martyr the Blessed John Ogilvie and suggested that she pray to him for her husband's recovery. She did so, and gave the medal to her husband. By March, John Fagan's death was expected at any minute by the doctor. He could neither eat nor talk. Friends gathered round his bed and asked for the intercession of the Blessed John Ogilvie. Next morning Mrs Fagan was amazed to find her husband not dead but very much alive, hungry and asking for food. He soon made a complete recovery, and a medical committee testified that they could not explain how he could have recovered from terminal cancer. On 12 February 1976 Pope Paul VI issued a decree declaring that John Fagan had received a miracle cure due to the intercession of John Ogilvie, who was then entered into the calendar of Roman Catholic saints.[11]

Mental powers or subconscious forces (call them what you will, because no one can yet explain how they work) have been used to explain all the religious phenomena we have so far described, though there is of course considerable debate as to whether any external intelligence has any part to play in the continuing visions of the Blessed Virgin Mary. (We will not entangle ourselves in that debate here. Interested readers

Mary Jones, the Welsh evangelist preacher whose activities were accompanied by the appearance of strange lights.

should obtain a recent book which valiantly tackles a complex range of related phenomena and which includes a chapter on religious visions: *Visions, Apparitions, Alien Visitors* by Hilary Evans.) Of a similar nature, and equally puzzling, were the phenomena which accompanied the Welsh Methodist revival of 1905. An unnamed eyewitness wrote on 30 May 1905 an account of the phenomena he saw, which generally took the form of lights in the sky accompanying the evangelist preacher Mary Jones, who was active in the west coast area of Merionethshire (now part of Gwynedd) between Harlech and Barmouth. The eyewitness's experience took place on Saturday evening, 25 March 1905, when Mrs Jones was conducting a service in the Calvinistic Methodist chapel at Llanfair about 1½ miles south of Harlech.

My wife and myself went down that night specially to see if the light accompanied Mrs Jones from outside Egryn [where she lived]. We happened to reach Llanfair about 9.15 p.m.

It was a rather dark and damp evening. In nearing the chapel, which can be seen from a distance, we saw balls of light, deep red, ascending from one side of the chapel, the side which is in a field. There was nothing in this field to cause this phenomenon – *i.e.* no houses, etc. After that we walked to and fro on the main road for nearly two hours without seeing any light except from a distance in the direction of Llanbedr. This time it appeared brilliant, ascending high into the sky from amongst the trees where lives the well-known Rev. C.E. The distance between us and the light which appeared this time was about a mile. Then about eleven o'clock, when the service which Mrs Jones conducted was brought to a close, two balls of light ascended from the same place and of similar appearance to those we saw first. In a few minutes afterwards Mrs Jones was passing us home in her carriage, and in a few seconds after she passed, on the main road, and within a yard of us, there appeared a brilliant light twice, tinged with blue. In two or three seconds after this disappeared, on our right hand, within 150 or 200 yards, there appeared twice very huge balls of similar appearance as that which appeared on the road. It was so brilliant and powerful this time that we were dazed for a second or two. Then immediately there appeared a brilliant light ascending from the woods where the Rev. C.E. lives. It appeared twice this time. On the other side of the main road, close by, there appeared, ascending from a field high into the sky, three balls of light, deep red. Two of these appeared to split up, whilst the middle one remained unchanged. Then we left for home, having been watching these last phenomena for a quarter of an hour.[12]

We could quote many similar eyewitness accounts, but this one is representative of the rest. All manner of people saw the lights, and although many explanations were put forward, such as misidentification of bright planets like Venus, natural phenomena such as ball lightning (see Chapter 10) or marsh gas (see Chapter 23), a lighthouse, or hoaxers (men with lanterns), the overwhelming impression gained from reading through the reports is that the lights cannot be explained away so easily. There was definitely a strong link between their appearance and the presence of Mary Jones, and indeed she believed that the lights were created by her faith, and that they helped her to make converts. Journalist Beriah Evans wrote that a light would often seem to rest above a particular house, and that a convert or converts from that house would 'invariably turn up at the next meeting . . . It [the light] glows placidly on the roof of the chapel where her service is held, and when it does so the spiritual character of the meeting is very marked.'

There are some similarities between the 1905 religious revival lights and the unidentified flying objects or UFOs widely seen from the late 1940s to the present day (see Chapter 7). Often, and especially at night, UFOs appear as 'lights in the sky', just as did the revival lights. Whether the similarity extends to their nature and origins as well as their appearance is difficult to say. Both could be known (and therefore misidentified) or unknown natural phenomena; or manifestations of external intelligences; or expressions of energy emanating from a human being, in the Welsh case Mary Jones, in the case of

Egryn Chapel near Barmouth in west Wales, one of the places where unidentified lights appeared, sometimes on the roof, sometimes nearby. One witness saw three pillars of fire, from which smoke ascended before they disappeared.

UFOs, presumably, the witness/es. Also likely to be relevant to the last possibility is the frightening phenomenon known as the poltergeist, which is probably caused by explosions of pent-up human psychic energy and whose effects will be described more fully in Chapter 25. Researchers into the links between UFO sightings and geological fault lines have noted that many of the Welsh lights appeared very close to the Mochras Fault, Llanfair chapel being located directly on the fault, and that many of the reports describe lights ascending from the ground, as they would if they were forming as a result of geological activity.[13] Whatever their origins, the lights which accompanied Mary Jones were relatively short-lived, being first seen about December 1904 but never after July 1905. Other phenomena of a psychic nature were experienced by participants in the revival, and the Revd A. T. Fryer's study of the 'Psychological Aspects of the Welsh Revival: 1904–5', compiled at the time of the events, makes intriguing reading, as it contains many first-hand reports of strange phenomena, especially the lights.

3. Toad (and frog) in the hole

This chapter's title refers not to the savoury batter and sausage dish, but to the discovery of toads and frogs entombed inside solid rock, for how long no one knows. They bemusedly crawl out when the rock is accidentally broken open. Although not a common occurrence, there are enough reliable reports on record from around the world to demonstrate that, although apparently unbelievable, the phenomenon is factual. Of the British reports collected by various researchers, only nineteen are definitely known to date from the last hundred years, and none of them happened during the last fifty years. There are also a further two or three modern reports of toads found incarcerated inside trees.[1] It is not immediately clear why there should be so few modern reports, but perhaps it can be explained partly by the fact that mining, quarrying and stone-breaking are now mechanized, with few people around to notice any toads or frogs emerging from newly broken stones.

The oldest British report we have come across dates back to the late seventeenth century, in the form of a letter written in 1698 by Dr Richard Richardson describing how he saw work-men break open a stone 'wherein was contained a toad . . .

The toad found inside a piece of flint at Lewes (East Sussex) around 1900.

which, being laid upon the ground, crawled about as long as the sun shone warm upon it, but towards night died'. The location is not given.[2] A number of similar reports are recorded from the following 200 years, and then a few during the present century, of which the following are a sample. Around 1900 workmen in a quarry at Lewes (East Sussex) found a toad when they cracked open a flint nodule, but it was mummified, not alive. The toad and stone are both preserved in the Brighton Museum. Also at the turn of the century, a strange discovery was made at North Moreton (Oxfordshire), here described by the vicar: 'On July 20, while some repairs were being carried on in our church, a skeleton was discovered at a depth of about six feet under the pavement, and in the skull a large yellow toad. The theory of the man who found it is, that the creature was there in the man's lifetime and grew after his death!'[3] In 1905 it was reported very briefly in a newspaper that a live toad had been found embedded in a tree at Pulham St Mary (Norfolk), but it died a few minutes after being released.[4] Several toads were found entombed at Broseley (Shropshire) in two separate incidents in 1906. A small toad was found buried alive in solid clay six feet underground, and three toads were discovered 'in a cavity of a solid piece of rock' during the building of a hospital. One was struck by a workman's pick, one escaped, but the third was captured. Its mouth was found to be sealed so that it could not eat, and so was the mouth of the toad found earlier the same year.[5]

The entombment of toads and frogs is definitely not confined to one type of rocky environment. We have already mentioned flint and clay; they have also been found (in Britain) in coal, limestone/chalk, sandstone, conglomerate, slate, gravel, sand and concrete.[6] In 1910 someone in Leicestershire discovered a toad while breaking open a lump of coal: 'from the centre a live half-grown toad fell out on its back. I called the attention of my neighbours to it, and I thought it was dead: but in a few minutes it began to move about, so I took care of it, and have it now as well as the piece of coal. There is the cavity in the coal where it laid. I can vouch for its genuineness.'[7] Later in the decade (May 1919) and in the adjoining county, a miner working 200 yards below the surface in Netherseal Colliery

(Derbyshire) found a 3-inch live toad in a pocket in the coal. It was dirty brown in colour. 'Its eyes were open, but it was obvious that it could not see at first. Two days afterwards, it gave indications of returning to normal. The toad has no mouth, but there are evidences that it once possessed this useful member. On the same day as the sight began to return the toad started to leap about in a clumsy manner. The webbed feet differ from the present well-known varieties.'[8]

Around 1929 two men blasting in a slate mine in Gwynedd

> noticed blood oozing out of the rock quite near to where they were working. One man was rather alarmed and called to his partner. Both together they scraped and saw two eyes and with a little hook scraped more until the frog was free and jumped out . . . There was no fault or crevice, and the spot was at least 200 to 250 feet from the nearest outcrop. To all appearances the rock was certainly solid and the frog had made a little nest which appeared like the hole found in limestone when a big shell is loosened.[9]

A later report is undated, but the events described by a witness, gas-fitter Eric Mackley, took place some years before 1972 when he sent this account to *Animals*:

> It became desirable to widen the Barnstaple–Ilfracombe

A live toad found embedded in a piece of coal by W. J. Clarke of Rugby (Warwickshire), date unknown. The coal had been on the fire for more than an hour when the toad was discovered, but it was still alive. It appeared to have no mouth or rectum, yet it lived for five weeks after discovery.

29

road some years ago, taking in part of the long gardens in front of a row of bungalows which had gas meters housed just inside the front gates; these of course had to be moved back to the new front wall line. The meter-houses were brick-walled but rather massively concrete-floored, and the concrete had to be broken up to allow me to get at the pipes for extension. My mate was at work with a sledge hammer when he dropped it suddenly and said, 'That looks like a frog's leg.' We both bent down and there was the frog. Being fond of animals the sledge was set aside and I cut the rest of the block carefully. We released 23 perfectly formed but minute frogs which all hopped away to the flower garden.

Mr Mackley's theory to explain this mystery was that 'whoever originally mixed the concrete took up frog spawn with the water from the stagnant stream opposite; the spawn found its way into the middle of the concrete base; and when the tadpoles hatched they cannibalized until the hole was completely filled with small but perfectly formed frogs.' As Bob Rickard commented in *Fortean Times*,

> The merits of this theory we leave for the criticism of others, but we would have thought that the concrete would have set around the relatively small mass of the spawn-cluster (if that's the way it happened) long before the critters hatched, not giving them much room. Secondly, they would have to survive the added hazards of the toxicity of liquid concrete and the heat generated by the setting process on top of the rough and tumble of mixing, pouring, and compacting. Another interesting point, says Mackley, is the speed with which the little sleepers roused from their torpid state and hopped away 'after over a quarter of a century'.[10]

Each report of this phenomenon seems to provide its own mysterious aspects, and none can be easily explained. A 1982 report from New Zealand is worth quoting in full, as it proves that toads and frogs are still being discovered inside solid rock, and shows that such reports cannot be ascribed to the unscientific and credulous attitudes of previous generations.

A Railways bridge gang discovered two frogs while working on the main trunk railway south of Te Kuiti last month. Under normal circumstances perhaps not a significant discovery, but the frogs were sealed under four metres of rock, and after close inspection were found to be alive. The 'black-as-black' specimens were found at Waimiha . . . by workmen laying a culvert. The first frog was found by a member of the gang who was trimming a rock face of sedimentary mudstone with his shovel. He saw the frog in a cavity in the rock, and placed the lump of rock containing the frog on his shovel. It soon became obvious that the frog was alive after it had been shaken from the rock on to the shovel. A Railways bridge inspector, Mr L. Andrews, who was with the gang, said he began to believe the claim when the workman stuck to his story. The frog was moist, but not exactly bouncing about, he said, and as the gang was busy, the find was left on a bank. Later the same day another frog in similar condition was uncovered by the drilling machine which was working at a depth of four metres. Mr Andrews is certain neither frog could have fallen with loose rock. Before resuming work the frog was placed near a stream, but workmen were unable to find either frog when they checked later.

The phenomenon of live frogs encased in rock is known in the scientific world, though debate has taken place over the age of the frogs. The professor of biological sciences at Walkato University, Dr J. Pendergrast, said he was certain the Waimiha frogs had managed to crawl through small cracks in the rock, which could later have closed with earth movements. 'Frogs can go into a very quiescent (dormant) state', he said, 'and are able to survive for many weeks without food.'[11]

Dr Pendergrast's explanation of how the frogs came to be inside the rock is a familiar one, but even if it is appropriate in some cases it cannot apply to all. In 1865 workmen at Hartlepool (Cleveland) found a toad embedded in a block of magnesium limestone which was 25 feet deep, and the 1919 Netherseal toad was found 200 yards down. It seems most unlikely that any toad could climb down to those depths. The Hartlepool toad was in a cavity which fitted its body snugly, suggesting that the rock had been formed around it. A contemporary press report described the creature:

> The toad's eyes shone with unusual brilliancy and it was full of vivacity upon its liberation. It appeared when first discovered desirous to perform the process of respiration but evidently experienced some difficulty and the only sign of success consisted of a 'barking' noise which it continues to make at present upon being touched . . . On a minute examination its mouth is found to be completely closed, and the barking noise it makes proceeds from its nostrils. The claws of its forefeet are turned inwards, and its hind ones of extraordinary length, and unlike the present English toad . . . The toad when first released was of a pale colour and not easily distinguished from the stone, but shortly its colour grew darker to a fine olive brown.[12]

Other entombed toads and frogs have been found to have a permanently closed mouth, including the Broseley toads described earlier, a feature which suggests long incarceration. Some frogs found during the 1920s in Oklahoma, USA, were entombed along with the bones of mammoths and sabre-toothed tigers, and it is tempting to speculate that they were all living at the same time.[13] Toads and frogs are known to be able to survive for a considerable time in a torpid state, but could they really survive for millions of years? Experimenters found that toads deliberately buried were most likely to survive if the tomb was only just big enough to hold the toad, but it has not of course been possible to undertake an experiment lasting longer than thirty or so years. In 1897 a horned toad was sealed up in a cavity in a marble cornerstone of a new courthouse being built at Eastland, Texas, USA, and in 1928 when the building was demolished, it was released alive from its cell. Will Wood, who performed the experiment, took 'Old Rip' on a national tour, including a visit to the President, and after its death a year later the toad was put on display in a casket at Eastland.[14] Whether any toads and frogs have really survived entombed over millions of years from the time when their muddy environment solidified into rock is likely to remain debatable for some time.

Earlier we mentioned a toad found inside a tree. This is not an isolated occurrence, frogs also having been found, as well as: live fieldmice in Staffordshire, a mummified marmoset at Bosham Mill (West Sussex), and 1,500 live fishes in gallons of water inside a tree-trunk being sawn up in California, USA, in 1954.[15] In 1969 a Finnish farmer found a dried fish about 16 inches long inside a log he had split open.[16] Snakes and shellfish have also been discovered alive inside stones, and in 1818 Dr E. D. Clarke, a geologist, discovered some live newts while searching for fossils in a chalk-pit. The newts were inside a lump of chalk stone, and began to move when placed in the sunlight. Two died, but a third was so active when placed in water that it escaped. The newts could not be identified, and did not resemble any of the species known in the neighbourhood.[17] This fact and other details retrieved from world-wide accounts of similar entombments hint at a phenomenon most worthy of intensive study, to try to ascertain whether survival over aeons is really feasible. But without many more new finds to work on, this mystery is likely to remain unsolved.

4. *Ghostly people*

. . . the strangest part of it all is that, though he was apparently walking slowly, I never could get any closer than within a few yards, for in but a moment he seemed to *float or skim away*. Presently he suddenly came to a stand-still, and I began to feel very much afraid, and stopped also . . . He turned round and gazed at me with a vacant expression, and the same ghastly, pallid features . . . Moving on a few steps he again stood and looked back for a second time, finally fading from view at his usual spot by the hedge to the right.[1]

Miss Louisa Scott is describing a ghost she saw on 12 June 1893, the same ghost she and her sister had seen twice the previous year, in the same place, and which others had seen too. Their ghost exhibited some typical characteristics of the species: the first time they saw him, walking along a road near St Boswells (Borders Region), they thought he was just an ordinary man dressed in black – until he vanished. On their second encounter a few weeks later, the sisters recognized him and so watched him intently, and they saw him fade away towards the roadside bank. When Miss Scott saw him again a year later, she ran after him in order to get a closer look at him, but as she described in her account quoted above, she couldn't seem to get close to him, and he again faded away from her vision.

In many accounts of encounters with ghosts, the witness reports that the figure looked like a normal human being – until it walked through a hedge or a fence or a door, or simply vanished. The phantom nun of Princethorpe (Warwickshire), seen by Walter Barlow in 1952 and again some time later, caused him some momentary alarm on the second occasion when he realized that she was moving towards him along a path through the woods. He stopped and waited as she walked up to him, and then passed right through him. He felt a 'brushing sensation, a shiver, and what he can only describe as something like a magnetic thrill passing through him'. When he turned, she had vanished.[2]

But we can only guess how many times people see a ghost without realizing that the figure is not a living, breathing person, because the witness does not actually see the ghost do anything contrary to known physical laws. The same applies to other types of ghosts, like ghostly animals, vehicles and even houses. These will be described in a later chapter, as will phantom armies, phantom hitch-hikers and poltergeists. Here we concentrate on the ghosts of individual people.

Contrary to popular belief, ghosts are not a phenomenon solely of past centuries, nor are they seen only in old buildings like churches and castles. The entries in our Chronological List of Strange Events demonstrate that ghosts are still being seen frequently as we approach the twenty-first century. A particularly memorable ghost of recent years was the mournful woman seen by several people near Llanidloes (Powys). Primary school headmaster Bill Hopkins was driving home one night in May 1973 when, as he approached the Red Bridge, an old railway bridge 2 miles out of Llanidloes on the road to Newtown, a girl stepped straight out of the hedge into his path. He later reported:

> I braked hard. All I could think was 'I am going to kill this woman'. But there was no impact, I could see her face looking straight at me and it seemed to pass through the car. She must have turned around as I could still see her face in the mirror. I didn't bother to stop; I was really frightened I can tell you . . . It all happened so quickly. All I can remember is her face. It was so sorrowful and she was looking straight at me.[3]

When his experience was publicized other people revealed that they had seen the same ghost in previous years, and a few weeks later, early in July 1973, she was seen by a chef who was looking for the road back to Llanidloes, having got lost after taking his girlfriend home. Abderrahman Sennah said later:

> I wasn't sure which way to turn when I came to the main road. Then as I approached a corner I saw the wall of a bridge and suddenly the head and shoulders of a woman came out towards me. It came straight at the windscreen and passed through the car on the passenger's side. I was alone but I shouted 'I'm on the Red Bridge' and then drove straight home. I was really frightened and was shaking.[4]

Many ghosts, indeed most of them, are not 'one-off' events, but appear over a period of time to a variety of witnesses. Another example comes from Norfolk, and it is a haunting similar to that at the Red Bridge. On the A12 road near Hopton, several motorists have been surprised by the appearance of a ghostly old man, and some have even collided with him. On

Andrew Cutajar points to where he saw the A12 ghost near Hopton (Norfolk) on 2 November 1981.

2 November 1981, Andrew Cutajar was driving along the A12 towards Great Yarmouth on a wet and dismal night. He noticed what appeared to be a 'grey mist' in the middle of the carriageway, and as he got closer he could see the figure of a man – 'tall, and dressed in a long coat or cape, coming well past his knees. He had on old-fashioned heavy, lace-up boots, and had long, straggly grey hair.' The figure did not move as the car approached it, and Mr Cutajar braked to avoid colliding with it. His car began to skid, and a collision seemed inevitable, but the car passed straight through the figure, 'just like going through a cloud'. Mr Cutajar lost control of the car, which spun right round and came to rest on the grass verge, but he was uninjured. The A12 in the vicinity of Hopton has been the scene of many unexplained traffic accidents involving single vehicles, and it may be that Mr Cutajar is only one of many drivers who have come into contact with the ghostly old man of the A12.[5]

What we might call 'non-existent road accidents', in which a driver unavoidably collides with a figure which steps out into the road, only to find on stopping and investigating that there is no body and no trace of a collision, are surprisingly frequent. The ghost of an elderly lady crosses Maidstone Road in Sevenoaks (Kent) on the anniversary of her fatal accident there on 14 June 1959, and in 1979 she was 'hit' by a driver who had no time to avoid her when she stepped out in front of him. Of course there was no body, and another driver who had witnessed the 'accident' was equally puzzled.[6] A few years earlier, in 1976, a driver on the A22 in Willingdon (East Sussex) had a similar strange experience, which was repeated a year later:

I nearly had a heart attack the first time, for suddenly this woman was in front of my car and I had absolutely no chance of avoiding her. But when I finally stopped, with a feeling of horror at having killed a pedestrian, and went back to the spot, there was nothing to be seen. The second time was nearly a year later when I had forgotten that first weird incident, and exactly the same thing happened. It was a few days after that I heard the woman had often been seen.[7]

These events may sometimes be re-enactments of fatal accidents, but they are not necessarily all explainable in this way, and often no one can remember an accident at that spot.

So far we have talked only of ghosts seen outdoors. Of course many ghosts are seen inside buildings, and in a great variety of buildings too. Many famous historic buildings are haunted, such as Hampton Court Palace, the Tower of London, Arundel Castle (West Sussex) and the dungeon at Winchester Castle (Hampshire), and many old churches, which is only to be expected. But ghosts have also been reliably reported in pubs and hotels, in theatres, in museums and schools, in factories and power stations, and in modern houses and council flats. Examples of all these can be found in the Gazetteer. One particularly interesting indoor ghost was seen or heard on several occasions in late 1953 in the library of York Museum (North Yorkshire). The caretaker was checking the building one evening when he saw a man apparently searching for a

The Tower of London, possibly the most haunted place in Britain.

The eerie Roman Steps (Gwynedd) where Redfern Thomas saw the ghost of a Welsh girl.

book along the bookshelves. He was dressed in an old-fashioned style, with a frock coat, drainpipe trousers without turn-ups, and elastic-sided boots. He was saying, 'I must find it, I must find it!' The caretaker, having no reason to think the man was a ghost, went up to him and spoke, reaching out his hand to touch the man's arm. To his great surprise, the man disappeared. He had dropped a book, *Antiquities and Curiosities of the Church*. A month later the caretaker saw him again, and another month after that, he and a friend heard pages being turned and saw the same book fall to the floor. In December a small group gathered in the library at the appropriate time, and they heard a rubbing sound and saw the same book move out of its place on the shelf and fall to the floor. But the ghost has not been seen again.[8]

This case has two particularly interesting features: the ghost was heard to speak; and it was seen to move a solid object. Both features are rare, especially the latter – usually, objects moved by ghosts, such as doors opened when they enter rooms, are afterwards found to have remained untouched, showing that the witness visually hallucinated the object's movement. Ghosts do occasionally speak, however, as happened to Redfern Thomas and his son in the late 1920s when they were in the Rhinog mountains near Harlech (Gwynedd), having just climbed the 'Roman Steps'. The mountain-top was deserted except for sheep and birds; then suddenly they became aware of the presence of a nicely dressed young girl, who approached them and greeted them in Welsh. Mr Thomas replied, and then she suddenly disappeared. Although they searched, they could find no trace of her.[9]

The ghost of Grandfather Bull also spoke briefly, once calling his wife by her name, Jane. Samuel Bull was a chimney-sweep who died in 1931 in his cottage in Oxford Street, Ramsbury (Wiltshire). During February to April 1932 his ghost appeared many times to the members of his family still living in the cottage, once remaining visible for as long as half an hour. He looked solid, and twice laid his hand on his widow's forehead as she lay in bed; the hand felt 'firm but cold'. It is a pity that no one in the cottage thought of trying to hold a conversation with this strongly energized ghost. Researchers investigating the nature of ghosts seem to have progressed only a short distance along the problem-strewn path leading to a complete understanding of the phenomenon, and they would probably be overjoyed to have an opportunity to observe and even converse with a ghost such as that of Grandfather Bull. Unfortunately the Society for Psychical Research slipped up in that particular case, representatives from the Society arriving on the scene after the family had left the cottage and the haunting had ceased.[10]

Many theories have been offered in an attempt to explain ghosts, ranging from misinterpretation of natural phenomena such as mist, through hallucinations, to contact with the spirit world. Many ghosts appear to be re-enacting major lifetime events, like sorrowful times or sudden death, or ordinary mundane lifetime rituals, and it has been suggested that these events, in certain circumstances (which no one has yet identified) can be imprinted on to the surroundings, to be replayed at times in the future. The trigger that sets off the replay is again indefinable, but perhaps requires certain atmospheric conditions, or the presence of a person of the requisite sensitivity, who unintentionally activates the recording and thus visualizes the historic event. Whatever the mechanism that brings a ghost into view, it cannot be entirely subjective on the part of the witness, because there are many occasions when multiple witnesses have shared an experience (such events being sometimes explained as a shared hallucination, an explanation which becomes more strained the larger the number of witnesses), and when the witnesses have included animals, which are always very quick to sense subtle influences. A corgi walking with its owner across the Downs near Beachy Head (East Sussex) in 1976 apparently saw a ghostly woman in grey who was also seen by the owner. The dog stopped and began to growl, quivering with fright. When the ghost bent down,

Sybell Corbet photographed the library at Combermere Hall (Cheshire) on 5 December 1891 and when she developed the photograph was astonished to see a figure sitting in a chair. The figure was later identified as Lord Combermere – but at the time the photograph was taken, during the afternoon, he was being buried four miles away.

41

seemingly to stroke the dog, the terrified animal ran off howling, whereupon the ghost vanished.[11] In the late 1920s a horse pulling a baker's cart near West Ashby (Lincolnshire) reared up and began to gallop down the road, at the same time as the driver saw the ghost of a man on a bicycle.[12] When a normally friendly dog in Chipping (Lancashire) encountered a trio of ghosts one evening in December 1966, it turned into a savage, snarling beast, attacking the vanishing figures before racing home terror-stricken. A few days later the dog died, although the vet could find nothing physically wrong with it.[13]

Some people are convinced that ghosts are visitors from the spirit world, and some reports do contain features which, if correctly reported, suggest that certain ghosts at least are rather more than mere recordings. We refer now to cases where ghosts interact in some way with the present environment, perhaps by speaking to witnesses or moving physical objects. But they may not possess a full consciousness as we do, only a lingering urge to fulfil some task not completed while they were alive. Full discussion of the implications of ghostly phenomena could easily occupy the whole of this book, and indeed many books have been devoted solely to this subject (a few are listed in the Bibliography – see Bennett, Green & McCreery, MacKenzie).

A man looking like a vicar appeared on a photograph of Eastry church (Kent) taken by a bank manager, Mr Bootman, in 1956, though the only other people present at the time were his wife and a cleaner. He later learned that a similar ghost had been seen in the church in the 1940s.

5. *Phantom black dogs*

Many folklore tales are clearly fantasies or allegories of past events, such as those describing the activities of giants and dragon-slayers, but in the case of the phantom black dog, the creatures described in folklore are still being seen today. These mysterious dogs are well established in the folklore of many parts of Britain, and have been given different names in different areas, for example Black Shuck (Norfolk), Gallytrot (Suffolk), Trash (Lancashire), Barghest (Yorkshire Dales), Padfoot (Staffordshire and Wakefield). In folklore the straight-forward appearances of black dogs have often been embellished by fictional details to make an appealing story, but the basic scenario is usually the same as that reported by modern witnesses: the observer, walking alone at night, or occasionally during the daytime, is suddenly aware of the presence of a large black dog which usually at first gives no hint of being a phantom. Then something happens to alert the witness to the dog's unreality: it might suddenly vanish, or nothing is felt when the witness reaches out to pat it. The encounters are usually brief, but the witness retains a clear memory of the dog. Usually it is black, though other colours, notably white and grey, have been reliably reported. It is always large, bigger than the biggest dog and often described as calf-size. The coat is often shaggy, and the other main feature often described is the creature's eyes, said to be glowing or even red or fiery. Some typical reports from the last hundred years will give a clearer picture of these uncanny encounters.

Ernest Whiteland saw a black dog in 1938 at Ditchingham in Norfolk, when he was walking home after an evening spent with friends in Bungay. About half-way between the Maltings and Ditchingham Station,

*Leiston churchyard
(Suffolk) where a
black dog was seen by
two ladies earlier
this century.*

I saw a black object roughly seventy-five yards away, coming towards me. I was on the left-hand side of the road, close to the hedge. As it came close, I could see it was a large black dog, trotting along the same side of the road as I was on. It was a lovely evening – no wind, and everything so quiet and still. As it came to about nine or ten yards away, I could see that it had a long, black, shaggy coat, and was about 28 or 30 inches tall. I moved into the middle of the road to let it pass. When it got level with me, it vanished. I looked round to see if I had made a mistake – to see if it was still running along, but could not see it. I then went and looked over the hedge, expecting to see it on the meadow, or hear it, but could do neither. I stopped, it seemed to me, for some minutes. Then a sudden fear came over me, and it did not take me long to cover the distance to my home.

He later discovered that the area was known to be haunted by Black Shuck.[1]

There had also been sightings of a black dog along a certain lane near Upper Booth in Derbyshire, though young Greta Shirt did not know this at the time she saw the creature in 1930. She was going home in the evening around 8 p.m. along the lonely lane when in the moonlight she saw a large black dog. It passed close to her, so she put her hand out to stroke it, but could feel nothing beneath her fingers. She was further disconcerted when the creature 'merged through the close, criss-cross wires of the fence, which could not possibly have let its body through'. When Greta arrived home and told her father about her experience, he revealed that he too had seen the black dog.[2]

These two accounts are similar, and are representative of many others. Variations do occasionally occur, however, as in this report by a trained observer, coastguard Graham Grant, who was on duty at the Gorleston rescue headquarters (Norfolk) on 19 April 1972.

> Looking to the north, at about 04.45, at daybreak, on Wednesday last, April 19th, I saw a large, black hound-type dog on the beach, about a quarter of a mile north of the look-out. What made me look was that the dog was running, then stopping, as if looking for someone. I watched it for one to two minutes and then it vanished before my eyes. I kept on looking for a time, but it did not reappear . . . One moment it was there, the next it had gone.

He had never heard of Black Shuck until a colleague told him, after his experience.[3] This report is unusual in that the dog generally materializes much closer to the witness, as if appearing for him alone.

In complete contrast to the reports we have given so far, we now tell the tale sent to us by Mr H. Holmes, who had the most unusual experience of seeing over twenty of these mysterious creatures. He was cycling home late at night in 1931 from a church service in Swaledale, and had reached Barton Quarry (North Yorkshire) after midnight. Suddenly he saw a 'dog-like figure'.

> Dismounting, I sat down. Lo and behold, I watched a big grey dog with eyes flashing like sparklers, also its tongue was flashing and frothing; the next dog was black. They were running about 5 yards apart. After 20 had passed I

decided to dive at one, being on the dole. I thought I could sell it at Darlington Market, but alas I ended up in a bed of nettles. They made no noise, and were like Old English sheepdogs only much larger, being about a metre in height. Their coats were shaggy and they had big heads. The whole apparition appeared to build up like a film show. I was not frightened in the least.[4]

As these four reports demonstrate, black dogs are usually seen in quiet rural locations. More specifically, they seem to favour lanes or ancient trackways, with hedges and trees around, churchyards, ancient sites, and their frequent proximity to water has also been noted, there often being a pond close by, or the dog frequents a bridge or path crossing a stream. They very often patrol a set route, so that it becomes known as a black dog haunt, and this spot sometimes coincides with a county boundary, as at the Devil's Bridge at Aston Dingle on the Powys/Shropshire border near Bishops Castle, or a lane at Uplyme following the Devon/Dorset border. They also favour certain gates, stiles or hedge gaps. All these facts must be significant, but it is a very difficult mystery to unravel. The liking for water, and especially bridges crossing water, is paralleled by our findings concerning female ghosts, as described in our book *Sacred Waters*. There we surmised that the bridge may symbolize the connection between this life and

The Black Dog Hotel at Uplyme on the Devon/Dorset border commemorates the phantom black dog which haunts the green lane following the county boundary.

the next. At death one crosses the bridge into unknown realms, but the ghosts are tied to this world and unable to cross over. It was also a traditional belief that spirits and supernatural beings could not cross running water. There may also be some way in which the ghosts are formed through the energy produced by running water.

So far as black dogs are concerned, some of them do have a connection with death, for they occasionally seem to act as death omens. In 1927 a man met a black dog near Ramsey on the Isle of Man. It had long shaggy hair and eyes like coals of fire, and would not let him pass. The witness's father died soon afterwards.[5] The death was simultaneous in a case from Norfolk. In 1930 a man saw a black dog on the road near Buxton Lamas church. It appeared seemingly from nowhere, and disappeared again as the witness reached out to pat it. He heard later that his brother had died at the same time as he had seen the dog.[6] A more recent instance of a dog foretelling a death took place on 6 January 1978, when the witnesses, a married couple, were driving home from Minehead (Somerset), on a misty evening.

One approaches Exford down a long, straight hill and as we got there it was already quite dusky. I was driving and I had the headlamps on.

Then we saw, coming up the hill towards us on the right-hand side of the road, the most extraordinary dog. It was alsatian type but with long dirty white hair which stood up around it in spikes, as if frozen. It looked almost transparent. Its eyes were red and glowing, the headlights could have accounted for this of course, but not for its baleful look, head down and staring at us sideways as it plodded along. Not many dogs make you exclaim as you pass them and still, when I think of it, it gives me goose shivers.

We were busy and forgot about it but my husband died in horrible circumstances later that year and my life changed drastically and unpleasantly.

I later met briefly someone else who said they had seen this dog and that it also presaged death.[7]

Notice in this report that the dog looked at the witnesses. This also happened in the 1927 Isle of Man encounter, and has been noted by other witnesses. It is as if there is some personal connection between apparition and witness, as there certainly is when the dog's appearance foretells a death. But the experience cannot be entirely subjective: there is sometimes more than one witness, and there are instances where living animals have shown fear at the presence of the ghostly animal. Although the black dog in its role of death omen may seem frightening, there have been many occasions when its presence has been comforting. It has often accompanied solitary women on their lonely walk home, acting as protector against assault or robbery because would-be assailants have kept away on seeing the dog. Interestingly, the Buxton Lamas witness felt no fear of the dog, reaching out to pat it; though it later proved to have been a death omen. So the dog's appearance can be either helpful or ominous, depending on the circumstances, and also depending on the part of the country, for the black dog tends to be regarded differently in different areas. Often, though, its appearance seems to have no personal significance at all for the witness.

That the phantom dog creates a genuine link between past folklore and present phenomena is shown by the way it shades over into the 'big cat' mystery described in Chapter 11. Some researchers have wondered if both creatures are in fact the same, that so-called 'black dogs' are actually specimens of out-of-place big cats reported so often in most areas of Britain at the present time. This is doubtful, because the cats seem to be living creatures, whereas the dogs are usually seen to be non-physical, the main evidence for this being the fact that they vanish in front of the startled witness. But there are also puzzling aspects to some creatures classified as 'black dogs', aspects which make the researcher familiar with both types of report wonder if there may be an overlap in some cases. To demonstrate this, here are a few cases.

The Carr Lane Cat of Hambleton (Lancashire) behaves very much like the classic black dog, but is described as a puma-like animal about 2½ feet tall with long, smoky-grey fur and bright yellow eyes. It was often seen in the village, and has appeared as recently as 1981. It would walk beside people, but when they reached out to stroke it their hands touched only empty air. Our informant, earth mysteries researcher Daresbury Hatton, has seen it fleetingly from behind: 'It trotted in a most life-like manner, but resembled a shadow projected on the night air.'[8] Equally mysterious is the animal seen in January 1947 at Chilham (Kent) by a man staying in the Woolpack Inn there. From the bedroom window he saw one afternoon an animal moving across the Pilgrim's Way towards the Neolithic long barrow known as Julliberrie's Grave.

> It aroused my interest, because it was black, and it appeared quite big. It was not as big as a calf, as I have seen mentioned in your book [*Alien Animals*]. I should have described it as being a 'big dog', if it wasn't for the fact that it was 'loping' along, with that sort of sinuous lope one connects with cats rather than dogs. It went behind the mound, or barrow, and I waited for it to appear at the other side, but it didn't. I watched for a while, but my wife being ready, we went out. And I never thought any more about it.[9]

There is nothing in this report to suggest whether the animal was a ghost or physical, but it is intriguing that the witness was not sure whether it was a dog or a cat. In 1928 a young man on holiday in County Derry (Northern Ireland) was similarly puzzled. While fishing in the river he saw a huge black animal padding along in the shallow water. It had blazing red eyes and bared its teeth as it looked up at the witness, who had by now taken refuge in a tree. Although it was daytime and he got a good look at the animal, he could not decide if it was a dog or a cat.[10] This echoes the experience of a number of witnesses of today's so-called 'big cats'.

Another phenomenon which is today usually ascribed to the cunning, strength and litheness of big cats or feral dogs, involves cases where some unknown creature has got into an apparently predator-proof cage holding birds or rabbits or other pets and has killed the occupants. One strange case in this category was sent to us by someone personally involved in the events which happened during the late 1940s at Alphamstone (Essex). The family living at Sycamore Farm bred chickens which they kept in a paddock surrounded by strong wire netting buried several feet in the earth and curved on top to prevent anyone climbing over. The doors were solid and padlocked. On the night in question the family were woken by the noise of the chickens. Looking through the bedroom window, the farmer saw what he described as a grey greyhound moving round the chicken huts in the centre of the paddock. It was a really big dog. He seized his gun and fired at it, whereupon it disappeared through the netting and into the hedgerow. The man went out to find the hole where it had entered, but meticulous searches then and during the following day failed to reveal any break in the netting. Nor could they find any tracks where the dog was seen. Our informant was present at the daytime searches, and she was positive that 'the entire paddock was totally dog and fox proof and even man proof'.[11] The conclusion must be either that the farmer was mistaken when he thought he saw a dog inside the netting, or the animal was a ghost.

6. *Mysterious deaths and injuries*

The majority of murders are straightforward. Domestic disagreements which get out of hand account for many tragic deaths; rivalry, jealousy and greed bring about others; the catalogue of human cruelties is unpleasant yet predictable. In most cases of murder the victim is easily identified, as is the cause of death and the motive, and the murderer is found without too much difficulty. But there are also plenty of more puzzling cases where people are found murdered and the police are unable to identify the victim. As people constantly go missing in Britain, this is perhaps not surprising. We shall not concern ourselves with such cases here, unless the death is surrounded by mystery for some other reason. We shall however write about some puzzling disappearances in Chapter 15.

In some murder cases the murderer is never found, and the case may also have some puzzling features. John Dawson was a farmer living at Bashall Eaves near Clitheroe (Lancashire). One Sunday evening in the spring of 1934 he was returning home from the pub when he felt a sharp pain on his back. He looked round but saw no one. Overnight his shoulder became very painful, and next day his sister discovered a large wound there. Dawson was taken to hospital immediately, but died three days later. Police discovered that he had been shot with a large home-made bullet cut on a lathe from a piece of steel, but although they made intensive searches in the area, no clues were discovered that indicated where the bullet was made or by whom. It was later said that John Dawson's ghost haunted the road to his farm, searching for the murderer.[1]

Another murder victim whose murderer was never identified, despite an intensive police investigation, was farm-worker Charles Walton. He was found dead on 14 February 1945 in a field on Meon Hill near Lower Quinton (Warwickshire): he had been killed by his own pitchfork, with slashes on his chest and throat forming a cross-shape. 'Fabian of the Yard', a famous Scotland Yard detective, headed the investigation, but nevertheless the mystery of who killed Charles Walton and why has never been solved. Many theories have been offered, the most popular involving witchcraft, and the full story can be read in Donald McCormick's book *Murder by Witchcraft*.[2] The Walton murder case was famous in its day, but even more famous, and still being written about today, are the murders committed by 'Jack the Ripper', though there is still no absolute certainty who 'Jack' was, and it is unlikely that we shall ever be sure of his identity. He murdered at least five women, all prostitutes, in London's East End in 1888, and left various clues, including mutilations showing surgical precision. In the century since the murders took place, many suggested identifications of 'Jack' have been made, including a gang of

Some of the events of 1888 when 'Jack the Ripper' murdered five women in London's East End.

Freemasons acting on behalf of the British Prime Minister and led by the ageing Sir William Gull, physician to Queen Victoria; a skilled astrologer, Dr Donstan, who was in search of occult power, and believed by Aleister Crowley to be Jack the Ripper; the Duke of Clarence, grandson of Queen Victoria; Virginia Woolf's cousin J. K. Stephen; the amateur cricketer M. J. Druitt; and others who all proved impossible to bring to justice.[3]

There can be no doubt that Jack the Ripper's victims, with their bodies slit open, were murdered. But what happened to Lavinia Farrar, who was found dead on the kitchen floor at her home in Cambridge in March 1901? There are numerous instances of strange deaths where it is not clear whether a murder has been committed, or if the victim died as a result of some freak accident. On the face of it, Lavinia Farrar's death sounds like murder, but . . . at the inquest the jury returned an open verdict. She was found lying on the floor with her face bruised and her nose broken. Beside her body lay a bloodstained knife and a few drops of blood. No wound could be seen, and it was not until her clothes were removed for a post-mortem examination that it was discovered she had been stabbed to the heart. She wore four garments, but none was damaged by the knife, and it could not have been inserted through the fastenings, which were not in a line. The wound was almost bloodless, with only a little staining of the innermost garment; the blood on the floor was said not to have come from the wound. There was no robbery or other apparent motive for this murder, if murder it was. But if not a murder, was it a suicide? Unlikely, because Lavinia Farrar was seventy-two and blind, and could not have undressed, stabbed herself and then dressed again, because she died almost instantly after receiving the injury.[4]

Equally puzzling was the fatal injuring of 69-year-old veterinary surgeon Sebastian Salaman, on the night of 26 May 1975. He was found next morning lying in the lane outside a friend's cottage at Nayland (Suffolk), and he died a day later without regaining consciousness. He had taken Mrs Alice Hawes home from a church social, around 11 p.m. All she remembered after returning home was falling and breaking a leg shortly after Mr

Salaman left – she also was discovered next morning. Mr Salaman was discovered by people living across the lane, who found him lying 15 feet from his car and half in the road. There was blood on the rockery, on the fence and on the car, and the cottage door was open. Mr Salaman had a fractured skull, a broken pelvis and broken ribs, but none of the neighbours had heard any disturbance.[5]

Some kind of hit-and-run road accident may have been the cause of Sebastian Salaman's death, as it may also have been the cause of our next victim's death, but in both cases this 'solution' is not totally satisfactory. The known facts about fifteen-year-old Peter Watts's last hours are these. On the afternoon of Sunday 18 January 1976 he left his home in Colwyn Bay (Clwyd) and possibly caught a train to Chester, after having left a note for his parents saying he intended to go and help a schoolfriend with revision. He then must have travelled to London, because at 1.30 a.m. on Monday 19 January he was found dying in the westbound carriageway of the Euston Road underpass. He had multiple injuries to the brain, lungs, liver, spleen and kidneys, and a major fracture of the skull, as if he had fallen from a great height. If Peter had travelled all the way to London by train, he would have arrived at Euston Station at 9.15 p.m., four and a quarter hours before his body was found not far from the station. Where was he during that time? It is clear that he fell – or was dumped – on the road only a short time before he was discovered, as three drivers using the underpass between 1 and 1.30 a.m. did not see him. No one has been found who saw Peter at Colwyn Bay Station (where he would have waited an hour for the Chester train), except for the ticket clerk to whom he gave £10 for a return ticket to Chester. No one remembers seeing him after that, until he was found dying, so no one knows where he was during those nine hours. Also, what happened to his watch, his ring, his keys, his comb, handkerchief and glasses, and his money? At the inquest in May 1976, the coroner said that he thought suicide was unlikely, but more likely was the possibility that Peter had been injured elsewhere and then dumped in the underpass. The jury's verdict was 'murder by person or persons unknown'.[6]

It is even less clear whether an act of murder led to our next mysterious death, though in outline the events are vaguely similar: victim goes missing unexpectedly, not seen again until discovered dead or dying, possibly dropped from some height. The victim was Zigmund Jan Adamski, who lived at Tingley near Wakefield (West Yorkshire). The 56-year-old Pole was a coal miner who wanted to take early retirement in order to look after his disabled wife, and also because his own health was poor. On 6 June 1980 he left home after lunch for a short walk to the local shops and never returned. It was thought most unlikely that he would have voluntarily disappeared, because he was looking forward to giving away his god-daughter at her wedding the next day. Five days after his disappearance his body was found perched on top of a pile of coal in a coal yard at Todmorden twenty miles away. Trevor Parker, the son of the yard's owner, found the body at 3.45 p.m. and he stated that it had not been there at 8.15 that morning. The pathologist estimated that death had occurred between 11.15 a.m. and 1.15 p.m. that day. So where was Adamski for the five days before his death, and how did he get on top of the coal heap? There was no evidence to suggest he had scrambled up the heap before dying, though it is possible that he could have done so and then died from his exertions. The post-mortem revealed no obvious cause of death. The only physical injuries were small cuts on the hands and knees, an abrasion on the right thigh, and a peculiar burn below the ear and reaching to his collarbone, as if caused by some corrosive substance. The pathologist was sure this burn had occurred two days before death, and it appeared to have been treated with some ointment. There were no internal injuries.

Adamski had apparently not been sleeping rough. Although he had not eaten on the day he died, he had eaten during the five days of his disappearance, he had only one day's growth of beard, and was not looking unkempt or scruffy, although he was not wearing a shirt. His watch was also missing. The pathologist concluded that death was due to natural causes, heart failure probably resulting from Adamski's long-standing ill-health and the stress of whatever had happened to him during the five missing days. At the inquest the coroner gave an open verdict, as there was no evidence to show whether others had been involved in Adamski's death, or whether he had suffered some unusual accident, perhaps combined with loss of memory. Speculation of course was rife, and much of it concerned a possible UFO involvement. Admittedly there are several strange coincidences in this case which could suggest a UFO connection:

1. Adamski is a name not uncommon in Poland, but rather less common in English-speaking communities. It was the name of a famous UFO 'contactee' in America, George Adamski, who claimed to have travelled to distant planets aboard flying saucers in the 1950s.
2. One of the two policemen who attended the coal yard on the discovery of Adamski's body was PC Alan Godfrey, who five months later claimed to have been taken aboard a UFO only half a mile away from where Adamski's body was found (see Chapter 14).
3. During 7–10 June unusual lights in the sky were seen in West Yorkshire, around Todmorden and Bradford.
4. The police could find no one who had seen Adamski during the five days between his disappearance and the discovery of his body.
5. Adamski suffered an unusual burn which might have been caused by exposure to whatever energy source is given off by UFOs.

The easy assumption is that Zigmund Jan Adamski was abducted by a UFO, sustained an injury during his five days' disappearance, and was finally dropped from the UFO into the coal yard at Todmorden. But however satisfactory this conclusion might seem, in that it appears to solve all the mysteries surrounding Adamski's death, it is of course only speculation and is suspect because it attempts to explain one mystery by invoking another. So we shall probably never know what really happened to him during 6–11 June.[7]

Death strikes some people like a bolt from the blue: our next victim apparently died as he was about to shave. This unidentified man was found lying by a stream on the southern side of Ben Avon near Braemar (Grampian Region) on 19

September 1938, about two months after he died. He was most unsuitably clad for mountain walking: he had on a dark suit, and close by were a walking-stick, a bowler hat and an attaché case containing pyjama trousers, two collars, a toilet roll, scissors and matches. His shaving gear was set out on a rock ledge.[8] Another mystery man died in somewhat similar circumstances early in 1976, his body being discovered in a shallow crevice on Dartmoor (Devon) more than a mile from the nearest road. He wore a grey suit and shoes that were unsuitable for walking on the moor. Despite intensive investigation he could not be identified – he had no driving licence nor other documents. All he had on him was a small amount of money, an Ordnance Survey map, a bottle of sweet-and-sour sauce, a bottle of poisonous laburnum seeds and twelve capsules of cyanide. There was no trace of poison in his body, and despite extensive forensic tests the cause of death remained unknown.[9]

Also unidentified was the body of a man which had fallen from the West Botley flyover near Oxford in 1975. Like the Dartmoor victim, he carried no papers, and the manufacturers' labels had even been removed from his clothes – he was wearing a neatly pressed pinstripe suit. He did have in his pockets five handkerchiefs with the letter M on them, and fifteen tablets of a drug called Vivalan. To add to the mystery, this drug was so new at the time that few doctors knew about it, they had only prescribed it to women, and none of them knew who 'M' was.[10]

Our catalogue of strange deaths ends with one that may have been a suicide with a difference. The victim was 60-year-old Michael Townsend from Bath. One afternoon in April 1982 a policeman watched with binoculars as a man, presumably Townsend, walked into the sea at Woolacombe (Devon). The policeman thought it strange that the man did not start to swim, but when he lost sight of him he thought he must have returned to shore. Twenty-five minutes later, Townsend's body was found on the beach. He was wearing only underpants, and he was in a kneeling position, with his head buried in the sand.[11]

A death took place in 1907 which seemed straightforward at first, but later became complicated. Albert Steer's body was taken from the River Thames near Chelsea Bridge in London, the day after he had left home in Bickley (London) saying he was going to Surrey. His son and daughter identified the body, which was not difficult as Steer had several unusual physical features – he had lost one eye, one toe had been crushed, and there was a dent over his eyebrow where some bone had been removed. Two months after his burial, Albert Steer turned up safe and well, saying he had been working as a gardener. So who was the drowned double who not only looked like Albert Steer but had also suffered the same injuries?[12]

Occasionally there are reports of mysterious injuries received by people who have survived to tell the tale, though in the case of Mrs Santuzza Campbell there was nothing to tell because whatever or whoever attacked her did so from behind. She was alone on the cliffs at Bridlington (Humberside) one day early in September 1954 when she was hit on the head and knocked unconscious. Nothing was found to account for the blow.[13] Many years earlier, in April 1911, three soldiers stationed at Colchester (Essex) were on different nights 'struck senseless by an unseen assailant' and seriously injured, but none of them could give any clues as to what had happened.[14]

Our next subject, who prefers to remain anonymous, does remember what happened to him. He was driving along the A422 road near Haselor (Warwickshire), returning home from Worcester to Stratford at night on 13 March 1980, when he saw a strange object in the star-filled sky. It was white and cigar-shaped, with a red light at either end, and appeared huge, filling the whole width of the car windscreen at its nearest approach. It moved across the sky ahead of him and disappeared at great speed. It made no sound, and the car engine and lights were not affected by its presence, but the steering wheel became very hot and burned the driver's hands. It soon went back to its normal temperature as the object sped out of sight.[15] There are several cases on record, both in Britain and abroad, where people have received burns through being in fairly close proximity to a UFO. Occasionally the burning seems deliberate rather than simply a side-effect of the closeness. Twenty-three-year-old Denise Bishop suffered a burn which she claims was caused by a UFO which shone a pencil-

Denise Bishop as she stood on the night in 1981 when she was struck on the hand by a green beam from a UFO. The resulting burn can be seen.

beam of green light on to the back of her hand. She was returning to her home in Plymouth (Devon) at 11.15 p.m. on 10 September 1981 when she noticed a huge UFO hovering over nearby houses. She later described what happened:

The object was unlit, and a dark metallic grey, but coming from underneath it and shining down on the rooftops beneath it were six or seven broad shafts of light. These were in lovely pastel shades of pink and purple, and there was also white. I saw all this in an instant, and I was terrified. I hurriedly reached for the door, but as I put my hand on the handle, from the unlit side of the craft a lime-green-coloured pencil beam of light came down and hit the back of my hand. As soon as it touched my hand I couldn't move but was stopped dead in my tracks. The beam stayed on my hand for at least thirty seconds, in which time I could only stand and watch the UFO. I was very frightened, although the UFO was a fantastic sight to see. It was huge and silent. In fact the whole area around about seemed very quiet. The green beam, which gave off no illumination and was rather like a rod of light, then switched off, and I continued to open the back door. It was in fact as though a film had been stopped and then started again. I had been stopped in mid-stride, and when the beam went off I continued with the same movement as before. I opened the door and rushed

59

into the house. As I did so I saw the UFO lift up into the sky slightly and then begin moving away out of my sight. Rubbing my hand, I ran and told my sister. Together we went outside again, but there was now nothing to be seen. We went in again, and my sister examined my hand, but there was nothing there to see. I sat down, and a few minutes later my sister's dog began sniffing at the hand, and made it sting. On looking at it again I now noticed spots of blood on it, and after I had washed it I saw that it was a burn.

Denise was interviewed in the early hours of 11 September by UFO investigator Robert Boyd, who photographed the burn then and later. Three months afterwards it was still visible.[16]

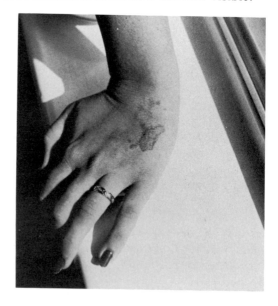

A closer view of the burn Denise claimed was caused by a UFO, photographed only thirty-six hours after the event.

7. Unidentified flying objects

UFOs, or flying saucers as they used to be called, seem to be a relatively recent phenomenon, having been in the public consciousness only during the last forty years. The concept of alien craft flitting about the skies originated in the USA during the late 1940s, after pilot Kenneth Arnold had a sighting of a formation of 'flying saucers' while he was flying over Mount Rainier in Washington State on 24 June 1947. Researchers have since shown that Arnold's was not the first sighting of unexplained objects in the sky, but his was the sighting which caught the attention of the media, with the result that 'flying saucer' became a household phrase overnight. Of course the mania soon spread overseas, including to Britain, and we would need a whole book to chart the subject of UFOs in Britain over the last four decades. In brief, there have been periods of great public interest, usually following an upsurge in sightings such as happened in the late 1960s with the many sightings of 'flying crosses' (explained away officially as jets refuelling in mid-air), and there have been periods of public apathy, usually after the subject has been overexposed in the media. The sightings themselves seem to have ebbed and flowed, but reports have never dried up altogether, even when public interest was at its lowest.

Ufology, as the study of UFOs is called, has become an extremely complex subject, and there are a number of dedicated researchers in Britain who soldier on trying to make sense of what in many respects is actually a nonsensical subject. Ufology is generally ignored by 'conventional' scientists, but it is clear that once the outer fringes of lunacy are stripped off there remains a hard core of genuinely puzzling reports from eyewitnesses who appear to be both trustworthy and intelligent enough not to be mistaking Venus or the moon or an aircraft for something more outlandish. What that 'something' might be, the researchers have yet to determine, but it is clear that there are meteorological phenomena which as yet we know little about, and some of these may be reported as UFOs. (See Chapter 23 for descriptions of some meteorological mysteries.) Only a very small proportion of UFO reports are actually genuine 'unknowns', or 'true UFOs', and some researchers would argue that none of them are, all sightings being explainable in natural terms if only we had enough knowledge of the natural world. But let us suppose that some sightings are indeed of alien spacecraft. To wonder whether the aliens are from other planets, from much closer to home, for example hidden terrestrial bases, or from other dimensions or other time-scales, is to tread a highly speculative path where many writers have trodden before. We will refrain from following them, and instead will concentrate on presenting a cross-section of 'typical' British UFO reports, to build up a picture of what is being seen in our skies today.

First, though, a few pre-1947 reports. In America during 1896–7 there was a wave of airship sighting reports, at a time when airship development was not sufficiently advanced for

A contemporary illustration of the Peterborough 'airship' of 1909.

these sightings to be of early terrestrial airships. There was a similar outbreak of reports in Britain in 1909 and intermittently in the years before World War I, the widespread public fear being that the airships were from Germany. A typical sighting, and one of the most famous, was that of PC Kettle in Peterborough (Cambridgeshire) in the early morning of 23 March 1909. He heard 'the steady buzz of a high power engine', and looking up saw a long oblong shape with a bright light attached. The 'airship' moved fast and was soon lost to view. More dramatic was C. Lethbridge's encounter with a landed airship two months later. The witness was walking home over Caerphilly Mountain (Mid Glamorgan) on the night of 18 May 1909, and later told reporters what he had seen.

> You know that the top of the mountain is a very lonely spot. I reached it about 11 p.m., and when turning the bend at the summit I was surprised to see a long, tube-shaped affair lying on the grass at the roadside, with two men busily engaged with something nearby. They attracted my close attention because of their peculiar get-up; they appeared to have big, heavy fur coats and fur caps fitting tightly over their heads. I was rather frightened, but I continued to go on until I was within twenty yards of them and then my idea as to their clothing was confirmed. The noise of my little spring-cart seemed to attract them and when they saw me they jumped up and jabbered furiously to each other in a strange lingo – Welsh or something else; it was certainly not English. They hurriedly collected something from the ground, and then I was really frightened. The long thing on the ground rose up slowly. I was standing still all the time, quite amazed, and when it was hanging a few feet off the ground the men jumped into a kind of little carriage suspended from it, and gradually the whole affair and the men rose in the air in a zig-zag fashion. When they had cleared the telegraph wires that pass over the mountain, two lights like electric lamps shone out, and the thing went higher into the air and sailed away towards Cardiff.[1]

Lethbridge found various items at the place where the airship had landed, including newspaper clippings referring to airship sightings and items on the German army, and it may well be that the airships were indeed carrying German spies, although there are a number of reasons why airship experts think this is unlikely.

Even more puzzling is a report which dates from the middle of World War I. The witness was looking out of the window of her home in Aldeburgh (Suffolk) just before midday. She saw a round platform with a handrail around it, moving silently at a height of about 30 feet above the ground, from the direction of nearby marshes and disappearing behind some houses in the direction of the sea. Standing on the platform were eight to twelve men, wearing blue uniforms and little round hats like sailors' hats. They stood close together and stared straight ahead, holding tightly on to the brass handrail. There was a second rail at knee height. This strange vehicle was in the witness's view for about five minutes.[2]

Another early UFO was of a more conventional design. This was seen near Brockworth (Gloucestershire) during November

Reliable photographs of UFOs are exceedingly rare. Thirteen-year-old Stephen Darbishire took this photograph at Coniston (Cumbria) *on 15 February 1954, but one investigator believed it to be a UFO painted on paper and then photographed.*

1939 by a man who was involved in building an extension to an aircraft factory at Brockworth; he was driving there at the time of his sighting, early on a Monday morning. Passing a farm, he noticed that it looked unusually deserted; then he heard a high-pitched humming noise and looked for its source. In a field behind the farm he saw hovering at a height of 20 feet a grey, bell-shaped object with a lower curtain of pale green light. He thought it was about 20 feet high by 25–30 feet wide, and only 100 feet away from him. As he watched, the light faded and the object tilted to one side and moved away. The witness then drove on to the factory, but soon returned to the farm to look for evidence of this strange experience. He found nothing, and as the weeks passed he became concerned for the people who had lived at the farm. It remained deserted, and he wondered if their disappearance had anything to do with the strange craft he had seen. Over forty years later, UFO investigator Mark Brown heard about the sighting and made exhaustive enquiries, but was unable to find any solution to the mystery.[3]

These reports indicate that UFOs/strange craft in the sky were being seen long before the flying saucer era began in the late 1940s. It is likely that many other sightings have been made during the last hundred years, and even earlier, but witnesses would have kept quiet about their experiences, not knowing where to report them, and also probably not wanting to face ridicule, a reaction which is still prevalent today. In a way it is understandable, because the events described by witnesses often sound too incredible for belief, however serious the witnesses may seem. There is usually, however, no apparent reason why the witness should tell a tall tale and invite ridicule. For example, pilot Leslie Groves was teaching a pupil in a Cessna F150 on 11 December 1979, and flying over Bolton (Greater Manchester), when he noticed a bright circular object, sharp in outline, moving below him. His pupil also saw it briefly. A few minutes later the pilot saw two more moving in the opposite direction. He estimated they were about 35 feet across and moving at 250 m.p.h. The investigator ruled out one possible explanation, reflections off seagulls, and the objects remain unidentified.[4]

When the reported sighting is much more dramatic, there is even *less* reason for the witness to make up such a fantastic experience, if he wants to be believed when he tells people about it. Therefore we can generally assume, unless the witness shows signs of mental disturbance, that witnesses who report strange UFO experiences genuinely believe that they saw what they describe. Such a witness is security guard John Byrne, who was on duty at Cairo Mill in Oldham (Greater Manchester) on the night of 8 October 1972 when he heard a humming sound. (This is often reported by witnesses; the 1939 Brockworth sighting reported earlier is one instance, and there will be others later in this chapter.) Alerted by the humming, John Byrne looked round and saw a strange object hovering beside the mill building. It was about 100 feet in diameter and seemed to fill the sky completely. It had a large window in front, brightly lit with a blue-white light, but nothing was visible through it. After five minutes, the craft turned on edge and John Byrne could see that it was saucer-shaped with a large dome; then it shot straight up into the air 'at a rate of knots which was absolutely fantastic'. John Byrne was understandably transfixed with fear and during the sighting did not call out to a colleague close by. He commented later: 'I've never seen anything like it and I don't want to see anything like it again.' In case anyone might be wondering if John Byrne could have imagined the whole experience, since his colleague noticed nothing strange, then if this was the case the factory cat shared his 'hallucination', for it ran away terrified and hid for several hours.[5]

Farmer Arthur Johnson also had a close sighting of a strange craft, in December 1977, when at about 10 p.m. he got out his car to collect his wife from her work. He was only yards from his home at Tittensor (Staffordshire) when he saw two bright lights and pulled up to look for the helicopter (as he thought it was). Instead he saw a cigar-shaped object about 40 feet long and with a small dome on top, travelling very low (about 100 feet) above the ground. It was in view for about half a minute, as it crossed the lane ahead of him at a distance of about 50 yards, passing just above the hedge and the telephone wires. It seemed to be metallic, and was glowing white from light emitted by the dome and from a grille or bars on the underside of the craft. The light also lit up the ground below. As the craft moved silently away towards the village, Mr Johnson got back into his car and resumed his journey, a very puzzled man.[6]

Lights often feature in UFO sightings, which may at first seem natural for craft travelling at night (though we should note that not all sightings occur at night). Cars use lights, ships use lights, aircraft use lights, so why shouldn't UFOs also use lights? However, this reasoning breaks down when you realize that UFOs have no need of lights. These craft are obviously so advanced that they could easily outmanœuvre any terrestrial aircraft which might be in danger of running into them, if they were travelling through the night sky unlit. If they are here for some purpose not concerning us, then why do they advertise themselves – for their lights can only be a form of advertisement. Presumably they cover themselves in flashing coloured lights because they wish us to see them. Before we find ourselves deep in a discussion of why UFOs wish us to see them, we will give another example of an illuminated UFO, just one from very many cases. The UFO seen by four girls on 12 December 1977 at Clifton Campville (Staffordshire) carried two flashing lights, red and blue. The girls heard a humming noise as the UFO passed overhead; then after descending into Lullington Woods it suddenly shot straight up into the sky.[7] Intriguingly, this UFO appeared in the same month as the craft seen by Mr Johnson 30 miles away and described earlier, but the physical appearance of the two UFOs was completely different.

Often UFOs appear to take no notice of the frightened observers, even though their light display seems designed to attract attention. Sometimes, however, a UFO will shine a beam of light directly on to witnesses as happened at Saltfleet (Lincolnshire) on 22 April 1984. The witnesses were a mother and daughter and her two young sons, staying on a caravan site by the sea. After 10 p.m. they saw an oval, domed UFO with a circle of nine white lights and red, blue and green lights above. Suddenly more lights appeared and the whole object began to revolve, with the lights flashing and then blurring with the speed of revolution. The UFO manœuvred for a while, then headed straight for the witnesses, came down to about 100 feet, and shone a beam of light on to them so that they were illuminated as in a spotlight. When the light dimmed they could see the craft very clearly. It finally flew out to sea, but not before other witnesses had seen it. The whole experience lasted about an hour.[8]

We have not heard whether the Saltfleet witnesses suffered any ill-effects from their exposure in a UFO's light beam, but our knowledge of such events would cause us to keep well away from any UFO that we might encounter. In the previous chapter we told of two instances of injury caused by UFOs, and there are others on record, including a horrifying case in America where two women and a young boy suffered serious injuries, including possible radiation damage, after having been too close to a UFO. There are also reports of deaths

Another UFO photograph with a possible mundane explanation. Wilfred Power saw nothing unusual in the sky when he photographed a giraffe at Plymouth Zoo (Devon) in August 1972, but the photograph revealed a UFO-like object. However, it could be a film or processing fault, which is often the explanation for 'UFO' photographs when nothing was seen at the time. Alternatively, Mr Power may have been too busy taking the photograph to notice the UFO whizzing by.

having occurred. In Britain we know of no injuries so serious, but two UFO witnesses in Cornwall (Newmill, 17 September 1977) suffered from vomiting, muscular pains and headaches after their sighting,[9] and two witnesses in Lancashire (Nelson, 9 March 1977) developed headaches, and one had watering eyes also.[10] In this latter case, Brian Grimshawe and his friend experienced a downwards pressure as the huge UFO hovered above them, and a tingling sensation as if they were being affected by an electromagnetic field. Paul Green had the same kind of experience at Langenhoe (Essex) on 14 September 1965, when he was travelling home on his motorcycle at 1 a.m. A domed UFO 'about as big as a gasometer' with flashing blue lights and making a high-pitched humming noise hovered overhead. The witness had by now dismounted, and felt unable to move. 'The flashing blue light became so intense that it was painful, and it appeared to fluctuate in rhythm with my heart beat and hit against my chest. I felt myself tingling all over, rather like the electric shock one gets when handling an electrified cattle fence.'[11]

We could continue indefinitely giving details of cases as weird as these. It is clear that many people in Britain have seen UFOs, and although not all of them have been as close to the craft as John Byrne, Brian Grimshawe, Paul Green and other witnesses in this chapter, they have noted enough peculiarities in the UFOs' behaviour to demonstrate that they were not watching the moon or Venus or satellite debris or an aircraft or helicopters or birds. All these have been mistaken for UFOs, and it is probable that some sightings at present marked 'unexplained' would become IFOs (identified flying objects) if we knew more about natural phenomena like ball lightning and plasmas. Two cases follow which for us are on the borderline between UFOs and IFOs, and illustrate very well the difficulty of distinguishing between the two. On 4 October 1974 George Longworth was driving past Bala Lake (Gwynedd) when a light like a 'blinding sun' flashed over his car, leaving behind a grey powder on his vehicle. Mr Longworth said he saw antenna-like protrusions on the object. Dr Patrick Willmore of the Global Seismology Unit in Edinburgh said: 'The description could fit that of a fireball, which is a floating, bright, electrical object – but the odd thing is the grey powder which fell from it. I just don't know about that.'[12] Equally puzzling was the 'red fiery circular object' which dropped out of the sky at Whitleigh, Plymouth (Devon), at 1.30 a.m. on 13 February 1983 before the startled eyes of a couple walking home from a party. The object hovered at the base of a lamppost for 30 seconds before shooting up into the sky again, leaving a patch of burnt grass.[13]

Both these 'UFOs' are totally unlike the awe-inspiring illuminated craft described earlier, and it seems almost certain that they were natural phenomena of some kind. Paul Devereux in his book *Earth Lights* describes his research into the possibility that many 'UFOs' are lights released by the earth at the site of faulting in the rock strata, and there is now strong evidence to support this hypothesis. However, lights of this kind could not be responsible for the craft described by some witnesses. Were these witnesses having hallucinations, or seeing some mundane object like the moon and from that stimulus unconsciously fantasizing an alien craft? It is possible . . . but how do we account for the multi-witness cases, of which there are many? A shared hallucination between two people is perhaps conceivable, but between sixty-seven? One of the best multi-witness sightings took place on the evening of 23 October 1978. Investigators Mark Brown and Graham Hall received sixty-seven independent reports covering the period from 6 p.m. until just before midnight, and an area of 425 square miles in western Leicestershire and extending as far as Burton-on-Trent and Nuneaton. Having analysed the reports very thoroughly, Brown and Hall decided that some people had been mistaken about the time, and that the 'fly-past' was of one UFO only, which travelled very slowly from south-south-east to north-north-west around 6.45 p.m. It was at a height of 2,000 feet, travelling at around 100 m.p.h., was very large, and it carried very bright lights, all these details accounting for the great number of witnesses. One report will suffice to describe what they saw.

I noticed three white lights travelling towards me. I thought at first it was an aeroplane going to land at Castle Donington with landing lights on. As it got nearer the lights got very bright and formed a triangle. This in itself seemed an unusual formation. I slowed down to view it more safely and realized there were no other lights as on normal aircraft . . . as it got closer . . . I could see the shape as a black silhouette. It was like a Vulcan bomber, triangular and with a light on each point and large. The other strange thing was that I heard no noise at all. After it passed the lights were no longer visible . . . I have never seen the like before and that includes three years in the RAF when I saw aircraft night and day.

One witness shot some movie film which showed three lights in a triangular form, thus confirming the many descriptions and proving that this was no hallucination. Brown and Hall investigated the possibility of a Vulcan bomber having flown over the area, but none of the bases from which Vulcans flew had one up at that time and flights over populated areas were not allowed. Local airport radar detected nothing unusual, and the Senior Air Traffic Controller at the East Midlands airport, in which direction the UFO was travelling, was very puzzled. The night of 23/24 October had been quiet and no military manoeuvres had been reported to him. It could not have been a Vulcan, because it was silent, except for some reports of a soft noise like a humming or whining, and no Vulcan travelling slowly at below 2,500 feet would have been inaudible. Nor were the lights at all similar to Vulcan lights. The object remains unidentified.[14]

The huge, low-flying UFOs with bright lights have been seen more frequently over the last fifteen years than the smaller domed discs which were once the most familiar type, but we cannot tell why this trend should be happening. It is only one of many mysteries in ufology. The subject becomes infinitely more mysterious when we start to analyse the close encounter cases, where people claim to have seen UFOs on the ground, sometimes with entities emerging and performing strange actions. Some people even claim to have spoken to UFO entities, or to have been abducted into the craft, and we will describe all these aspects of the UFO experience in Chapter 14.

8. Phantom soldiers, armies and battles

Considering how many battles have been fought on English, Welsh and Scottish soil, and how many armies must have marched thousands of miles in the course of their duties, it is really surprising that there are not more reports of the kind we include in this chapter. If strong emotion is in some part responsible for the creation of ghostly after-images, there must surely have been an abundance of emotion created when battles were fought, as men died sudden deaths and others struggled to retain their hold on life.

In fact some of the greatest accounts of phantom armies date from before 1885 and therefore strictly speaking do not qualify for inclusion in this book, but we will mention them briefly, as no account of phantom armies is complete without them. The Civil War Battle of Edgehill was fought on 23 October 1642 on the plain below Edge Hill near Kineton (Warwickshire), where on the following 23 December a phantom battle was fought lasting several hours. This was repeated several times in the days following, and King Charles who was in Oxford sent representatives to the scene to verify the stories he heard. They too saw the battle and even recognized some of the ghosts of people whom they had known in life. Ghosts have reportedly been seen on the battlefield in recent years, including a phantom horse seen in 1947 and again in the 1950s near communal graves where those killed in the battle were buried.[1] Ghosts have also been reported from the battlefields of Sedgemoor (Somerset),[2] Culloden (Highland Region) and Naseby (Northamptonshire), where for about a century after 1645 the battle was replayed annually in the sky above the battlefield.[3] In the mid-eighteenth century a vast army of men and followers was seen marching near Inveraray (Strathclyde

Region),[4] and a troop of phantom horsemen with carriages and marching soldiers was seen several times on Souther Fell (Cumbria). The appearances were on Midsummer Eve, 23 June, and on this day in 1745 twenty-six people watched the great army which covered half a mile on the fell.[5] These are just a few of the places where phantom armies have been seen, or phantom battles refought, and many other battlefields have been, or still are, haunted.

If we move forward in time to the present century, we find that reports of ghostly armies persist. A number of reports describe soldiers from Roman times, so the strength of the after-image in such cases is obviously very strong. At the White Sands on the Isle of Iona (Strathclyde Region) a ghostly fleet of Viking longboats has reportedly been seen on more than one occasion. John MacMillan was one witness. He saw fourteen ships land and the Viking occupants attack and slaughter a

A memorial to the Battle of Naseby (Northamptonshire) on the haunted battlefield.

group of monks standing on shore, before seizing their cattle and possessions from the nearby abbey and setting the building alight, then sailing out to sea again. This seems to be a rerun of events which took place in AD 986.[6] Also in Scotland, an even earlier military event was witnessed in 1950 by Miss E. F. Smith, who saw the aftermath of the Battle of Nechtanesmere 1,265 years after it took place in AD 685. She was returning home to Letham (Tayside Region) after attending a party in Brechin, when her car skidded on the icy road and landed in the ditch, so that Miss Smith had to leave it and walk the remaining eight miles home. As she approached Letham the time was 2 a.m. and she was very tired, partly because she was having to carry her small dog. She saw people carrying flaming torches, and the dog obviously saw them too because he began to growl. The apparition lasted for twelve minutes, and Miss Smith felt that the figures she saw were looking for their dead. She said: '. . . the one I was watching, the one nearest the roadside, would bend down and turn a body over and, if he didn't like the look of it, he just turned it back on its face and went on to the next one . . . There were several of them . . . I supposed they were going to bury them.' She described their clothing to the investigator, and it matched very closely the dress of a Pictish warrior carved on an ancient stone. In fact all the details she gave fitted the known facts very well, even to the location of the events in relation to a loch which no longer exists, all this information being unknown to Miss Smith at the time of her experience.[7]

One of the most vivid apparitions of soldiers on record was that seen in 1953 by eighteen-year-old Harry Martindale, then working as an apprentice plumber installing central heating in the Treasurer's House, York (North Yorkshire). He was knocking a hole in the ceiling when a Roman soldier stepped out of the wall. Mr Martindale did not realize at the time that his ladder was standing on the course of an old Roman road. He later described his experience as follows:

> I heard a sound – the only way I can describe it is the sound of a musical note. It was just like a trumpet blaring out – no tune, just a blare. At the same time, a figure came out of

A recent photograph of Harry Martindale, who in 1953 saw phantom Roman soldiers in the cellar of a house in York (North Yorkshire).

the wall. And the head of the figure was in line with my waist, with a shining helmet. I knew that it shouldn't be here, and when I say that I was terrified, I mean that I *was* terrified. I fell off the ladder and scrambled into the corner . . . and from there, I got a bird's eye view of what it was. It was the head of a Roman soldier.

The figure crossed the room at a slight angle and disappeared into the opposite pillar. He was immediately followed by another Roman soldier on horseback, Harry said, and behind the horse Roman soldiers in twos, walking side by side.

Now I was in no fit state to count them, but as I say, at the time I took a count of between 12 and 20. I was suffering from severe shock, and the immediate relief I got was that not one of them looked in my direction. You couldn't see through them. I saw them exactly as what you and I are.

The soldiers were small men, 'about five feet, in want of a good wash and shave. Nothing smart about them.' They were dressed in handmade uniforms, 'like shirts, made of cloth, in various shades of green'.

When they came through the wall, I couldn't see even the horse from the knees down. The road had only been excavated in the centre of the cellar. The surface is 18 inches below, and I couldn't see them from the feet up until they were walking on the centre of the cellar.

They all had the same helmets on, with the plumes coming out of the back, down the neck. They all carried a short sword on the right-hand side. I used to think that Roman soldiers carried a long sword, but it was like an over-sized dagger on the right-hand side.

The horse I can only describe as a great big cart horse – not like the chargers that they use nowadays on the television. And they came as quick as they went. When they were in the centre of the cellar, I could hear a murmuring, no speech, just a murmuring.

The terrified witness collapsed at the top of the cellar steps, where he was found by the museum curator, who said: 'By the look of you you've seen the Roman soldiers.' The curator himself had also seen them, seven years before, and in the late 1930s an American professor had gone into the cellar specifically to see them and had done so, which indicates that others before him had also seen them.[8]

Mr Martindale's Roman soldiers must date back at least 1,500 years, and possibly as much as 1,900 years, for the first Roman fortress in York dates from around AD 71. However, even these are not the oldest ghosts seen in Britain. The oldest we know of is the horseman, possibly a soldier, who is thought to be a ghost from the Bronze Age, almost 3,000 years ago. Several people have seen him, but archaeologist R. C. Clay was able to date him from his clothing, when he got a close sight of him in 1924. The ghost haunted Bottlebush Down in north Dorset, and Mr Clay saw him galloping along the road parallel to his car. The horseman was using no bridle or stirrups. He wore a long flowing cloak and waved a weapon above his head. He vanished near to a burial mound.[9]

Not all witnesses of phantom battles actually see the events being re-enacted; sometimes only the sounds of battle are heard. Offham Hill near Lewes (East Sussex) was the site of a great battle over 700 years ago, when 3,000 men died, and in late May, around the anniversary of the battle, people have reported hearing strange noises in the area, men shouting and horses whinnying, with no apparent physical source for these sounds.[10] A couple living at Holme Hale (Norfolk) actually found themselves in the midst of a phantom battle in the small hours of the morning when they returned home from visiting friends. They heard shouting, running feet and galloping horses, but could see nothing as they walked into the village street to investigate. Suddenly the noises seemed much nearer, and the couple felt themselves to be surrounded by a battle which gradually moved away into a field. Researchers could find no record of a large-scale battle at Holme Hale, but there had been several smaller disturbances, from attacks by the Danes in the eleventh century to rioting during Ket's Rebellion in 1549.[11]

A well-known battle site where ghosts have been seen on several occasions in this century is Marston Moor (North Yorkshire). In November 1932, Tom Horner and Arthur

A memorial on Marston Moor battlefield (North Yorkshire) where ghosts have been seen more than once.

Wright were driving across the battlefield on a misty evening when they both saw two men in the car headlights. Mr Horner described them as wearing large soft hats, dark plum-coloured cloaks and leggings. Mr Wright said:

> They seemed two fine fellows about six foot high, and built proportionately. The one I saw most clearly had on a long brown cloak, dark brown top boots, long hair, and a large hat, turned up at the side with a cockade. The other was dressed likewise, but being in the shade appeared to be in black.

Mr Horner dipped his headlights for a bus approaching, and when he put his lights up again the road was empty. 'Being alarmed we got out of the car and searched the road everywhere. There was no hedge or wall, and nowhere for these men to have gone.'[12] Other people crossing the battlefield have also seen ghosts. In 1968 a car driver and his passengers saw five or six men in strange clothing, possibly of the seventeenth century, stumbling along a ditch. Five years later they were seen again.[13]

In November 1960 Dorothy Strong and the driver of the taxi in which she was travelling saw phantom soldiers at the site of the Battle of Otterburn (Northumberland), fought in August 1388. Mrs Strong said: 'Suddenly the engine died, the fare-meter went haywire and the taxi felt as if it was being forced against an invisible wall. The soldiers seemed to close in on us then fade into thin air.' This was apparently not the first time phantom soldiers had been seen at this spot, and indeed Mrs Strong herself saw them three times altogether.[14]

Peter Zinovieff and Patrick Skipwith may also have seen ghosts from the fourteenth century when they were doing geological work on the Isle of Skye (Highland Region) in November 1956. They were camping in Harta Corrie in the Cuillin Mountains, and in the early hours of one morning they saw dozens of kilted men scrambling along the mountainside in total silence, and watched them for several minutes. On another night soon afterwards they saw them again, this time retreating in disorder towards the Bloody Stone which marks the scene of a battle in 1395. Whether the two men witnessed part of this battle, or a later clash of Highlanders, perhaps during the '45 Rebellion, is uncertain, but they were adamant that they had seen the phantom Highlanders and, on reporting their experiences locally, were told that Harta Corrie was known to be haunted.[15]

We end this tour of ancient battlefields with a possible ghostly echo of the most recent conflict to touch British shores. According to a report in the *US News and World Report* in 1978, sounds from World War II battles may be echoing round the North Atlantic. The US Navy has a network of super-sensitive hydrophones called SOSUS – Sound Surveillance System – buried on the ocean floor, and linked to land stations scattered along the coasts, where armies of listeners compare the incoming sounds with computerized libraries of submarine sounds and engine noises. According to the report, strange and unaccountable faint sounds have been picked up since SOSUS was installed in 1952. It was suggested that these sounds, like distant explosions and cannon fire, were being perpetuated by freak conditions under the sea in much the same way as a coil immersed in liquid helium becomes 'super-conductive', losing all resistance and allowing any current to flow virtually unobstructed for a very long time. One expert on undersea surveillance thought the cause might be deep channels, known to exist, which 'act like huge natural telephone cables. Sound seems to be able to travel along them without deterioration in the signal. The sound goes back and forth, losing hardly any of its strength . . .' Strange currents and temperature conditions seem to create these 'deep sound channels', but there is a snag to this theory, as this expert admitted: 'Not all sounds are "stored" in this way for years. The sounds apparently have to have occurred at the right place . . . but how sounds get into this "system" remains a mystery.' It is well known that the sounds of undersea earthquakes and volcanic activity can carry extraordinary distances in the sea, and some critics have indeed explained these sounds in this way. But the SOSUS experts could hardly have overlooked such an obvious explanation (if relevant) before coming out with their remarkable theory.[16]

If sounds really are perpetuated in water in this way, does this offer any clues as to how images as well as sounds can be perpetuated out of water for long periods of time, several thousand years in some cases? One popular theory is that images of the events are somehow trapped in the surroundings either indefinitely or for a limited period of time under certain conditions, and are released or replayed, again when the conditions are favourable. But there are so many unknowns in this theory that it is quite inadequate in explaining ghosts, be they of soldiers or everyday people like Grandfather Bull who featured in Chapter 4. Unfortunately researchers seem to shy away from tackling ghostly phenomena, though there are surely enough well-authenticated cases now on record to convince anyone that ghosts are a valid subject worthy of investigation.

9. Out-of-place animals roaming the countryside

Bertie the giant bat is proving a handful for RSPCA staff at Exeter. The bat, which has a 3 ft wing-span, was found [in September 1984] clinging to the radiator of a car in the city.

The driver went straight to the RSPCA kennels, where helpers gingerly avoided Bertie's sharp teeth and made him a temporary home in a large cat cage.

Now officials want to know how the tropical fruit bat – probably from New Guinea – reached Exeter.

Assistant manageress Teresa Joslin (22) said: 'He's been tucking into bananas and apples. He seems as tame as he can be and we want to find the owner, if he's got one, because we haven't really got the space to keep him here.'[1]

Bertie the bat is but one of many specimens of immigrant wildlife recorded in Britain over the last hundred years. The creatures seen range from crocodiles to hyenas, from a Japanese sea squirt (found in the Helford estuary, Cornwall) to New Zealand stick insects (which are naturalized in Cornwall).[2] Because there are logical ways of explaining how the smaller immigrants, such as insects, butterflies, molluscs, crustaceans, and smaller reptiles, arrived here (hidden among imported goods, or in some cases perhaps even brought here as unusual pets, later discarded), and because birds are often zoo escapes or wanderers flying well off course, and because fish are sometimes known to swim long distances from their native waters if confused by abnormal weather conditions, we shall not include them in this chapter, but will concentrate on the larger species whose presence here is rather more difficult to explain.

There is no shortage of explanations, of course, but rarely are they supported by evidence, and it is interesting that the same explanations are trotted out again and again. The most popular explanations given for sightings of alien wildlife are:

1. Zoo escapes – but often local zoos claim that all their inmates of that species are safely in their cages; also zoo escapes are widely publicized and the escapees usually quickly caught, as they are not used to running free and can become frightened and hungry.
2. Escapes from travelling circuses – this old chestnut is usually offered when monkeys or bears, for example, are reportedly seen, even if any local circus has lost no animals, and also sometimes when there is no circus within miles.
3. Escaped or abandoned pets – another popular explanation, especially for puma sightings, and sometimes likely to be true, but as with zoo escapees, ex-pets may no longer have the ability to fend for themselves in the wild, whereas the true immigrant wildlife seems to be very successful at surviving.
4. Misidentification of native animals – this probably does apply in some cases, especially in poor light conditions or when the animal is only briefly seen, but such a suggestion is an insult to a witness who has seen a strange creature at close quarters and in good light.

There are also some rather more exotic explanations for out-of-place animals, but these are unlikely to appeal to the authorities whose job it is to capture these creatures or to reassure the public that there is no danger – which they may do by suggesting, for example, that the lynx reportedly seen prowling around someone's garden was really only a domestic tabby.

1. Teleportation – a concept which, if it could be shown to be valid, would provide an explanation for many mysteries. It means, in brief, the instant relocation of an object or living creature from one place to another, by a mechanism as yet unknown. It has certain attractions as an explanation for some reports of immigrant wildlife, those where only one animal is seen, briefly, which then fails to be seen again in the locality. Or, if it is caught, its origin cannot be traced.

Teleportation may seem a far-fetched concept, but some cases very suggestive of its occurrence will be given in Chapter 15.

2. Ghosts – some immigrant wildlife may only appear to be physical and solid, just as the black dogs of Chapter 5 seemed like living dogs, until the witnesses reached out to touch them. In most cases, witnesses of immigrant wildlife never get close enough to touch the boar, or crocodile, or whatever it may be, and so its apparitional nature may go undetected.

3. Spontaneous revivals – a theory, offered by John Michell and Bob Rickard in their books *Phenomena* and *Living Wonders*, that creatures which once inhabited an area and then became extinct can sometimes re-establish themselves there. In their own words: 'We note the tendency of animals all over the world to recur in places which were once their native haunts, and we are drawn to reconsider the ancient belief that every part of the earth naturally produces the life-forms which are characteristic of it.'[3]

So much for the explanations; now let us look at some of the sighting reports. The animals most often seen (apart from big cats, sightings of which greatly outnumber all other species – they will have Chapter 11 to themselves) are boars, bears, crocodiles and wallabies, with many others putting in occasional appearances, for example wolves, porcupines, jackals, monkeys, hyenas, Arctic foxes, raccoons, Nilgai antelopes, yaks. Some of these are known to have established successful breeding colonies, such as the Tasmanian wallabies which have colonized the Derbyshire and Staffordshire Peak District since about 1940, when the estate where they were kept was neglected. There is also a colony of wallabies in the Ashdown Forest (East Sussex), and there are occasional sightings in Kent/Sussex/Hampshire which may be connected with this. On 16 November 1984 a wallaby was seen in the town centre of Henley-on-Thames (Oxfordshire) and others have been seen in the countryside nearby, said to be escapees from a private collection of twelve wallabies, which lived confined in a 70-acre park surrounded by a 6-foot-high fence, but tunnelled to freedom.[4] It seems that wallabies are frequent escapees, and pretty good at keeping concealed and surviving. A 'kangaroo' (we suspect it was really a wallaby) was seen in fields in Bedfordshire in mid-April 1978, and police caught up with it at Hockliffe, but it got away. None of the local zoos was missing a kangaroo or wallaby.[5] Hockliffe is not too far distant from Whipsnade Zoo, where a wallaby was run over on the public highway nearby in early August 1975. But the zoo said it was not one of theirs.[6] These two sightings suggest there may be another colony of wallabies living in Bedfordshire, possibly escapees from years past that the zoo has quietly forgotten about?

Other animals which have established successful colonies include porcupines, following the escape of a pair of Indian crested porcupines from a wildlife park, the Pine Valley Zoo, in Devon around 1970. In the early 1970s they were breeding happily in woodland near Okehampton, eating tubers (especially bluebell bulbs), roots and fruit;[7] and another colony has been reportedly discovered in Wiltshire. Raccoons also seem to have successfully adapted to an environment different from that in their native North America, having become feral in a number of areas, including Kent. One was found near Daventry (Northamptonshire) in 1976,[8] and another in North Wales seven years later. Farmer's wife Mrs Mair James of Pen y Glannau Farm, Gellilydan (Gwynedd), was woken in the early hours of 24 October 1983 by the barking of her dogs. Something had disturbed the chickens, so she went out and let the dogs loose. She spotted a greyish-brown, bushy-tailed animal with a sharp snout and thought at first it must be a cat. It ran up a tree and when she shone her torch on it, she soon realized it was not a cat. She called the RSPCA and their local inspector came immediately. He said:

When I was given the description it fitted that of a raccoon but I just could not believe it. Nevertheless when I got to the farm, I saw that it was a raccoon. I had one devil of a job to get it down. Raccoons are normally confined to North America and I understand that they are classed as dangerous wild animals in this country. Anyone keeping them as pets should have a special licence. But on checking, no such licences have been issued to anyone in this area. How the raccoon came to be in the area is a mystery to me and the police.[9]

The animal was taken to the North Wales Mountain Zoo at Colwyn Bay where they commented: 'Although he seems well we think he was probably running wild in the hills for a long time. It will certainly be a lot better for him here.'[10] Perhaps there is another colony of raccoons living in Snowdonia?

Surprising though the successful colonies of porcupines and raccoons might be, even more surprising is that wild boars appear to be living wild quite happily in Britain. Boars were once common, but are believed to have become extinct around the seventeenth century. However, perhaps they never did become totally extinct? In the summer of 1972 there were several sightings, including a capture and a killing, in Hampshire. The capture was made in a garden at Odiham, where a 200-pound boar was eating young trees and generally making a nuisance of itself. No zoos or other keepers of exotic beasts in the south of England admitted to having lost a boar. A few days later another was seen near Odiham, running into woods, but police with dogs found nothing. The same happened after another sighting was reported later in August. Then on 2 September a farmer saw one eating his barley, and shot it.[11] Four years later, in March 1976, a year-old wild boar was run over and killed on a forestry road near Nairn (Highland Region), but the Highland Wildlife Park which had a breeding pair claimed that no boars of theirs had gone missing.[12] Boars seem to be attracted to domestic gardens. In December 1979

One of the gardens at Basildon (Essex), thoroughly 'dug over' by a wild boar in December 1979. He left his signature in clear hoof-prints.

85

one was causing annoyance to householders by rooting about in gardens in Basildon (Essex) during the night. It was never caught, though it was seen several times, once grazing in a field with some horses.[13]

We must look back quite a few centuries to find any trace of native bears. They lived successfully in Britain before the last glaciation, along with elk, lynx, wolf and wolverine (the last three of which have also, interestingly, been reported seen in Britain within the last hundred years despite being officially extinct). But we also have recent reports of bears being seen in North Yorkshire, Bedfordshire, Norfolk and Greater London. The earliest of these reports is from February 1975, when milkman David Bowlby thought he saw a bear in woods on Skipwith Common near Riccall (North Yorkshire). He was within 20 yards of it before it ran away, and he said: 'I'm sure it was a bear, not fully grown. It was brown with black foot-pads; standing by a tree. It was about as big as an Alsatian dog on all fours; on its hind legs it was about as tall as a 10-year-old child.' He saw it again a few minutes later, and claimed that others had seen it too. No zoos or circuses in North Yorkshire had lost a bear, but one zoo suggested the animal might be a raccoon, as one of theirs had disappeared. But the animal seen by David Bowlby stood 4 feet 6 inches tall, and does not sound much like a raccoon.[14]

In the following year, but many miles away, children playing in a sandpit in Leighton Buzzard (Bedfordshire) ran home shouting that they had seen a huge, hairy animal, a bear, in the sandpit. Mrs Maureen Walsh went back with them and found large pawprints in the sand. She also saw 'a large black object trundle into the woods'. The police could find no trace of any bear, and the local press were inclined to explain away the report.[15] This sighting was on 12 June 1976 and, strangely enough, eight years later another bear sighting was made only a mile away, at Heath-and-Reach. Early in December 1984 a brown bear was spotted in a sand quarry, being seen by three people. Although the police took the report seriously and maintained an all-night vigil, nothing was found, only foot-prints which were identified as belonging to deer, and the experts were inclined to believe that it was a deer that had been seen.[16] However, the sightings were made in daylight, and would three separate people mistake a deer for a bear? It seems unlikely. But the strangest aspect of these reports is the fact that on both occasions the bears were seen in sand pits only a mile apart. Is there a bear, living wild in Bedfordshire, that likes playing in sand? In June 1979, motorists on the A1066 road at Snare Hill, Thetford (Norfolk), reported seeing a bear in the forest, which was said to have escaped from a travelling circus. As Bob Rickard aptly commented when reporting this case in *Fortean Times*: 'I wish I had £1 for every travelling circus that's sneaking along our byways distributing exotic aliens.'[17]

Bears lurking in the English countryside are strange enough, but in the eastern suburbs of London? On 27 December 1981 four boys aged nine to thirteen said they had seen a 'giant great growling hairy thing' on the 5,000 acres of scrubland called Hackney Marshes. Thirteen-year-old Tommy Murray saw it rear up on its hind legs, and he fled. The boys had earlier seen strange tracks in the snow, which they thought looked like a bear's pawprints. Fifty police with dogs, marksmen and a helicopter searched the marshes, but found only more of the strange tracks. A hoax was suspected, and one of the chief inspectors organizing the search commented:

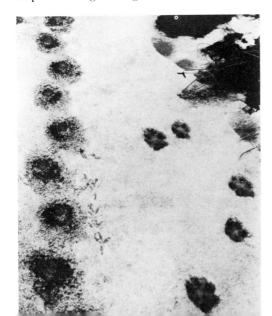

Pawprints left in the snow at Hackney Marshes in December 1981.

87

Although I didn't see the boys myself, I'm reliably informed that they were very frightened by what they saw. They were not hoaxers, although, of course, they may have been hoaxed. The search itself was interesting . . . it was winter and there was about two inches [of snow]. I saw three sets of prints that to me were very strange. One line of prints [was] on an island which had a perimeter fence and a locked gate. The other two lots were near marshalling yards. All three were on virgin snow and could not have been made by a [hoaxer] because no other prints were near them or led to or from them. *But* these prints could easily have been misinterpreted by all who saw them [because] the snow had begun to melt and then re-frozen. A man went to London Zoo and secured a footprint of a bear on a piece of cardboard. When this was placed next to a [mystery] print there was little similarity. The real bear print was bigger and a slightly different shape. Police dogs which usually go bananas at a whiff of a Kray Twin, took no notice whatsoever. The searches were inconclusive but that was not necessarily the reason they stopped, nor was the alleged confession by the alleged hoaxer. The trouble with a live bear is that, unlike most things police search for, it is not static and can cover 15 miles in a night. There are so many ways off Hackney Marshes if you're a bear that after one full day of searching a second would be pointless without a further sighting to assist . . . There were no more credible witnesses. In my opinion the boys were frightened by something that was probably someone dressed up as a bear.

An inconclusive termination to a definite mystery, made more mysterious by the discovery earlier in December of two bear corpses in the River Lea in Hackney. They had been skinned and decapitated. And even if the 'bear' was someone dressed in a bearskin, how were the footprints made, and by whom or what?[18]

It seems unlikely that crocodilians could ever live comfortably in the British climate, but there have been several sightings of these creatures, which are hard to mistake for anything else. In March 1962 'a lizard-like four-footed animal, three feet long, weighing about 10 lbs, sandy coloured, and with a black stripe along its back' was killed in a road accident in Friern Road, East Dulwich (Greater London), and the corpse, being unidentified and therefore an embarrassment to police and RSPCA, was buried. In August 1966 an alligator was found in a garden in Westleigh Avenue, Leicester, while in June 1970 a 4-foot crocodile was seen on the bank of the River Ouse at Little Barford (Bedfordshire). There were two reports in 1975, of a crocodile seen basking on the bank of the River Stour at Sandwich (Kent) in July, and a baby alligator found on a road at Stevenage (Hertfordshire) in August. In March 1978 twelve-year-old Kay Hall found a 5-foot-long dead crocodile behind her house and took it to school, in Caerphilly (Mid Glamorgan).[19] As if these reports weren't strange enough, on 16 May 1980 three motorists reported seeing a 6-foot crocodile crossing the M55 motorway near Preston (Lancashire), and one even claimed to have run over its tail. Police and dogs searched in vain.[20]

We close this chapter with some reports of creatures seen less often, and first of all an older report, from 1905, which shows that immigrant wildlife is not just a phenomenon of the last twenty years. Other earlier reports will be found in the Chronological List and Gazetteer. In early 1905 farmers in Kent, in the countryside between Tonbridge and Sevenoaks, were suffering mysterious attacks on their sheep.

> Sometimes three or four sheep would be found dying in one flock, having in nearly every case been bitten in the shoulder and disembowelled. Many persons had caught sight of the animal, and one man had shot at it. The inhabitants were living in a state of terror, and so, on the first of March, a search party of 60 guns beat the woods, in an endeavour to put an end to the depredations.

The animal was located and killed, and identified as an Indian jackal. The body was stuffed and displayed in the studio of a Derby taxidermist.[21]

Not far away in distance, but some 66 years later in time, another strange animal was causing problems on a farm at

Nutley on the edge of the Ashdown Forest (East Sussex). It was in the area for several months from spring to autumn 1971, and although it spent much time in the fields where the sheep were grazing, it never attacked them. Farmer Alistair Whitley described it as a 'very heavy strong dog with fierce eyes and round pricked ears, yellowish in colour splotched with darker marks', and said that it was living on wild rabbits. He was eventually able to get a shot at it and it crawled into dense undergrowth and was never seen again. Before that, it had been identified from pawprints and hairs as an African spotted hyena.[22]

Another large and distinctive animal was killed by the witness's dog at Saltaire (West Yorkshire) in March 1983. David Bottomley and Sheba, a collie, were walking by the River Aire when Sheba flushed an unusual prey from the undergrowth. The two fought, Mr Bottomley being unable to separate them, and when Sheba had killed her opponent, David Bottomley was puzzled by what he saw. The animal had a small head, a long thin dog-like muzzle, small rounded ears, long wolf-like fangs and a handsome silky snow-white coat. From a wildlife book he identified it as an Arctic fox, and this identification was later confirmed by a zoologist.[23]

If the thought of all these potentially fearsome wild beasts roaming around the United Kingdom is frightening, be consoled by the thought that none of them has been known to attack human beings. If cornered and provoked, of course they would attack in self-defence, but if left alone they will only be concerned to slink away under cover – and the same goes for the big cats we will meet in Chapter 11. So do not panic if you see an out-of-place animal. Keep still, observe the creature, and then send us the details – with a photograph if you have the opportunity to take one.

10. Ball lightning: mysterious exploding spheres

Some scientists do not admit the existence of ball lightning: others suggest that it is quite common. But no one can yet explain what it is and how it is formed. It is usually, but not always, seen during thunderstorms, and can take a number of different forms. A diameter of 5–15 inches is most common, though the ball can be as small as a pea or bigger than a house. It is luminous, usually spherical, and yellow, red or bluish-white in colour, though green and purple 'fireballs' have been reported. It usually falls or descends from the sky and moves around for a few seconds, often entering houses, and it usually disappears with an explosion which can cause damage. When ball lightning enters a house, it sometimes moves around a room as if exploring it, almost as if directed by some form

No one is sure what this photograph shows – but it might be ball lightning. When M. R. Lyons of Nottingham took the photograph in the hills of Derbyshire in the early summer of 1972 he noticed nothing unusual. He took several photographs of the same scene at intervals of about fifteen seconds, but the light-ball appeared on only one frame, so it was either short-lived or moving fast. It doesn't appear to be caused by lens-flare or a film or processing fault.

of intelligence, and naturally this causes some consternation to witnesses. A few representative reports of ball lightning entering houses will show what might be seen next time a thunderstorm strikes your area.

On the afternoon of May 28 last, whilst I was in the kitchen of my house in the country during a most violent thunderstorm, my housekeeper sitting on one side of a window, the top sash of which was open and I on the other, simultaneously with a very heavy peal of thunder a red-hot bolt the size of a small rocket flew in through the open window, followed by a stream of sparks. When in the middle of the kitchen the bolt exploded with a bright flash and sharp crack as of a pistol. Stranger still, this was followed in about 15 seconds by two more similar bolts, one of which came through the back door and one through the front door, both of which were open. There was no smell or after-effect noticeable.[1]

This took place on 28 May 1901 in Liverpool (Merseyside).

Two ladies sitting at a table at 8 p.m. on 17 August 1921 in Eastbourne (East Sussex) were privileged to see a rarer example of miniature ball lightning. Although it was raining at the time, there was no thunderstorm nearer than about fifty miles.

As one of the ladies took up a knife to cut bread the ball of light was seen to flash past the knife (without touching it) on to the table, travelling a distance of about 9 inches at an average height of about 3 inches from the table, but moving toward the latter. When the ball touched the tablecloth it 'went out with a spitting sound', leaving no mark or trace of any sort . . . As to the appearance of the ball itself, it was 'about the size of a pea, the light encircling it being about the size of a golf ball. The light was white and intensely bright, like electricity. Too dazzling to see through.'[2]

The brilliant blue ball of flame, 'a sort of bluey electric colour with sparkling flashes', seen by Miss Edith Foster in February 1981 inside her flat at Warminster (Wiltshire) seems to have been attracted to her electric oven. Miss Foster was standing at the oven cooking, when she saw the marble-sized light floating through the door from the dining-room. It missed her face by inches and settled on one of the cooker rings, where it burned fiercely until she turned off the electricity at the mains. Afterwards the cooker was still working, but that ring was burned out.[3]

Ball lightning does not always cause damage when it enters a house, but when it explodes indoors the result can be unpleasant for the householder. In Suffolk on 20 July 1897 ball lightning entered a cottage and went upstairs, where it exploded in a small bedroom. The plaster was cracked, the wallpaper torn, and whitewash covered the bed and the floor. The house was also filled with a strong smell of sulphur.[4] When a fireball exploded in a beach café at Crail (Fife Region) in August 1966, the thick cast-iron top of the café's stove was split from end to end.[5] Buildings can be damaged, too, when outdoor ball lightning explodes close to them. On 11 April 1894 near Dunstable (Bedfordshire) a fireball which was seen to fall from the clouds during a thunderstorm severely damaged a barn,[6] while in Coventry (West Midlands) on 10 November 1940 a pale blue-green ball about 2 feet across and seemingly 'made of a mass of writhing strings of light, about ¼ inch in diameter' exploded behind a public house, causing much damage.[7] A huge fireball wrecked the east end of Barsham church (Suffolk) on 8 February 1906, during a thunderstorm. An eyewitness told of 'a huge circle of light' appearing in the sky, two or three times the diameter of the setting sun and yellow or white in colour. It was visible for some time and seemed to travel over the house, which was 100 yards away from the church. It may have collided with the church, for the witnesses heard 'an appalling crash . . . like the bursting of a big shell immediately overhead', which they later assumed was the moment when the church had been damaged.[8]

Giant ball lightning of this kind is comparatively rare, but another example was reported from Dyfed on 8 June 1977, when a brilliant, yellow-green transparent ball as big as a bus and with a fuzzy outline came from the cumulus cloud hanging over Garn Fawr mountain, Fishguard, and floated down the hillside, rotating and seeming to bounce off projections on the ground. It gave off an intense light for three seconds before flickering out. It caused static on the radio, and witnesses also noticed that cattle and seabirds close by seemed disturbed.[9]

Fortunately, ball lightning rarely causes physical injury to living creatures, perhaps because most people do not touch it. One witness who did touch a 4-inch ball of bright blue or purple light which appeared in her kitchen described what happened: 'The ball seemed to hit me below the belt, as it were, and I automatically brushed it from me and it just disappeared. Where I brushed it away there appeared a redness and swelling on my left hand. It seemed as if my gold wedding ring was burning into my finger.' It had moved straight towards her after appearing above the cooker during a thunderstorm at Warley (West Midlands) on 8 August 1975. She also noticed that it gave off a singeing smell and made a rattling noise, but this all happened very quickly since the time from its

This illustration of a fireball landing shows the sort of event which is attributable to ball lightning.

appearance to when she brushed it away was only about one second. It also damaged her clothing where it had struck her.[10]

On 15 August 1974 a climber was struck by ball lightning in Glencoe (Highland Region). John Graham and Jimmy Alexander were climbing Bidean-nam-Bfan when a thunderstorm began to rage. Mr Alexander describes what happened.

> I was about a yard behind John. I saw this thing, about the size of an orange and the same colour, only very bright as if it were lit from the inside. It seemed to be darting up the ridge towards us like a bouncing rubber ball. Then there was a blinding flash and a cracking noise and John went down with a bump. The next thing I knew I was on my knees – I thought I had been driven into the ground.

He was however able to fetch help in the form of another party of climbers and Mr Graham was taken off the mountain. In fact his injuries were amazingly slight: a small purple spot on his bald head, with a fiery ring around it, and a one-inch-deep wound on his heel.[11]

There are also occasional reports of unusual ball lightning (as if the 'normal' sort were not unusual enough). Sometimes it appears to have projections or spikes, and a particularly well observed instance of this took place on 3 December 1979 at Fleetwood (Lancashire):

> On the evening in question there was an intermittent thunderstorm with rain in heavy showers. My son Michael had just come in from the college and had gone into the room and was standing watching the TV. The time would be a little before 6.00 p.m. I said something to the effect that his meal would be ready and he'd better wash his hands, so he turned the television off, although it remained plugged in . . . At this point a spherical object about six inches (15 cm) in diameter floated down the (sealed) chimney and into the room. It appeared to be rather like a soap bubble but was dull purple in colour covered or rather made up of a furry/ spiky emission all over. The coating seemed to be about one

inch (2.5 cm) thick with spikes of two inches here and there but changing all the time. It was quite dim and appeared to be semi-transparent, in so much as I could see through to the *inside* of the opposite side, which appeared quite smooth – all the spikes pointing outwards from the surface. It appeared to me to be insubstantial and made no sound. It drifted between the two of us towards the television screen at about 30 inches (75 cm) from the floor, covering the six feet (2 m) in about four seconds. When about eight inches from the screen it disappeared (imploded?) with a fairly loud crack/pop sound leaving behind a smell as of an electrical discharge.[12]

Of a similar nature to the projections or spikes may be the streamers or rays which are sometimes seen emerging from ball lightning, as in London, c.1915, when a fireball which struck a house was giving off fanlike rays of lightning. Sometimes the fireball bursts or disintegrates or shoots off smaller short-lived balls, as was seen to happen in Essex on 13 April 1904. A thunderstorm was raging in the early hours of the morning, when a blinding flash was followed by a crashing explosion. One witness saw a ball of fire explode, 'casting darts' in all directions. In daylight, three sets of circular holes were discovered in a field, ranging from 9 inches to 1 inch in diameter. They were 'as clean cut as though bored with an auger'.[13]

Other unusual and rarely seen features include rod-shaped ball lightning, double and triple ball lightning (two or three balls of lightning connected by a luminous rod-like structure) and black ball lightning. Someone watching a thunderstorm on 13 May 1906 at Morchard Bishop (Devon) described seeing a dark fireball which exploded:

I leaned forward to have a wider range through the open window, when I saw a large, dark egg-shaped ball swiftly falling straight down from the sky in the open space between two elm trees on the lawn and a fir tree. When the ball came to about the height of the latter, it suddenly collapsed and sparks of fire flew about in all directions like a magnificent firework . . . When the ball split, a solid lump of rather light-looking fire (like the colour of a blaze) issued forth, at first more from the bottom than the sides, and this emitted thousands of red-hot (bright deep red) sparks which flew in all directions, taking a circular shape.[14]

With this spectacular demonstration we will conclude our examples of the phenomenon of ball lightning and turn to some of the explanations which have been offered. First of all, one which will be quite unacceptable to such as the Morchard Bishop witness: that ball lightning is non-existent, being merely an illusion created by the witness's eye and brain. Treating that suggestion with the contempt it deserves, we will move on to the complex field of plasma physics, which is where explanations for ball lightning are being sought today. It is obvious from the damage that can be caused that considerable energy is contained within an often very small sphere, and the old idea that ball lightning was formed from a combustible gas is no longer entertained. Because ball lightning is closely connected with thunderstorms, sometimes shows an attraction for electrical equipment, sometimes gives off the smell of ozone and sometimes sends out showers of sparks, it would appear to be an electrical phenomenon of some kind, but the electromagnetic effects which would be expected have not been reported. Another mystery is that ball lightning has been reliably reported as appearing inside electrically shielded structures, such as aircraft, which it presumably could not do if it were itself an electrical phenomenon. We will leave this problem with the physicists for the time being. At least this is one mystery which is now acknowledged by science and is being investigated, though the scientists are unlikely to be concerning themselves with ball lightning's UFO links, with which we will conclude this chapter. Since ball lightning is often seen outdoors and in the sky, it is clear that a witness, especially if interested in UFOs, might believe he or she was seeing a 'true UFO', that is an unidentified object, rather than a natural phenomenon. So some sightings of UFOs could in fact be sightings of ball lightning; though conversely, some sightings ascribed to ball lightning could be UFO events. Four reports follow which illustrate this ambiguity: depending on your viewpoint, the objects seen could be described as either UFOs or as ball lightning.

In Warminster (Wiltshire) in the 1960s there was a plethora of UFO reports. Sightings of alleged flying saucers were given so much publicity that hundreds of eager UFO-spotters converged on the town to see for themselves, and every aerial phenomenon became a UFO, from planets and satellites to army flares. Probably very few if any of the reported events involved true UFOs. Consider this sighting reported by Terry Pell, who was approaching Warminster in his lorry at 4.36 a.m. on 10 August 1965. His wife and young daughter were asleep in the cab beside him. Suddenly Mr Pell was dazzled by 'a brilliant crimson ball' which flew at his windscreen. It seemed larger than the truck, and vibrated as it touched the glass, but amazingly it did no damage to the truck, not even breaking the windscreen. Mr Pell braked and almost crashed his lorry, but he and his family were unhurt as the fireball took off again. At the time, amid the UFO fervour, this incident was viewed as a close encounter with an alien craft getting a 'close-up view of humanity in an Earth mechanical contrivance', but we have our doubts about that.[15]

One day in October 1969, Alastair Mackenzie was drinking coffee with his wife and daughter at their hotel in Bournemouth (Dorset) when they noticed something strange fluttering on the veranda. They went out and saw a shape resembling a jellyfish, about 5 inches across and glowing slightly. After a few seconds it began to move out to sea, at a height of about 25–30 inches above the water. Mr Mackenzie interpreted this strange sighting in UFO terms, but could it have been a form of ball lightning?[16] And what about the Smiths, returning home from a party in the small hours of 13 February 1983? They were walking back to their house in Whitleigh, Plymouth (Devon), when they saw a 'red fiery circular object' dropping quickly out of the sky. It hovered around the base of a lamppost for about 30 seconds before shooting up into the sky again, leaving a funny smell and a burned area of grass.[17] Ball lightning?

In the summer of 1984 two men hiking in the Derbyshire

Peak District saw a very strange sight which is difficult to pigeon-hole – ball lightning, UFO, earth light . . . or what? The morning of 27 August 1984 was bright and clear though cloudy. It was 11 a.m. when one of the two caught sight of a shining ball of light moving down the slope from Nether Moor. He thought at first it was a piece of plastic, but was puzzled when it did not get caught in barbed wire on top of a stone wall, but seemed to pass through it. He pointed the light out to his colleague. Sheep were undisturbed as it drifted across their pasture; then it passed through a barbed-wire fence and ascended to the top of some trees, where it hovered for a few seconds before proceeding along a road, having changed its direction of travel from north–south to east–west. It began to climb fast into the sky, and was finally lost to view in the clouds.[18] There are too many anomalous sightings of this kind for them all to be attributable to illusions; or else we are living in a world composed of hallucinations and fantasy!

11. *Alien big cats or an unknown native species?*

Judged simply by the sheer volume of reports, the greatest mystery of the last twenty-five years must surely be the British big cat. To present a detailed overview of this phenomenon in one short chapter is an impossibility. We have already given considerable coverage to these creatures in the chapter 'Cats that can't be caught' in our book *Alien Animals*, giving the situation to the end of the 1970s, and others have also written on this subject, notably Di Francis in *Cat Country* and Graham McEwan in *Mystery Animals of Britain and Ireland*. We will therefore in this chapter concentrate on sightings during the period 1980–5, and will thus be able to go into more detail on some of the recent well-researched cases. At least a hundred sightings covering earlier decades can be found in the Gazetteer. In some areas where there have been large numbers of sightings, it has proved impossible to mention more than a few

A possible photograph of the 'Surrey puma', taken by an ex-police photographer at Worplesdon (Surrey) in 1966 from a distance of 35 yards. The two witnesses were certain the animal was not a feral cat.

100

representative ones. This refers particularly to the Surrey/ Hampshire area, where the phenomenon seems to have emerged into the national consciousness in the early 1960s with the many sightings of the so-called 'Surrey puma'; to Devon, where on the north Devon/Somerset border the 'Exmoor Beast' was a major media star in 1983; and to Scotland, where there have been several pockets of major activity during the 1970s and early 1980s, and from where have come the only corpses of these mystery cats.

In October 1980 attention was focused on the Cannich area south-west of Inverness (Highland Region), where a live puma was actually captured in a cage, the trap having been baited with a sheep's head. There had been many sightings of strange cats in the area around Miss Janet Chisholm's isolated cottage, black ones, yellow ones, adults and cubs, so this was where farmer Ted Noble decided to place his trap. The puma he caught was a fully grown female, about ten years old and weighing approximately 80 pounds. Eddie Orbell, director of the Highland Wildlife Park, gave as his opinion that it was a tame animal that had never fended for itself in the wild, but an analysis of its droppings taken within hours of capture showed that it had been living wild for some time, eating deer, rabbit and sheep. However the consensus was that the animal had lived in captivity earlier, and so was presumably a former pet that had escaped or been abandoned. Felicity, as she was named, became a favourite attraction at the Highland Wildlife Park until she died of old age early in 1985.[1]

Earlier in 1980 a big cat had been reliably sighted in the apparently unlikely environment of Wolverhampton (West Midlands/Staffordshire border). Actually these sightings illustrate the fact that industrial areas can be wildlife havens, as they always include many acres of derelict and overgrown land, in this case a disused railway line. One of the witnesses was a superintendent at Dudley Zoo, Mike Williams, who kindly sent us an account of the events.

In July this year at Wolverhampton, a school teacher on holiday was walking near a disused railway line and saw an animal come out onto the grass field alongside. He had a good view of it for nearly 5 minutes. A lady exercising her dog also saw it, she ran off exclaiming that it was a wild animal and the gentleman concerned agreed and phoned the local police. He was *adamant* that what he had seen was a Puma, I was called in and the description which he gave me certainly fitted that of a Puma, round cat-like head, pricked ears, short thick legs, heavy tail held low, brown in colour and the size of a large dog. His attention was drawn by the sound of crows mobbing it, the animal bounded down the field for 30 yards then came back and lay in the long grass at the side of the railway track watching him, then disappeared, he was about 50 yards away at the time. The teacher claimed to be an amateur naturalist and had seen foxes etc many times, so there was no doubt in his mind that what he had seen was not a fox or dog. As you can imagine over the next few days various sightings were reported along about 3 miles of this disused railway line.

After a reported incident whereby a large brown animal had attacked a dog whilst being walked by a child, I was called out again, with me was our Senior cat keeper with over 10 years experience of Lions, Tigers, etc. We were on our own, searching along the same disused railway line, but about 2 miles from the original sighting by the teacher, when we noticed something looking at us about 200 yards further on. It disappeared and then we heard birds mobbing something in the thick cover and an animal emerged onto the track about 300 yards in front. It was a large animal which had a round head, was level across the back, heavy tail held low, and when it turned to look at us it was very narrow, everything about it was cat like, but we couldn't get nearer than about 300 yards.

I left Alan our cat keeper watching it whilst I ran back to alert the police of a possible sighting. The police organised a search and within 10 minutes they had observers on roads and bridges in the area. Alan had followed the animal for about 15 minutes and then lost it. The subsequent search by police of this section of the railway track was blank. Both Alan and myself were of the opinion that the animal we saw was much too large to be a fox, and had a lot of typical cat characteristics about it, but as we could not get close enough we could not give the police a positive identification. If it had been a large brown dog it would surely have been found during the big police search.[2]

The report is fairly typical, in that the animal is seen by several witnesses, including in this instance people very familiar with big cats, but a police search fails to find any trace of the beast which seems to have vanished into thin air. This ability to 'melt away' could explain how the big cats have lived so successfully for so long in our overcrowded island. They do not disturb us, are only seen accidentally when going about their food-gathering, and are obviously quite able to live and even to thrive here. That they sometimes achieve this by taking livestock as prey is unfortunate for the farmers concerned, and

Farmer Michael Nash of Llangurig (Powys) telling Janet Bord about the strange animal which had been hiding in his barn until a few days before. The box beneath his foot is protecting the one surviving footprint, and on the right-hand side of the photograph, to the right of the upright and just above the piece of wooden gate, is a hole which Mr Nash thought was the animal's way into the bales of straw.

if they were to content themselves with rabbits and carrion – as they often do, sheep or cattle killing being exceptional – no one could complain about them or need to hunt them. They are certainly not a danger to humans, unless provoked.

At the end of August 1980 a cat-like animal was being seen in the Handforth area of Cheshire. One farmer witness thought the animal was a four-year-old stag until he was able to see it more clearly, which gives some indication of its size. Another witness said: 'the size of an Alsatian with pointed ears, a cat-like body and tail'.[3] A couple of months later we were able to become involved ourselves in a big cat investigation, when sightings were reported from our mid-Wales area. At Churchstoke (Powys) on the England/Wales border, a district nurse on her rounds was startled by the appearance of a lynx-like animal. She had parked her car and was walking along the lane to a farm at about midday on 29 September 1980 when she saw a large cat-like animal ahead of her. 'I stayed rooted to the spot,' she said. 'I shut my eyes and opened them and it was still there, about 40 yards away. I remember thinking "God, what *is* it?" It looked like one of those Scottish wild cats. I just saw the front half of it and I didn't step any nearer. I was really quite frightened.' The same size as an Alsatian dog, the animal was described as having grey fur with black spots, and large pointed ears with tufts of hair – a clear description of a lynx. The nurse retreated to her car, where she sat for five minutes before plucking up the courage to walk again along the lane. This time no animal was to be seen, and no one at the farm knew of any pet of that description in the area. It was the publicity surrounding the events of a month later which finally decided the nurse to reveal her sighting. At the end of October, Michael Nash, who works a remote 1,500-acre sheep farm near Llangurig (Powys), contacted the police to report what he believed was a strange animal lurking in his barn among the bales of straw. He had heard unusual snoring noises coming from the barn, he had found large footprints in the mud, and four of his 3,000 sheep had been killed in a way not typical of dogs or foxes.

Armed police went to the farm and kept watch throughout the night of 23 October. Using subtle tactics, they 'hammered hell' (in the farmer's words) out of the side of the barn when they heard the animal snoring. At midday on the 24th they decided to go in and, not surprisingly, found that the beast had flown. The farmer later told us that some bales were wet, as if with urine, that strange droppings 3–4 inches long were found, and that there was a strong smell. But no one ever saw any animal, and the only visible evidence of the presence of anything out of the ordinary, apart from the sheep carcases, was a large footprint 5 inches long which we were able to photograph.

A month after the Llangurig stake-out, the local papers reported that the 'Powys beast' had actually been seen, on 25

The footprint at the Llangurig farm, identified as dog-like by experts, but possibly made by a big cat, since this unknown species often leaves dog-like tracks.

November, on a farm at Cwmbelan near Llanidloes only six miles from Llangurig. Ernie Lloyd, the farmer who saw it as it bounded across the fields, said it was cat-like, and definitely not a dog. He said:

> The animal was a dark colour with some white on it. It was difficult to see what part was white because it was moving. It was the size of a large dog. The animal moved very quickly and ran in leaps and bounds like a cheetah. It looked as if it was scared and stopped from time to time and looked around. I haven't got any idea what it was but it was definitely wild and not a dog. The tracks left by the animal were the size of a small palm with claws about the size of a finger.

Although Mr Lloyd did not actually see the animal make the tracks that were found, plaster casts were taken of them, and members of the staff at Dudley Zoo in the West Midlands said the prints could have been made by a large dog. Back in October, we had photographed the one preserved paw print at the Llangurig farm, and this too was the size of a small palm, five inches long by three inches wide. After seeing our photographs, the Llangurig print was also pronounced dog-like by the Dudley Zoo superintendent. He was the person who saw a possible puma at Wolverhampton in July, as reported earlier in this chapter.

Was the 'Powys beast' perhaps only a large dog? At Llangurig, of course, no animal was seen, and after the event the police tried to explain it all away. The paw print was made by a large dog; the snoring noise was made by owls; the 'droppings' (unfortunately not kept for examination) were owl pellets – all reasonable assumptions in the absence of any sightings or a corpse. We are left with four dead sheep, killed in a manner said to be untypical of dogs. It is indeed true that sheep farmers in this area are plagued by dogs worrying their animals. Some are domestic pets, others are former pets living wild after having been abandoned by uncaring owners. These dogs turn naturally to the plentiful livestock for their food. Perhaps the 'Powys beast' was a dog; but we remain doubtful about this explanation. There were no reports of sheep-killings in the

Llanidloes area around the time the 'beast' was seen there, and Ernie Lloyd, the Cwmbelan farmer who saw the animal, said it was definitely *not* a dog. There were also one or two other sightings, but none added any clarification to the mystery, and by the end of the year peace had returned to the remote mid-Wales countryside.[4]

The centre of activity had shifted east to Warwickshire, where in the south of the county two sightings of a big black cat had been reported at Long Marston. On 23 November a man walking along a road saw the animal seize a moorhen by a pond and run off. He described it as 'jet black, as big as a fox, and with a long bushy tail'. On 3 December a resident of Long Marston saw 'a jet black animal, about 3 feet long, with a long tail', which ran off at speed. He commented: 'It was definitely not a dog, but more cat-like in appearance.'[5] Intriguingly, Long Marston is close to Meon Hill, where in 1885 Charles Walton saw a phantom black dog nine times, and then in 1945 was murdered on the hill in mysterious circumstances (see Chapter 6). So the black cat of 1980 was appearing in black dog country – is this only a coincidence, or are the two animals linked?

Now into 1981, when in February two young boys saw a black cat in woods near their home at Tedburn St Mary (Devon), just one example of the continuous stream of reports emerging from that county. During March there was another sighting in the Wolverhampton area, this time at Perton just over the county boundary in Staffordshire. This follows several sightings in July 1980 (see earlier) from the same area, specifically Compton, Aldersley, Lower Penn and Wombourne.[6]

We have sighting reports from three areas in June 1981 – Bedfordshire, Dyfed and South Glamorgan – all at the same time of the month. On 9 June, chiropodist Adrian Grier was driving along the Toddington–Tebworth road (Bedfordshire) at 1.30 a.m. when he saw a large animal in his headlights. From a distance it looked like a Great Dane dog, but as he got nearer Mr Grier changed his identification to 'lioness'! He slowed down and was 10 yards from it when it broke into a trot and turned into a field. He drove to Luton Police Station, where officers received his report with scepticism. 'They asked

107

me if it could have been a deer or a large dog; they even said "Was it a cow?" but I'm sure it was a lion. It must have been six feet long, more than 3½ feet tall, very powerfully built and the colour of a Great Dane. It had bloody great feet, and was loping along. It didn't look like a cow!' But no zoos or wildlife parks had lost any lions, and farmers had not reported attacks on their livestock. However, after Mr Grier's report was published in the press, other people claimed to have seen a similar creature, including a man who was followed by it in Luton one night. When he got home as white as a sheet, he told his wife that

> he had just seen the largest dog he had ever seen. It was similar to a Great Dane but the coat was different. It was a bit like an Irish Wolfhound that had had its coat cut. He assumed it must be a dog because he couldn't think what else it could be. It followed him and he said he dare not run in case it went for him. He was really scared.[7]

Of course no lion was ever found, and this case parallels closely the events of July 1976 when there was a massive police search for the 'Nottingham Lion' after two reliable sighting reports. Full details can be found in our earlier book *Alien Animals*.

The day after Mr Grier saw a lion, Peter Coburn saw a lion-like animal many miles away at Leckwith (South Glamorgan). On 10 June 1981 he was driving home in the rain at 11 p.m. when he saw the animal in the car headlights, sitting on the lawn. It was about 3 feet tall and brown-tan in colour and Mr Coburn was not particularly alarmed, as he had already seen it or a similar one twice before. Others had also reported sightings in Leckwith Woods.[8] Further north in Wales, around Ysbyty Ystwyth (Dyfed), east of Aberystwyth and only 12 miles west of Llangurig, where a big cat was thought to be lurking the previous autumn, seven ewes and five lambs were savaged between 11 and 14 June, large paw prints being left at the scene. The animal was also seen: a jet-black cat, about 2 feet 6 inches tall.[9]

The cat seen by Mr and Mrs Maggs at Tonmawr (West Glamorgan) in South Wales was striped grey and black, but was again about 2 feet 6 inches tall and 6 feet long. Anne Maggs thought it rather ugly, with 'a rather bulldog-like muzzle'. It crossed the road ahead of their vehicle some time in November 1981 and disappeared into the undergrowth.[10] As Di Francis reveals in her book *Cat Country*, this was just one of several cats known to be living wild in the Tonmawr area, and local resident Steve Joyce managed to get close-up photographs of one of them taking baits he had left out for them (the photographs can be seen in *Cat Country*). Di Francis was also lucky enough to see the cats for herself, and she photographed a black cat from a distance.

Towards the end of 1981 a report came from the North Yorkshire coast town of Whitby, where a man had seen what he thought was two cats fighting. When one seemed to be attacking the other with unusual ferocity, the man threw a rock at it. It turned to face him before running away, and he saw that it was much bigger than a normal cat, with long legs and pointed ears. It bared large dog-like fangs at him but did not attack him. This sighting may be linked to something that had happened the previous night in Whitby, when a woman heard a banging noise in the early hours of the morning. It was coming from the back garden gate, but as she and her young sons were alone in the house, she decided not to investigate. Next morning she found that the whole of the bottom of the gate had been chewed away by an animal which had left blood and fur on what remained of the gate. She believed the animal had jumped into the garden over the wall and found it could not escape; the garden is much lower than the street outside, so it could not jump up over the wall and had to chew its way out through the wooden gate.[11] There have been other reports of animals penetrating quite formidable barriers, like the creature that ripped open a 6-foot wire fence to get at some geese a few miles south of Glasgow (Strathclyde Region) in August 1976.[12] If pumas really are capable of such behaviour, then one would expect them to be able to escape easily from the wire compounds in which they are kept at zoos.

We have fewer reports for 1982, though this does not mean of course that no big cats were being seen, as not all sightings are reported and we do not hear of all those that are. It is almost certain that big cat sightings were continuing in Scotland, Devon and Surrey, and probably elsewhere too. In Essex Mrs Annette Redhouse and her niece saw what they thought was a lioness. This was on 29 May at Billericay, where they were in Mrs Redhouse's garden during the afternoon. At first they thought the animal in the field opposite was a cow, but when they looked at it through binoculars they decided it was a lioness. It was 'a champagne colour with a face exactly like a lion'. Mr Redhouse saw a similar animal later that evening, but a police search found nothing, except for a large white domestic cat.[13] In July, brewery worker Albert Sellars saw a big black cat from his home at Eaton Bray in Bedfordshire. He reported:

> My wife first thought it was a hare. I looked down the field and said 'No, it's too big – maybe it's a sheep.' But it was too dark for a sheep. It looked like a cat from the way it was sitting, but it was too big to be a domestic cat. Then I went to the bottom of the garden and looked at it from 200 yards for about a minute, before it moved and slouched into the undergrowth like a cat.[14]

The following month, a big cat popped up further east, being seen on 12 and 25 August 1982 at Fobbing (Essex), which is just north of the Thames estuary. Foreman Bill Watt saw it on 12 August at the Waterworks Depot where he worked. It shot out from behind a pile of wooden pallets with a cat-like growl and Mr Watt got a sight of it from only three paces away. It was the height of a large Alsatian, but longer and more streamlined. It was sandy-grey in colour with a thick, roughish coat and a very long tail. He noticed a pungent, urine-like smell from where the cat had been lying. On 25 August it was seen again, not far away, by a Mr Brazier who was walking to work. It was 5 a.m. and still semi-dark, but Mr Brazier was still able to make out some detail in the animal which dashed out in front of him and ran off into undergrowth. His description ties in very closely with Mr Watt's.[15]

At the end of the year there was a brief sighting of what the witness described as a 'cheetah', lying down on its front paws on a grassy bank beside the junction of Mill and Dyke Roads in Brighton (East Sussex). It got up and ran off towards some houses. This was around 10 p.m. on 23 December.[16]

Since 1982 the big cats seem to have become even more active than they were before; at least there are more reports and from a wider area. There could be a number of reasons for this. Perhaps the cats are breeding successfully and are therefore increasing in numbers; or the media are taking more interest and publishing more reports; or the cats are being seen more often because more people are exploring the countryside. The last is less likely to be the answer, for, as this chapter shows, most sightings are made by people going about their daily business, not by hikers and tourists. There is evidence, to be described later, that the cats are in fact breeding and multiplying very successfully in many areas of Britain. In 1983 there were reports from England, Wales and Scotland, but the main attention was centred on Exmoor, especially that part along the Somerset/Devon boundary, where in February the 'Exmoor Beast' began its terrible depredations among the flocks of sheep and lambs. This creature killed over 200 sheep, but despite numerous sightings and the presence in the area of a team of Royal Marines with special equipment for seeing and shooting in the dark, it was never captured or killed. Big cats were being seen in other parts of Devon throughout 1983, and we also have reports from Derbyshire (February), Dorset (March), Buckinghamshire (April–May), Dyfed (August), Hertfordshire (May, August–October), Powys (October) and Essex (November). Sightings also continued in Surrey and Scotland, and through 1984 and 1985 in these areas and in Devon. Also in 1984 big cats were seen in Lancashire (August) and Cornwall (December and into January 1985). In 1984 and 1985 there were many sightings in the Isle of Wight, and in April 1985 reports came from the Norfolk/Suffolk border, in May from Hampshire, in August from Kent and in November from Gloucestershire. More details of these sightings can be found under the relevant county in the Gazetteer.

This necessarily brief listing of sightings is also of course incomplete, for, as we mentioned earlier, it is unlikely that we have heard about all the sightings throughout the country. The

111

quantity of sightings shows that this phenomenon cannot be ignored. What exactly are the witnesses seeing? Some may be misinterpreting other animals, such as dogs, foxes, deer, domestic cats run wild (these feral cats are often bigger than ordinary domestic cats), especially where the creature is seen only fleetingly. Some may be animals escaped from zoos or circuses, though such escapes are usually widely reported, with warnings to people to look out for potentially dangerous animals which will be frightened by their unexpected freedom, and they are usually speedily recaptured. Some of these sightings could be of phantom animals, of course, possibly even of the black dogs described in Chapter 5. There is a possible overlap between phantom black dogs and alien black cats which needs closer study; it has been suggested that the black 'dogs' may in fact be black cats, but this cannot be the case because so many witnesses of the dogs have reached out to touch them and found nothing there. The dogs are certainly ghosts, but the cats seem, so far as we can tell, to be certainly alive.

It is likely that at least a number of the big cats are escaped or abandoned pets, usually pumas. But they do not all look like pumas, and so many witnesses have been unable to identify what they are seeing. They describe the animal as being the size of an Alsatian dog, but cat-like. However, when tracks are found they usually show claws; and as all big cats (with the exception of the cheetah) walk with their claws retracted, cat prints do not show claws. Therefore, argue the experts, the prints were made by a large dog, and that is what witnesses have seen. This mystery has puzzled researchers for some years, but there is now a solution to it, as we shall shortly reveal.

Since the animals people are describing often do not resemble known animals, some people have suggested that we have an unknown species on our hands. In *Cat Country* Di Francis put forward the idea that the cat is a living fossil:

But could a cat exist in the British Isles that is different from any other existing cats: not just a British leopard or a British lynx, but one with characteristics of a number of other animals? An animal that is either the only survivor of a

A mystery black cat shot on the Kellas estate at Dallas (Grampian Region) in 1983 by land-owner Tomas Christie, who had the animal stuffed and is seen here (left) discussing the animal with David Morgan, editor of the Forres Gazette.

species that has been destroyed elsewhere, or one that has evolved in isolation over thousands of years to produce a species that is unique to the British Isles.[17]

Her question has yet to be answered, but the answer may soon be forthcoming. So far, researchers have been hampered by the lack of a corpse to study. Now corpses are beginning to be available, following the killing of several black cats in Scotland during 1983–5. They have all been killed in Moray (Grampian and Highland Regions), two of them in the Dallas area, and it would seem that these animals, all very similar in appearance, are breeding successfully. The cats are jet black in colour, dog-sized – the adults around 43 inches long from nose to tail – with a slender body, long legs, a long tail and large fangs. At the time of writing (late 1985) they have not been identified, but they are thought to represent either a rare melanistic (black) Scottish wild cat, or even a new strain of cat, possibly a cross between a feral cat and a wild cat. However, the resulting animal is larger than either of these, so perhaps the original cross was between a feral cat (or a wild cat) and an abandoned pet puma, or even some other exotic member of the cat family. In view of the many sightings of the same kind of animal in parts of Britain long distances from Moray, it would seem that this same cross-breeding has also happened elsewhere. Since wild cats now live only in Scotland, it is unlikely that they are mating with feral cats elsewhere in

113

Britain. Also, the great increase in numbers of sightings in all areas during the 1970s and 1980s seems to follow on from the great popularity of pumas and other big cats as pets during the 1950s and 1960s, and the possible subsequent abandonment of many of these pets when their owners tired of them, and when stricter licensing came into force. There is one other clear link between the Moray cats and those seen elsewhere, which suggests that whatever cross-breeding took place in Moray also happened elsewhere. The Moray cats walk with their claws out and therefore leave claw marks in their paw-prints, just as do so many of the mystery cats of Britain.[18]

The exciting discovery that the Moray cats are different from all other known cats goes some way towards vindicating the people who report strange sightings or strange happenings. A large proportion of these witnesses have clearly seen what they claim to have seen, and we should bear this message of 'the Moray cats affair' in mind when we consider the validity of the variety of weird events reported in the other chapters of this book.

This cat was shot while stalking pheasants at Dallas (Grampian Region), on 14 October 1985. It is a young male, with a spaniel-sized body, about 36 inches from nose to tail. As the photograph clearly shows, its body is longer and slimmer, its legs longer, and its tail longer and bushier, than a domestic cat's.

12. *Ghostly houses and vehicles*

. . . suddenly, we both stopped dead of one accord and gasped. 'Where's the wall?' we queried simultaneously. It was not there. The road was flanked by nothing but a ditch, and beyond the ditch lay a wilderness of tumbled earth, weeds, mounds, all overgrown with the trees which we had seen on our first visit.

The reason Miss Wynne and Miss Allington were so surprised by the scene which lay before them was that four or five months earlier, when they had last walked that way, they had seen a wall with wrought-iron gates, a drive, and beyond the trees a large Georgian house. The date was October 1926, and the place was Bradfield St George in Suffolk. Since then other people have retraced the steps of the two ladies, but have been unable to find any explanation for their experience – no other house that they might have seen and then mislocated; indeed, no evidence that there ever was a house on the site where they saw one.[1]

If this was just an isolated incident, we might suspect that Miss Wynne and Miss Allington had simply forgotten where they saw the house and so were at the wrong place on their second walk. However, there are a number of other accounts of phantom houses on record, of which the following are just a selection. About 1946 Mr and Mrs MacMahon saw an 'imposing Georgian house' near Hadleigh in Essex, which no one could ever find again, despite extensive research.[2] A visitor to South Cadbury in Somerset, just after the end of World War II, saw a beautiful old house standing in a field. Outside stood a man and a small boy, dressed in period costume whose century she could not identify. As she wondered who they were, they suddenly vanished, though the house was still visible. On returning to the house where she was staying, she asked who lived at the big house, and was told that there was no house in that field. When she returned to the spot, the field was indeed empty of buildings. Research showed that during wars in the twelfth century, Prince Henry (the future King Henry II) had been sent to Somerset for safety and had been hidden at a house near South Cadbury Castle, though the exact location of the house was unknown. So it would appear that on this occasion the phantom house may once have existed on the site where it was seen 800 years later.[3]

There was no record of a large manor house ever having stood near Start, not far from Kingsbridge in South Devon, but such a house was seen one misty day in November 1939 by two ladies who were walking in the lanes. One of the witnesses lived nearby and knew that there was no house on the site; also, 'it did not *look* real', and as they watched it gradually faded away.[4] Also unreal was a cottage seen in the 1960s by several separate witnesses on the eastern edge of Dartmoor (Devon) near Haytor, in fact not very far away from the previous example. Ruth St Leger-Gordon included details of the sightings in the first edition of her book *The Witchcraft and Folklore of Dartmoor*, and after it was published she received a visit from a surveyor for the Ordnance Survey who was working in the Haytor area. As she reported in her second edition,

> Looking down on this terrain from a high vantage point to check his map, he noticed one cottage that he had apparently missed. Smoke was rising from the chimneys and clothes blowing on a line. To remedy the omission he pinpointed and walked down to the exact spot. He toothcombed the vicinity but could find no cottage or trace of any building. Encountering a lady exercising her dog, he enquired where this cottage might be. Her reply surprised him. She, too, had seen it – once – but had never been able to locate it again.

When he returned puzzled to his lodging, he chanced on a copy of the book and read about the phantom cottage. Convinced it was the cottage he had seen, he went to visit Miss St Leger-Gordon and they agreed that he had indeed seen the phantom cottage.[5]

It is understandable that people should occasionally see the ghosts of houses that used to exist, but very puzzling when they see houses that have never existed – and not just one witness, but several, at different times and not knowing of the other sightings. How can this be? Equally puzzling are phantom landscapes, such as that seen in March 1938 by a Mr Bates on the south coast at Mansands near Dartmouth (Devon). He was walking along a cliff path and saw his path crossing a vista of fields. He climbed over a stile to follow the path and found he was nearly falling over the edge of the cliff – the fields were a phantasm.[6]

In 1952 the Swain family, on holiday in the New Forest (Hampshire), came across a lake. About 50 yards from the shore was a boulder with a sword embedded in it, which they thought was a memorial to King Arthur. They were so fascinated by the scene that they made more than 200 trips from their home in Somerset to try to find the lake again. Seventeen years later, they were still searching for it.[7] Presumably what the Swains saw was a phantom lake, though where Excalibur came from is anybody's guess. Had the Swains been reading about King Arthur before their experience? All these ghostly phenomena are characterized by the apparent randomness of the vision of unreality vouchsafed to the witness. A particularly good example of this is Arthur Slater's experience on 1 February 1976. He was walking home from church in Southwold (Suffolk) and it was dark on the Green as he approached his house. As he reported later, 'I was startled to see between me and the houses what appeared to be a leafless thorn hedge, waist high and covered in raindrops. I knew very well that there was no hedge there, for the path is asphalted over from the Green's edge to the house walls.' There was in fact a double hedge running parallel in front of him for about 40 yards.

I swung my walking stick against the hedge and saw the

stems give way to the impact and felt a slight resistance through the stick. I next tried to grasp the hedge with my hand, but though it remained visible I could feel nothing, so I walked the remaining steps to my home with the hedges close to me on both sides until I reached the entrance to my flat, where, on looking back, everything was in its normal state.

Why should Mr Slater hallucinate a non-existent hedge?[8]

All ghost sightings, whether animate or inanimate, could be explained as hallucinations, but this still does not explain why the witness should suddenly hallucinate in this way. People seeing the ghosts of dead people, a subject covered in Chapters 4 and 8, are possibly 'tuning in' to some residual traces of those persons' lives, and an extension of this idea could also apply to buildings which once existed, but we must look elsewhere for an explanation of phantom houses that never were, and also of Mr Slater's hedge. Also for an explanation of the phantom road seen by a driver on the Sevenoaks bypass (Kent). Mrs Babs Davidson had an unnerving experience one night in March 1979, when she saw the road ahead blacked out and another road leading away to her right. She kept driving left into the darkness, where she knew the real road to be. Had she followed the 'phantom road' she would have driven into the path of oncoming traffic, and her experience, which she has had three times altogether, has been suggested as an explanation for four fatal accidents on the same stretch of road since November 1977, when drivers inexplicably swerved across the grass-covered central reservation of the dual carriageway. Experts were trying to ascertain whether moonlight, or the headlights of oncoming traffic, might have caused some kind of illusion which led the drivers to steer in the wrong direction.[9]

From phantom roads we turn to phantom vehicles. These have been widely reported, but of course it is impossible to tell whether they represent real vehicles which once drove along the stretches of road where the ghosts are now seen. The traditional view of ghosts as restless spirits can hardly apply to wheeled vehicles, unless we credit them with souls which can survive the crushing machine. Nor is it at all easy to imagine an inanimate object like a car leaving in its wake an aura which can be picked up by some sensitive passer-by in later years, who then hallucinates an image of its original appearance. But if this does not happen, why do witnesses see the ghosts of these vehicles, and even more puzzling, how can individual witnesses see identical ghosts at the same place on different occasions, sometimes years apart? Often these witnesses do not know until later that someone else has seen that same ghost. Perhaps the theory that ghosts are an imprint of the person or object which is inadvertently recorded at the location, and is later sensed and converted into a visual image by a person with psychic sensitivity, is not always correct. Possibly these witnesses are in fact experiencing a timeslip, and are momentarily mentally aware of the visual appearance of a person or object which existed at some other time than their own. But there is still the question of how or why the witness experiences

This fine phantom equipage is typical of ghostly transport as it appeared last century. Now phantom cars and lorries are seen more often than carriages.

the timeslip, and why all the images seem to be of past times and none of the future; but this is leading us into the deeper waters of precognition.

Whatever the actual mechanism of a ghost sighting, it all seems very real to the witness at the time. An important feature supporting the view that a ghost is neither hallucination nor timeslip is the fact that the experience is often shared. The following case illustrates both these points very clearly. The witnesses were Colonel Leland and his chauffeur Mr Webber, who was driving the car on this particular night in November 1915. They had just left the Colonel's house in Watersplash Road, Sunbury-on-Thames (Surrey); the Colonel takes up the story.

> . . . after we had gone two or three hundred yards, I noticed a moving light on my left; concluding that this was a horse-driven vehicle coming in to our road, I told Webber to slow down and let it come in ahead. This was done and the vehicle, which was very indistinct, drew in and turned the way we were going. I told Webber to go up behind it and not pass. He did so and we kept behind it, close behind, for about two hundred yards. I could plainly see the back of the vehicle, which was black and appeared to be a hearse; it was moving at a trot. The queer part was I could see no driver, and the two panels at the back and the keyhole for locking the doors showed up most distinctly under the rays of our lamps. The road is, or was, narrow with a bend in it. I told Webber to slow down and crawl letting the other go ahead, and when we got round the corner, I said, 'push on'. We did so, and the road before us was empty. We accelerated but there was nothing to be seen, and Webber said, 'Lord, sir, what was that!' We went down and around Sunbury but did not see any vehicle. It was a wet night too by the way. I can assure you that the vehicle, whatever it was, only rounded the corner a few yards ahead of us, and there was nowhere it could have gone.[10]

Mr Webber confirmed Colonel Leland's story.

A ghostly horse-drawn vehicle was seen in Milton Combe

(Devon) in 1962 by a car driver entering the village down a steep hill.

> At the bottom there is a sharp right-hand bend shaded by trees. I was halfway down, when suddenly I saw a horse and cart coming round the bend at the bottom. It did not strike me as strange at the time, though afterwards I realised that I had not seen such a thing since before the war. I could see the old horse's head going up and down with each step as he plodded up. 'Hell,' I thought, 'the poor old chap will never get past. I shall have to back up the hill to that gateway on the left.' Watching the horse and cart, I got into reverse, and was just going to back when the horse and cart emerging into the sunlight round the bend, gradually faded away. At the inn I told this to the landlady who served me. 'Oh,' said she, 'that is the last of the carters. Over there by the fire is the chair he used to sit in and that is his whip hanging on the wall.'[11]

In this case the witness was made aware of the insubstantial nature of the event by the fact that the horse and cart faded away before his eyes. The same thing happened in 1976 to a Mrs Willis who was in her car at Ealing Common, London, when she heard the sound of wheels and horses' hooves. An old black coach pulled by two grey horses dashed past, and then, as they neared the traffic-filled Uxbridge Road, coach and horses vanished.[12] Later Mrs Willis found that she had seen the apparition on what had once been a route for horse-drawn coaches.

Still in London, the ghost bus of North Kensington was well known in the 1930s, and many people saw it speeding along St Mark's Road to the junction with Cambridge Gardens. Some motorists had to swerve to avoid what they thought was a real bus: 'I was turning the corner and saw a bus tearing towards me. The lights of the top and bottom decks and the headlights were full on but I could see no sign of crew or passengers. I yanked my steering wheel hard over, and mounted the pavement, scraping the roadside wall. The bus just vanished.' The bus was widely held responsible for a number of accidents at this spot, some of them fatal, though as the bend where the two roads met was itself a dangerous one, it is uncertain whether this or the ghost bus was the worse hazard. Once the bend had been modified the bus was no longer seen.[13]

There were also many witnesses to the phantom lorry which hurtled along the A45 Rugby–Coventry road in the 1950s, again said to be responsible for numerous accidents on the stretch over Knightlow Hill (Warwickshire). One witness was Police Constable G. Forsythe, who had heard of the phantom lorry but was inclined to disbelieve the stories. One winter's night, when he was living in a house beside the A45, there was a pile-up and he went out to assist as one vehicle after another ran into the crash. All the uninjured men available quickly lit bonfires in the road to alert approaching traffic, and when they saw a lorry speeding towards them, they were sure it would crash. As it sped past, Mr Forsythe noticed that he could still see the light from the bonfires through the body of the lorry. Not realizing the significance of this, he ran along behind it through the snow, fully expecting to hear a crash, but there was no crash and the lorry had disappeared.[14] A phantom lorry was also said to haunt the main Edinburgh road near Stow (Borders Region), and one sunny afternoon in 1956 it was seen by May Caig as it drove over Watherston Hill along a sheep track, and then joined the main road. It came so close to her that she had to jump aside, to the surprise of her husband and a neighbour who were standing nearby, since they could not see any lorry.[15]

Phantom cars have also been reported, not unexpectedly. Several witnesses have seen the driverless 1934 Austin which used to speed along a road near Sligachan on the Isle of Skye (Highland Region) with its lights ablaze. Dr Allan MacDonald saw it in 1941, but postman Neil MacDiarmid gave the eeriest description of the ghost car:

> I had been out with mail to Sligachan. There had been a full moon but it had gone down. As I drove along a cold chill suddenly swept over me. I looked to the shore side and saw an old Austin travelling very fast with one light burning

bright at the front and a kind of dim glow inside the car. I could plainly see that there was nobody at the wheel. It tore ahead of me and veered to the right; and then just disappeared.[16]

A Daimler Landaulette of 1920s vintage was seen by several witnesses in the 1960s and 1970s on a stretch of road between Modbury and Gara Bridge in Devon. Mr and Mrs Stephen Bale saw it several times at the same spot, but others saw it too.[17] In Seaford (East Sussex), Mr and Mrs Gordon Spooner saw a ghost car which swerved off the road and through a 3-foot sea wall, leaving no trace of its collision. This happened in October 1976.[18]

We must not close this catalogue of ghostly vehicles without mentioning aircraft. Ghostly planes have reportedly been seen above wartime airfields like Biggin Hill (Greater London) and Montrose (Tayside Region), but the most intriguing phantom aircraft is the Wellington bomber which has been seen more than once flying down the Towy valley between Llandeilo and Llandovery (Dyfed). The writer Martin Green saw it in 1979 and again a few weeks later in company with other witnesses. On the first occasion it was flying at treetop height but was completely silent. In the local pub Martin Green found other people who had seen the same plane, which cannot be a real 'live' plane as there are only one or two Wellingtons still in existence, and they are not flying. However, they did train in the Towy valley area during World War II, and this one is obviously some kind of psychic legacy of those days.[19]

We have in this chapter described phantom horses and carts/coaches (and maybe a hearse), a bus, lorries, cars from Austin to Daimler, and aircraft. There is a ghostly man on a ghostly bicycle in Chapter 4, and ghosts on horseback in Chapter 8. Somewhere in Britain ghosts of other forms of transport have doubtless been seen – ships and boats, trains and trams, motorcycles and mopeds, maybe also tandems, pennyfarthings and trolleybuses. We would love to hear of any sightings of phantom vehicles, even if more mundane than these.

13. *Morgawr and other sea monsters*

People first started recording sightings of sea monsters in the early seventeenth century, and since then many hundreds of sightings have been claimed around the world, especially during the nineteenth century. Fewer reports in recent years may not be due to the demise of the species, but because long-distance travel is now by air and there are far fewer ships with crew and passengers to see the creatures. Also, the high-powered ships of today cause far more noise in the water than did the sailing ships of earlier centuries, and timid sea creatures would be frightened away. Most sightings nowadays are made from land, when the monsters come close inshore. In this chapter we will make a tour around the British coastline to pinpoint the many sightings close to our shores, but first it is relevant briefly to note pre-1885 sightings in British coastal waters. In June 1808 there were sightings off Coll and Canna (Highland Region), and also off Shetland in the early part of the century. A few years before the middle of the century, a woman living by Greiss Bay, Sutherland (Highland Region), saw a sea monster swimming close to the shore, alarming the fish, which were leaping out of the water ahead of it. It was shot or wounded by fishermen, and rested partially out of the water on some rocks until boats approached, whereupon it slid into the water and disappeared out to sea.[1] In August 1872 there were sightings off Skye and in Loch Duich, a sea-loch a short distance to the east of Skye (Highland Region), and in September 1873 off Dunrobin and Golspie in Sutherland (Highland Region). On 18 November 1873 some 120 people watched a large black animal over 100 feet long as it disported itself in the Firth of Forth. In 1882 there were sightings off the Butt of Lewis (Western Isles), Llandudno (Gwynedd),

Bude (Cornwall) and in the Bristol Channel.[2] Of course there were probably many more unreported sightings before 1885. Neither do we claim to have all the post-1885 sightings on record, but the reports which follow will give a representative picture of the sort of creatures that have been seen in Britain's coastal waters, and indeed are still being seen.

We begin in Wales, where one of several sightings was made of a sea monster actually out of the water and wandering about on the beach. The witnesses in this case were six schoolgirls, all aged twelve, who were walking on Barmouth beach (Gwynedd) at dusk on 2 March 1975. The creature they saw about 200 yards away was 'about 10 feet long, with a long tail, a long neck and huge green eyes'. Its 'feet were like huge saucers with three long pointed protruding nails . . . Its skin was black, patchy and baggy – it was not like anything we have seen before.' It was making its way back into the sea as the girls ran away, and when they looked back they could see its eyes above the surface of the water. Although this was the only sighting of a sea monster in this area at this time, around the early 1970s other people reported seeing strange footprints on the beaches and strange creatures in the sea off north-west Wales.[3] There was also a sighting from Llandudno pier on 3 September 1882 by several worthy citizens from Leicester and Manchester of a large black snake-like creature travelling very fast across the mouth of the bay,[4] and in August 1963 a man on holiday at New Quay (Dyfed) on the west coast of Wales saw a large creature whose presence was disturbing a colony of seals. It had a large body, four small 'paddles', a long neck and small head which were above the water. It was 30–40 feet long and 8 feet wide by comparison with the seals, and dark in colour.[5]

Moving further north, we have no reports for the Irish Sea off Merseyside, Lancashire, Cumbria, or Dumfries and Galloway Region, but several from the waters of Strathclyde Region. A 30-foot monster with a camel's head, giraffe's neck and a tail covered with long hairs was seen by fishermen in the Firth of Clyde in August 1953,[6] and early in February 1962 Mr Jack Hay who was walking his dog on the beach at Helensburgh at midnight saw a 30–40-foot monster out of the water.

His dog alerted him to the creature's presence by suddenly cowering behind him. Mr Hay reported his experience as follows:

> I saw the thing – about 40 yards away. I made out a massive bulk with a sort of luminous glow from the street-lamps on the esplanade. It did not move for about a minute, then seemed to bound and slithered into the water. I saw the thing swim out. It had a long body and neck, and a head about 3 feet long. I watched until it was well out in the water and had disappeared. There was a strong pungent smell in the air. I was really scared and Roy started to sniff the ground. I shielded a match in my hand, and saw where the sand was scuffed – and there was a giant footprint. It looked like three huge pads, with a spur at the back. The thing was not a seal. I have been a sailor – but it was not like anything I have ever seen.[7]

Two years later, early in June 1964, a man living on the Isle of Jura (Strathclyde Region) saw a sea monster travelling south along the Sound of Jura. The witness drove as close as he could, so that it was 250 yards away at its nearest approach, and he saw that the visible part looked like a cow's head. Through a telescope he could see that it had large white humps on each side of the head, but no sign of eyes or ears. The skin was smooth and grey. The overall length of the creature was about 25 feet. It swam parallel to the shore and was visible for about two miles, but the witness could not tell how it propelled itself. It left no wake or disturbance as it moved, its speed being about 6 m.p.h.[8] A short distance to the north, but many years earlier, two naturalists saw a strange creature in the sea off the island of Shuna (Strathclyde Region). They were cruising in a yacht, when on the morning of 30 July 1887 the steward interrupted their breakfast to point out a sea-serpent. A fourth witness was a deckhand. Professor M. F. Heddle and J. A. Harvie Brown independently wrote down their descriptions of what they had seen, which was a creature with ten to thirteen humps and a low, flat head, moving very quickly through the water. Both men observed it through binoculars, but Mr Brown would not accept that he had seen a sea-serpent and ascribed the sighting to a 'tide-rip or tidal wave', a conclusion not accepted by Professor Heddle who was able to disprove it.[9]

The sightings increase as we move further north. There have been at least two sightings in the large sea-loch Linnhe (bordered by both Highland and Strathclyde Regions), Mrs B. E. Cox seeing a long-necked creature from 20 feet away in the 1940s,[10] and Eric Robinson seeing a three-humped creature 'ploughing along the surface' at a speed of 30–35 m.p.h. and followed by a 'terrific churning of water at the rear', on 21 July 1954.[11] In September 1893, Dr Farquhar Matheson had a strange experience while on a boat trip with his wife in Loch Alsh, a sea-loch to the east of Skye (Highland Region). Dr Matheson's account appeared in the *Strand Magazine* in August 1895:

It was a beautiful day, clear as possible, the sun shining brightly, and without clouds. The time was between one and two.

Our sail was up and we were going gaily along, when suddenly I saw something rise out of the Loch in front of us – a long, straight, neck-like thing as tall as my mast. I could not think what it was at first. I fancied it might be something on land, and directed my wife's attention to it. I said, 'Do you see that?' She said she did, and asked what it could be, and was rather scared. It was then 200 yards away, and was moving towards us.

Then it began to draw its neck down, and I saw clearly that it was a large sea-monster – of the saurian type, I should think. It was brown in colour, shining, and with a sort of ruffle at the junction of the head and neck. I can think of nothing to which to compare it so well as the head and neck of the giraffe, only the neck was much longer, and the head was not set upon the neck like that of a giraffe; that is, it was not so much at right angles to it as a continuation of it in the same line. It moved its head from side to side, and I saw the reflection of the light from its wet skin . . . I saw no body – only a ripple of water where the line of the body should be. I should judge, however, that there must have been a large base of body to support such a neck.[12]

A few years earlier, in the summer of 1886, there had also been a sighting in the adjoining sea-loch, Duich.[13]

The southern coast of the Isle of Skye (Highland Region) seems to be a favourite area for sea monsters. In the early years of this century a boy and two men fishing from a skiff in Loch Scavaig saw an object 20 or more feet high rise from the water and move about in the air. They could also see a dark mass below the water, presumably the creature's body. As the tall column (its neck?) slowly sank back into the water, the boat began to rock as if in the wake of a steamer, and the men rowed back to shore as fast as they could.[14] A similar sight was seen in nearby Loch Brittle in the summer of 1917, and also a few

Loch Duich (Highland Region), one of numerous Scottish sea-lochs where monsters have been seen.

miles south off Rhum, some time early in the century.[15] More recently but still in the same area south of Skye, on 13 September 1959, shark fisherman Tex Geddes and his fishing companion James Gavin saw a strange creature while out fishing for mackerel off Soay. As it moved slowly towards them, they could see what Tex Geddes later described as 'some hellish monster of prehistoric times'.

> The head was definitely reptilian, about two feet six high with large protruding eyes. There were no visible nasal organs, but a large red gash of a mouth which seemed to cut the head in half and which appeared to have distinct lips. There was at least two feet of clear water behind the neck, less than a foot of which we could see, and the creature's back which rose sharply to its highest point some three to four feet out of the water and fell away gradually towards the after end. I would say we saw 8 to 10 ft of back on the water line.

Mr Gavin's description largely agreed with Mr Geddes':

> The head was rather like that of a tortoise with a snake-like flattened cranium running forward to a rounded face. Relatively it was as big as the head of a donkey. I saw one laterally placed eye, large and round like that of a cow. When the mouth was opened I got the impression of large blubbery lips and could see a number of tendril-like growths hanging from the palate. Head and neck arose to a height of about two feet. At intervals the head and neck went forward and submerged. They would then re-emerge, the large gaping mouth would open (giving the impression of a large melon with a quarter removed) and there would be a series of very loud roaring whistling noises as it breathed.

It was as close as 45–60 feet and dived and swam close to them for an hour. Despite Mr Geddes' wide experience of sea creatures, he could not identify this one. Dr Bernard Heuvelmans, whose book *In the Wake of the Sea-Serpents* is essential reading for anyone interested in sea monsters, wondered whether the men had seen some giant sea-turtle, such as are known to have lived in prehistoric times.[16]

The inhabitants of the Scottish islands further out from the mainland have also reported seeing sea monsters, such as the 'huge hornless bull' seen off Bernera on the Isle of Lewis (Western Isles) in January 1895. It was about 60 feet long. A few days later, a kirk minister saw from the Butt of Lewis a creature with a 15-foot neck, two great staring eyes and a segmented body about 120 feet long.[17] Further north, in the Orkneys, J. Mackintosh Bell, a Scottish lawyer on holiday in Hoy in August 1919, saw a long-necked sea monster while out fishing with local fishermen, who told him they had seen it many times before. They would not let him shoot at it, in case it attacked them, and his camera would not work, so he could not get a photograph of it. It had four paddles or fins, and on top of its 6–7-foot neck, which had rough-looking skin like elephant's hide, was a head somewhat like a dog's, with black whiskers and small black eyes. Dr Heuvelmans felt that what Mr Bell had seen was 'a sort of huge seal or sea-lion with a very long neck'.[18]

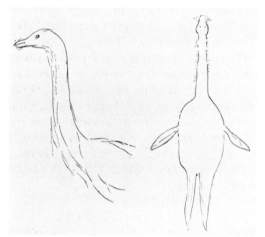

Drawings of the Hoy sea-monster based on sketches by the witness J. Mackintosh Bell, who had a close sighting of this creature in August 1919.

A long way south, now, to the Tay estuary on Scotland's east coast. On 3 October 1892 fishermen at Broughty Ferry (Tayside Region) saw a 40-foot monster with a round, blackish-brown head and a slaty-blue tail with a white tip.[19]

Many years later, on 30 September 1965, two motorists on the A85 road east of Perth (Tayside Region) saw a strange creature beside the road, very close to the banks of the River Tay. It was late at night, and they both saw the creature by the light of their headlamps. Mrs Maureen Ford saw 'a long grey shape. It had no legs but I'm sure I saw long pointed ears.' Travelling along the same road an hour and a half later, Robert Swankie saw what was presumably the same creature, but on the opposite side of the road. He reported: 'The head was more than two feet long. It seemed to have pointed ears. The body, which was about 20 feet long, was humped like a giant caterpillar. It was moving very slowly and made a noise like someone dragging a heavy weight through the grass.'[20] If all this sounds unbelievable, don't forget that we have already reported two sightings of a sea monster on shore, and there are two more to come, not to mention the several land sightings of the Loch Ness Monster and cousins, which will be described in Chapter 19.

On several days at the beginning of July 1939, a number of people saw a sea monster in the Firth of Forth, off West Wemyss (Fife Region) and Dunbar (Lothian Region). Fishermen described a brown creature with a horse's head and large eyes.[21] Five years earlier, on 28 February 1934, a much more dramatic encounter had taken place many miles to the south at Filey Brig on the North Yorkshire coast. Coastguard Wilkinson Herbert was walking along the shore on a dark moonless night when he heard a loud growling noise ahead. He switched on his torch and saw 'a huge neck, six yards ahead of me, rearing up 8 feet high!' He also saw the head on top of the neck. It was 'a startling sight – huge, tortoise eyes, like saucers, glaring at me, the creature's mouth was a foot wide and its neck would be a yard round'. His report continued:

The Monster appeared as startled as I was. Shining my torch along the ground, I saw a body about 30 feet long. I thought 'this is no place for me' and from a distance I threw stones at the creature. It moved away growling fiercely, and I saw the huge black body had two humps on it and four short legs with huge flappers on them. I could not see any tail. It moved quickly, rolling from side to side, and went into the sea. From the cliff top I looked down and saw two eyes like torchlights shining out to sea 300 yards away. It was a most gruesome and thrilling experience. I have seen big animals abroad, but nothing like this.

Despite its melodramatic quality, Dr Heuvelmans was prepared to accept this report as genuine, because the description agrees very closely (except for the shining eyes, which he felt may have been an exaggeration) with so many others of the long-necked category of sea monster.[22] This is a good point to describe another very close sighting of a similar creature, on Herm in the Channel Islands, in August 1923. The fourteen witnesses were exploring the beach at low tide when they came across 'drag marks' 5–6 feet wide which led into a large pool. As they stood and wondered what could have made the marks,

slowly, away in the middle of the pool, a large head appeared and a huge neck – but we did not see the body; there it stayed with its great black eyes gazing at us without fear – then slowly it sank back into the water. It was evident it had never seen a human being before. We joined hands and all stepped into the pool, to see if we could disturb the creature, but it was too large and deep for us to make any real impression.

They could not stay any longer, as the tide was coming in fast.[23]

Over the years there have been a number of sightings along the east coast of England. Shortly after World War II, Mrs Joan Borgeest saw a sea monster off the coast of Humberside from the beach near Easington: 'Suddenly I saw a huge creature rise, it was of a green colour, with a flat head, protruding eyes, and a long flat mouth which opened and shut as it breathed; it was a great length and moved along with a humped glide.' When she shouted out to people nearby, the noise seemed to alarm the monster, which dived and did not resurface.[24] Only a few miles north of her sighting, the Baylis family saw the head and four or five rounded humps of a sea monster off

Hilston in early August 1945. It was moving rapidly along close inshore, travelling against a northerly wind.[25] On the other side of the Humber estuary, in Lincolnshire, another sighting of a creature with four or five humps had been made in the summer of 1937 or 1938 at Trusthorpe,[26] while in mid-October 1966, Mr and Mrs George Ashton saw a monster less than 100 yards offshore at Chapel St Leonards.

It had a head like a serpent and six or seven pointed humps trailing behind. At first I thought it was a log but it was travelling at about 8 m.p.h. and going parallel with the shore. We watched it for some time coming from the direction of Chapel Point until it disappeared out of sight towards Ingoldmells.

I just didn't believe in these things and tried to convince myself it was a flight of birds just above the water. I even thought of a miniature submarine but after watching it for some time I knew it couldn't be.

There was no noise. It just skimmed through the water.[27]

A few miles further south, the steward on a small coaster saw a long-necked sea monster when their ship was north of the Norfolk coast. This was in 1930.[28] A few years later, in August 1936, two couples strolling on the beach at Mundesley (Norfolk) saw a long-necked monster with five humps, travelling 'at a terrific speed'.[29] There was a very similar sighting on 5 August 1936 at Eccles (Norfolk), also in the evening, when a former lord mayor of Norwich, an MP, a former MP and three other people saw a 30–40-foot monster 'skimming the surface of the water in a wormlike movement. Its speed was terrific. It would not be an exaggeration to say it was anything from ninety to 100 miles an hour.'[30] If by any chance the Mundesley sighting was also on 5 August, then it is likely that the two groups of people saw the same monster at different points along the Norfolk coast.

Most of the east coast witnesses have reported very similar creatures, even though their reports are sometimes made years apart. An early one (July 1912) comes from Kessingland in Suffolk, where two of Rider Haggard's daughters saw a many-humped monster about 60 feet long and travelling parallel with the shore at a great speed.[31] Three women at Thorpeness (Suffolk) saw a many-humped creature moving very fast in June 1931,[32] and on 21 October 1938 two fishermen from Southwold (Suffolk) who were laying nets saw a fast-moving creature, grey in colour and about 60 feet long, whose head had suddenly risen out of the water 40 yards away. The vicar of Southwold said he too had seen it.[33]

A sighting was recorded in the Thames estuary in August 1923 (an 8–10-foot neck) and one off Cliftonville (Kent) in the summer of 1950 (a head with ears like a horse's),[34] but the English Channel seems to be a no-go area for sea monsters until we reach the south-west peninsula, where a number of sightings have been reported from Devon and Cornwall. On 5 July 1912, the captain, first officer and an Elbe pilot on board a German ship saw a sea monster off Prawle Point. It was 20 feet long and 12–18 inches thick, and seemed to be fighting another creature, for its tail was causing a violent disturbance. Dr Heuvelmans thought it sounded like a 'monstrous eel'.[35] A few years earlier, in August 1906, two officers and a passenger on a transatlantic liner saw a sea monster off Land's End (Cornwall),[36] and on 5 July 1949 writer on mysteries Harold T. Wilkins and a companion saw two 15–20-foot monsters off East Looe (Cornwall), apparently chasing fish in the creek. They had bottle-green snake-like heads and ridged and serrated dorsal parts.[37]

But for the most dramatic sightings we must come much closer to the present day, and to the south-coast town of Falmouth (Cornwall), for round the shores of Falmouth Bay a great number of sightings of one or more sea monsters have been made since 1975. The first sighting was made from Pendennis Point in September 1975 by Mrs Scott and Mr Riley, who saw a humped creature with 'stumpy horns' and bristles down the back of its long neck. This creature dived and resurfaced with a live conger eel in its mouth.[38] There were many sightings throughout the long hot summer of 1976 and into 1977, and the creature became known as Morgawr, or sea-giant, though we must not assume that only one creature is being seen. An anonymous witness took two excellent photographs of Morgawr in February 1976, showing the long neck and humps that so many witnesses around Britain have described. She wrote a letter to the press describing her experience:

> It looked like an elephant waving its trunk, but the trunk was a long neck with a small head on the end, like a snake's head. It had humps on the back which moved in a funny way. The colour was black or very dark brown, and the skin seemed to be like a sealion's . . . the animal frightened me. I would not like to see it any closer. I do not like the way it moved when swimming.[39]

One of the February 1976 photographs of Morgawr.

In *Alien Animals* we described the mid-1970s sightings of Morgawr in some detail. For nearly ten years it kept a low profile, until suddenly resurfacing during the summer of 1985. In July of that year Jenny Halstead and Alice Lee, on a cycling and camping holiday, saw Morgawr one evening from Rosemullion Head. It looked 'rather like a massive overgrown black slug' and they watched it for 10 seconds before it sank and did not reappear. They did not think to use the camera they had with them, but the sketch Jenny drew shows the now

135

familiar long, sinuous neck and small head.[40] Several other holiday-makers saw Morgawr during the summer of 1985, but little scientific interest has been shown in what may well be an unknown sea creature.

Dr Bernard Heuvelmans is one of the few scientists to take an active interest in sea monster sightings. He has differentiated nine types of large unknown sea animals, the most frequently seen being the long-necked, the merhorse and the many-humped, all represented among the reports quoted in this chapter. More details of the characteristics of these and the other six types can be found in his book *In the Wake of the Sea-Serpents*, over 600 pages long and fascinating reading. In Chapter 19 we shall be describing British lake monsters, and an interesting question is whether the lake monsters are related to the sea monsters, even whether they are the same species, or whether they are entirely different. Some of the Scottish lakes where monsters are seen do link by river or canal to the sea-lochs where sea monsters have been seen, and both types have been reliably reported out of water. What does seem certain is that, despite attempts by the disbelievers to explain all the sea monster sightings away, as misidentification of

Jenny Halstead's drawing of Morgawr, which she saw in July 1985 from Rosemullion Head, the same location as the February 1976 photographs were taken from. Despite the nine-year gap in time, the creatures are clearly of the same species.

known sea creatures, or sea birds, waves or hoaxes, there are enough reliable reports by competent people to prove beyond doubt that the sea still holds some monstrous surprises for us.

14. *UFO close encounters: landings, entities and abductions*

The question of what people have actually seen when they report UFO sightings – stars and planets, natural phenomena, aircraft lights, hallucinations, meteors, satellites, maybe even alien spacecraft? – must still be asked even when witnesses claim to have seen UFOs on the ground and at close quarters. The people who report such encounters are not usually obviously insane, and their reports usually sound very convincing. The matter becomes even more puzzling when they claim to have seen entities, to have spoken to those entities, to have been abducted aboard a UFO by the entities. Faced with an earnest witness, telling you in all seriousness that he or she has been abducted into a UFO, what are you to think? Such stories are all so amazing, and the witnesses themselves usually so apparently truthful, that the investigator's only sensible course of action is to take a non-committal line and investigate the claim from all possible angles. Unfortunately too many investigators are often unwittingly biased towards a belief in visitors from other planets, and any bias, including one in the opposite direction towards complete disbelief, will inevitably influence the impartiality of the investigation and the value of the final result. Therefore in the accounts which follow we will merely present the facts as recounted by the witnesses, and will refrain from labelling any case a hoax unless that is the consensus of a number of investigators. But agreement among investigators occurs rarely, and the majority of these cases still carry question-marks.

First, an example of a landed UFO from which no entities were seen to emerge. The witnesses were two teenage girls, sledging on a steep hill near their home at Meanwood (West Yorkshire). It was 6.45 p.m. on 22 February 1979, and therefore dark. The girls saw red and green lights and heard a humming noise above them, and thought the craft must be a helicopter. But as it began to spiral down towards the ground they were not so sure. It landed just below them on the hill-slope, and they could see that it was about the size of a small car, grey and egg-shaped, with two 'fins' at either end. The girls were, not unnaturally, very scared and ran back up the hill, stopping at the top to look back at the object. It was stationary on the ground for about three minutes, giving off red and green light, before rising into the air and moving towards them, then settling on the ground again about 80 feet away. A minute later it took off and was soon lost to sight in the sky. Investigators who visited the site three days later found E-shaped marks in the hard snow and ice at the two places where the object had stood. Black material found in the marks was analysed and found to be carbon crushed by a heavy weight. There were other UFO sightings in the area around that time.[1] Assuming that the girls were telling the truth, and their father attested that they arrived home very frightened, there seems to be no obvious explanation for their sighting.

Another landing case from the same year does have a possible explanation, but remains puzzling nevertheless. The witness was 61-year-old foreman forester Robert Taylor, who in the morning of 9 November 1979 was inspecting young forest plantations at Livingston (Lothian Region) on foot, ac-

Robert Taylor, who had a very strange encounter in the forest at Livingston, on 9 November 1979.

companied by his dog. In a clearing surrounded by trees he came upon a large dome-shaped object, dark grey in colour, hovering just above the ground. The surface texture seemed to be periodically changing from something like emery paper to smooth and shining. The object was about 13 feet high and 20 feet in diameter. There was a rim around it, like a hat brim, from which emerged small projections like propellers. Only seconds after first seeing this strange object, Mr Taylor became aware of two smaller spheres which emerged from close to the larger one and rolled quickly towards him. They may have been around 3 feet in diameter, and had spikes around them which touched the grass with a sucking or plopping noise. When they reached him, each sphere attached itself to his trousers just below the pockets and he felt himself being tugged towards the larger object. His wellington boots were dragging on the ground as he tried to resist the pull, and he was being overcome by an acrid choking smell. He lost consciousness and fell forward on to the ground.

When he opened his eyes the objects had gone and his dog

Robert Taylor stands at the site of his experience; the object he saw, and the marks it left, were within the area which was afterwards fenced off.

was running round him barking. Mr Taylor could neither speak nor stand at first, so he began to crawl towards his truck, and then was able to walk the rest of the way. He then accidentally ran the truck into soft ground and had to walk home, where he told his wife of his experience. He complained of a bad headache and was thirsty, his chin was painful, he felt sick and could still taste the acrid smell. The only visible injuries were a graze on his chin and others on his thighs, and his trousers were torn below the pockets. When he felt better Mr Taylor accompanied his supervisor back into the forest, and the location was fenced off. On examination, marks were found on the ground, ladder-like 'tracks' across flattened grass, and forty holes surrounding the 'tracks', not more than four inches deep. The grass was not burned or otherwise damaged. An intensive investigation was conducted into all aspects of the witness's reported encounter, and investigator Steuart Campbell concluded that Mr Taylor had encountered some form of ball lightning rather than an alien spacecraft, which was what the press had wildly reported.

Thinking back to the sightings of ball lightning reported in Chapter 10, it is clear that the objects Mr Taylor saw have certain similarities, ball lightning giving off smaller spheres and ball lightning with projections being two of them. Steuart Campbell postulated that the spheres moved 'as a natural result of the influence of magnetic fields', were attracted to Mr Taylor by a vacuum, and when for some reason they reversed direction, they could not detach themselves and therefore seemed to be dragging him with them. Although this looks on the surface like an attempted alien kidnap, the ball lightning hypothesis has many features in its favour. A whole chapter could easily be devoted to discussion of this intriguing case, which clearly demonstrates the overlap between UFOs as alien craft and UFOs as natural phenomena. Readers who wish to know more details of the case and the investigation are advised to read Steuart Campbell's report.[2] Early in 1986, Steuart Campbell abandoned the ball lightning explanation, preferring to believe that Robert Taylor saw a planet, or a mirage of a planet, on the horizon, this being the stimulus for an epileptic seizure. He hallucinated the attack by the spiky spheres, and

141

the damage to his clothes was caused by his dog who was excited or confused on seeing his master thrashing about on the ground. The marks in the grass could have been caused by water board vehicles which had been working close by. Both the ball lightning and astronomical hypotheses have points in their favour, so we will reserve our judgement for the time being.

However useful ball lightning might be as an explanation for certain UFO events, it has never been known to disgorge entities! Many witnesses of UFOs at close quarters describe seeing entities, either in the craft or outside on the ground. Mrs Jessie Roestenberg and her two young sons saw a round UFO hovering over their cottage at Ranton (Staffordshire) on 21 October 1954. Inside were two men, and the craft was tipped forward as if to enable them to see her better. They had high foreheads, white skin and long hair, wore blue clothes and transparent helmets, and were gazing down as if sternly or compassionately.[3] When entities are seen on the ground, they are usually doing nothing, or doing something unexpected or incomprehensible. Two entities from a silvery UFO seen by four young poachers on the banks of the River Weaver near Frodsham (Cheshire) on 27 January 1978 were carrying a cage or framework of silvery material which they then placed around an uncomplaining cow standing in the field. They began to move parts of the cage as if carrying out measurements. The poachers left the scene at this point, fearing they might be next.[4]

Children are often UFO witnesses, and in one way could be thought of as good witnesses because their minds are free of many adult preconceptions. But with today's emphasis on space travel in so much of the media, their reports cannot be unquestioningly accepted as they might once have been. Nevertheless, children's reports are often convincing for various reasons, and they are observant witnesses. In 1980 we published a book of 'True UFO sightings by children around the world', entitled *Are We Being Watched?*, which contains many intriguing reports, and here is one of the many British accounts. Three children aged around ten, two boys and a girl, were playing on waste ground at North Reddish (Greater

Manchester) at lunchtime one day late in August 1976. Seeing a flash of silver and hearing a crackling noise, the two boys looked in that direction and saw a strange figure coming out of a bush. He wore a one-piece suit, silvery in colour, but looked human, with long yellowish hair and a short grey beard. However, he was also floating about six inches above the ground. After a few seconds, he suddenly vanished. One of the boys said: 'It was like a light bulb being switched off; one minute he was there, the next he was gone.' The girl saw none of this as she was in a shed, but she was the next to see the strange visitor. While the boys were still wondering where he had disappeared to, he had reappeared behind them and only a few feet away from the surprised girl who was looking at him face to face through the shed window. As she looked, he took a shovel from his belt and began to dig up soil, transferring it into plastic bags on his waistband. Scared, she shouted to the boys, and at this the man disappeared again. When she told the boys what she had seen, they realized they had all seen the same figure. They soon saw him again, stooping down apparently gathering more samples. He disappeared again, this time as if 'down into the ground', and the children saw a silver disc-shaped object rising up. Such reports as this are very puzzling. Were the children lying? It seems unlikely, because there have been reports of this sample-gathering behaviour by UFO entities around the world, though not widely published. Also the investigator pointed out the similarity between their description of the figure and an entity seen near Winchester (Hampshire) in November 1976, only three months later.[5]

Because UFOs have received so much publicity in recent years it is impossible to find anyone, adult or child, who does not have some rudimentary knowledge of the subject. 'Uncontaminated' witnesses are the most valuable, which is why genuine UFO reports predating the widespread media interest in the subject from the late 1940s onward are so important. Our next sighting is alleged to have taken place in 1901, when the witness was a child of ten, but unfortunately the details were not revealed until the late 1970s, so this is not a genuinely uncontaminated report. However, it is still most interesting. The witness was returning home to Bournebrook

(West Midlands) on a summer evening when he saw a strange object on the grass in the back garden. It was about 4 feet high and 5–6 feet long, and was box-shaped with a central turret. There was a small door but no windows. Two small entities came out through the door and one walked cautiously towards the boy, waving at him as if to say 'Keep back!' The figures wore grey-green close-fitting uniforms with dark helmets that had two 'wires' sticking out on either side. They went back into the object, which lit up all round before streaking upwards with a loud whooshing noise.[6]

Although some of the witnesses so far described were seen by the UFO entities, there was no spoken communication. However there are plenty of reports in which witnesses claim to have talked, sometimes at length, with UFO entities. It is interesting that of the thirteen cases we have on record (discounting abduction reports which will be dealt with later), six took place in the 1950s, at a time when the American 'contactee' George Adamski became world-famous as a result of his claim to have met space people and travelled in their craft. His best-known book *Flying Saucers Have Landed* (with Desmond Leslie) was first published in 1953. In 1981 Mrs Nellie Thomas revealed that her late husband had talked to the occupants of a UFO in 1952 near Castlemartin (Dyfed). She said:

My husband was taking an after lunch walk when he saw the UFO shining very brightly in a sheltered spot amongst the sand dunes. Naturally, he went nearer to investigate and saw the occupants on top of the 'Saucer'. One of them who was obviously the captain of the crew spoke to him in perfect English and told him not to approach any nearer because he was not wearing protective clothing like they were and therefore could be injured by the strong rays emitted by their craft which was then in the process of being recharged by the Sun's rays . . . He told me that they looked just like we did and they said that they had been travelling to and around our Planet for five years and were then about to make their return journey. They told him the name of their Planet but I cannot remember it . . . They said that their crafts had been landing on the waste lands in America for hundreds of years because they were less likely to be interrupted there in their examination of the soil and terrain which is exactly what our craft have been doing on the Moon, etc., in recent years. They were very concerned that our 'Earth' was on a course of self-destruction and wished that they could be allowed to help prevent this. They said that as scientists their knowledge was far in advance of ours on this planet . . .[7]

This agrees generally with the content of messages allegedly given by UFO entities to other contactees, especially with regard to our planet being 'on a course of self-destruction'.

In 1954 Cedric Allingham wrote that while he was walking near Lossiemouth (Grampian Region) he met a man from Mars, but they had difficulty in communicating because they did not speak the same language and Allingham had to draw diagrams on a piece of paper and get the Martian's nod of agreement. (He did not explain how the Martian knew that we nod our heads to mean 'Yes'.) Other contactees did not have this communication problem, as the aliens they met either could communicate telepathically or were able to speak good English. After the publication of Allingham's book *Flying Saucers From Mars*, no one could trace the author, and there were many doubts about the reported encounter, here voiced by *Sunday Express* science correspondent Robert Chapman:

The 'Martian' whom Cedric Allingham met and photographed near Lossiemouth on 18 February 1954.

I am certain in my own mind that Cedric Allingham, if an author of that name ever really existed, did *not* have the experience he claimed – or anything like it. As for his 'death' in Switzerland, I suggest this was no more than a device to put an end to inquiries for him.

In my view, there is a strong likelihood that 'Cedric Allingham' is still alive, in excellent health and far from repentant at having pulled a fast one on thousands of credulous saucerers.[8]

In 1957 Mrs Cynthia Appleton had the first of several encounters with UFO entities, and they communicated by telepathy. An entity materialized in her home in Aston (West Midlands) on 18 November 1957. At first he looked blurred, then the image cleared and she saw a tall, fair man in a tight garment. She said that he informed her that he was from another world, where they lived in peace and harmony, and he was here searching for a substance that sounded like 'titium', though it might have been titanium. He travelled in a saucer-like craft and in a larger 'Master' craft. At the end of their meeting he suddenly disappeared. Two figures appeared in a similar fashion on 7 January 1958, and this time they spoke. Other visits followed, and on one occasion she was asked to treat the wounded hand of one of the entities. This sounds an unlikely event, but UFO contact reports are not noted for their logic.[9]

Contacts of this nature between humans and UFO entities are very rarely reported in Britain these days. The aliens' attitude towards us seems to have changed. The usual fate nowadays of people who come into close contact with UFOs and entities is to be abducted: we have a record of ten such cases, all but two having occurred in the 1970s and 1980s. Many more abductions have been reported abroad, principally in the USA. The earliest in Britain allegedly took place in 1942, though the details were not reported until the early 1970s, by which time UFO abductions were in the public consciousness, following the world-wide media coverage given to the American case of Betty and Barney Hill. Another abduction claimed for 1954 was not reported until 1977, so we unfortunately have no abduction reports which genuinely predate the Hill case. The abduction scenario is fairly standard: the abductees are travelling by car at night, see a bright light which they think may be a UFO, and later discover that they have spent time on their journey for which they cannot account. UFO investigators are alerted to the possibility of an abduction and the witnesses agree to be hypnotized to see if any details can be revealed of what happened during the missing time. Under hypnosis the witnesses give details of their abduction and medical examination by UFO entities. We do not have the space to describe all ten of the English (none known elsewhere in Britain) abduction cases, so we will concentrate on one of the most recent; it is possibly also the most intriguing and convincing abduction case. The others are briefly noted in the Gazetteer.

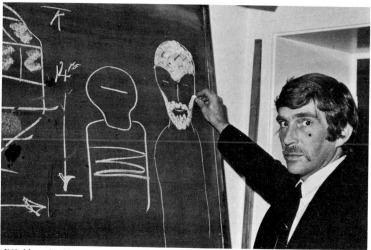

PC Alan Godfrey drawing one of the entities he saw when he was abducted into a UFO in November 1980.

Five months after the mysterious death of Zigmund Adamski (see Chapter 6), one of the policemen who was involved in the case, 33-year-old PC Alan Godfrey, found himself at the centre of another mystery in Todmorden (West Yorkshire), this time a UFO abduction in which he was the victim. It was 28 November 1980 and PC Godfrey was on duty. About 5 a.m. he was patrolling in his car when he saw a bright light on the road ahead. He soon discovered it was not a bus, as he had at first thought, but a dome-shaped object with five dark 'windows'. His car headlights were reflecting off what appeared to be a metallic surface. He sat and watched for a short while, then tried to report the sighting to base through his radio, but could not make contact. So he sketched the object, though he did not get out of the car to do this. The next thing he knew, he was still sitting in the car, but further along the road, and the object had gone. Back at the police station he realized that he could not account for some of the time he had been away, but was not really concerned about this. Then he began to get flashes of memory. He recalled hearing a voice inside his head, while he was sitting in the car watching the UFO. It said: 'You should not be seeing this. It is not for your eyes.' He was encouraged to learn that others had reported seeing UFOs in the area on that same night, including three other police officers.

After PC Godfrey's sighting came to the notice of a local UFO group, hypnosis sessions were arranged, and it was during these that the abduction came to light. The fear the witness expressed as he relived the strange events convinced those present that he had indeed experienced something very unusual. Having seen a video recording of one of these sessions, and met PC Godfrey himself, we can confirm that he certainly believed that the events had occurred as described. During the hypnosis sessions he experienced a mental blockage and intense pain in his head as he tried to recall and describe the machinery in the UFO, and it never was described. But much detail was revealed, and a full description of this case can be found in Jenny Randles's book *The Pennine UFO Mystery*.

What is the explanation for the strange events the UFO witnesses describe? There are probably several explanations. Some witnesses are liars making up stories to gain attention; others are mentally unbalanced and are literally 'seeing things'; others are experiencing hallucinations not brought on by mental illness but precipitated by factors such as stress, fear of the unknown, a surfeit of space imagery in the media, disassociation which can happen when travelling by car at night and seeing a planet as a UFO; others may even have undergone a genuine UFO encounter. But just as no one can say exactly what a genuine UFO encounter is and at what level of consciousness it takes place, so also it is usually impossible to categorize other experiences reported as UFO encounters.

15. *Mysterious disappearances – and sometimes reappearances*

Children and adults disappear in their thousands in Britain every year. Some return home or notify their anxious relatives of their whereabouts, but many are never heard of again. Of these, it is probable that a large proportion are people who for various reasons wish to make a new start in life, but also some of them have been abducted and murdered, and their bodies destroyed or hidden. Others may even have been teleported out of this world . . . Teleportation, a word derived from the Greek *tele*, 'far', and Latin *portare*, 'to carry', is the instantaneous transportation of a person or object from one location to another, and, although according to our present scientific understanding this process is impossible, there are some strange events on record for which teleportation would appear to be the only explanation. It might be argued that teleportees would make themselves known at their new locations, and in fact there are reports where this has occurred, but these do not fall within our present brief of *British* mysteries. One totally untestable hypothesis is that untraced individuals may have been teleported into another dimension of existence, one not discernible to our earthly senses. Whether or not this is a valid or useful hypothesis, one thing we can be sure of is that people do disappear without trace, and that there is some intriguing evidence for the reality of teleportation.

The obvious first question is, could teleportation occur? Recent (1985) research involving the use of a high-resolution electron microscope, with a magnification of 30,000,000, has shown that the atoms on the surfaces of gold crystals are in constant motion.[1] Extending this finding, all 'solid' objects could in reality be dynamic and fluid, and therefore under certain circumstances possibly capable of extraordinary behaviour, such as teleportation. What these circumstances might be is, of course, wide open to conjecture.

One of the most famous unexplained disappearances in Britain takes us back to December 1900, and out to the furthest outpost of Scotland, the tiny Flannan Isles west of Lewis (Western Isles). Three men disappeared from the lighthouse on Eilean Mor around the middle of the month, leaving behind only enigmatic entries in the log. A bad storm was described, though none had been experienced on Lewis only twenty miles away, and there was mention of the men weeping and praying, but no reason given for why they should behave in such an unusual way. It was conjectured that one man may have gone mad and killed the other two, pushing their bodies into the sea before jumping after them, but the knives, hammers and axes were all untouched, and the men's living quarters were undisturbed, giving no clue to what had befallen them. Even the lighthouse lamps were ready for lighting. The mystery remains unsolved.[2]

Eilean Mor lighthouse, from which three men mysteriously disappeared in 1900.

Still at sea, we move to southern coastal waters, where in 1919 two schooners were found abandoned. The *Mary Celeste* is by no means the only ship found deserted in mysterious circumstances, though it is certainly the most famous. One schooner found north of the Scilly Isles was in good condition, with all her boats on board, the sails furled, but entirely without crew. Another, the *Lucienne* from St Malo, was found stranded on the Goodwin Sands off Kent. A half-eaten meal was still on the table, but a boat was missing, and so were the crew, though there was no apparent reason for their having abandoned ship in such haste.[3]

Now we have several more recent cases of adults and children disappearing without apparent reason and without trace. Nineteen-year-old Alex Cleghorn was first-footing with his two elder brothers in the early hours of 1 January 1966 in Glasgow (Strathclyde Region). They were walking along Govan Road when suddenly Alex was no longer there. In 1971 he was still missing, and his brothers were planning to repeat the journey of six years before 'in the vain hope that somehow he may return'. We have not heard whether he was ever seen again.[4]

When young children disappear, it is naturally assumed that they have been abducted and killed, but sometimes the disappearance takes place as if by magic, in that there are other people not far away who see or hear nothing untoward. When thirteen-year-old April Fabb disappeared on 8 April 1969, she was cycling down the lane from Metton to Roughton (Norfolk) in the afternoon. Her abandoned cycle was found, within earshot of picnickers and people working in the fields, only nine minutes after she had left home.[5] Similarly, thirteen-year-old Genette Tate's abandoned bicycle was found by her friends only five or ten minutes after they had been talking to her. She had gone ahead of them along the lane at Aylesbeare (Devon) to deliver newspapers, and the mystery began only 300 yards along the lane from where they had talked, when they found the bicycle lying in the road, with some of the newspapers spilled on to the ground, but no trace of Genette. One car had passed them since she went on ahead, and that was never traced either. Genette disappeared on 19 August 1978 and is still missing.[6]

Mysterious disappearances – and sometimes reappearances

Although adults often disappear voluntarily, it is doubtful if this is always the explanation, as family, friends and working colleagues in many cases can think of no reason for the disappearance. The Revd Philip R. M. Smith was a minister of the United Reformed Church working as a catering officer and counsellor at the YMCA in St Helens (Merseyside). On 27 March 1984 he had lunched at the hostel, and colleagues say he was laughing and joking. He was planning a day in the country for his wife and children the following weekend, and was also planning to buy his wife a record. After lunch he drove off to a discount warehouse and bought the record. No one seems to have seen him after that. When he did not arrive home, his wife phoned the police, who found his car parked in a lay-by on the Rainford bypass. A front tyre was flat, and the obvious conclusion is that he had to stop on the way home to change the wheel. But what could have happened to him on this busy dual carriageway? The car doors and bonnet were unlocked, the hatchback was partly open, a jack handle lay on the parcel shelf and the record for his wife was on the back seat. But no one remembered seeing Mr Smith, and when we contacted the Merseyside Police eight months later, they confirmed that he had still not been found.[7]

Now a few cases suggestive of teleportation, though we are of course unable to vouch that the events took place exactly as reported by the participants, and it should be borne in mind that, were all the facts known, there could be a mundane explanation for these apparent mysteries. In June and July 1887 poltergeist phenomena (see Chapter 25) were occurring in the home of the Revd David Phillips of Swansea (West Glamorgan). During this time, a woman working in the Phillips household was carried (teleported?) semi-conscious over a wall and towards a brook.[8] Many years later, mystic Wellesley Tudor Pole claimed in his book *The Silent Road* (1962) that he had been teleported to his home.

On a wet and stormy night in December 1952, I found myself at a country station some mile and a half from my Sussex home. The train from London had arrived late, the bus had gone and no taxis were available. The rain was

153

heavy and incessant. The time was 5.55 p.m. and I was expecting an important trunk call from overseas at 6 p.m. at home. The situation seemed desperate. To make matters worse, the station call box was out of order and some trouble on the line made access to the railway telephone impossible. In despair I sat down in the waiting-room and having nothing better to do, I compared my watch with the station clock. Allowing for the fact that this is always kept two minutes in advance, I was able to confirm the fact that the exact time was 5.57 p.m. Three minutes to zero hour! What happened next I cannot say. When I came to myself I was standing in my hall at home, a good twenty minutes walk away, and the clock was striking six. My telephone call duly came through a few minutes later. Having finished my call, I awoke to the realization that something very strange had happened. Then much to my surprise, I found that my shoes were dry and free from mud, and that my clothes showed no sign of damp or damage.[9]

There are rare reports of people disappearing, then reappearing in the same location – have they been teleported briefly elsewhere or 'merely' become invisible? The victims are unable to clarify their apparent disappearance. One such occurrence was reported in 1968 in a letter to the *Manchester Evening News*. The writer described camping holidays when his family were young, at the upper reaches of the River Wharfe (North Yorkshire).

I will never forget one such occasion, when we had climbed up over the moors. The children played around, while my wife and I rested among the heather, basking in the sunshine. Whether I dozed off or not, I do not know, but suddenly I became aware that my wife was not with us. I called the children and asked them where she had gone, but they could not tell me anything. I got the queerest impression that she had been spirited away by the 'fairies' – there was nowhere on the moors that she could have hidden, and I began to get panicky . . . We began to get really worried, and even Paddy our dog, who always accompanied us on our outings, started to whimper, and appeared very distressed. Suddenly, apparently from nowhere, my wife was with us again, and there was a faraway smile on her face. We questioned her as to where she had been, but she could offer no explanation, and had no recollection of having been away from us at all. There is no doubt in my mind that something very odd had happened – something associated with the 'farawayness and remoteness' of the place.[10]

In July 1966 a four-year-old girl, Dawn Chester, disappeared in a similar way from her bed at home in Chatham (Kent). The family searched the bedroom thoroughly, stripping the beds and pulling out drawers, but there was no sign of her there or elsewhere in the house, and the doors were locked. Neighbours helped in another search of the house, and an hour later, when Mr Chester was on his way to phone the police, he heard a voice in his right ear: 'We have returned her.' He rushed home and found Dawn sitting on the bed, rubbing her eyes. Fifteen years later, when asked about the experience, she replied that she remembered nothing of what had happened, except 'going to sleep and waking up to a lot of people making a lot of fuss'.[11]

Teleportation, if that is what is happening, can happen also to animals, and to inanimate objects. In February 1956 a man working on power-lines at Brockworth (Gloucestershire) stopped for lunch and discovered that he had left his knife at home. Then he noticed a knife at his feet which he was sure had not been there before. It was not his knife, but a brand-new table-knife, and he kept it. It is said that the knife disappeared when the man died.[12]

Earlier we described a possible teleportation in Swansea having taken place where poltergeist phenomena were also occurring. In May 1906 at Furnace Mill, Lamberhurst (Kent), poltergeist-type phenomena were also happening – heavy barrels of lime being thrown downstairs, a water butt knocked over, locked and bolted doors opened . . . One morning the miller found the horses turned around in their stalls, and one was missing. It was in the adjoining hay room, the door to which was only just wide enough for a man to enter, and a partition had to be removed to get the horse out again.[13] Teleportation is the explanation that has been attached to this event, but that is, of course, simply explaining one unknown by invoking another.

The next case also suggests teleportation, for again there was no access for the interloper. Joe Castle of Sheffield (South Yorkshire) reported in 1975 that when the meter reader came, he was unable to read the gas meter because the dials were hidden. The obstruction was found to be 'a cabbage white butterfly, its wings fully open and obliterating almost all the dials'. Gas board officials were puzzled, saying that the gas meters were sealed at the factory and, apart from gas entering at the inlet, it was impossible for anything to get inside.[14] A similar mystery was reported by Bryon Harvey in the summer of 1977. He found a live bird inside his burst tyre when he went to get a new inner tube for it. The only possible explanation he could think of was that the bird had been drawn into the tyre at the moment of its bursting when he was driving on a Midlands motorway, but it seems inconceivable that the bird could have survived inside the tyre as it still kept moving. The bird was cheeping when released, had feathers missing and bits of rubber on its feet 'like small wellies', and those present were convinced that the bird had been inside the tyre.[15] This happening reminded the authors of *Living Wonders* of the strange reports of toads and frogs incarcerated inside stones (see Chapter 3), and they commented: 'Is it not as reasonable to wonder if the same inscrutable force which can place toads inside cavities in rocks, placed this little bird inside its inhospitable prison?'

Finally, a most puzzling case, of recent date, which will perhaps convince even the most determined doubter that perhaps teleportation can happen. One morning in January 1984 farmer Derek Steedman opened the door of a shed housing twelve Hereford calves and was amazed to find thirteen animals inside. The interloper was a small white bull calf, a Charolais crossbred only about a fortnight old. The night before, Mr Steedman had checked the calves and locked the shed door, so how did the white calf get inside, and where had it come from? It had no ear tag or markings to identify it, and despite much publicity no one came forward to claim it. It was still at Mr Steedman's farm at Chillerton on the Isle of Wight ten months later, when we received a letter from Mr Steedman confirming the details of the press report which had alerted us to this mystery. He wrote: 'The sudden appearance of the calf remains a mystery despite repeated attempts to ascertain its origin. It has now taken its place as the only white beast amongst the rest of the herd on my farm.'[16]

16. *Phantom hitch-hikers*

Phantom road accidents, in which a real car runs into a phantom figure and the driver thinks he has hit a live person, until he gets out of the car and can find no body, have already been mentioned in this book (see Chapter 4). Here we have a variant on that theme, where drivers pick up hitch-hikers who then vanish from the vehicle. This is not a uniquely British phenomenon. Michael Goss, who has turned this subject inside-out in his book *The Evidence for Phantom Hitch-Hikers*, quotes similar stories from many countries. At first sight one might think this was an example of what have become known as urban legends – for example, 'The spider in the hairdo', 'The Kentucky fried rat', 'The killer in the back seat', 'The baby in the oven'.[1] Probably some of the hitch-hiker tales are no more than legends that are still being transmitted from person to person, especially those stories in which the hitch-hiker gives the driver a message or in some other way induces him to call at the hitch-hiker's home address, only to be told that the hitch-hiker has been dead for some years, having been killed in a road accident at the very spot where the driver picked him or her up. But nevertheless it is apparent that at least some of the legends are based on factual experiences, for in Roy Fulton we have a real live witness who in 1979 had the misfortune to give a lift to a ghostly hitch-hiker.

On 12 October 1979 he was going home after a darts match at the pub. He had had only two pints of lager, and denies that he was drunk. In any case, drunkenness would be unlikely to cause a hallucination of a phantom hitch-hiker. As he drove through Stanbridge (Bedfordshire) he saw a figure standing beside the road thumbing a lift, so he stopped. The man walked towards the van, and in its headlights Mr Fulton could see that he was wearing dark trousers and jumper, and a white open-necked shirt. He opened the door and got in, but when Mr Fulton asked where he was going, he did not reply, only pointed along the road. After driving for several minutes in silence, Mr Fulton turned to offer his passenger a cigarette, and found there was no one beside him. He checked that the man had not climbed over into the back, nor was it possible for him to have got out of the van at 40 m.p.h. without the driver's noticing.[2] We have not heard of any other similar reports from the Stanbridge area, so it does not look as though this hitch-hiker is haunting the locality. Most phantom hitch-hikers are seen over a number of years by more than one witness, though lorry-driver Harold Unsworth had the misfortune to see the phantom hitch-hiker of the A38 around Wellington (Somerset) on several occasions in 1958.

The first meeting was in the early hours of a wet morning. Mr Unsworth picked up a middle-aged man in a light raincoat who had been standing near the Blackbird Inn a mile west of Heatherton Grange. During the four-mile journey to his indicated destination, the passenger spoke of recent road accidents. A few days later, Mr Unsworth came across the same man, again wandering along the A38 with a torch in the middle of the night, and picked him up again. The same thing happened a month later. During these encounters there was nothing to suggest that the man was anything other than a living person. But in November 1958 Mr Unsworth became enlightened as to the true nature of his weird passenger, who he had thought might be mentally ill. He stopped as usual for the hitch-hiker, who said he needed to collect some cases. Mr Unsworth waited for him to fetch them, but after twenty minutes he gave up and drove on. Three miles along the road, he saw a torch being waved and in the headlights spotted his friend the hitch-hiker. Apprehensive because he did not understand how the man could have got to this spot, since no other traffic had passed along the road, Mr Unsworth decided not to stop. He drove on, whereupon the man threw himself in front of the lorry. Mr Unsworth stopped and got out, but there had been no accident – the man was standing in the road shaking his fist, angry at Mr Unsworth's refusal to pick him up. Then he turned away and vanished. Understandably, Mr Unsworth did not linger there either.[3] Other drivers on the A38 also reported encounters with this same phantom hitch-hiker in 1970, and some collided with him, only to find no body in the road.

The other major location of such tales or reports, whichever they may be, is Blue Bell Hill on the A229 south of Chatham (Kent). Reports seem to have begun in 1968, often of phantom road accidents rather than of drivers picking up phantom hitch-hikers, though there were reports of a ghostly girl (perhaps a bride-to-be or bridesmaid who was killed in a car crash at the foot of the hill in 1965) flagging down cars and asking for a lift. The reports are mostly vague and second-hand, but one from 1974 is clearer, and very puzzling. Maurice Goodenough was driving on the hill after midnight on 13 July 1974 when a girl appeared in his headlights and the car collided with her. Mr Goodenough got out and found a young girl about ten years old, with a bleeding forehead and knees, lying in the road. He carried her to the pavement and wrapped her in a rug or blanket before driving to Rochester Police Station. When police arrived at the scene, the victim had disappeared, leaving only the blanket and no trace whatsoever of any accident. This mystery was never solved: was she a ghost, or was she a real girl who was not badly hurt and, having good reasons for avoiding publicity, just got up and went on her way?[4]

The factor which links all these strange tales is that the witnesses are all driving vehicles on lonely roads at night. This factor also links them to a great many UFO witnesses, and especially those who claim to have been abducted into UFOs (see Chapter 14). Anyone who has driven alone at night, especially late at night when they are tired, will know that the mind can reach a state of disassociation that borders on a hypnotic trance, and they are then driving on 'automatic pilot'. It may be that witnesses of all these strange events are in another state of consciousness, without realizing it, and vulnerable to both self-engendered hallucinations and psychic experiences.

17. *Mysterious images*

Photographs of 'ghosts' rarely look convincing: white blotches on photographs could have various mundane causes, such as lens flare or stray light causing fogging. But when a recognizable figure can be discerned, other answers must be considered – hoax? inadvertent double-exposure? Or perhaps there really was a ghost in front of the lens, unseen by the cameraman. The ghosts which turn up on photographs are usually unseen at the time the exposure was made. The three shown here are all in this category. The ghost inside Newby church

The ghost of Newby church.

(North Yorkshire) was not seen by the Revd K. F. Lord, a keen amateur photographer, when he was photographing the interior of his church in the early 1960s. It is a strange menacing figure, standing on the steps to the right of the altar, apparently aware of the photographer and almost posing for him. The ghost dog of Tingewick (Buckinghamshire) is also posing nicely beside the trio of ladies engaged in a garden tea-party during World War I (*c.*1916). The photographer was Arthur Springer, a retired CID inspector from Scotland Yard, and neither he nor the ladies saw any dog in the garden, nor did it appear on any of the other photographs of the scene, nor was any living or dead dog recognized from the image on the

The ghost dog of Tingewick.

photograph. Equally puzzling is the 'spaceman' photograph taken in May 1964 by Jim Templeton. He photographed his young daughter in a field by the Solway Firth (Cumbria), and one of the prints showed what looked like a figure in a spacesuit standing in the field behind the girl's head, though Mr Templeton saw no one else in the field when he was taking the pictures. This figure was interpreted as a 'spaceman' because the photo-

*Elizabeth Templeton
and the mysterious
'entity' behind her
head.*

graph was seen by UFO researchers, but it could just as easily
be any old ghost dressed in white clothes – or it might not even
be a human figure at all. What could be arms are discernible,
and a head and torso, but from the waist downwards is hidden
by the girl's head. Perhaps a fault in the film just happened to
take a human shape. It is well known that the mind will always
try to make visual sense of random shapes, and form them into
a recognizable shape, most often a human image.

A puzzling image turned up on one of our own photographs
a few years ago. On 4 July 1983 we were photographing a
summer scene on the Worcester and Birmingham Canal. We
both took a number of photographs in black and white and
colour, and after the colour film had been processed we noticed
a strange shape in the sky at the top edge of one of the colour
transparencies. We were about to reject the photograph as
spoiled, but, looking at it more closely, we realized that the
image could be interpreted as a UFO. Unfortunately we cannot

reproduce it in this book because it is hard to discern the image in black and white. It shows up much more clearly in colour: a white misty cylinder like a thin cigar tilted at a slight angle in a strong blue sky. There are no clouds to be seen in the rest of the sky, and the shape of the 'object' is too regular for it to be a cloud. Also, nothing at all appears in any of the other photographs, all taken in quick succession. Nor did either of us see anything unusual in the sky at the time, no planes or birds, or even UFOs. It does not appear to be a fault in the film or a processing fault. We are unable to explain this anomalous image, unless a UFO did momentarily materialize. This image could provide clues to the nature of the UFO; equally it could have a perfectly mundane explanation.

Occasionally a photograph is taken of a visible ghostly figure, as happened at Raynham Hall (Norfolk) on 19 September 1936, though of the two men present only one could see the

The Brown Lady of Raynham.

ghost. Mr Shira and Captain Provand were photographing the interior of the Hall, when Mr Shira saw an indistinct figure moving down the old staircase. He told Captain Provand that they must take a photograph of the stairs immediately, and they were in time to capture the ghost on film, though Captain Provand did not believe Mr Shira's story until he saw the photograph.[1] The Hall was known to be haunted by the so-called Brown Lady of Raynham, who was the ghost of Dorothy Walpole wearing a brown brocade dress. She was often seen, and Captain Marryat, who wrote *Mr Midshipman Easy* and other novels, fired his pistol at her. The ghost disappeared and the bullet was found lodged in the door behind where she had stood.[2]

In writing of ghostly images on photographs we must also mention the so-called 'spirit photographs' which purported to show living sitters accompanied by their dead friends and relatives. At the end of the nineteenth century and earlier this century, these photographs were much in vogue and there were a number of skilled practitioners who seemed to have no difficulty in persuading ghostly extras to reveal themselves on photographic plates. Some of them were, however, caught out in fraud and some admitted to secretly putting images on to the photographic plates before photographing the sitters. It is impossible to know whether any of the 'spirit photographs' show genuine images of the dead, but it seems very doubtful.

Strange images have sometimes appeared without the medium of photography. There is some evidence that in certain circumstances lightning can produce photographic images, and nineteenth-century scientists referred to this phenomenon as keranography. Some examples of lightning photographs from around the world are described in Michell and Rickard's *Phenomena*,[3] but we have found only one example in Britain in the last hundred years. This took place in an office in Mincing Lane, London, during the night of 9/10 July 1923 when there was a storm. Next morning the staff arrived to find a detailed, bleached 'photographic' image of a wicker waste-paper basket on the bare unpolished floorboards. Lightning had apparently made the image through the clear glass roof above. The boards were cut out and taken to the Science

Museum, but the image appeared to be fading soon after the event.[4]

We referred earlier to the mind's tendency to see recognizable images in random shapes. There are many examples of this tendency to be discovered in the shapes supplied by Nature: rock outcrops looking like giant stone heads, faces in the clouds, in gnarled tree bark, on prehistoric standing stones . . . the image seen is usually the human head and/or face. Many examples are illustrated in John Michell's book *Simulacra*.[5] When such images of human faces suddenly reveal themselves in unexpected places, they are often considered to be miraculous, and the face is interpreted as that of Christ or some other religious figure. Two weeks after the death in 1897 of John Vaughan, the Dean of Llandaff Cathedral (South Glamorgan), a damp spot on the west wall of the cathedral formed itself into an image of the Dean, and even the initials DV could be

A photograph of Dean Liddell when alive.

seen. A photograph was taken, but unfortunately the plate has since been lost. The image eventually dried out.[6] In the early 1920s a similar thing happened in Christ Church Cathedral, Oxford, a white stain on the wall plaster gradually forming itself into a clear image of Dean Liddell, who had been Dean of the cathedral and who had died in 1898. An investigator discovered other faces near to that of Dean Liddell, and was told that others had appeared over the years in various parts of the building. Apparently a long-lasting rift in the Liddell family had only been healed in 1921, being followed by a marriage in the cathedral, and the image of the Dean had begun to form after this event.[7]

The image of Dean Liddell which formed on the wall of Christ Church Cathedral, Oxford.

We often read reports of miraculous images appearing in various parts of the world, and of crowds of pilgrims flocking to see them. This type of phenomenon apparently satisfies a

167

subconscious desire in people to experience the miraculous. In 1976 such an event occurred in Britain when an image of Christ was said to have appeared on a henhouse wall at a poultry farm at St Ives near Bournemouth (Dorset). It was first noticed by a farmworker in mid-August, on a stained fifteen-year-old asbestos wall. A photograph shows grey patches on a white wall, in which a possible face can be discerned. When details of the image were published in the *Sunday People* the farm was inundated by visitors wishing to see the image, and the paper received many letters from readers describing what they could see in the photograph, all the interpretations being very different, thus proving that all is in the eye of the beholder.[8] Perhaps not quite always, though, for the image of Dean Liddell was very clear, and also closely resembled his photograph. Might it be that sometimes a 'supernatural force' (for want of a better term) can imprint ghostly images, just as lightning can make photographic images when the circumstances are right?

18. *The Little People*

Folklore and fairy tales are, perhaps surprisingly, not the only haunts of the Little People. If we can believe the witness reports, humans are still seeing the Little People, and in everyday environments. The encounters are usually short-lived and always unexpected. In the majority of reports we have collected the witnesses are children, but there is usually more than one witness of each event, and the children seem to be sincere when they describe what they have seen. The encounter is sometimes recollected in adulthood, as is this account given by Mrs G. Herbert in 1928:

> I saw the pixy under an overhanging boulder close to Shaugh Bridge (on the southern edge of Dartmoor) in the afternoon. I . . . remember running in to my mother after an afternoon walk and saying I had seen a pixy – and being laughed at. This was in 1897.
>
> It was like a little wizened man . . . eighteen inches or possibly two feet high, but I incline to the lesser height. It had a little pointed hat, slightly curved to the front, a doublet, and little short knicker things. My impression is of some contrasting colours, but I cannot now remember what colours, though I think they were red and blue. Its face was brown and wrinkled and wizened. I saw it for a moment, and it vanished. It was under the boulder when I looked, and then vanished.[1]

Mrs Herbert probably saw what may be termed a 'nature spirit'; meetings with these are usually fleeting and happen when the witness is alone or with a sympathetic companion. In the famous affair of the Cottingley fairies (West Yorkshire),

*One of the Cottingley
fairy photographs,
taken in July 1917. It
has recently been
shown that the
original photograph
was heavily
retouched before its
release.*

which began in the early years of this century when two young
girls claimed to have photographed fairies, their experiments
with a camera and cut-out fairy figures were inspired by the
fairies, probably nature spirits, that they saw in the glen at
Cottingley. Even after their recent admission that they faked
the photographs, they still claimed to have seen the fairies,
and to have taken the photographs in order to convince the
adults, who did not believe them. The transitoriness of encounters with nature spirits does not necessarily mean that the
experience is subjective, but as in our present age of 'enlighten-
ment' beings such as fairies are considered to be merely a
legacy from the ignorant and bucolic past, such reports as Mrs
Herbert's are now disregarded, and the revelations as to the

real nature of the Cottingley photographs have been greeted with great relief by the sceptics who have conveniently ignored their basic stimulus – the fairies in the glen. The fact remains that people still see nature spirits today, in the late twentieth century, and accounts come from prosaic people whose thoughts are not for ever dwelling on ethereal matters.

Nature spirits seem to be solitary creatures, while another category of Little People are gregarious and appear to enjoy themselves in sometimes unexpected activities. In the summer of 1964 children in Liverpool (Merseyside) reported that they had seen 'little green men in white hats throwing stones and tiny clods of earth at one another on the bowling green'.[2] A witness on the Isle of Man, T. C. Kermode, saw 'a great crowd of little beings' in 1911. They were dressed in red and looked like soldiers drilling as they marched back and forth.[3] The creatures W. E. Thorner saw during World War II on the remote island of Hoy (Orkney) appeared to be dancing on the cliff-edge. The weather was stormy and Mr Thorner found it difficult to keep his footing. Looking up, he was surprised to see 'a dozen or more "wild men" dancing about'. They were small and had long, dark, bedraggled hair, and Mr Thorner felt he was 'a witness to some ritual dance of a tribe of primitive man'.[4]

One of the strangest reports of recent years comes from Wollaton Park, Nottingham, where in late September 1979 four children aged between eight and ten claimed to have seen about sixty Little People riding around in little red and white cars. Angela Elliott described what happened:

We heard this tinkly bell. We started running and these little men in cars came out of the bushes. There were about 60 of them in 30 cars like bubble cars. They were half my size and looked old. They had greenish faces with crinkles in them and long white beards with a bit of red on the end. They were laughing in a funny way and driving over swamps near the lake. We were frightened and ran to the gate. I don't think they liked the lights outside because they didn't follow us into the street.

Andrew Pearce felt something drop on him out of the trees: 'I think it was one of the men and I fell into the swamp.' Patrick Olive also tripped and fell into the swamp. Despite the children's fear, and the feeling that they were being chased, Angela described the creatures as 'friendly and joyful'. They were wearing yellow tights or trousers, thin blue tops, and caps with bobbles on the end like Victorian nightcaps. Angela also recalled having seen them before in the summer holidays a few weeks earlier: 'We saw them first in the bushes and they ran off.'[5]

One fact which struck us as we read through the reports of encounters with Little People was the number of times they were seen using some form of transport. The Little People of Wollaton Park were in little red and white cars, and many years earlier, around 1940, three girls saw one little man riding around the yard at their home in Kilkhampton (Cornwall) in a tiny red car. It was night-time and the girls were sleeping together in one bedroom when they were woken by a noise. One heard a buzzing noise, another the sound of music and bells, but on looking out of the window they all saw 'a little man in a tiny red car driving around in circles'. He had a white beard and a 'red droopy pointed hat' and 'in particular was *very happy* looking'. The similarities between this and the Wollaton Park sighting are intriguing: the car, red and white at Wollaton, red at Kilkhampton; the apparent happiness of the Little People; their long white beards and their similar-sounding caps. Were these merely projections of the traditional gnome image, or were these children all seeing some kind of

The children who saw the fairies at Wollaton Park being interviewed soon afterwards by their headmaster.

real creatures? What is certain is that one report could not have been influenced by the other: the Kilkhampton report came to us in a letter from one of the witnesses in 1973, six years before the Wollaton Park report appeared in the press, and we have not published it until now.[6]

In 1929 a five-year-old girl and her eight-year-old brother saw a tiny pilot in a tiny plane. They were in the garden of their home in Hertford when they heard the noise of an engine and saw a small aeroplane like a biplane with a wingspan of 12–15 inches swoop down over the garden fence. It landed briefly, almost hitting the dustbin, and then took off again and flew away. The pilot wore a leather flying helmet, and he waved at the children as he took off.[7] We have no other reports similar to this, but one witness described a ship in the clouds, which she and a friend saw earlier this century in St Merryn (Cornwall). The ship was red, and held many little dwarf-like people who were looking down at the girls, chattering and laughing and pointing.[8]

Also in the early years of this century, around 1912, two boys at the other end of these islands saw a 'faery boat', this time sailing in the sea. The two MacDonald boys were searching for driftwood on the beach of the island of Muck (Highland Region) and found a tin. They were trying to open it with a stone when 'two tiny boys with green vests' appeared and asked what they were doing. They talked in English and Gaelic, the Little People apparently able to speak both perfectly. The boys then saw a tiny boat lying alongside the cove. On board was a tiny woman dressed in green, and a dog the size of a rat. She invited them aboard, but they refused, and so she gave them some walnut-sized loaves of bread, which they ate and enjoyed. After announcing that they were now leaving, and that 'others of our race will be coming', the Little People sailed away. Their sister found the two boys sitting on the rocks gazing out to sea; she broke the spell and brought them back to reality. They then began to tremble and were afraid, but when they had been in the company of the Little People they had been 'awfully happy'.[9]

Such stories as these almost defy belief, yet are they any stranger than the stories of UFO entities which we described in Chapter 14? Perhaps they are not only equally strange, but have some features in common. While in some respects the modern tales of the Little People hark back to the fairy traditions of past centuries, they also have clear links with the twentieth-century reports of UFO entities. Both travel in vehicles of various kinds, both are other-worldly, and often both are smaller in size than average human beings. There are a few cases where the links seem very clear, and sometimes one type of entity is indistinguishable from the other. On 28 January 1967 seven boys aged ten and eleven were playing on Studham Common (Bedfordshire) on their way back to school after lunch. It was raining and there was a flash of lightning. A few minutes later, Alex Butler saw 'a little blue man with a tall hat and a beard' standing about twenty yards away. Alex called to his friends and they ran towards the little man, whereupon he vanished 'in a puff of smoke'. They searched, saw him again twenty yards away, and the events were repeated, the entity disappearing as they approached. The third time they saw him, they also heard voices, foreign-sounding and babbling, and they were more cautious, watching the little man who stood motionless. When the teacher's whistle called them back to school, they ran off and immediately told their teacher what they had seen. They thought the little man was 3 feet tall, and he wore a tall hat like a brimless bowler. On his broad black belt was a black box, and this may have been the source of the 'puff of smoke' which was in fact a yellowish-blue mist, giving off no noticeable smell. They described the man as blue because he seemed to be surrounded by a dim greyish-blue glow, which somewhat obscured his outline; his legs and feet were also unclear. Although this little man had strange headgear like the others we have described, he also had a 'space-age' gadget in the form of a black box and behaved in such a way as possibly to place him in the 'UFO entity' category, though no UFO was seen (unless the flash of lightning emanated from a UFO?).[10]

Around Gateshead (Tyne and Wear) UFOs as well as entities were seen, and the witnesses were again children. At the end of May 1964 children and adults were seeing discs and flashing lights, and then on 2 June fourteen-year-old David Wilson saw ten 'children' standing near a haystack, and another six or eight on top of the stack. They were around 2½ feet tall and dressed in green, and they were digging in the stack as if searching for something. Other children also saw small beings – on a barn roof, or riding on a cow.[11]

An air of unreality pervades these reports, and by that we do not mean to suggest that the witnesses were fabricating them. They may all have been under a spell, as the boys on Muck appear to have been; perhaps children are more susceptible, and fall more easily under the influence of the Little People, the UFO entities, or whatever these creatures are. Possibly they are all from the same place as the entities we will describe in Chapter 22, 'Beings from another world?'

19. The Loch Ness Monster and other lake creatures

I saw this thing coming. I thought it was a man standing in a boat but as I got nearer I saw it was something coming out of the water. I tried to get up close to it with the outboard motor and what I saw was a long neck five or six feet out of the water with a small head on it, dark in colour, coming quite slowly down the loch. When I got to about 300 yards of it, it turned off into the deep and just settled down slowly into the loch out of sight.

John MacVarish, a barman at the Morar Hotel and very highly respected in the area, was describing his sighting of a monster in Loch Morar (Highland Region) on 27 August 1968. He was in a boat in deep water off Lettermorar Point and watched the monster for about ten minutes as it moved slowly as if paddling itself along, though he could not see how it was moving. He could make out no features on the head, either.[1] This is a fairly typical Scottish lake monster sighting, of which there have been many over the years. Loch Ness is by no means the only lake where strange creatures have been seen, although Loch Ness gets all the publicity. We are including only inland lakes in this chapter, though some of them are directly linked to the sea by rivers. The monsters seen in Scotland's many sea-lochs have already been described in Chapter 13.

This chapter concentrates almost exclusively on Scotland, because there are no reports of monsters in England's lakes, which are either not large enough or have been interfered with by man too much for unknown creatures of any size to thrive there. In Wales where there are a few sizeable lakes, the only one to have any suspicion of monster life in recent years is the 4 miles long and 150 feet deep Lake Bala (Llyn Tegid) in

Gwynedd. Mrs Anne Jones saw something strange as she was being driven by the lake in October 1979. She briefly saw a large hump-backed creature which came out of the foaming water. When she told greengrocer John Rowlands in Bala of her sighting, he replied with an even closer sighting of his own, which he had had while fishing with his cousin. They saw something coming towards them:

> It had a large head like a football and rather big eyes. We could see the body which was nearly 8 ft long. It wasn't aggressive at all. It swam towards us to within a few yards and then turned and disappeared. I wouldn't say I had seen a monster. It was just a large being. But I have caught some rather big pike in the lake before now and it was bigger than any of those.

The lake warden, Dewi Bowen, also claimed to have seen a hump-backed creature in the lake. But we have not heard of any sightings since 1979, and if there really is something strange in the lake, it is surprising it is not seen more often, in view of the large amount of water-sporting activity that happens there.[2]

Loch Ness is a much bigger lake than Bala, being around 25 miles long, a mile wide and up to 900 feet deep in parts, although about 430 feet deep on average, so there is plenty of room for a family of monsters to live relatively undisturbed in spite of the passing boats, the tourists, and the ubiquitous monster hunters who have persistently surveyed the lake since the 1950s. There have been several hundred sightings reported over the years, many of them explicable in mundane terms by people with years of experience at the loch – boats and boat wakes, rotting vegetation and dead wood, deer, otters, water birds and hoaxes being the most common explanations. The sceptics would say that these answers cover *all* the sightings, but not everyone would agree with that, especially those people who have seen a monster at close quarters. A number of photographs of varying quality have been produced as evidence for the monster's existence, the best in our view being two taken by Anthony Shiels on 21 May 1977 from Urquhart

Castle. The details of the circumstances in which they were taken, and the photographer's description of what he saw, are given in our earlier book *Alien Animals* and so we will not repeat them here, though one of the photographs is reproduced here. Nor will we give details of the many other sightings of Nessie, as she is affectionately known (there must of course be more than one monster to account for sightings over generations, and indeed some witnesses think they have seen more than one monster at a time). Most people see either a hump in the water, looking like an upturned boat, or several humps,

Two photographs which may possibly show Morag, the monster in Loch Morar. They were taken by Miss M. Lindsay on 31 January 1977, and a comparison of the trees shows that the same shoreline appears on both photographs, the creature having moved its position between exposures.

or a long pole-like neck and head. The best accounts can be found in the several books on the Loch Ness Monster listed in our Bibliography (Costello, Dinsdale, Gould, Holiday, Mackal, Whyte, Witchell, or, for a sceptical approach, Binns and Campbell), together with details of the last twenty-five years of investigations.

We will concentrate here on those reports which indicate that water monsters may be rather more mobile than is generally realized, with special reference to Loch Ness where there have been several sightings of monsters *out of the water*. In Ireland, where there are many lakes in remote areas, there is also a rich catalogue of water monster sightings. Some of the Irish lakes where there have been reliable sightings are quite small, so in the 1960s a group of investigators decided to net a small lake where good sightings had been made, in an attempt to catch the creature. But they were unable to find any trace of a monster, and this may be indicative of the creature's ability to move overland from lake to lake; or maybe they go back to the sea, or come inland to freshwater lakes from the sea.[3] Although

there is as yet no firm evidence to support this theory, it is possible that some sea monsters (there are several kinds) and lake monsters can live in both fresh and salt water, and the same type of creature may have been reported from both environments. This would explain sightings like Mr and Mrs Y. H. Hallam's, who saw two humps and a head moving fast down the River Ness (Highland Region) towards the sea, in June 1936.[4] There was another sighting in the River Ness on 30 July 1965,[5] but if this journey was happening regularly we would expect far more sightings, as the river passes through Inverness. However, the journeys may take place under cover of darkness: remember the strange creature seen late at night close to the A85 road near Perth, described in Chapter 13.

The earliest land sighting of Nessie dates from the late 1870s, when a group of children on the north shore saw a strange creature coming down the hillside and waddling into the loch. It was the same colour as an elephant, and had a long neck with a small head which turned from side to side. It passed only a few yards away from them.[6] In 1880 two children had a similar sighting of a creature with four legs which waddled out of woodland and into the loch.[7] In the early years of this century, Mrs Cameron, then a young girl, was with some friends near Cherry Island when they heard a crashing sound 100 yards away across a small bay, and then saw a large

The Loch Ness Monster as photographed by Anthony Shiels on 21 May 1977.

animal come out of the woods. It was elephant-grey in colour, it had a head like a horse's, and thick legs. It moved like a caterpillar, and the children were frightened by it.[8]

In April 1923, Alfred Cruickshank saw a khaki-coloured creature by the light of his car headlamps. Its body was 10–12 feet long, and it had a tail the same length. Its four legs were thick and ended in webbed feet. This creature was heard to bark like a dog. Ten years later, in 1933, three possible land sightings were reported, the closest being experienced by Mr and Mrs F. T. G. Spicer when the monster crossed the road ahead of them in daylight. Mr Spicer described the event as follows:

> . . . it was on July 22nd, 1933, that my wife and I were motoring along Loch Ness between Dores and Foyers when we suddenly saw a trunk-like thing come out of the bracken from the hillside on our left. We were about 200 yards away, and as it crossed the road we could see this trunk was really a very long neck which moved very rapidly up and down in

This photograph of the Loch Ness Monster was taken by a woman on a cycling holiday in mid-September 1983. She stopped by the loch near Achnahannet to take photographs and the monster came up. She saw 3–4 feet of neck, smooth and dark brown, and it sank straight down after a few seconds. The similarity between this and the Shiels photograph is startling.

curves, that were 2 or 3 feet in height from the ground. We did not see any feet . . . There is no doubt he came down from the hillside and when he was broadside on he took up all the road; which I have had measured, and it is 20 feet wide. He was elephantine in colour, and before we reached him he had disappeared into the loch, which was only 20 feet down on our right.

I got out of the car and could see the traces of where he had gone through the bracken, but there was no sign of him in the water. I might say it was a lovely summer's day. The creature was quite big enough to have upset our car . . . The neck moved very rapidly and the body followed in jerks . . .[9]

Only a week later, early in August 1933, Mrs McLennan saw a dark grey mass 20–25 feet long on the beach. It had short thick legs and large hoofs. When it moved it kept its hind legs on the ground.

Three land sightings were also made in the following year, 1934, but one may have been a misidentification of a deer or other large animal, as may a sighting in December 1933.[10] The first reliable sighting of 1934 was on 4 or 5 January, the witness being Arthur Grant who saw the creature cross the road in two bounds. It was 1 a.m., but there was bright moonlight.

I had a splendid view of the object. In fact I almost struck it with my motor cycle. It had a long neck and large oval-shaped eyes on the top of a small head. The tail would be from 5 to 6 feet long and very powerful; the curious thing about it was that the end was rounded off: it did not come to a point. The total length of the animal would be 15 to 20 feet. Knowing something of natural history I can say that I have never seen anything in my life like the animal I saw. It looked like a hybrid. I jumped off my cycle and followed the animal, which had entered the loch with great speed. There was a huge splash and from the disturbance of the surface it had evidently made away before I reached the shore.[11]

On 5 June 1934, Margaret Munro watched an animal 300 yards away through binoculars for twenty-five minutes. It was almost out of the water and she described it as follows:

> Giraffe-like neck and absurdly small head out of all proportion to the great dark-grey body – skin like an elephant – two very short fore-legs or flippers clearly seen. The animal kept turning itself in the sunshine and at times arched its back into one or more humps. [Finally] it lowered its head, quietly entered the water and disappeared.[12]

There were also two further sightings at some unspecified time in the 1930s: some schoolchildren at Drumnadrochit saw a strange and frightening animal in the bushy swamp in Urquhart Bay, and Alec Muir saw a monster cross the road in front of his car near Inverfarigaig.[13] Twenty-five years were to pass before the next (and most recent, though now twenty-five years ago) land sighting, made by Torquil MacLeod. He observed through binoculars a grey-black creature about 45 feet long which was on the opposite shore of the loch. It had flippers and ended the sighting by flopping into the water.[14]

These reports provide striking evidence for the existence of an unknown creature in Loch Ness which can live both in and out of the water. Some time earlier this century there was also a possible land sighting of Morag, the monster of Loch Morar. A party of schoolchildren travelling by boat from Meoble to Morar saw something said to have been as big as an elephant, and they watched it plunge off the rocks, making a terrific splash as it hit the water.[15] Loch Morar is rather more inaccessible than Loch Ness, but nevertheless there are a considerable number of close sightings on record, the witnesses often being local people who know the loch and its fauna, rather than tourists who are in an unfamiliar environment and therefore more likely to misinterpret what they see, especially if they are hoping to see a monster, as most visitors to Loch Ness are these days. Elizabeth Montgomery Campbell has recorded many sightings of Morag up to 1971 in her book *The Search for Morag*, and a particularly intriguing one was that made by Robert Duff, a regular visitor to the loch. On 8 July 1969 he was fishing in Meoble Bay in very clear water about 16 feet deep. He was looking over the side of the boat and could easily see the bottom. Lying there was a 'monster lizard' about 20 feet long. It was looking up at him, and he was so shocked he got away from the spot as quickly as possible. He had time however to notice a snake-like head with eyes like slots, four legs with three digits on each foot, and a grey-brown skin which was 'rough like burnt coke'.[16]

With so many clear sightings on record, it may seem strange that the existence of lake monsters is still not scientifically recognized. The existence of these creatures has been known for centuries, in the areas where they appear frequently, and they have taken their place in folklore as 'water-horse', 'water-bull', and 'kelpie', strange creatures of the lakes and rivers that could be mistaken for normal horses and cattle. Father Allan McDonald, collecting accounts of strange happenings from Hebridean natives at the end of the last century, was told by Ewen MacMillan of Eriskay (Western Isles) of his own encounter with a water-horse in 1893, a tale which links folklore accounts with modern-day factual reports, and makes us realize that, even if sometimes embroidered in retelling, folklore tales were often based on factual happenings. It was 9 or 10 p.m. in late May or early June and Mr MacMillan had gone to look at a horse and foal. Over near Loch Duvat he saw his neighbours' horses, and then saw what he thought was his own mare. The light was hazy and he could not see the animal clearly, but as he approached within twenty yards it gave a hideous and unearthly scream which terrified MacMillan and the grazing horses too. They took to their heels, and they and MacMillan didn't stop running till they reached home. It was not usual for the horses to go home, so they were obviously badly frightened by whatever had been out there by the loch. The scream reminds us of the barking noise made by the monster seen by Alfred Cruickshank in 1923, though these creatures are rarely heard to make any noise.[17]

Of recent years, the reports of lake monsters have not been so dramatic as in the 1930s, the decade when so many land sightings were made. Either the creatures are dying out, or they are now much more cautious about showing themselves.

Nevertheless, long-time researchers continue with regular surveys at Loch Ness, and their dedication and ingenious use of limited funds must be admired. Despite their efforts, and many attempts to identify the monsters through analysis of the hundreds of sighting reports, there is no consensus as to the creatures' identity, and different researchers have their favourite theories. Theories they are likely to remain, until the scientists have a corpse to examine. But obtaining a corpse, or even a skin sample, or a sharp and detailed photograph of unquestioned authenticity, will not be easy, as researchers have discovered during the last twenty-five years. So unless someone is willing to invest large amounts of money, Nessie and her cousins will retain their mystery for many years to come.

The search for the Loch Ness Monster continues. In June 1982 the Goodyear airship carried a group of researchers silently over the loch, seen here above Urquhart Castle. Also in the photograph is Adrian Shine's Loch Ness Project research barge.

20. *An assortment of mysteries – including some possible illusions*

The hum

Many press reports were published in the 1970s and early 1980s about people who were plagued by a continuous but unidentifiable humming noise. Not everyone could hear it, but many people were apparently suffering from it in various parts of Britain. Some people do get noises in the head (an illness called tinnitus), and we all sometimes hear internal noises which could be the blood pulsing through our veins; but the humming noise is definitely an external sound. Sufferers describe it as a constant throbbing hum, like a lorry engine idling, and it seems loudest in the early hours of the morning, when all other environmental noises are quiet. That the problem is widespread was shown by the reaction of readers when the *Sunday Mirror* in 1978 published a story about the hum. They received over 800 letters from people claiming that they too could hear such a noise. The reports we have on file cover a wide area of Britain, but show that the problem seems to be the same everywhere. In 1972 Paul Wallace of Poole (Dorset) had been hearing the noise for five years:

> Everyone who hears the noise agrees it's like having a dynamo in the head. It's a ringing hum, a vibration which is very painful. It gives me headaches and migraine and I can never get a good night's sleep because of it. Earplugs seem to make it worse. My hearing is A1. When I'm out of the area the noise is faint or non-existent. So it's not me.[1]

There were other people in the Bournemouth and Poole areas suffering in the same way. In 1975 Donald Wood, a water authority technician and former Post Office engineer, and his wife, living in Dorstone (Hereford and Worcester), were finding the hum very distressing: 'We have even walked around in the middle of the night trying to locate it, but it seems to be everywhere. We have heard it over a wide area of Herefordshire, Monmouth, and Gwent. It is always more intense indoors than outdoors, but pillows and ear muffs are no protection from it.'[2] In 1976 Lydia Gilbert of Bognor Regis (West Sussex) recorded on tape the sounds which had been disturbing her on and off for years, and it was like 'a low-pitched throbbing dynamo'.[3] In the late 1970s, experiments were conducted to try to trace the source of the noise which was affecting many Bristol (Avon) residents. In 1982 it was the turn of Worlingham (Suffolk), where only women seemed to hear the 'low-key pulsating sound which seems to go right through you'.[4] In 1984 people in Aldershot (Hampshire) were hearing an intense high-pitched sound which was waking them up in the early hours of the morning. One of the victims was welder Tom Chuter, who said: 'I am a very level-headed person, and I definitely heard this noise. I have never heard anything like it before. I was surprised that no one else living near me heard it, because it was so loud. It was filling up the whole atmosphere.'[5]

In 1978 and 1979 we sometimes heard a strange noise which may have been 'the hum' in our house on the Welsh border, usually in the early hours of the morning, so we can sympathize with the many thousands of victims. Fortunately for us, the sound in our house was very localized, being confined to a corner of the first-floor landing. It was a high note of steady pitch and volume, not very loud, but sometimes louder than at other times. We thought it might be something to do with the electrical wiring, so we tried switching off the mains electric supply, but this made no difference to the sound which continued as before. Perhaps the oddest thing occurred on the last occasion that we heard the noise, at 9.45 p.m. on 27 October 1979. We quote from Colin's report written at the time:

We discovered that as I swivelled my head from side to side in order to hear the noise come and go, Janet, who could independently hear no noise and was standing about 2 feet away and keeping quite still, could hear the noise come and go in unison with my movements. It was as though she could hear the noise being relayed through my brain or skull. We tried it several times and as I turned my head from side to side she could tell me whether I could hear the noise or not, and whether it was loud or faint. Again as before the noise could be heard best with my ears in an east/west direction and not at all in a north/south one. We did not have time to reverse the experiment, with Janet standing in the 'reception' area and me reporting what she could hear, because the note soon became fainter and stopped altogether. We have not heard it since.

According to S. L. Birchby, who in 1979 was researching into 'the hum', this problem was also publicized in the media in the 1950s and 1960s, though no explanation was then forthcoming. More research located letters in a Manchester paper in 1878 about a mysterious noise called 'The Humma-druz' (=hum+drone+buzz) and there were even found cases dating back to 1727, so this does not seem to be a problem with twentieth-century origins.[6] Many explanations have been offered in recent years, and perhaps most are valid to a degree: factory machinery, ship engines, intelligent beings deep in space beaming noises to earth, a noise generated by the surface of the sea creating large movements of air mass, noise from the jet stream (a mass of air flowing fast at a height of 15,000 metres) interacting with lower atmospheric strata, gas turbine noise, the sound of natural gas flowing up from the sea bed, insects, electric power grid substations . . . Mysterious humming noises are by no means unique to Britain. Similar sounds have been heard in the Arctic, the Caribbean, the Australian desert, the Middle East, China, the USA, the USSR – in fact it is a world-wide phenomenon. Its long history and wide coverage suggest that this is a natural atmospheric noise, to which some people are unfortunately sensitive.[7]

Booms and bangs

More strange noises, this time in the form of explosions or
noises like the rumbling of thunder, were being heard, mostly
in south-west England but also elsewhere, in the 1970s. They
were explained away as sonic booms caused by Concorde, but
although this could account for some of the noises, it by no
means accounted for all of them, such as those which did not
coincide with a Concorde flight. Experts said that the sonic
booms could be carried through the air after Concorde had
slowed to subsonic speed, and that weather and wind conditions could sometimes cause the sound to be carried for
unexpected distances. But none of this could explain the story
of a man from Porlock (Somerset) who claimed to have been
hearing the bangs at about 9 p.m. for over twenty years, since
long before Concorde was built. The noise from military firing
ranges has also been blamed, and earthquakes are sometimes
accompanied by aerial explosions, but there may also be unknown atmospheric effects to account for many of these explosions. In other parts of the world, mysterious detonations
have been known for many years, like the 'Barisal Guns' of the
Ganges Delta in India, which were being heard regularly
in the nineteenth century and remain unexplained. In 1978
atmospheric booms throughout the east coast of North America
were puzzling scientists, and again Concorde was the obvious
scapegoat, but not all scientists agreed, some blaming 'the
sudden eruption of gas from high-pressure sources in the
ground'. Closer to home, a phenomenon that sailors used to call
'mistpouffers' was often experienced in the English Channel, in
the North Sea, and elsewhere in Europe. The noise was like
cannon fire, and in the last century was blamed on military
operations, just as Concorde is blamed today.

> Sometimes on shipboard the sailors hear strange detonations
> which give a painful impression to the ear; the noise does
> not seem to come from any definite point of the horizon,
> but seems to emerge as a muffled tone from the depths of
> the water about the vessel. Nevertheless, it does not give the
> impression of being produced near at hand, and seems to

originate from a far-off place. Another remarkable point is that the zone in which such sounds are produced does not seem to be confined to the sea region, for numerous observers claim to have heard them at a considerable distance inland, for instance in Italy and in some parts of the Alps. The causes of such phenomena are little known.[8]

It would seem, therefore, that the explosions heard in Britain in the 1970s had two probable explanations: some, occurring at the times when Concorde was in the air, could be sonic booms, while others were 'natural phenomena' as yet unexplained, but possibly of seismic or atmospheric origin.

One particularly mysterious explosion occurred in the Berwyn Mountains near Llandrillo (Clwyd) at 8.38 p.m. on 23 January 1974. An earth tremor of magnitude 3.5 to 4 on the Richter scale was recorded by the Global Seismology Unit of the Institute of Geological Science in Edinburgh, and it was clearly felt for some distance from Llandrillo. This in itself is not puzzling, since earth tremors are not rare in Britain. The mystery arises from the fact that a blue-green streak of light was seen crossing the sky immediately before the explosion was heard, as if something had crashed into the mountain. It might have been a plane crash, so police went out to search,

The Berwyn mountains, scene of mystery explosions.

190

but nothing was found. The other alternative was a meteorite, but it would have had to be a very large meteorite to have caused such a large tremor, and no trace of any such impact was found on the mountain. Perhaps there was no meteorite, the aerial lights being part of the earthquake activity and originating from inside the earth. The events on the Berwyns certainly had the experts baffled.[9] A repetition of these events two years later received little press publicity. An explosion on the night of 6 August 1976 was heard over about a ten-mile radius, and witnesses saw aerial lights. V. C. Worthington said: 'The explosion was extremely loud, but had a dull, muffled sound. The earth shook as though from a heavy impact. The sky lit up brightly, and stayed like that for several minutes.' Nothing was reported found on the mountain to account for the explosion.[10]

Corny circles

It seems that every summer since 1980 the press has had a field-day over the flattened circles in cornfields in the south of England. These have been dubbed 'UFO nests' and seen as evidence of alien visitations by supporters of the belief that UFOs contain people from outer space, especially since the first circles to come to widespread notice appeared at Warminster in Wiltshire, which in the 1960s and 1970s was a focus of pilgrimage for sky-watchers where much UFO activity was believed to be occurring. It is extremely unlikely that UFOs are the cause: no one has claimed to have seen UFOs at the scene of the circles. Far more likely is that the majority are caused by localized fair-weather whirlwinds. In the summer, small-scale whirlwinds are common, and we have seen them ourselves in calm, hot weather. The circles are often found in fields close to the foot of a concave steep hill, and it is thought that the hill stops the moving whirlwind which then concentrates its force on one spot, hence flattened circles in the corn.[11] An alternative theory is that the circles are man-made, either as part of pagan rituals or as a hoax. It is probable that the earliest circles were made by whirlwinds, and that the media publicity given to them has prompted hoaxers to try their hands at making even more elaborate designs. One appeared on 3 July 1983 at Westbury (Wiltshire) which consisted of a large central circle surrounded by four smaller satellite circles equally spaced. A surveyor helped a group of men from the *Daily Mirror* armed with a long chain to fabricate a similar design beside the original one, and the two groups of circles were indistinguishable.[12] It is not necessary to blame alien visitors for this mystery, for which two perfectly adequate terrestrial explanations exist.

Space message

Alien visitors were thought to be involved in another mystery from southern England, when a 'voice from outer space' broke into a news bulletin on Southern TV at 5.12 p.m. on 26 November 1977 and broadcast a message 5½ minutes long which drowned out the news bulletin. The message began:

> This is the voice of Gramaha the representative of the Asta Galactic Command [there is some disagreement over these names, which were transcribed from tape-recordings of the announcement] speaking to you. For many years now you have seen us as lights in the skies. We speak to you now in peace and wisdom as we have done to your brothers and sisters all over this, your planet earth. We come to warn you of the destiny of your race and your worlds so that you may communicate to your fellow beings the course you must take to avoid the disasters which threaten your worlds, and the beings on our worlds around you. This is in order that you may share in the great awakening, as the planet passes into the New Age of Aquarius. The New Age can be a time of great peace and evolution for your race, but only if your rulers are made aware of the evil forces that can overshadow their judgements . . .[13]

The voice continued with warnings against nuclear energy and weapons, and false prophets, and indeed spoke much good sense. Hundreds of worried viewers, believing the end was nigh, telephoned the police or Southern TV, a reaction reminiscent of what happened when Orson Welles broadcast his adaptation of H. G. Wells's *The War of the Worlds* in the United States in 1938, which listeners believed to be factual and which caused thousands to flee into the streets in panic. The Southern TV 'space message' was immediately officially denounced as a hoax (what else could they say?) by 'students', but if so it was a very elaborate one, and no one was ever apprehended or charged with what the authorities undoubtedly consider to be a very serious offence. In the past, radio broadcasts had been broken into, but this was the first time a TV programme was taken over. Television stations are heavily guarded by electronic devices that monitor the signal and are supposed to detect interference. Very sophisticated equipment would have been needed to achieve what the 'hoaxers' did achieve, and it would also have had to be very high powered to put their signal into the relay station at Hannington (Hampshire). The authorities were uncertain as to how it had been done, despite their apparent confidence that it was a hoax.[14] Perhaps it wasn't a hoax at all; perhaps it really was our interplanetary neighbours, concerned about the way we are threatening to destroy our planet, and injuring them in the process. Theirs was the same message that the 'space people' have been giving to UFO 'contactees' for decades – perhaps they now decided they would have to relay it to a wider audience, before it is too late . . .

Electromagnetic mysteries

The interaction of electric and magnetic fields, though 'natural', is still pretty mysterious, and electromagnetism probably has a part to play in many happenings which appear inexplicable. We cannot delve too deeply into this aspect of mysteries, since our knowledge of physics is basic, to put it charitably, so we will leave the theorizing to those better equipped. But we would not be surprised to find that electromagnetism is involved somewhere in producing phenomena like ghosts

(Chapters 4, 8, 12, 16), black dogs (Chapter 5), UFOs (Chapters 7, 14), ball lightning (Chapter 10), poltergeists (Chapter 25) and some of the meteorological mysteries in Chapter 23, as well as the strange events to be described below.

Some time in 1978, the liner *QE2* received a mysterious radio signal. The message was in Morse and read: GKS GBTT QSX AREA 1A. This message was received by the radio officer Alan Holmes, when the *QE2* was in the Atlantic on its way to America. Mr Holmes recognized that the message was coded in a procedure no longer in use, and deciphered it as a routine position check from the old liner *Queen Mary* to the Portishead Radio Station at Burnham (Somerset). But the message was in an obsolete code and seemed to have been sent out by the *Queen Mary* more than eleven years before. The *Queen Mary* had in 1967 become a stationary floating conference centre, and her GKS call sign had been inherited by the *QE2*. Mr Holmes's explanation for the late message was that the radio signal must have bounced off something in space and come back to earth; that being strange enough, it becomes even more unbelievable for the message to have been received by the very ship which inherited the GKS call sign. Station manager Donald Mulholland just could not accept this, and said that someone must have hoaxed Mr Holmes, but Mr Holmes said he was not alone when he received the message, and it 'really did come in. I was listening out on a frequency used for radio telephone calls. I can't explain it.' He said that if it was a hoax, 'it's an elaborate hoax, rather difficult to lay on, and hardly worth the bother of laying on. The hoaxer would have had to know exactly what frequency we were listening out on, and when.'[15]

We have already mentioned, in Chapter 8, the possibility that the sound of World War II battles has been 'recorded' under the sea. In 1978 a press report described how a tape of home-recorded music was found to have extraneous sounds on it – a crashing noise, screaming, groaning, a boy whimpering, and a voice calling 'Is there anybody down there?' Then a muffled voice says something about dead bodies and the music comes back on again. Mrs Joyce McCarthy commented: 'We recorded the music some time ago and there was nothing like that on the tape. We have played it dozens of times before without hearing these dreadful noises. The ghostly voices suddenly appeared – the mystery has completely baffled us.' The McCarthys live in a coal-mining area (Whiteheath, Birmingham, West Midlands), and the sounds on the tape are reminiscent of an underground accident, so a check was made locally and it was discovered that the Black Bat mine nearby had been closed in 1883, five years after several men and boys had been killed in a roof fall.[16] If it is true that the sounds on the tape are a recording of the disaster exactly a hundred years before, we cannot begin to explain how the events came to be imprinted on a tape in 1978. There may be some connection with the EVP or 'electronic voice phenomenon' whereby the dead allegedly imprint their voices on tape, and also with Spiricom, where the dead are said to hold tape-recorded conversations with the living, via audio frequencies in both cases.

Finally in this section, an electromagnetic mystery which is a potential hazard to air traffic. We all remember the 'Bermuda Triangle', the mysterious area which is not triangular nor centred on Bermuda, where ships and planes have disappeared without trace, some of them having reported trouble with their instruments. A similar problem was being encountered in 1978 over the English Channel. In October of that year Malcolm Montgomerie was flying with his daughter and another pilot to Alderney in the Channel Islands. In patchy cloud and failing light 25 miles south of Bournemouth (Dorset), the cockpit instruments suddenly went berserk. The compass and direction indicator spun 100 degrees in the same direction, and the pilot had to fly by taking navigational fixes with his radio direction finder. After twelve minutes the instruments suddenly returned to normal and they made a safe landing. On their return trip, the same thing happened in the same area though with only a 20-degree deviation. It led them to wander more than twenty miles off course, and on both occasions if Mr Montgomerie had followed the false course indicated, he would have flown over Portland (Dorset). His co-pilot wondered: 'Was something secret being tested at Portland Naval Base? Could there have been a nuclear submarine in the vicinity with some sort of weapon on board which might affect the magnetic field?' Predictably the Ministry of Defence replied: 'We know of nothing which might have caused this.'[17]

Illusion or reality?

Magic tricks performed by conjurers are, as we all know, illusions masquerading as reality, and so too is the Indian Rope Trick . . . or is it? Detailed explanations have been published on how it is done – the rope held up by fine wires manipulated by assistants, the fakir working under cover of twilight, using lights at ground level to keep his audience's attention from straying upwards; or using a 'rope' constructed of sheep's vertebrae covered with cord which when expertly handled can appear as a normal rope but then becomes a solid stick up which a boy can climb. These are just two ways in which the audience can be fooled into believing that they are seeing

The Indian Rope Trick as performed on 7 January 1935 by Karachi and Kyder.

something other than what is really happening. In his entertaining book *Confessions of a Ghost-Hunter*, Harry Price describes how Karachi (Arthur Claud Darby), aided by his eleven-year-old son Kyder, performed the Indian Rope Trick at Wheathampstead (Hertfordshire) on 7 January 1935 in the presence of Price and other psychic researchers, and also in the book he quotes a full account by occultist Erik Jan Hanussen of the Indian Rope Trick he saw performed near Babylon in the 1920s. Although it is virtually certain that in all cases an illusion was skilfully created, a lingering doubt (or hope?) remains that it was not an illusion every time, but that sometimes the fakir really had the skill to give a momentary twist to our reality.[18]

We now describe some strange events which may also have been either illusions or momentary twists of reality. Let us start with the strange case of John Lee, the man who could not be hanged. Lee was condemned to death for the murder of his employer Mrs Keyse. He was her 22-year-old footman,

John Lee, the man they could not hang.

197

whom she had employed despite his criminal record as a thief. He insisted that he was innocent of her murder, and on the night before the day set for his execution at Exeter (Devon), 23 February 1885, he dreamed that the trap would fail to function three times. In fact three unsuccessful attempts were made to hang him, and the Governor postponed the execution, the sentence later being changed to life imprisonment. Lee was released after serving some years in prison. Divine intervention? Or did Lee's grandmother, who was believed to have strange powers, manage to gain control of the trap and stop it working? We shall never know what really happened.[19]

Still in Devon, a stretch of road leading into Postbridge got a reputation for being dangerous, after several serious accidents there in 1921. Dr Helby, doctor at Dartmoor prison, was flung off his motor cycle and died of a broken neck in March, and a few weeks later a motor coach drove on to the grassy bank and several passengers were thrown out. The driver said he had felt invisible hands pulling at the wheel. Two men on a motor cycle had trouble with their steering while coming down the hill, and on 26 August a young army officer on a motor cycle was slightly injured when he was thrown onto the grass verge. He later commented:

It was not my fault. Believe it or not, something drove me off the road. A pair of hairy hands closed over mine. I felt them as plainly as ever I felt anything in my life – large, muscular, hairy hands. I fought them for all I was worth, but they were too strong for me. They forced the machine into the turf at the edge of the road, and I knew no more till I came to myself, lying a few feet away on my face on the turf.

The 'hairy hands' have also been blamed for other accidents in the area, but perhaps this happened after the army officer's experience was publicized. Local people blamed the accidents on excessive speed and the camber of the road. But Devon folklorist Theo Brown was told by a man who was in the habit of wandering on Dartmoor at night that he had heard, very near the hill where the accidents occurred, an awful scream, unlike the noise made by any wild animal. In 1924 Miss Brown's mother actually saw the hairy hands, clawing at the window of a caravan where the family were spending the summer, half a mile away from the notorious road. Were the 'hairy hands' really objective, or did the awkward camber of the road give the impression that a vehicle's steering was being controlled by some unknown presence, which the army officer interpreted as 'hairy hands', which then passed into the folklore of the area, to be visualized at night in a half-asleep state by Mrs Brown? Decide for yourself whether illusion was to blame for the 'hairy hands' of Dartmoor.[20]

In 1936 Sir Alexander Hay Seton and his wife Zeyla visited Egypt, and Lady Seton took a small bone from a tomb near the Pyramids. When they were back home in Edinburgh (Lothian Region) strange things began to happen and Sir Alexander came to the conclusion that the bone had brought a curse into the household. A ghostly figure in robes was seen by servants and visitors, furniture was thrown around and banging noises were heard as in poltergeist outbreaks. Such events took place on several occasions, and finally Sir Alexander destroyed the bone by burning it, without his wife's knowledge. As well as the domestic disturbances, Sir Alexander also suffered ill-health and financial problems, and felt that the bone was to blame. He wrote: 'The curse did not end with the destruction of the Bone. From 1936 onwards trouble always seemed to beset me. Zeyla never forgave me for destroying the Bone and it did not help our already rocky marriage.' A similar case will be described in Chapter 22, of a ghost which materialized in a house where a possible Celtic stone head had been taken in the 1970s, and it is quite possible that the removal of the bone from the tomb did somehow activate the ghostly phenomena. But whether Sir Alexander was right to blame *all* his misfortunes on the bone is another matter, and he may have been using it as a scapegoat. It is possible also that the poltergeist phenomena developed as a result of family tensions, rather than being caused by the bone. As we shall see in Chapter 25, poltergeists are closely linked to the emotions of family members.[21]

In the late 1940s, what can only be classed as a visual illusion, or some kind of shared hallucination, was experienced by the Revd Dr A. T. P. Byles and his wife, at his parish church in Yealmpton (Devon). The vicar was walking up the path to the church at twilight to meet his wife who was arranging the altar flowers. He came upon a hole in the path, about a yard wide, and went into the church to fetch his wife. She also saw the hole. The vicar threw a stone down it and heard it hit stonework, which looked like part of a wall. Anxious that there should be no accidents, they hurried off to fetch planks to cover the hole, and brought back with them a local builder. To their total surprise, there was no hole to be seen – the path looked normal, with no signs of disturbance. Whether the vicar and his wife were momentarily experiencing a timeslip similar to those described later in this chapter, it is impossible to tell.[22] It is a pity that they both went off to fetch the planks. If one of them had stood guard by the hole, the outcome to this story might have been different.

Our final illusion, if an illusion it be, was shared by several different young people in 1976 and 1978. The first to see 'the Owlman' were June and Vicky Melling, aged twelve and nine. On 17 April 1976 they saw a big feathered birdman hovering over Mawnan church tower (Cornwall). On 3 July 1976, fourteen-year-old Sally Chapman and Barbara Perry saw him in the woods nearby. Sally described 'the Owlman':

Sally Chapman's drawing of 'the Owlman'.

I saw this monster bird last night. It stood like a man then it flew up through the trees. It is as big as a man. Its eyes are red and shine brightly.

Sally Chapman 4/7/76.

It was like a big owl with pointed ears, as big as a man. The eyes were red and glowing. At first, I thought it was someone dressed up, playing a joke, trying to scare us. I laughed at it, we both did, then it went up in the air and we both screamed. When it went up, you could see its feet were like pincers.

Next day, Jane Greenwood saw him in the woods, then he kept a low profile until 1978 when there were two further reports. When we wrote *Alien Animals* we were inclined to accept the strange nature of these sightings, in view of the fact that other strange things were happening in the area in 1976, like UFO sightings and sightings of Morgawr the sea monster (see Chapter 13). But since then one of us (Janet) has seen a similar sight many miles away from Mawnan, in Hafren Forest (Powys).

I was sitting in a car when my attention was caught by a disturbance in the trees across a stream. I saw a large bird, definitely an owl, rise up vertically, facing me with its whole face and body visible, its legs and feet hanging down. It rose straight up above the trees and flapped off, in broad daylight.

Apart from the human-like touches on the children's drawings, the owl seen in Hafren Forest very closely resembles what the children described and drew. The name 'Owlman', and also Sally's description, acknowledge the creature's similarity to an owl. We therefore now feel that what the children saw at Mawnan was a large owl. The Long-eared Owl has prominent ear tufts which it holds erect when nervous, and all the children's drawings show definite ears sticking up. Children don't often see owls close to in daylight. We have a resident tawny owl in our conifer plantation, and it is quite frightening to come face to face with it, as it sits watching us from a safe perch. No wonder the children spoke of the Owlman being 'horrible, a nasty owl-face with big ears and big red eyes'; and 'It was so strange, like something in a horror film.' We do not know what species of owl they could have seen, since two of the witnesses call it man-sized, but we must allow for some exaggeration here. Owls normally seen in Britain are usually no bigger than 14–15 inches long. There are bigger owls, like the Eagle Owl and the Great Grey Owl which are 27 inches long, but they are not native to Britain – unless an aviary bird had escaped and was living in the Mawnan area?[23]

Timeslips

So-called timeslips might also be explained away as illusions, but they are complex and not easy to understand. To begin with, the word 'timeslip' can cover more than one type of experience. Anna Petherbridge was walking along a side street in Covent Garden, London, early in the morning one autumn day in 1982 when she saw a young man running towards her. She noticed him particularly because 'he seemed wild-eyed and was panting heavily', though no one seemed to be chasing him. He dashed past and was lost to sight behind a parked van. Ms Petherbridge had only walked on a few yards when the same young man came round the corner and again ran towards her. But Ms Petherbridge says it would have been impossible for him to have doubled back in such a short time.[24] Was she mistaken? Was this a timeslip? Or was she perhaps seeing a ghost, not a living man at all, and did she see it go through its 'routine' twice, rather than once as usually happens? Ghosts and timeslips do overlap considerably. For example, people seeing what appear to be ghostly buildings or events may actually have somehow gone back in time and be eavesdropping on the past. Consider Mrs Edna Hedges' strange experience some time in the 1930s. Then a young girl, she was cycling along the Roman road Ermine Street just outside Swindon (Wiltshire). When a storm began to threaten, she called at a thatched cottage for shelter and was invited inside by the old man who answered the door. She saw an old-fashioned interior with a lighted fire, but could hear no sound inside the cottage, and the old man never spoke. Then, without knowing how she got there, she found herself back on her cycle, dry despite the rain. When she told people of her experience, they said that there was only a derelict cottage at that spot, so eventually she went back to see for herself and found the derelict cottage which had obviously not been lived in for many years.[25] Did Mrs Hedges really take shelter inside the derelict cottage, but imagined it as it might have been when occupied, or did she somehow slip back to a time when the cottage really had been inhabited? A couple who had been exploring Wotton church in Surrey during the summer of 1954 wandered into a non-existent landscape when they left the churchyard. While sitting on a bench feeling uneasy for no apparent reason, the wife 'saw' three figures standing behind her, and was unable to turn her head to view them directly. On a later occasion when the couple returned to Wotton, the landscape was completely different and bore no relation to what they had seen before. The events were closely investigated, and it was decided that the couple had had some kind of shared psychic experience. They too may have stepped back in time, but into an imaginary time as the landscape at Wotton could never have been as they saw it.[26]

Timeslips may not be so rare, for readers of *The Unexplained* reported their own experiences of apparent timeslips, including Mrs E. Hall who, when living in Kent in the 1950s, walked past a man sitting in his car talking to someone. She knew the driver, who lived nearby. A few seconds later she turned a corner and saw the same man's car in the drive of his bungalow. When she had seen the car seconds before, it was pointing away from his home, and it would have been impossible for him to move it from one location to the other in such a short space of time. What she should have done, of course, was quickly to retrace her steps and see if the driver was still sitting where she had first seen him. She should also have made sure that it was the same car, and not another car of the same model and colour.[27] We suspect that most 'timeslips' may have perfectly straightforward explanations . . . but it is easy for us to say that, because we have never experienced one!

21. Spontaneous human combustion

According to a report in the *British Medical Journal* (1905) on the death of 'an elderly woman of intemperate habits', the authorities broke into her house when smoke was seen coming from it, and they found

> a small pyramidal heap of broken calcinated human bones, on the top of which was a skull, on the floor in front of a chair. All the bones were completely bleached and brittle; every particle of soft tissue had been consumed, and yet a tablecloth within three feet of the remains was not even scorched.

These are the classic signs of spontaneous human combustion: fire suddenly overwhelms the victim, who rarely has time to call for help; the fire burns so fiercely that the flesh is completely consumed, and only a few charred bones are left, or sometimes a limb or two also survives. Great heat is obviously needed to burn a body so completely (in a crematorium a temperature of 2,500–3,000°F is needed for up to four hours), yet the burning is so localized that objects nearby are untouched. If the victim was sitting in a chair, that usually survives the fire. These are strange facts indeed, so strange that doctors and scientists cannot accept them but will go to great lengths to explain away such a death, as we will see. Yet spontaneous human combustion has been occurring for centuries, and researchers have unearthed many old cases which baffled the experts of the time. Dickens had the villain Krook die such a mysterious death in *Bleak House*:

> Call the death by any name . . . attribute it to whom you

will, or say it might have been prevented how you will, it is the same death eternally – inborn, inbred, engendered in the corrupt humours of the vicious body itself, and that only – Spontaneous Combustion, and none other of all the deaths that can be died.

The majority of cases reported in Britain today do not involve the complete combustion of the body. Usually the victim bursts unexpectedly into flames, which are then extinguished by other people, leaving the victims with burns but still alive, though sometimes they are so badly burned that they die later in hospital. Again the experts are left with the job of explaining the sudden igniting of the victim, which they achieve with varying degrees of success. We will present the major cases of possible spontaneous human combustion during the last hundred years in chronological order, to build up a clearer picture of this mysterious phenomenon.

On 19 February 1888 a 65-year-old man, referred to as an 'old soldier', was burned to death in the loft of a stable in Aberdeen (Grampian Region). University lecturer Dr J. Mackenzie Booth who was called to the scene found a charred corpse with most of the flesh burned away. The surrounding

The corpse of the 'old soldier', a possible victim of spontaneous human combustion, who died in Aberdeen in February 1888.

floor had also been burned, and the fire had evidently burned upwards as the roof was damaged and slates had fallen on to the body. However, hay and dry woodwork close by did not catch fire. The night before, the 'old soldier' had been seen taking a lamp and a bottle into the loft, but the lamp was seen to go out shortly afterwards, and no fire was seen during the night, so it is unlikely that the lamp was the cause of the fire.[1]

The widow of Thomas Cochrane was found dead at her home in Falkirk (Central Region) on the morning of 16 December 1904. The corpse, 'burned almost beyond recognition', was sitting in a chair surrounded by pillows and cushions which had not burned. There was no fire in the grate.[2]

The next case introduces another aspect of spontaneous human combustion, a possible link with poltergeist phenomena. Mysterious fires are one way in which a poltergeist manifests itself, and at Binbrook Farm, Binbrook (Lincolnshire), objects had been falling from shelves and moving around of their own accord, in addition to which the farmer had lost almost 250 hens, all killed in the same strange way, four or five at a time, despite a watch being kept on the henhouse. It was the servant girl who became the fire victim in this case, as here described by the farmer:

> Our servant girl, whom we had taken from the workhouse, and who had neither kin nor friend in the world that she knows of, was sweeping the kitchen. There was a very small fire in the grate: there was a guard there, so that no one can come within two feet or more of the fire, and she was at the other end of the room, and had not been near. I suddenly came into the kitchen, and there she was, sweeping away, while the back of her dress was afire. She looked around, as I shouted, and, seeing the flames, rushed through the door. She tripped, and I smothered the fire out with wet sacks. But she was terribly burned, and she is at the Louth Hospital now, in terrible pain.[3]

This happened in January 1905, and only a month later, during the night of 25/26 February 1905, an elderly couple living in Hampshire died from burning at their home in Butlock's

Heath, in somewhat strange circumstances. A scratching noise early in the morning of 26 February alerted neighbours who broke in and found the house on fire. They also found John Kiley lying dead on the sitting-room floor, and his wife also dead, sitting in a chair. Their bodies were 'charred but recognizable'. Although a table had been overturned and an oil-lamp lay smashed on the floor, it was clear that this could not have caused the fire, and a verdict of 'Accidental Death – but by what means we are unable to say' was brought in. The most puzzling fact is that the Kileys were fully dressed, as if they had not gone to bed. So if they had died in the evening before going to bed, how was it that a general fire did not break out until the next morning? And why had they not called for help? The chair Mrs Kiley was sitting in was undamaged: even the loose chintz cover was unburnt.[4]

Retired schoolteacher Wilhelmina Dewar, who lived with her sister Margaret, also a schoolteacher and well respected, at Whitley Bay (Tyne and Wear) died in mysterious circumstances on 22 March 1908. Margaret found her dead in bed, her body and legs badly charred but the bedclothes undamaged. The coroner could not believe her story, and under great pressure she said that she had found her sister burned but alive downstairs and had helped her up to bed. This satisfied the court and the case was closed. They did not consider how Wilhelmina could have managed to get upstairs with her body so badly burned, nor the fact that there was no sign of burning elsewhere in the house.[5]

In 1919 the author J. Temple Thurston died mysteriously at his home, Hawley Manor near Dartford (Kent). Just before 3 a.m. on 7 April firemen were called to a fire there, and Thurston was found dead inside his room. But, strangely, there was no fire inside that room. Thurston was not in his nightclothes, and his body was scorched on the thighs and lower legs. The inquest verdict was that he died from heart failure caused by inhaling smoke. Because he was still dressed in his day clothes, it may be that he died hours before the main fire broke out, just as seems to have happened to Mr and Mrs Kiley in 1905. The firemen found the fire burning fiercely outside Thurston's room, but there was no fireplace nearby, and no sign of how it began, no trace of arson, and there had been no burglary. Nor was there any indication that Thurston tried to get help when he was first burned.[6] In so many cases the victims fail to cry for help when they realize they are burning; in fact in some cases, as with the Binbrook servant girl, they do not at first realize that they are on fire. The fact that victims are found still sitting in a chair, with no sign of any struggle to escape or beat out the flames, suggests either that they were in a trance-like state when the fire struck, or that the events happened so quickly there was no time to even move before they died.

Death quickly overcame Mrs Euphemia Johnson while she drank a cup of tea. Mrs Johnson was a 68-year-old widow living alone in Sydenham (Greater London), and she had returned from a shopping trip on a hot summer's day in 1922. She made a cup of tea and sat down at the table to drink it – but she left it unfinished. Her remains – a pile of calcined bones – were found on the floor beside the table and her overturned chair, but though a great heat was obviously required so completely to consume her body, there was only a slight bubbling of the varnish on her chair, and the rubberized tablecloth which hung within nine inches of the remains was only slightly yellowed. The linoleum upon which the bones lay was only slightly charred. Most amazing of all is the fact that the calcined bones were lying inside her unburned clothes. Being a hot day there was no fire in the fireplace, and Mrs Johnson had turned off the gas after making her tea.[7]

Twenty-two-year-old Phyllis Newcombe's crinoline-style dress burst into flames when she was leaving the dance floor with her fiancé at Chelmsford (Essex) on 27 August 1938 and, although the fire was extinguished, Phyllis died in hospital a few hours later. It was thought that the accident could have been caused by a lighted cigarette, but although the material of her dress could be ignited with a lighter, when cigarettes were used the material would not burn.[8] Note that in this case, in contrast with the earlier cases where many of the victims were apparently burned from the inside out, the clothes being undamaged, Phyllis and certain other victims were burned from the outside in, the fire starting in their clothing.

The charred remains of a widow who died on 29 January 1958, a possible victim of spontaneous human combustion.

The case of Mrs Madge Knight is very similar to that of Wilhelmina Dewar. Like her, Mrs Knight was in bed when she was burned. She was sleeping in the spare room of her home at Aldingbourne (West Sussex) on 19 November 1943 when her screams brought other family members running to her aid. They found her in great pain, with most of her back so badly burned that the skin had come away. She said she had woken feeling as if she was on fire, but could throw no more light on the mystery before her death on 6 December. Because there were no signs of burning on the sheets, and no smell of burning, a specialist said the burning must have been caused by a corrosive liquid, though no trace of any was found in the room.[9]

So far we have only described cases of spontaneous combustion of humans, but can it also attack other creatures? A suggestive event took place in Jarrow (Tyne and Wear) on 6 February 1978, involving a four-month-old golden retriever called Hayes. Mrs Jean Payne, the dog's owner, heard it yelping and went to the front window from where she saw it 'on the pathway with flames leaping up from his belly. A man was

All that remained of an 85-year-old woman after her mysterious death, possibly from spontaneous human combustion, were her charred remains and one unburnt foot. She died in Yorkshire in November 1963.

passing and he grabbed Hayes and rolled him in a puddle and on the grass. I was so upset I didn't even have time to thank the man or find out who he was.' The dog fortunately recovered after veterinary treatment. No one seems to have seen anyone running away, so was Hayes really set alight by someone using matches or a lighter, as the authorities supposed? The dog alerted Mrs Payne immediately it felt the pain of burning; would it have hung around and allowed anyone to set light to it?[10]

On 12 November 1978 a possible case of spontaneous human combustion occurred in Reading (Berkshire) where Mrs Lucy Gmiterek was found lying on the basement floor by her young daughter. Her body was charred and she died of shock caused by extensive burning. Police and fire experts were puzzled that the rest of the room showed little fire damage, a circumstance which is by now familiar to us.[11]

Only two months later, another mysterious death by fire was reported, from North Yorkshire. The victim was Mrs Lily Smith, a 76-year-old widow who lived alone at Hutton-Le-Hole, whose body was discovered after a fire at her home on 25 January 1979. (Do you notice how often the victims are women? Out of nineteen human victims described in this chapter, only five are male. We do not yet know the significance of this, but women victims also outnumber men elsewhere in the world.) Mrs Smith had been reduced to a pile of bones on a chair seat, though her legs were found lying under the chair. The chair, though made of wood, was intact. The fire officer gave as his explanation for the tragedy that 'something fell either out of the fireplace or down the chimney', but since he also said that Mrs Smith was in the habit of sitting with her feet on the hearth, wouldn't her legs and feet have been the first to burn, rather than surviving intact?[12]

A year later, 73-year-old Henry Thomas was found dead in similar circumstances. He lived alone at Ebbw Vale (Gwent) and on 6 January 1980 failed to arrive at his daughter's for Sunday lunch. On investigating, his family found a pile of clothes and charred bones on the fireside rug in his smoke-filled living room. Police officer John Heymer was called to the fire, and said that although it was a very cold day, he was struck by the warmth of the house. The living room was like an oven, and he noted smoke stains on the wall. The room also had a strange orange-red glow. He continued:

Condensation was running down the window. The walls were generating heat; the window and lightbulb were covered in an orange substance. The lightbulb was bare because the plastic shade had melted. There was an open grate, but it was undisturbed. The settee still had its loose covers. The carpet was largely undamaged. The knobs of the TV had melted, but it was still on.

On the floor was a pair of human feet clothed in socks. They were attached to the lower portion of the body; this was clad in trousers, undamaged as far as a distinct burn-line. From the trousers protruded the calcinated bone, and just

211

beyond the knees this disintegrated into an amorphous mass of ash.[13]

In November 1980 another dance-hall fire occurred similar to that at Chelmsford in 1938, but fortunately nineteen-year-old Vicky Gilmour survived, though she needed extensive skin grafts to her face and body. She was in the powder-room of a disco at Darlington (Durham) when she burst into flames. Later experiments to ignite an Indian cotton dress like the one she was wearing, using cigarettes, showed that the material only smouldered.[14] Not many weeks later, on 4 December 1980, Mrs Frances Kenworthy was found dead in her home at Lockwood near Huddersfield (West Yorkshire). She lay on the kitchen floor badly burned, but her clothing was not marked. There was no sign of a serious outbreak of fire, though there was a burnt hole in the hearthrug and a few objects in the room were scorched.[15]

We wondered earlier if animals could spontaneously combust: what about inanimate objects? On 22 March 1981, caretaker Victor Webber opened up the Leasowes Sports Centre in Halesowen (West Midlands), smelled smoke, and called the fire brigade, who found a mop blazing in a broom cupboard. Nothing else was burning, and there was no obvious way the mop could have been set alight. It had not been used recently.[16]

Mrs Sandra Braddock was among the lucky survivors of a mysterious outbreak of fire. She was lighting a cigarette when she, or her clothes, burst into flames. She received burns but was not badly injured. This happened on 3 May 1981 at her home at Wath upon Dearne (South Yorkshire).[17]

On Christmas Eve 1984, Mrs Christine Middlehurst was rushed to hospital suffering from 50 per cent burns. An early press report told how she was sitting in the lounge late in the evening after friends had gone home, and her common-law husband was upstairs. He came down to find her in flames. He threw water over her, shouted for help, and got his hands, arms and body burned as he tried to put out the flames. Mrs Middlehurst ran outside screaming and a neighbour took her upstairs and put her into a bath of water, where her skin 'floated off'. The house at Newton Abbot (Devon) was virtually untouched by the fire.[18]

Seventeen-year-old Jacqueline Fitzsimon, though suffering only 13 per cent burns to her back and buttocks, sadly died from shock to the lungs after her mysterious burning. She was a cookery student at Halton College of Further Education in Widnes (Cheshire) and had had an examination on 28 January 1985. She left the examination room with friends and was chatting with them on the stairs when she suddenly began to burn. After the flames had been beaten out she was rushed to hospital, where she died on 12 February. There was conflicting evidence at the inquest as to whether the gas rings had been left on to heat the room. Jacqueline and her friends had spent the time after the examination leaning against the worktops and cookers, but when they left the room a friend who was behind Jacqueline noticed no evidence of burning or smouldering on her back. It was several minutes later that Jacqueline called out 'My back's hot. Am I on fire?' and was then surrounded by flames. Jacqueline's fellow students gave contradictory evidence at the inquest, which did not help to sort out the confusion over what actually happened before and during the conflagration, but two mature male students who were passing by at the time of the fire gave a clearer account of the events. When they passed Jacqueline and her friends there was no sign of fire, no smoke, no smouldering, yet thirty seconds later they heard cries and turned to see Jacqueline ablaze – 'like a stunt man on TV'. The two men helped to put out the fire, and Jacqueline seemed relatively unharmed, only complaining of a burned finger. To add to the mystery, a hairdressing student who had also passed Jacqueline on the stairs said she had seen a strange glowing light above Jacqueline's right shoulder, which had appeared in mid-air and fallen down her back seconds before Jacqueline burst into flames. Despite all the strange facts, including the results of scientific tests on a catering jacket which showed that it would *not* smoulder for minutes then burst into flames, the coroner refused even to consider 'spontaneous human combustion' as an explanation for the tragedy, and a verdict of 'misadventure' was brought in by the jury.[19]

Paul Hayes was luckier than Jacqueline Fitzsimon, because he survived an 'attack' of spontaneous human combustion. Paul, a nineteen-year-old computer operator living in London, was walking along a quiet road in Stepney Green late on the night of 25 May 1985. Suddenly he found himself surrounded by intense flames from the waist up, as if he had been doused with petrol and set alight. He later reported his horrifying experience:

> It was indescribable . . . like being plunged into the heat of a furnace . . . My arms felt as though they were being prodded by red-hot pokers, from my shoulders to my wrists. My cheeks were red-hot, my ears were numb. My chest felt like boiling water had been poured over it. I thought I could hear my brains bubbling.

He tried to escape the flames by running, but fell on to the pavement and curled up into a ball, thinking he was dying. Then, about thirty seconds after it began, his ordeal was over. 'I opened my eyes. There was no flame, no smoke. For a few minutes I lay still, terrified. I began to shiver with shock.' He managed to stumble to a nearby hospital, where he was treated in casualty for burns to his hands, forearms, face, neck and ears.[20]

This gruesome catalogue of mysterious deaths by burning contains certain repetitive features which suggest that there is much that is not understood about the properties of fire and the process of combustion. In the nineteenth century it was thought that all victims were heavy drinkers, and their alcohol-sodden bodies ignited easily, but surely anyone in that state would have died of alcohol poisoning first. Professor David Gee has been examining reported cases of spontaneous human combustion for twenty-two years and believes that 99 per cent have straightforward explanations and that only 1 per cent are truly inexplicable. The hypothesis he favours is that the victims collapse and fall near the fire, the body catches alight, and the heat and flames are drawn up the chimney. The strong draught involved helps the body to burn up fiercely, and also keeps the flames from damaging the rest of the room. The fatty tissue melts in the heat and turns the body into a human wick. He believes that in this way, temperatures sufficiently high to burn a body totally can be achieved.[20] Although in theory his explanation is feasible, and could account for some cases, in practice there are many cases which do not conform to his suggestions on some essential points. Even though victims often have been sitting before an open grate, there is not always a fire burning in it to start the conflagration. Often no source of fire is found, sometimes a chair in which the victim's body has burned does not get damaged, and in some cases the victim's clothes are relatively untouched. What about those cases where the victim apparently died hours before a general fire began to burn? How do people lying in bed burn, and without damaging the bedclothes? One answer seriously presented to explain such cases is that the victims used a corrosive liquid to burn themselves or covered themselves with a flammable liquid which ignited, but left no chemical trace. Wouldn't it be simpler to accept that spontaneous human combustion really might occur, and then to start a scientifically organized investigation of this mystery?

Looking at more esoteric possibilities, Livingstone Gearhart noticed that a significant number of spontaneous human combustion cases world-wide took place when the force of the Earth's geomagnetism was at a high point. One US witness found a fireball hovering over a victim, and also one witness of the Widnes tragedy claimed to see a strange light descend on to Jacqueline Fitzsimon. It has been suggested that ball lightning (see Chapter 10) may be responsible in some way for some of the deaths. In his series of articles on spontaneous combustion in *The Unexplained*, Bob Rickard offered a sequence in which spontaneous human combustion could take place:

> Age and sex seem less important than the victim's psychic and physiological state. We may imagine a lonely, sedentary person, incapacitated by illness or injury, or physically by despair, fear, depression and perhaps resentment. This incapacity may psychosomatically affect the body and its metabolism, causing an imbalance of phosphagens and erratic

behaviour in the body's heat-regulating mechanisms. Normally, this state would pass unnoticed. But imagine that it should happen a few days after intense sunspot activity, with a magnetic storm pushing up the value of the geomagnetic field to abnormal heights for the victim's locality. Now all that is needed is a trigger: a cosmic ray, a natural burst of low-frequency energy, or a lightning ball. And then we have a human bonfire.[22]

This does not take account of those victims who are young and not in a depressed state; and if spontaneous human combustion is more likely to occur at high points on the geomagnetic scale, we would expect to find cases clustering together at these points, as there must be many people who are in the appropriate physical and mental state, who would combust if the necessary triggering mechanism were applied to them. Perhaps the combination of a suitable human, the correct geophysical location and the appropriate triggering phenomenon is sufficiently rare to cause the events to occur on an apparently random basis.

22. Beings from another world?

Having already examined the characteristics of UFO entities, ghosts and the Little People (Chapters 14, 4, 18), there yet remain other reports of enigmatic entities which do not obviously fit any of these categories. This uncategorized group of entities sometimes possesses characteristics which are associated with the above-mentioned categories – a witness reports seeing a UFO entity, but no UFO is seen; some entities are of small stature, but are they the same as the Little People, even though in other respects their appearance is quite different?; some entities have ghost-like tendencies, but cannot happily be categorized as ghosts because of definite unghostlike aspects. We also include here some entities which are semi-animal, and others that fit into no category so far mentioned. Which suggests that all such categories may have no intrinsic significance but are simply useful labels used by researchers to keep reports tidy and that correlations between various groups are always possible and should be looked for.

Our first two cases will begin to show the complexities, for they both involve small entities which could, if one wished to slot them into categories, be classed either as Little People or as UFO entities. Ernest Suddards was driving his lorry near his home in Bradford (West Yorkshire) at 4 a.m. on 16 August 1955 when he and his passenger, his thirteen-year-old son, both saw a small black creature around 4 feet tall illuminated in the headlights. It wore skin-tight black clothes and held its arms by its sides and its feet together, moving forward jerkily. The two amazed witnesses also saw a circular perforated silver disk on its chest below its throat. The entity went out of sight down a passage, and the witnesses were too shaken to pursue it. They did eventually alert the police, but nothing was found.

However Mr Suddards was later told by a man in a pub that he had seen a bright bullet-shaped object about 12 feet tall standing upright in a field, giving off a high-pitched buzz – though this was three days after Mr Suddards's entity sighting and may not have been connected with it.[1]

About four years later a similar entity was encountered in Staffordshire by a man, his wife and a woman friend, who were driving home from work. It was the winter of 1959–60, and the car had reached Brocton when it began to falter going up a hill. When it stalled, the driver 'tickled' the erratic petrol-pump which he believed to be the cause of the break-down, but after a few yards the car stopped again. The two passengers were preparing to push when they suddenly became aware that they had been joined by a small figure around 3 feet 6 inches tall and dressed in tight blackish clothing. It had a large head, three or four times bigger than normal, covered by a transparent bowl. The entity asked if they were in trouble, and on learning of the car's breakdown began to push. The car, weighing over a ton, moved quickly uphill. The driver was able to start the engine again, but when he turned to thank their helper, he was nowhere to be seen.[2]

In the next few cases the entities were all much taller, were all lurking in fields or gardens, and were in certain respects similar in appearance. Two entities seen late at night by Mrs Wood and her two teenage sons in September 1971 (approximately) at Oulton near Stone (Staffordshire) were at least 6 feet tall, dressed in 'diving suits' and moving like 'astronauts on the moon' in a field close to the Woods' house. One of the entities strode around and kept squatting as if looking for something; the other was mostly stationary. They were luminous in the darkness, and one glowed more brightly than the other. Mrs Wood watched the figures for almost ten minutes, her sons for less, until they faded and disappeared.[3] Strikingly similar is the encounter reported over six years later from Shotton in Clwyd by a 22-year-old man who was taking his dog for a walk at about midnight (the Oulton sighting was twenty minutes before midnight) on (probably) 10 December 1977. The dog saw the tall white figure first of all, and drew its master's attention to it by stopping dead and raising its hackles. Only a few yards away, behind a fence, was an 8-foot figure in a white, apparently padded, 'astronaut's' suit, possibly self-luminous and with a visor. It walked stiffly with one arm raised, but the witness stayed to watch only for a minute before rushing home, closely followed by the dog which then spent the rest of the night under a chair.[4]

Similar entities to these have also been seen in gardens, as happened in a very strange case at Huyton (Merseyside) early in 1977. When he went out to empty a waste bin at 4.30 p.m. on a winter afternoon, Mrs Street's twelve-year-old son saw a head among the bushes at the end of the garden. Mrs Street investigated and saw a pair of legs belonging to an entity she estimated was 9 feet tall, wearing a white suit and a helmet with a visor. She shouted at it, but it just stared at her, whereupon she panicked and ran indoors. She watched through the window as it floated towards the house. Soon a friend arrived and also saw the figure. She ran out at it waving a broom and shouting, but she too retreated when the figure simply stared at her. Other friends arrived, one of whom fetched the police, but as the two policemen went out to confront the figure, it disappeared.[5] A ten-year-old boy was the only witness to another gardening entity, this one appearing in the Handsworth district of Sheffield (South Yorkshire) on 4 October 1979. In the early evening he saw a 7-foot silver figure drilling a hole in the ground with a tube. The watching boy moved and the entity spotted him, his reaction being to disappear in a puff of pink smoke. An investigator who was taken to the spot soon afterwards found four inhuman foot-prints and a small hole, but rain obliterated them before he could take plaster casts.[6]

All these tall entities in white clothing were seen during the 1970s, during which decade there were also three brief sightings by passing motorists of similar figures at the road-side. On 10 July 1975 Mr and Mrs Taylor were driving along the A55 at Ewloe (Clwyd) during daylight hours when they saw a tall (possibly 7 feet) figure in a bright silver 'cross between a diving suit and a boiler suit' and a balaclava-like helmet. It stood at the foot of an embankment and had its arms stretched up. It turned to face them as they drove past, at the same time bending as if to pick something up with the left hand.[7] A few years later and many miles away on the Isle of Sheppey (Kent), Frank Rossien was driving along Sheppey Way on 22 March 1979 at 10.30 p.m. when he saw a stocky, silver-suited figure loping down a bank beside the road. Its suit and helmet were all in one piece, and some sort of visor was noted as Mr Rossien drove past. Other motorists also reported seeing this figure, and earlier that evening a couple had seen a red light with revolving white lights in the sky above the Isle of Sheppey.[8]

Perhaps the weirdest report of a roadside entity came from service engineer Ken Edwards, who was driving home very late on the night of 17 March 1978. At Risley (Cheshire) his route passed an atomic energy reactor. As he approached it he saw a strange figure in the headlights. The figure seemed to be climbing down an embankment, but stooping and with its arms stretched out. It was about 7 feet tall, and silvery, with a dark head. It walked into the road and stopped. As it turned towards Ken Edwards, two slim beams of light shot from its eyes and touched him, as he sat in his now stationary van, watching. After a minute the figure continued across the road, and then walked straight through a 10-foot-high security fence topped with barbed wire. Ken Edwards drove home, badly shaken. Afterwards the radio transmitter and receiver in the van were out of action, and found to have been extensively damaged as if by a massive power surge. Two years after this strange experience, Ken Edwards was diagnosed as having cancer; in 1982 he died, in his late thirties. We shall never know if he was the first person in Britain to have died as a result of encountering a UFO entity; we do not know who or what the figure was, and we do not know if his encounter with it caused the cancer to develop.[9]

We have reported these seven cases in detail because of the very suggestive similarities in the appearance of the entities seen, and also on occasion their behaviour. It is unlikely that any of the witnesses were aware of earlier reports of this kind, which are only circulated among the ufological fraternity. Silver-suited entities were reported by a number of people during the 1970s, but usually in conjunction with UFOs. If the entities we have described were UFO entities, where were their UFOs during the times of the sightings? Can the UFOs become invisible or dematerialize, as the entities themselves seem able to do? At present these questions remain un-answered, but it does seem clear that ordinary people in Britain were seeing strange entities during the 1970s (see the Chronological List of Strange Events for the extent of these sightings) and although it is possible that some of the reports are hoaxes or misperceptions, it is unlikely that all of them are. With regard to misperceptions, motorists who have brief sightings of apparently strange creatures or events should really go back and check on what they think they have seen. We were driving one Sunday in the hills near Llangollen (Clwyd) when we caught a brief glimpse down a side lane of what appeared to be a gaggle of weird orange-suited entities with oversized heads. Not wishing to remain for ever uncertain about whether or not we had seen alien beings, we turned the car round and cautiously drove down the lane, to confront the entities – who turned out to be a group of hikers swathed in fluorescent cagoules and hoods against the wet weather. We wonder how many other reports of aliens would disintegrate if the witnesses had summoned the courage to move closer; but conversely such a venture could prove foolhardy if an entity of uncertain temper and unknown abilities should decide to attack an inter-fering human, not to mention the possibility of radiation dangers, Ken Edwards's unfortunate encounter being a poss-ible case in point. Witnesses are advised to observe unseen and from a safe distance, using binoculars if available.

It is uncertain whether or not the entities so far described were part of what is now known as the UFO phenomenon; and equally difficult to categorize is this report made by an eight-year-old boy, for the entities he saw did not *need* a UFO – they appeared to be self-propelled. The sighting took place in the autumn of 1976 at Baddeley Green (Staffordshire). The witness was in bed at around 9 or 10 p.m. when he heard a humming or whirring noise and looked out of the window. He saw that the noise was coming from two men who were flying at walking pace past his window, only feet away from him. They seemed to be 4 feet tall and dressed in white one-piece suits without separate boots. They also wore white helmets with dark visors. Their flying position was horizontal, with legs straight and together, and arms at 90 degrees to the body. The witness could see them clearly, because they were so close and were also well lit by the street lighting. Each had a white rectangular box on his back, with a small cube and a button on it.[10] Lest readers dismiss this report as too weird and the flying men obviously a figment of the boy's imagination, we should say that it is not unique, though similar reports are admittedly rare.

The strangest case in this chapter deserves far more space than we are able to devote to it. It is a classic example of the strange experiences so often reported by children, who sometimes seem able to see things denied to their elders. This is not in any way to belittle their experiences, which are so obviously real to them; children 'uncontaminated' by adult concerns may well see through windows on to other realities. Chapter 18 on the Little People contains several strange experiences reported by children, and this one could well join them, except that the entity was nearly 7 feet tall. The encounter between a seven-year-old girl, a boy of about the same age and a colourful entity took place early in May 1973 not far from Sandown Airport on the Isle of Wight. The entity spoke to the children and showed them around the interior of a windowless metallic hut, which he said he had just made. It had two levels, the lower containing an electric heater and simple wooden furniture and with the walls 'papered' in a blue-green with a pattern of dials, the upper less spacious and with a metallic floor. The entity wore a yellow pointed hat which joined on to the red collar of his green tunic. On top of his hat were a round black knob and antennae. He wore white trousers with 'wooden slats' protruding from the bottom and from his sleeves. On his white face he had triangular marks for eyes, a square brown nose and yellow lips which did not move. He had only three fingers on each hand, which were covered by blue gloves, and only three toes on his bare white feet. The children asked if he was a ghost and he replied, 'Well, not really, but I am in an odd sort of way.' When they pressed the point, asking 'What are you then?', he would only say, 'You know', and nothing more. He said he had no name and that there were others of his kind. He drank river water after cleaning it, and ate berries.

On being told the story the girl's father did not at first believe her, but later became convinced that she was telling the truth, and the boy also confirmed that he had seen the entity. However on what level did the children see him? They were talking to him for over half an hour, during which time two workmen were repairing a post nearby, and they paid no attention to the entity or his hut, as if they could not see him.[11]

The next five entity reports are presented in chronological order and without any attempt at categorization, since none fits easily into any of our familiar categories. In November 1951, William Routledge was working in a ship-breaking yard in Garston, Liverpool (Merseyside), when he saw a creature wearing tight plum-coloured breeches who 'looked at least six-foot-six, and I was particularly struck by his hair which stood up from his head in a great brush four or five inches high'. (An early punk?) It walked with an ape-like gait through car headlights without breaking the beam, and could be seen by only two out of three people present.[12] A few years later, on 26 June 1959, a Mr R. Taylor was walking along Alexander Avenue in Whitefield (Greater Manchester) when he noticed two men who were walking ahead of him. They were 6 feet tall and had long blond hair (unusual in 1959) and were wearing tight trousers and heavy boots. They turned a corner, and when Mr Taylor followed, he was surprised to find that they had disappeared.[13]

The next report is the only one of the five not to come from the north of England. In Caterham (Surrey) on 28 July 1963 passing motorists were bewildered by the sight of eight men wearing thick black cowls who were 'running and leaping across the road to the dual carriageway' but their movements were 'silent and most odd'.[14] Equally puzzling to the witness, a nineteen-year-old farm worker, was the figure he saw while camping with a friend beside Clowbridge Reservoir, Dunnock-shawe (Lancashire), on 28 July 1977 (which lovers of coincidence will note was exactly fourteen years after the previous report). At 2.30 a.m., as dawn approached, he went to get some drinking water and saw a figure 8 feet tall with a beard and bushy hair and wearing a long white robe standing about a hundred yards away and gazing out over the reservoir. It vanished when the witness called to his friend.[15] The witnesses in our fifth case, a married couple walking their dog, were frightened by their entity sighting. They were on Carleton Moor (North Yorkshire) early in the 1980s, when they saw two men with their arms stretched out over some hawthorn bushes. The men were dressed in blue or green overalls, very tight, and had pale, thin faces with pointed chins and a waxy appearance. They were motionless and the couple felt that they were menacing. At this point the witnesses fled, but the husband looked back and found that the men had gone. When the couple returned to the spot they discovered that the men must have been over 7 feet tall to have been visible above the hedge.[16]

All the reports given so far have been isolated incidents. As we have seen, ghosts often repeatedly reveal themselves at one location, but this feature appearing in a case does not necessarily mean that the entity is a ghost. In the case of 'the Big Grey Man of Ben MacDhui' (Grampian Region) it is not possible to ascertain what was being seen and heard on the mountain, but it is clear that too many people experienced strange encounters there for them all to be mistaken. One of the earliest witnesses was Norman Collie, a professor of organic chemistry, who had a frightening experience while climbing alone on the mountain in 1890.

> I was returning from the cairn on the summit in a mist when I began to think I heard something else than merely the noise of my own footsteps. For every few steps I took I heard a crunch, and then another crunch as if someone was walking after me but taking steps three or four times the length of my own.
>
> I said to myself, 'This is all nonsense.' I listened and heard it again but could see nothing in the mist. As I walked on and the eerie crunch, crunch, sounded behind me I was seized with terror and took to my heels, staggering blindly among the boulders for four or five miles nearly down to Rothiemurchus Forest.

Whatever you make of it I do not know, but there is
something very queer about the top of Ben MacDhui and I
will not go back there again by myself I know.

In later years others heard the footsteps and had other
frightening experiences. One man, who was camping on the
mountain, said that he saw 'a great brown creature' swaggering
down the hill, and it appeared to be covered with shortish hair.
It had a large head, a thick neck, broad shoulders, relatively
slim hips, long arms and thick legs, but it did not resemble an
ape. It was at least 20 feet tall.[17] This fact, and the witness's
insistence that the creature was not apelike, dashes our hopes
of finding a surviving Gigantopithecus (such as the North
American Bigfoot might be) lurking in the Scottish mountains.
As we have written in our book *The Evidence for Bigfoot and
Other Man-Beasts*,[18] Europe is the only continent that does
not have a living tradition of man-beasts, though occasionally
vague but tantalizing reports are found; for example in May
1961 'two schoolgirls at Bilsington [Kent] . . . reported seeing
"something like the abominable snowman with a tail running
from the fields into the woods"'.[19] From time to time people
report Bigfoot-type entities which are clearly non-physical,
though these reports usally come from the USA. A group of
teenagers in Wollaton (Nottinghamshire) had an experience of
this kind in the autumn of 1966, at a time when they were
'UFO-orientated' and therefore somewhat susceptible to the
occurrence of strange events. The principal witness was Frank
Earp, who describes the figure which appeared at twilight near
a disused canal; the witnesses were already in a nervous state,
having just seen and been followed by two luminous spheres
surrounded by a mist.

> The figure [which was over 6 feet tall] did not appear to be
> three-dimensional, but looked flat, rather like a cardboard
> cut-out. It gave the overall impression of being hairy all
> over. Its head was mounted directly on its shoulder. No
> facial or other details were visible as we were seeing it lit
> from the back by the cloud. The shoulders were hunched
> up and its arms hung long by its side. The arms ended

without hands almost like a single finger which curled inwards. In each of these curved 'hooks' it held what I can only describe as a glowing rod. Each was about eight to ten inches long and thicker than the average pencil. They glowed red as if with heat. Its legs were straight, but disappeared from the knee down, not like the tapering arms. They actually faded out; the mist swirled around where its feet should have been. If one imagined the missing part of its legs in proportion to the rest of the body it would have been hovering a few inches above the ground.

Only two of the three boys present saw the figure, and they ran away, leaving the third, who had been within touching distance of it, to follow behind them, asking what was going on.[20]

Continuing with reports of entities with animal characteristics, we cannot omit the incredible saga of the 'Hexham Heads'. These were two small stone heads of Celtic appearance, unearthed in 1972 in a garden in Hexham (Northumberland). Poltergeist phenomena broke out at the home of the family

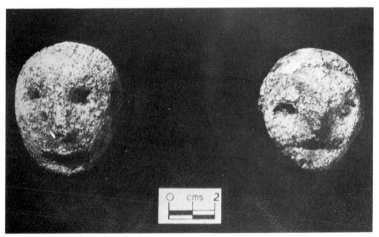

The two heads found in a back garden at Hexham in February 1972.

who found the heads, and the next-door neighbour was also drawn into the mystery, being terrified by the appearance of a half-man half-beast which came into a bedroom and then padded downstairs. The heads were sent to Southampton for examination by Dr Anne Ross, an expert in Celtic lore, and she too soon received an unwelcome visitor.

I woke up in the middle of the night. We always keep the hall light on and the doors open, because our small son is a bit frightened of the dark – so there's always a certain amount of light coming into our room – and I woke up, and felt *extremely* frightened . . . in fact, panic-stricken, and terribly, terribly cold. There was a sort of dreadful atmosphere of icy coldness all round me, and something made me look towards the door, and as I looked, I saw this . . . thing . . . going out of it. It was about 6 feet high, slightly stooping, and it was black, against the white door, and it was half-animal and half-man . . . the upper part, I would have said, was a wolf, and the lower part was human, and, I would have again said, that it was covered with a kind of black, very dark fur. It went out and I just saw it clearly, and then it disappeared, and something made me run after it, a thing I couldn't normally have done, but I felt compelled to run after it. I got out of bed, and I ran, and I could hear it going down the stairs, then it disappeared towards the back of the house. When I got to the bottom of the stairs I was terrified . . .

A few days after I saw it, we had to go up to London, and our teenage daughter had the key and came home from school about 4 p.m., and we got back from London about 6 p.m. When we opened the door, she came to it and looked *extremely* pale and terribly shaken. Finally I got it out of her what had happened. She had opened the front door and as she opened it, a black thing, which she described as being as near a werewolf as anything, jumped over the bannister and landed with a kind of plop, you know, like padded, heavy animal feet, and it rushed towards the back of the house, and *she* felt compelled to follow it. It disappeared in the music room, right at the end of the corridor, and when she got there it had gone, and suddenly she realised she was terrified. The day the heads were removed from the house everybody, including my husband, said it's as if a cloud had lifted; and since then there hasn't been, really a trace of it.[21]

There was talk of an ancient curse attached to the heads, but the whole affair became even more puzzling when Desmond Craigie announced that he had made the heads for his daughter about 1956, when the Craigie family had been living in the house in Hexham where the heads were found. That this was in fact the case was shown by Professor Dearman of the University of Newcastle, who sectioned them and showed that they were artificially moulded and not carved from natural stone. Nevertheless, they are remarkably similar to the stone heads produced by the Celts, of which many examples

On the left is a head made by Desmond Craigie in an attempt to prove that he had also made the original 'Hexham heads'; on the right is a head made by one of the boys shortly before he and his brother found the mystery heads in their garden.

have survived. But no one can explain why they should have attracted a non-physical entity into their aura.

We close this round-up of assorted entities with reports of a species of semi-human creature which most people think of as belonging solely to folklore, or as a fantasy arising from the misinterpretation of mirages or seals basking on rocks. We refer of course to merfolk – mermaids and mermen. It is intriguing to find that there are reports of close-up sightings which cannot be easily explained away, especially in the early nineteenth century and off the Scottish coast. We have space to describe only one of these earlier sightings, which was reported at the end of the century by 'persons still living who saw and touched this curious creature'. About 1830 on Benbecula (Western Isles) people cutting seaweed heard a splash and saw a creature a few feet away in the sea. It was 'in the form of a woman in miniature'. She resisted capture but was injured by stones thrown at her and a few days later she was found dead on the shore. She was described as being 'the size of a well-fed child of three or four years of age, with an abnormally developed breast. The hair was long, dark and glossy, while the skin was white, soft, and tender. The lower part of the body was like a salmon, but without scales.' The land-agent of the district must have been convinced that the creature was at least partly human, for he ordered a shroud and coffin and she was buried above the shore. If only that grave could be rediscovered![22]

Even more recent sightings have been recorded, again from Scotland. In 1900 a small landholder, Alexander Gunn, saw a mermaid in the district of Sandwood in Sutherland (Highland Region). His dog howled and drew his attention to the creature, who was lying on a ledge only feet away from them. She was described as human in size, beautiful to look at, with curly reddish-yellow hair, greenish-blue eyes and arched eyebrows. She gave Mr Gunn a frightened and angry look and he ran off. But he later insisted that he had seen her: 'What I saw was *real*. I actually encountered a mermaid.' She was apparently stranded and waiting for the tide to float her into the water. In 1947 an 80-year-old fisherman saw a mermaid in the sea not far off the island of Muck (Highland Region). She was sitting

A mermaid said to have been seen by mariner John Robinson on the Black Rock near Liverpool. The rest of the crew had perished in a storm, when the mermaid appeared and gave the lone sailor a compass, advising him to steer to the south-west, which he did and reached land safely.

on a floating herring box combing her hair, but she plunged into the sea when she realized she had been seen.[23]

In our late twentieth-century rationalist climate it is almost heretical to suggest that such creatures as mermaids could be living in the sea off Scotland, that phantom werewolves might appear inside a modern Southampton home, or that giant figures roam the British countryside at night. But people continue to report such inexplicable happenings despite the almost certain ridicule they will face, and we can only accept that they really believe they saw what they describe. To dismiss all these sightings as hallucinations explains nothing, is medically untenable and marks the escape route of the arch-sceptic. But mankind's knowledge of the workings of our mysterious planet is so limited that we can only guess at other levels of existence, phantom lands whose denizens may come and go at their will, leaving the occasional human witness amazed and terrified.

23. Mysteries above and below

Although our natural environment usually behaves in ways that are familiar to us, occasionally the unexpected – and perhaps also the inexplicable – happens. In Chapter 1 we wrote about lumps of ice falling from the sky, which is generally believed to be contrary to nature and is explained away as ice which formed on aircraft and then broke off. This may be true in a few cases, especially where the ice is coloured or has a chemical smell and is thought to be waste water leaking from the plane and freezing on the outside. But if all ice-falls are attributable to aircraft, then many aircraft are in a condition dangerous both to their passengers and to people on the ground, and these events should be investigated. A great many ice-falls are reported, and there are probably many others unseen and therefore unreported. It is more likely that most of the ice-falls are caused by some unknown natural process. We are familiar with small ice-falls – hailstones – and these are sometimes quite large, egg-sized for instance, but at what size does a lump of ice cease to be a hailstone and become an unexplained phenomenon? The lump of ice which fell into a garden in Kings Norton, Birmingham (West Midlands) during the night of 9/10 December 1980 was 12 inches in circumference and weighed 1 pound 6 ounces. Was this a hailstone, as the press called it, or an ice-fall as it was termed by the *Journal of Meteorology*?[1] In fact hailstones usually fall in showers, not singly, therefore this was probably an ice-fall – unless one large hailstone fell in a shower of normal-sized hailstones which had melted by the time the occupants found the large hailstone next morning.[2]

Ice-falls are reported so often that they have become almost a common phenomenon, despite the means of their formation being unexplained. A similar apparently inexplicable event which has often been observed is the falling of rain or snow from a clear, cloudless sky.

> On the 6th February [1895, in Surrey], at 9 a.m., light snow began to fall, sparkling in sunshine from a cloudless sky. Thinking that the snow might be blown off a roof, I went out on the common, clear of houses, and made no doubt that the fall was from the sky. Gradually it clouded over, and at 10 a.m. was quite overcast, the snow continuing as a natural shower for a short time longer.[3]

> On December 29th, 1929, following on a very stormy day, with gale, hail, sleet, heavy rain and lightning, the evening was fine, and the stars brilliant. At 21h. 40m. with the stars as bright as ever and not a trace of cloud visible, palpable drizzle fell for a few minutes.

The same observer noted two other instances of rain from a cloudless sky at the same location, Grayshott (Hampshire), early in January 1931 and on 3 January 1933.[4] On 20 January 1935 drizzle fell from a cloudless sky with the sun shining brightly at Benson (Oxfordshire),[5] and on 5 February 1955 there was twenty minutes of light rain falling from a cloudless, starlit sky following a normal shower, at Wrexham (Clwyd), followed ten days later by snow falling when only high cirrus clouds were visible.[6]

The rain which fell from a cloudless sky at Stevenage (Hertfordshire) on 22 July 1888 preceded a thunderstorm by an hour and a half. This rain was strange in appearance, falling in 'remarkably straight lines' and looking 'like a shower of luminous particles of a somewhat skim-milky appearance'. William R. Corliss felt this luminosity in some way resembled low-level auroras and auroral fogs, these being luminous fogs and mists seen during auroral activity.[7] A possible explanation for the phenomenon of rain or snow from a cloudless sky is that high-level winds may bring rain from clouds too far distant to be seen. When ice needles fall from a cloudless sky in very cold regions, this can be caused by the crystallization of water vapour at low temperatures.[8]

From anomalous precipitation we turn to light and darkness.

On 15 April 1904 it grew dark at Wimbledon (Greater London) during normal daylight hours. It was described as like a tunnel of darkness with light at either end, and it lasted for ten minutes. It was too dark to go outdoors, but the darkness was not accompanied by rain or thunder, so it was not caused by storm clouds. Such a phenomenon has been recorded all over the world and is totally inexplicable if there are no forest fires bringing smoke, no volcanic eruptions or dust storms bringing dust, and no heavy storm clouds. Sometimes the stars become visible during periods of abnormal darkness, and in this event the cause must be 'out there'; perhaps the sun is obscured temporarily by a passing comet.[9]

At the opposite extreme is the appearance of daylight during the night, or a 'false dawn'. Although not common, this happened to one witness on 7 January 1933 as he was travelling from London to Torquay, when he had reached the area of Shaftesbury (Dorset). He stopped for a rest.

> I got out of the car and found the rain had ceased and strolled up and down for a few minutes, when I suddenly realised that it was getting light, and at first I thought it was the dawn, but knowing it was only about 5 a.m. I realised I was mistaken, but very unfortunately I cannot give exact times. But the time was almost certainly about 5.10 a.m. It became so light that I was able to see the surrounding countryside. I could see the Dorsetshire hills sufficiently plainly to see that the clouds lay on their tops and that they were clear below, and I was able to turn off my headlights. The light was a general diffused light with no apparent focal point but I should say it was lighter towards the south and east, although I could quite well see towards the north and west – and here again I failed to note times; but this condition lasted probably for about 20 minutes, after which period, and about as suddenly as it appeared, it became quite dark again. I had to switch on my headlights and keep them on until Fairmile, which is 10 miles short of Exeter, at about 7.30 a.m., when the true dawn commenced.[10]

William R. Corliss feels that 'The zodiacal light probably

accounts for the phenomenon', though he is puzzled by the light's sudden disappearance.[11] The frequent mention of William R. Corliss in this chapter is due to the fact that his books (see Bibliography) are full of accounts of anomalous phenomena of this kind collected from scientific journals, and in his *Catalog of Geophysical Anomalies* he evaluates the data and provides possible explanations. Browsing through his books will soon convince even the most scientifically orientated reader that the world is a far stranger place than we ever imagined, with countless mysteries science has so far failed to explain. In this book of course we can only include British phenomena occurring between 1885 and 1985, but Corliss's coverage as regards time and place is unlimited, and therefore very rich in content.

In the afternoon of 24 October 1914, an observer at Mawnan (Cornwall) saw 'a most curious phenomenon', best described in his own words:

In a shallow cloudbank stretching across the horizon from south-east to south gradually appeared what seemed to be a line of coast, with woods, trees, fields, hedges, and houses in their natural colours.

At first I thought it was merely a peculiar arrangement of clouds, but soon I recognized that it was a complete reflected panorama of this coast, and I gradually identified St. Keverne with its church spire, the Helford River, Mawnan Church, Rosemullion, Falmouth Harbour, and St. Anthony.

Shortly before the whole scene faded away, a reflection of Pendennis Head with the castle and the military huts, emerging like some huge ship from a fog bank, appeared most distinctly and was visible for several minutes. Every detail of the whole scene was reversed as in a looking-glass and slightly magnified, for although the panorama seemed to be some twenty miles away, everything appeared as it would to an observer from the distance of only a mile or so. The colours were a little less bright than those of the real coast at the time.

The scene as a whole was visible all the time, but the

details of a small portion only were quite distinct at any one time, commencing in the south and gradually moving towards the east, the effect being that of a powerful search-light being very slowly turned from right to left on the opposite shore of a large lake. Nothing of it could be seen through a telescope; at least I found it impossible to get it into focus.[12]

A similar reflected coastal panorama was witnessed on the east coast, at Hunstanton (Norfolk) on 1 May 1949, again in the afternoon. The beach scene, with a group of beach huts and people walking about, was seen reflected on the sea about 1,500 yards away.[13]

Possibly related to the phenomena of reflections and mirages is the unusual 'mock sun', when a second sun appears alongside the real sun. They could be caused by sideways mirages. One was seen over Wales on 5 November 1896. The true sun was dark red, the mock sun looking as the moon does when seen during the daytime.[14]

Next some phenomena which sound as if they were caused by winds or air movements, though this is not necessarily the explanation. In 1887 strange noises were heard in Somerset:

On Wednesday evening last, at a little after 7 o'clock, I was somewhat startled at hearing a most peculiar noise. It began with a rushing sound as if a sudden gust of wind were shaking the trees. It being quite calm at the time, I looked in every direction, but could see no indication of the least disturbance. In a few seconds the noise changed to a very deep and subdued roar, and in a few seconds more with two or three distinctly separated sounds, with intervals of not more than half a second between each. It was quite impossible to judge from what direction the sounds came; in fact, there was something so peculiar about them, that although they were far from loud, I stopped to listen, and at once came to the conclusion that they were subterranean noises, and made the remark to one or two friends, who also heard them, that we must expect either an earthquake, or that we should soon hear of one having occurred elsewhere.

William R. Corliss comments that the only earthquake reported at that time was in Central Asia.[15] Similar in some ways was the sound like a rushing wind heard on 15 April 1974 by three people walking in the Prescelly Hills (Dyfed). It lasted for about 25 seconds, but they felt no wind, and the grass remained still.[16] Earthquake activity is again a possible source of the sound; William R. Corliss also suggests 'instantaneous meteor sounds' and 'the sound of the aurora'. But what explanation can be offered for a wind which came and went in seconds, and was totally silent? In July 1984 Mrs Neila Taylor, who lived near Cheddar (Somerset), hung out her washing on the rotary clothes-line and went indoors. The weather was mild and calm, with little wind. A few seconds later she went outside again and found most of the washing all over the garden, torn forcibly from the line, and some of it was wound round the pole, which had been bent.[17] A possible explanation is that a powerful vortex or whirlwind passed through the garden very quickly, but it is surprising that nothing was heard.

The next phenomenon did (or does, as it is probably still occurring) make a noise, a sound like breathing. The location is the 200-foot-high Brahan Rock at Dingwall (Highland Region), where it was reported that around midnight strange noises like breathing, whispering, snoring, panting or gasping could be heard. A press report published in 1968 said that people would drive out to listen for the noises. People living close to the rock said they often heard them, and one explanation is that warm air rising up from underground caverns is escaping through crevices in the rock. The noise was said to have been heard over many years, as far back as the end of the last century.[18] Noises of a more explosive kind were being heard at a Staffordshire cave in the second half of the nineteenth century. The location was Old Hannah's Cave in the Manifold valley, where many witnesses had heard the explosions and seen blue flashes erupting from the cave. Sir Thomas Wardle, who was conducting archaeological excavations in the cave, experienced the phenomena in the company of George Borrow of H.M. Geological Survey, on 10 December 1899. They heard a sound like rifle fire and saw a bluish flash and a column of 'aqueous vapour' erupt from a fissure in the cliff. Within minutes another explosion sounded from higher up the cliff and then 'several ones with crackling sounds producing semi-transparent wavy streaks in the air, not smoky in appearance'. They were unable to climb the cliff to investigate because a strong wind was blowing. It has been suggested that the decay of organic material carried underground by the River Manifold released flammable gases which filtered upwards and escaped through cracks in the rock, being ignited by static electricity caused by blowing dust. It was noted that there was always a strong wind blowing when the explosions occurred. The phenomena are no longer experienced at Old Hannah's Cave, since an earth slip blocked the flow of gas at the back of the cave.[19]

We close this chapter with what William R. Corliss prosaically calls 'low-level nocturnal lights' but which in folklore have names like corpse candle, will-o'-the-wisp, and jack-o'-lantern. These often appear like flames or candle-lights, sometimes globes, and tend to flicker and move about as if trying to entice the witness into following them. They are usually found in wet and marshy areas, hence the general belief that they are caused by marsh gas or methane igniting spontaneously. But in *Lightning, Auroras, Nocturnal Lights, and Related Luminous Phenomena* William R. Corliss presents many cases that cannot be explained in this way, and he suggests that there are several possible alternative explanations, such as phosphorescence and electro-chemical luminous phenomena. Luminous owls may also have a part to play. It is believed that in certain circumstances, owls' feathers may appear luminous when they have been in contact with phosphorescent fungi or bacteria, probably growing on a tree where the birds have perched, or resulting from a fungal disease of their feathers. When birds affected in this way fly around silently at night, they inadvertently mimic strange nocturnal lights. This explanation is useful ammunition for the sceptics, but no one is sure how valid an explanation it really is for will-o'-the-wisps.[20] There is also a supernatural aspect to these lights, as we shall demonstrate later. Recently a scientist, A. A. Mills, did some research into will-o'-the-wisps, to see if they really were caused by the spontaneous ignition of marsh gas. He constructed a 'swamp'

An illustration of will-o'-the-wisps seen at Issy in France, June 1871, showing how several columnar lights sometimes appear in a group.

in a one-gallon glass bottle, collected the marsh gas given off, but was unable to duplicate the familiar characteristics of will-o'-the-wisps.[21]

There are many reports of will-o'-the-wisps available, but we have room for only a small sample of particularly interesting cases. The flames seen at Blundellsands (Merseyside) on 5 June 1902 were especially dramatic, even if not a classic example of the phenomenon. A witness reported:

The evening was dull and grey, a strong north-westerly wind was blowing in from the sea and the tide was flowing in. In the distance we first saw smoke with frequent jets of fire bursting forth from the mud of a shallow canal. Drawing near, we perceived a strong sulphurous odour, and saw little flames of fire and heard a hissing sound as though a large quantity of phosphorus was being ignited. It was impossible to detect anything which caused the fire, only the water where the flames appeared had particles of a bluish hue floating on the surface. The area over which the tiny flames kept bursting forth was about 40 yards. A gentleman present stirred up the mud with his walking stick, and immediately large yellow flames nearly 2 feet in length and breadth burst forth. The phenomenon lasted some time, until the tide covered the part and quenched the fire. As we returned from our walk the atmosphere was impregnated with a strong odour of sulphur.[22]

The origin of the lights seen in the hills around Burton Dassett (Warwickshire) was not so easy to determine. They were clearly not emerging from marshy ground, and were seen to travel against the wind, so they were difficult to explain away as marsh gas which had spontaneously ignited. Many people saw the lights during 1923 and also during their reappearance in 1924, though because of the publicity that followed the initial reports, some of the sightings may have been of the torches of other watchers, and there were probably some hoaxers roaming the area too. Nevertheless, the lights were seen by many reliable witnesses, the following being extracted from a long report published in the *Birmingham Gazette*. The writer staged his vigil during the nights of 17 and 18 February 1923.

It is a globular glow of unusual brilliance, varying in size from a bright pinpoint of light to a radiance which looks like a small Chinese lantern. Rarely has it been seen stationary; the majority of the observers have seen it as I saw it, moving hither and thither all over the hills, sometimes with great rapidity. Its motion is undulatory, with sudden dives downwards, at which it generally disappears, to appear again perhaps five hundred yards away.

In its nightly dance on the hills the ghostly light has no definite orbit. It moves either with or against or across the wind with almost equal facility. On Saturday night, for instance, when the hills were being swept by quite a gale I saw it travelling dead against the wind at quite a good speed, the height of the light above the ground being that most usual to it – anything from two to thirty feet . . .

. . . Whereas a will o' the wisp is a faintly luminous haze in the surrounding darkness – a shapeless, shining patch in the blackness – the Burton Dassett ghost is a well-defined light, spherical in shape and without radiations.

It is brighter than any bicycle lamp, and glows with a dull yellow colour, tinged when seen near at hand, with red . . .

We were facing the Edgehills across the valley, and the light, well-defined and spherical, moved across our field of vision with its peculiar switchback motion from left to right, disappearing as quick as it had come. A few moments later we saw it again, a pin-point of light, which seemed to be growing larger every second, moving, however, hardly at all. 'It's coming at us,' gasped a nervous ghost hunter, and come it did until, like a dull yellow eye, it was glowering at us apparently from beneath a nearby tree. There was a concerted rush to the spot – the dog, the nervous ghosthunter and all. Through the mud and ditches we stumbled, determined to lay that ghost. And when we were at the foot of the tree and had flashed our electric torches on it, there was nothing at all – nothing anywhere except a derisive light, circling at the side of the ruin we had just left. After that we saw it again three or four times, in every quarter of the compass and flitting in every direction. Then the mist fell again, the rain began, and towards dawn a dissatisfied investigation party trudged back to the inn.[23]

A will-o'-the-wisp seen as a single bright light, this example appearing in Lincolnshire in 1811.

Following publication in 1982 of *Earth Lights* by Paul Devereux, a number of phenomena have been reassessed in view of the convincing evidence presented for the theory that lights can be produced from the earth as a result of geological stress in fault lines, and it is possible that the Burton Dassett lights originated in this way. It is certainly intriguing that the lights reappeared early in 1924, immediately following an earth tremor in Herefordshire and Worcestershire, not far away.

In country regions, where will-o'-the-wisps seem once to have been a much more familiar sight than they are now, the lights were often associated with death. An instance of the reason for this association took place in May 1890. James Campbell was returning home on a dark night on the island of Luing (Strathclyde Region) when he saw a bright light ahead. It was travelling at great speed towards him along the course of a stream. When it reached a bridge crossing the stream, not far from where Campbell was standing, it stopped, then vanished. Next day a young man riding a horse home from the smithy was killed when this same bridge collapsed as he was crossing it. He was pinned under the horse, the water in the stream rose against the obstruction, and the rider was drowned.[24]

Early this century two manservants walking in the evening near the village of Francis Well, Carmarthen (Dyfed), saw a will-o'-the-wisp and watched it travelling towards them from the village. One of the witnesses later described it: 'It looked like a bright candle flame, without the candle; and it kept on coming nearer and nearer to us. It passed by us, on the other side of the hedge, just where the footpath came up from the valley. It went on, hopping along a few inches above the ground, and then vanished in the distance.' Three days later, a funeral procession followed the same route to the nearest churchyard. This event explains clearly why the light was sometimes called 'corpse candle'. The same witness saw the will-o'-the-wisp again ten years later, and knew it was a portent of death. His neighbours also saw the light enter his house under the door, on more than one occasion. The farmer saw it from inside the house: it was 'a little light, like a candle flame'. It went upstairs and into the bedroom where two of his children lay ill. Seconds later it returned downstairs and out under the door. As the farmer expected, both children died.[25]

In their role of death portent, will-o'-the-wisps display intelligence, even precognition, which may seem hard to accept if these lights are a natural phenomenon such as burning marsh gas or earthquake lights. However, there is now a suggestion that will-o'-the-wisps and other unidentified balls of light, such as ball lightning, UFOs in the form of lights in the sky, and mountain lights, may even be living entities of an unknown kind, but native to our atmosphere and possessing some form of intelligence. This novel theory has been put forward by Hilary Evans, who on studying these phenomena noticed the intriguing similarities between apparently diverse kinds of light balls, which he gathered together under the heading 'balls of light' or BOLs. His accumulated evidence is intriguing but inconclusive. As he comments:

> It will not do to say that BOLs are 'simply' ball lightning or 'simply' field-generated electrical plasma or 'simply' anything at all. Whatever they are, BOLs are nothing simple. Whatever they are, they represent something unknown to science and that alone makes them an exciting study for the anomaly researcher.[26]

24. *Mysteries of nature*

Nature is overflowing with 'mysteries' – plant and animal behaviour we cannot understand; the incredible complexities of organisms too small for us to see with the naked eye – the study of which helps us to gain perspective on our own place in the natural scheme. Not being zoologists or botanists or arachnologists or any other kind of specialist, we will not attempt to delve into their microcosmic world, but will concentrate on a few of the larger-sized mysteries of nature which can be more easily comprehended by the 'ordinary' mortal. We realize that all these 'mysteries' must have logical explanations, and where they are known to us we give them.

Cat-owners will all extol the mystery of their chosen species, and certainly the cat's homing instinct is often difficult to understand, when they travel hundreds of miles across un-

The Wiveliscombe winged cat.

known territory in order to return to a familiar environment. Whisky is just one of many cats to do this: in 1973 he travelled 150 miles in twenty-five days to get back to his old home in Bingley (West Yorkshire) from Cambridge. Even stranger are the occasions, admittedly rare but still on record, when a cat has found its way to its owner's *new* home, where it has never been before.[1]

Also rare are 'winged' cats, of which we have six accounts, the earliest being a winged cat from Wiveliscombe (Somerset) whose portrait appeared in the *Strand Magazine* in November 1899.[2] Another winged cat was born in a workhouse in Leeds (West Yorkshire) in 1900, and became known as Thomas Bessie. After some time as a sideshow in a fairground, Thomas Bessie died, possibly of poisoning, and was stuffed. The 'wings' were said to be malformations of the rib structure.[3] In 1933 a press report described the writer's encounter with the Oxford winged cat:

I have just seen a cat that has on its back fully-developed fur-covered wings, with which, it is stated, it can fly. It is now housed in the Oxford Zoo, and it is one of the strangest of Nature's freaks – and the most pathetic. All the time it seems to be ashamed of its unusual appearance and tries to be as like a normal domestic cat as possible. When I approached him, the winged cat rolled over on his back and then frisked around an enclosed paddock.

Here is the strange history of the animal, which is puzzling eminent zoologists. A few days ago neighbours of Mrs Hughes Griffiths, of Summertown, Oxford, saw a strange black and white cat prowling round their gardens. Last evening Mrs Hughes Griffiths saw the animal in a room of her stables. 'I saw it move from the ground to a beam – a considerable distance, which I do not think it could have leaped – using its wings in a manner similar to that of a bird,' she said to me.

Mrs Hughes Griffiths at once telephoned to the Oxford Zoo, and Mr Frank Owen, the managing director, and Mr W. E. Sawyer, the curator, went to her house and captured the animal in a net. I carefully examined the cat tonight,

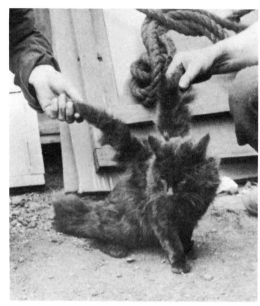

The Manchester winged cat.

and there is no doubt about the wings. They grow just in front of its hindquarters.[4]

Sally, the winged tomcat belonging to Mrs M. Roebuck of Attercliffe, Sheffield (South Yorkshire) in the late 1930s, had a 2-foot wingspan but could not fly, though he used the 'wings' to help him jump.[5] A winged cat called Sandy was exhibited at a carnival in Sutton-in-Ashfield (Nottinghamshire) in the 1950s,[6] and another made its home in a builder's yard at Trafford Park, Manchester, earlier this century (exact date unknown), having strayed there as a kitten. The 'wings', which developed as the cat grew, were about 11 inches from the shoulder-bone to the top, and the cat also had an unusual tail, broad and flat.[7] In 1985 a winged cat was discovered living on an Anglesey farm (Gwynedd). The 'wings', 7 inches long, were located just in front of its hindquarters and seemed to be made up of thick matted fur. They only began to grow when the cat was about four years old. It later shed the 'wings' which seems to support the idea that, in this instance at least, the 'wings' were no more than matted fur.

Unfortunately there seems to be no report on this phenomenon from someone with a good knowledge of cat anatomy who has examined a winged cat and can give a precise description of exactly how the 'wings' are formed, and whether they have proved of any use to the cats in chasing their prey.[8] The 'wings' on the Anglesey cat were seen to spread out when it jumped, but this is presumably caused by air currents lifting the 'wings', and they are not controlled by the cat.

Now some miscellaneous nature mysteries, starting with four unusual trees. In a wood at Wishaw near Glasgow (Strathclyde Region), a phosphorescent ash tree was discovered in 1908 by a group of young men who at first thought it was a ghost. The trunk was giving off so much light it was possible to read by it.[9] In 1939 an old birch tree at West Harling (Norfolk) was causing some amazement to the villagers, because clear water was trickling from it day and night. At the time of the press report, this had continued for about a month. First the trunk was seen to be dripping, then water ran from the branches. When one was sawn off, water ran from the cut. It was suspected that water from a spring was forcing its way upwards through the tree trunk, which may well have been hollow, as the tree was old.[10] In Peru there was said to be a 'rain-tree' whose leaves condensed atmospheric moisture and released it as rain. Water also oozed from the trunk, similar to the Norfolk tree. It was said that a square-mile grove of these trees could supply about 100,000 gallons of water daily. Such a tree would be a godsend to desert areas, but, sad to say, the tale was soon discredited by scientists, who offered other, more believable, explanations for the phenomenon of 'rain' falling from trees.[11]

In 1974 a smoking tree was reported on the Isle of Wight, near East Cowes. Firemen had been called to it three times in two days, but apparently it kept on smoking, with no obvious cause.[12] Perhaps it was not giving off smoke but gas. Trees being cut in the Ozark Mountains of America were found to be giving off gas from cavities at their bases, and it would burn with a faint yellow flame if ignited. The gas was found to be similar to natural gas, and was either resulting from decomposition in the trees' heartwood, or coming from underground supplies.[13]

The 'bleeding' yew at Nevern.

There is an old yew tree in Nevern churchyard (Dyfed), in a small thicket of yews, which 'bleeds' continuously, and this is one mystery we can confirm, having seen and photographed it for ourselves. The thick reddish liquid oozes from a gash in the trunk, and has apparently been doing so for decades, though yews do not usually give off resin like some other trees. It is said that a monk who was hanged in the churchyard for a crime which he claimed he had never committed, before his death swore that the yew would bleed to prove his innocence. But recently a man from the Forestry Commission explained that rainwater gets into the wood and causes decay which produces the reddish liquid.[14]

Plants and animals – and stones – sometimes turn up where least expected. In the summer of 1919 there were two cases of wheat appearing in fields where none had been sown. Close to the villages of Sturton and Stowe (Lincolnshire), some land had been left fallow, having previously grown a crop of barley.

Wheat had not been grown there for ten years. But in 1919 a fine crop of wheat sprang up, in better condition than the wheat sown in cultivated fields round about, and farmers came from far and wide to see it. Similarly, in a field near Ormskirk (Lancashire) an unexpected crop of wheat had appeared. Wheat had been growing there the previous year, but had died in a drought without yielding any crop worth harvesting. It is likely that it was the unharvested wheat which germinated, but surprisingly it was considered 'one of the best crops of vigorous, young wheat in West Lancashire, for the season'.[15]

Rather more puzzling are the fish which appeared in a pond at Newick (East Sussex) in 1921. Major Harding Cox had drained the pond, cleaned out the mud, and then in November 1920 refilled it. In May 1921 it was found to be teeming with tench, and thirty-seven were caught in one day. Where did they come from? It is not as if the pond had been a favourite habitat of tench. Major Cox said that no tench had ever been caught in the pond before.[16] Was this a case of teleportation (see Chapter 15), the fish being brought in by some unknown means to fill a void? There was more head-scratching on a farm near Chipping Sodbury (Avon) where in April 1975 Peter Lipiatt found thousands of little stone heaps in his barley field. Experts could not suggest any bird or animal that might have piled up the stones in this way.[17]

All pet-owners have tales to tell concerning the intelligence of their pets: others might say that the animals are merely acting instinctively, in pursuance of their self-interest. But are they still acting instinctively when they rescue their owners from dangerous situations, or do the pets really care about the safety of their human companions? And what of those instances where people have been helped by non-domestic animals, like dolphins? For some fascinating accounts of 'humanitarian' animals, see John Michell and Bob Rickard's *Living Wonders*.[18] Here we give a few recent examples of animals apparently displaying intelligence and compassion.

On Friday 13 May 1983, a chihuahua belonging to Christine Harrison of Barnsley (South Yorkshire) was run over and apparently killed. Christine buried the dog in a sack in the garden and went off to work. A while later, Mrs Harrison noticed that her dog Mick, a Jack Russell terrier, had dug out the grave and was pulling on the sack with all his strength. She went out with her husband and they saw Mick growling and dragging the sack towards them. Mr Harrison managed to take it from him and was refolding the pathetic bundle ready for reburial when he felt a slight movement. Opening up the sack, he found Percy the chihuahua still breathing, and later Christine was amazed to be greeted by him when she arrived home from work. It would be interesting to know if Mick was around when Percy was buried, and if so, how he had reacted then. Apparently the two dogs did not get on all that well together. Maybe Mick knew Percy was alive right from the start, but decided to teach him a lesson by letting him be buried for a few hours![19]

Another case of dog rescuing dog took place in December 1984 at Shipley (West Yorkshire). Rasputin the Alsatian and Scooby Doo the Yorkshire terrier had escaped from the garden of their home when the gate was left open. There was dense freezing fog about and Mrs Kerr was worried for the safety of her pets, but she could find no trace of them. Early next morning, workmen arrived at a 4-foot hole in the road half a mile from the Kerr home, to continue working on a water main, and found two dogs at the bottom of the hole. They were curled up together, a Yorkshire terrier peeping out from beneath an Alsatian. Scooby Doo had obviously fallen into the hole, and Rasputin had jumped in after her. He could easily have leapt out again, but would not leave the frail fifteen-year-old dog, and kept her warm all night. Rasputin snarled when the workmen came near and they had to telephone the dog warden, who got the dogs out. They were then luckily recognized by a passer-by and taken home. Mrs Kerr was delighted to see them:

Rasputin was wet, cold and bedraggled but Scooby Doo looked amazingly unscathed. She is an old lady now and has been ill for months. I have no doubt her big friend saved her life. The two of them eat, sleep, play and go everywhere together. After a good meal and a bath they both settled down for a comfortable sleep and seem none the worse for their experience.[20]

Also in December 1984, Pickle the cat saved his owners from possible death when their house in Halstead (Essex) caught fire. It was Pickle's habit to wake Mr Potter every morning at 6 a.m. by tapping him on the face with his paw, but on this particular morning he did it at 4 a.m., and Mr Potter told him to go away. But Pickle kept tapping on Mr and Mrs Potter's faces, and miaowing at them, so that they got up and then discovered the fire. Mrs Potter said: 'Pickle knew exactly what he was doing and the firemen told us that if he hadn't woken us when he did we would have been goners for certain.'[21]

In another house fire, in March 1985 in Whitehaven (Cumbria), Toby the labrador saved not only the family, but the cat too, in a particularly brave rescue. Using the same tactics as Pickle in the previous account, Toby went upstairs and began to lick Mr Phillip Robertson's face. When he took no notice,

Andrea Robertson with Toby the labrador and Sootica, whom Toby rescued from their burning home.

Toby seized the blankets in his teeth and started to pull them off the bed. Mr Robertson then noticed smoke billowing up the stairs, and quickly led his wife and four children outside, Toby following. Once they were all outside, Toby went round them all, nuzzling their hands – then he dashed back inside the house. They all shouted at him, but he did not reappear, and the house was now burning so strongly that they feared he was lost. Then he suddenly emerged, carrying Sootica the cat in his mouth. The Robertsons had only had Toby for a couple of months, having chosen him from an Animal Refuge Centre, and they had been told that there was a note on his record that he didn't like cats, but he certainly seems to have made an exception for Sootica.[22]

On 20 April 1985, golfers at Meriden (West Midlands) were the surprised witnesses of a drama involving geese, a stoat and a rabbit, here described by Jeremy Blyth, who was one of the golfers:

. . . We came to the tenth – not a hole to hook on, as the lake was on the left, and sure enough the fairway was littered with geese. Eventually we arrived at the fringe of the green when we were surprised to see a stoat run across the green carrying some hapless victim in his mouth.

Before we had had time to move forward a small rabbit dashed across the green hotly pursued by another stoat and disappeared into the bushes only to reappear almost immediately with the stoat gaining in every bound. A few yards and the rabbit was screaming loudly – we moved to help, but paused in amazement – six or seven of the geese left the flock and solidly marched on the stoat who turned tail and fled into the bushes.

The rabbit limped through the flock to the far side of the fairway where it rested, tired and hurt. But the stoat was not done yet and moved out of hiding to continue the chase; however, neither were the geese finished as they turned once more to the attack, and drove him back.

Before we left the green, he had tried another two or three times to cross the fairway, with the same result from the geese . . .[23]

251

Bird expert Peter Colston of the Natural History Museum commented:

> I have never heard of anything like this before. The geese obviously felt concern for the creature in distress and acted as if they were protecting one of their own young. It awakened their defensive and parental drive. They are the largest geese [Canada geese] in the world – as big as a turkey – and they must have been confident that the stoat – the size of a small rabbit – could do nothing against them. The rabbit just hung on to the only port in the storm.[24]

Finally two stories from Devon, both showing dogs' intelligence, especially the first, which tells of Suzy, a Jack Russell terrier who ran to fetch her master from work when burglars raided his home in May 1985. She ran 1½ miles, including crossing a busy main road and following forest tracks, along a route she had only ever travelled by car. Roy Dyer knew something was wrong when Suzy appeared, so he drove back to his home at Gulworthy, and found that burglars had stolen electrical gear worth £1,300. Not only did this dog know that something was wrong at home, but she also knew how to find her master at work.[25] A Border Collie named Abigail also proved herself a capable direction-finder, when she got lost on Dartmoor in May 1985, on a part of the moor where she had never been before. Search parties found no trace of her, and it was a week before she finally arrived home, having crossed 15 miles of moorland, 15 miles of villages and fields, and several roads including the M5 motorway.[26] Many accounts like these are published in the press each year, and we think they prove conclusively that domestic pets do not act solely according to instinct, but possess an intelligence greater than we realize; and sometimes they even demonstrate a sixth sense, when they set about locating people and places.

25. Poltergeists

'Poltergeist' means literally 'noisy spirit'; noisy they certainly can be, but opinions are divided as to whether spirits (i.e. non-physical intelligences) are really involved in poltergeist outbreaks. Each case is different, but certain similarities are apparent, and the kinds of things that happen include the movement of heavy furniture, footsteps, rappings, knockings and other noises including voices, the movement (often un-naturally slowly) of all manner of household objects through the air, smashing crockery and other damage and destruction, mischievous behaviour such as mixing up incompatible food-stuffs to render them useless, showers of stones, flows of water

The Runcorn (Cheshire) poltergeist of 1952 was fond of moving furniture around, and even when the police set traps and kept watch the disturbances continued. Here John Glynn surveys his wrecked bedroom.

and other liquids, materialization of apparitions. The activity often seems directed as if by an intelligence, written words and even messages sometimes appear, and the 'spirit' often seems to have a sense of humour.

In Coedkernew (Gwent) a poltergeist outbreak erupted in a farmhouse in 1904. A bundle of hay was thrown into the yard, pictures on the walls were turned round, two hundred pieces of crockery were dropped in the kitchen but none was broken, beds were moved and some carried partly downstairs, soda was put in a tub of lard, pickled cabbage was mixed with cream, and the name of the housewife's first husband was traced on the glass of a lamp. One night ten people sat up to watch for a ghost, but all was quiet, possibly because the village police-man was in attendance. Then a noise was heard, and a lump of butter hit the policeman right in the eye.[1] A few years earlier the Durweston (Dorset) poltergeist had also shown a sense of humour. One of the main witnesses of the 1894–5 outbreak was a gamekeeper named Newman. He was present one day when a boot flew into the afflicted cottage. The occupant threw it out, and Newman put his foot on it, saying 'I defy anything to move this boot.' When he took his foot away, the boot rose up behind him and knocked his hat off.[2] The ingenious Pontefract (West Yorkshire) poltergeist of the late 1960s once activated a pair of fur gloves and terrified the people in the room by making them appear at the top and bottom of the door like huge hands. Aunt Maude Pearce told them sternly to go away, but one of the gloves made a fist which it shook at her. She began to sing 'Onward Christian Soldiers', whereupon the glove began to beat time to her singing.[3]

Poltergeists are one of the best-established phenomena, be-ing experienced all over the world. The earliest known case dates back to AD 530, when the deacon Helpidius, living in Ravenna, Italy, complained that he was being assailed by showers of stones in his house. St Caesarius blessed the house with holy water, and the disturbance ended.[4] The same prob-lem of showers of stones is one of the most frequent types of poltergeist outbreak experienced today, as we shall show later; likewise the same remedy, blessing or exorcism, is still em-ployed, with varying degrees of success.

Apart from the actual movement of small objects and furniture, which is strange enough, some of the antics performed by poltergeists seem to defy natural laws. Objects are propelled through the air unnaturally slowly, as is described here by Mr Newman, the gamekeeper who witnessed the events at Durweston (Dorset) in 1894–5:

> I saw coming from behind the door a quantity of little shells. They came round the door from a height of about five feet. They came one at a time . . . They came very slowly, and when they hit me I could hardly feel them. They came so slowly, that in the ordinary way they would have dropped long before they reached me.[5]

Objects sometimes materialize as if out of thin air, and liquids appear from nowhere. In the Pontefract case, water appeared on the kitchen floor, more appearing as it was mopped up. The floor underneath the linoleum was dry, and there was no obvious source for the water.[6] During the haunting in Warrington (Cheshire) during the 1970s of a former school then being used as a shop, liquid appeared on the floor, and those who saw it had reason to believe it was urine. Stan Evans, Director of the tent manufacturers occupying the premises during the haunting, wrote to us concerning the urine:

> The puddles were there every morning for about 7 days and during the day it would dry up leaving a white ring stain. We had no cats and the shop was closed and locked each night. It was quite embarrassing as usually a customer would find it before our staff. We explained to one of our customers what we thought was causing the trouble and as she was quite religious she offered to pray for the phenomena to be taken away. About a fortnight later she came into the shop quite upset. The trouble had followed her home and her bed clothes were soaked with urine.
>
> The area where the pools appeared was on the lower floor and in the centre of the large tent exhibition room. As we had no rain leakage through the top floor and no piped water supply in the lower floor we were unable to accept that it

was water . . . We did not have the liquid analysed. We assumed that it was urine because it was reported that it was seen being produced from a height of approx 18″ and everything that happened [in the building] was connected with [ghostly] children.[7]

Many years earlier, the poltergeist outbreak at Swanton Novers rectory (Norfolk) (8 August to 8 September 1919) took the form of liquids flowing from the walls and ceilings. Paraffin and petrol were identified, also methylated spirits, sandalwood oil and water. Sometimes the liquid seeped out, sometimes it spurted, and a report dated 2 September said that about fifty gallons of oil had been collected that day. The rector, the Revd Hugh Guy, said to a reporter who had witnessed paraffin seepage: 'Next time it will be methylated spirit, or just water. I'm sorry you can't see it gushing . . . gallons of water came from that ceiling . . . the queer part is that the ceiling, the paper, and the laths are quite dry.'[8]

Equally strange things are still happening in the second half of the twentieth century and it is difficult to select from the many examples. There were plenty of witnesses to the antics of the haunted lift in the Palace Hotel, Birkdale, Southport (Merseyside), when it was being demolished in April 1969. The ten-man team were planning to sleep in the hotel, but they soon moved out into lodgings and would only work there in daylight hours, after they had heard strange noises in the night and the lift began to move of its own accord. Even when all the power to the building was cut off, the lift still moved up and down, its doors opening and closing and its indicator lights flashing. Even when the emergency winding handle was removed, the lift still moved. Workman Fred Wooley said: 'Nine of us came back one night and as we entered the foyer the lift doors slammed shut and it shot up to the second floor.' Another witness was Mrs K. Templeton, who was looking for antique mirrors in the hotel. She said:

While I was talking to the workmen the lift suddenly began to go up. There wasn't any sound from it – it was very eerie. It just glided up about 7 ft almost to the next floor and stopped. I ran all the way up to the winding room with one of the workmen, but there was just no way it could have been moved mechanically. The brake was still on.

When the men cut the lift cables, the lift did not fall. Neither did it fall when they cut through the main shafts. Nor even when they had struck at it with sledgehammers for twenty-five minutes – until suddenly it plunged down and buried itself four feet into the cellar.[9]

The poltergeist phenomenon is as active now towards the end of the twentieth century as ever it was. Several good cases in the last fifteen years include the Enfield (Greater London) poltergeist (described at length in Guy Lyon Playfair's book *This House is Haunted*) which plagued a family living in a council house for a year or more in 1977–9; the Handsworth, Birmingham (West Midlands), poltergeist which moved furniture in the home of a science technician and his wife during several weeks in 1976–7, finally being quietened by the Bishop of Aston and a priest who prayed there a number of times (the priest actually witnessing a bedspread that got off the bed and walked downstairs 'as if on legs' and threw itself against the front door);[10] another council house poltergeist at Ivybridge (Devon) which in November 1984 was terrifying the family of six with tappings, musty smells, a screaming noise, pacing footsteps, and 'vague forms like a smoke haze';[11] and the Reading (Berkshire) poltergeist which began in late 1979 and continued for eighteen months, a case well worth describing in more detail here.

The victims were Mrs Adams, in her eighties, and her fifty-year-old daughter Pauline. It began with the movement of furniture and often the breaking of objects, sometimes quite large, like television sets and radios (several of each being destroyed). Poltergeists are not usually so violent and destructive as this one. When the two women sat downstairs they were often bombarded with china and glassware. All their crockery was smashed in this way, though fortunately neither of them was hurt. Even furniture was smashed. The electricity would go off for no reason, clocks would stop, the bathroom flooded without reason, there was a gas leak which could not be traced

Mrs Adams with a sample of the crockery broken by the poltergeist at her home in Reading.

and later cleared up spontaneously, and the poltergeist even destroyed or dematerialized pound notes – Pauline's holiday savings were shredded and she lost £50 this way. Other people also experienced the poltergeist activity, among them Mrs Adams's seventeen-year-old grandson Stephen. One day he was standing in the living-room when his clothes flew off his body and disappeared, leaving him dressed only in his underpants. Not knowing what to do, they asked 'it' to return the garments, which it did. They reappeared one by one on top of the door. Stephen commented, 'I had to unbutton all the shirt buttons and unlace the shoes before I could put them on. They had disappeared all buttoned and laced up, just as I was wearing them.' Other items had disappeared over the

258

months, including seven pairs of Pauline's shoes – and thirteen of the missing shoes reappeared immediately after Stephen's clothes, falling one by one over the door. The fourteenth shoe is still missing. The dematerialization of items in this way reminds us of the cases of teleportation described in Chapter 15. This is one phenomenon that is definitely not acceptable to science – but it seems to happen nevertheless. There are many other examples in poltergeist lore.

Poltergeists rarely injure people physically, only frighten them. As noted before, the Reading poltergeist was particularly violent, and did cause injury on several occasions. A friend of the family was hit on the head by a packet of butter from her shopping basket, and on another occasion her husband was struck on the forehead by a house number which flew off the doorpost as he was about to photograph it. It originally belonged to the next house, but had removed itself to the Adamses' door, making their number 121 into 1231; and he was trying to photograph it as evidence, but the poltergeist obviously did not approve. Worst of all, Mrs Adams herself was struck on the head by a small medicine tablet box, and the wound needed two stitches.

The Adamses called in a priest to perform an exorcism, which worked temporarily, but the phenomena soon began again. They also called in mediums, who again had only limited success in quietening things down. Finally they moved into a new flat to escape their tormentor.[12]

Because of their extraordinary character reports of poltergeist activity are often received sceptically, the authorities tending to believe that children are to blame, causing mischief unknown to their parents. It is true that children sometimes try to help the manifestations along a little, especially if they are getting plenty of attention from visiting media people and psychic investigators, but experts feel that rarely are the children totally responsible for the events. Investigators are not always able to get to the scene in time to witness the phenomena, and sometimes they are not entirely impartial, being keen to see phenomena, which can cause hoaxers to play up to them even more, the investigators being too blinkered to see that they are being fooled. But in the case of the

Tydd St Mary (Lincolnshire) poltergeist in 1957, unbiased investigators from the Society for Psychical Research accompanied by journalists were able to vist Hannath Hall while the phenomena were still occurring. Alan Gauld and A. D. Cornell were two of the investigators, and they described their experiences in their book *Poltergeists*.[13] They heard rapping and knocking noises in the 'haunted room' where they were spending the night. Using a simple code, they found that the raps would answer questions, but the 'entity' was not particularly coherent, and claimed to be a woman who had been murdered in the house in 1906. They were not able to find any evidence for this event. Nothing was found to account for the raps, which would stop whenever a torch was flashed in their direction. Gauld and Cornell describe the thoroughness of their search for any way in which the raps could have been manually produced by a hoaxer, including examining the floorboards with a magnifying glass and looking under them for anything suspicious. Having watched each other during the rapping for signs of hoaxing, and seen none, the only alternative to the phenomena being genuine was that they had faked them together!

The mechanisms of a poltergeist outbreak have everyone baffled, though many investigators believe that the phenomena are brought about by a release of energy from one of the persons present, usually a young person or someone experiencing mental conflict or repressed emotion. The energy may be similar to that used in psychokinesis (PK), using the mind to influence matter, and it may be electromagnetic in nature, but much experimentation still needs to be done to find out what is going on in a poltergeist outbreak. Some investigators believe that underground water courses create movements in the earth and buildings that in turn cause all the noises and movements ascribed to the poltergeist, the 'geophysical theory', but it is surely impossible that all the poltergeist effects we have described could be accounted for in this way. The other popular theory is that there is some form of intelligence behind the poltergeist, which may come from a dead person, from some other kind of non-living entity, or indirectly from a living person. The 'simplest' explanation, though many questions obviously remain unanswered, is that a member of the family is unconsciously causing and directing the phenomena using PK energy, but we must stress that they are not actively in control of what is happening and cannot stop or start it at will. Most poltergeist cases do involve one person who could fit the role of agent, for example the Sauchie (Central Region) outbreak in November 1960 which was centred on eleven-year-old Virginia Campbell. She was a lonely girl, living temporarily in the home of her elder brother and sharing a room with nine-year-old Margaret, her niece, which apparently was not to her great liking. She was said by her teacher to be quiet, shy, above average intelligence. One evening, a noise like a bouncing ball was heard in the house, and next day the sideboard was seen to move a few inches and return to its usual position. Knocking noises were heard in her bedroom while she was in bed, and a heavy linen chest was seen to move. Strange movements of her bedclothes were also noted. The phenomena followed her to school, but they gradually faded as Virginia settled down.[14]

Another lonely girl was Voirrey Irving, who lived with her parents in an isolated farmhouse on the Isle of Man. She was thirteen when the phenomena began in 1931, and they continued until 1935, leaving us one of the strangest cases on record. The events centred on Gef, a talking mongoose who lived in the farmhouse. He was unseen by visitors, but all three Irvings had seen him and described him as yellow, with a long bushy tail, and a hedgehog-like face with flattened snout. He was nearly as big as a rat. Voirrey took some photographs of Gef, but they are all lacking in clarity. Only one visiting newspaperman heard him speak, and reported:

Does the solution of the mystery of the 'man-weasel' of Doarlish Cashen lie in the dual personality of the 13-year-old girl, Voirrey Irving? That is the question that leaps to my mind after hearing the piercing and uncanny voice attributed to the elusive little yellow beast with a weasel's body . . . Yesterday I heard several spoken sentences . . . The conversation was between the 'weasel-voice' and Mrs Irving, who was unseen to me in another room, while the girl sat motion-

Voirrey Irving at her home on the Isle of Man.

less in a chair at the table. I could see her reflection, although not very clearly, in a mirror on the other side of the room. She had her fingers to her lips . . . The lips did not move, so far as I could see, but they were partly hidden by her fingers. When I edged my way into the room the voice ceased. The little girl continued to sit motionless, without taking any notice of us. She was sucking a piece of string, I now saw.

The story is far too complex to detail here, but Harry Price and R. S. Lambert's book *The Haunting of Cashen's Gap* is recommended, though having been published in 1936 it is not easy to find.[15] In his articles on Gef in *The Unexplained*, Melvin Harris commented:

Gef never had a personality or existence independent of Voirrey. He brought home rabbits, as did Voirrey. His favourite foods were also Voirrey's favourites. He shared her strong interests in mechanical things. Moreover, Gef was never heard unless Voirrey was out of the room or so placed that her mouth could not be watched. The voice itself was described by one observer, who believed in Gef, as 'like a girl's voice of about 15 or 16 – a striking penetrating voice'. In other words, just the sort of voice Voirrey could easily assume.

Was it all a joke that got out of hand? Or did Gef begin life as Voirrey's invisible playmate, such as lonely children often have? Or was Gef an unusual expression of poltergeist phenomena? Whatever the truth, it is an entertaining story worth reading in full.

Mongooses don't feature very often in poltergeist cases, but as mentioned earlier, showers of stones do. We close this chapter on one of Britain's most intriguing and well-authenticated mysteries with details of recent and not so recent stone-throwing events, of which we have collected eight without much difficulty. In 1887 a mill on the River Eden near Appleby (Cumbria) was the centre of a poltergeist outbreak during May to September, during which stones were thrown through the windows. The first missile was found to be a large roundish pebble, still wet from the stream bed, but the source of the stones used in such cases is not usually so easily ascertained.[16] A shower of stones broke windows in a house in South Woodford (Greater London) on 9 August 1920, and other showers followed. On the 13th and 14th police kept watch on the house and its surroundings; on both nights the house was bombarded with stones, and forty policemen could not solve the mystery.[17] In May 1969 a council house in New Moston (Greater Manchester) was being bombarded with bricks, stones and milk bottles, but not on those nights when the police were on watch.[18] In October 1973 large stones were being aimed at a house in Croydon (Greater London), 150 of them having broken forty panes of glass over a week or so. The police felt a man with a giant catapult must be responsible, but they and their tracker dogs found nothing and no one.[19] Only a few months later, in April 1974, it was the turn of a house in Swallowfield (Berkshire), which had been hit with stones for nine weeks at the time of the press report.[20] During the Enfield (Greater London) poltergeist outbreak in 1977–9, stones were being thrown into the house, and one of the investigators collected some of the pieces, finding three that fitted together to form one large pebble. Interestingly, the smallest piece arrived several hours after the others.[21] During heavy rain on the night of 21/22 June 1980 houses in Hampshire Place, Peterlee (Durham), were showered with stone chippings, this being a once-only affair and therefore more akin to the sky-falls of Chapter 1 than to poltergeist phenomena. But can we be sure that sky-falls and stone-throwings are not in some way connected?[22]

Beginning about 1979 but continuing for several years, the Ward End, Birmingham (West Midlands), stone-throwing outbreak is one of the most interesting, because of its long persistence and because of the close involvement of the police. Five houses in Thornton Road were the focus of the attacks, the bombardment with large stones happening regularly, often nightly. The residents eventually had to board up their windows and erect screens of chicken wire. The stones thrown were the same as those found in the gardens, but they had no fingerprints on them, and no soil either, looking as if they had been washed clean. The police spent months on the case, and constables even spent cold nights huddled in sleeping bags in the back gardens. They heard the stones arriving, but could find no clues to where they had come from. They were using modern equipment including night-sights, image intensifiers and infra-red video, but they might as well have left them in the police station for all the help they were. At the end of 1982, after 3,500 man-hours of investigation, they admitted they were still 'completely baffled'.[23]

Stone-throwing poltergeists have a long history and a world-wide spread – but the same cannot be said of black-pudding throwing. We cannot close this chapter without relating the case of the phantom black-pudding thrower of Castleton (Derbyshire). For two years during 1977 and 1978 someone (or something) was throwing food at the old people's bungalows – black puddings, eggs, bacon, bread and tomatoes, even a leg of mutton early on in 1977. One of the pensioner victims, 74-year-old Fred Robinson, said: 'Black puddings, bacon, tomatoes and eggs have all been thrown at my house. The attacks were irregular. Every other night . . . then nothing for weeks on end. But he hasn't struck since the police were brought in. We hope it stays that way.' Mrs Ethel Bramley said: 'It's unreal, weird! If people want to give us food why not wrap it up and leave it on the doorstep?' Another added: 'There's not much you can do with an egg once it has hit a door!' The donor was generous too – he threw one-pound black puddings, whole loaves of bread, a dozen large eggs, all at once, but no food of this kind was reported stolen, and no one was buying extra quantities of black puddings in the area. It was – and will probably remain – a total mystery.[24]

Some concluding thoughts on Britain's mysteries

Do ghosts appear when there is no one there to see them? Or do their appearances depend on the presence of a witness? That witness may in fact be the trigger which brings the apparition into being. This same observation also applies to certain other categories of mysteries, apart from all the ghosts we have described: poltergeists and religious visions certainly, UFOs probably (except for those attributable to natural phenomena), and possibly also all the entities such as the Little People and those described in Chapter 22. If these phenomena do depend on the presence of a human witness, does that mean they are all subjective? Not necessarily. Some experiences in any of the categories may be totally subjective; others may be partially subjective, in that although there is only one witness, whose store of mental images may be drawn upon, the event does have some external stimulus independent of the witness; yet others may appear superficially subjective but in fact have a completely objective reality and be able to leave physical traces of their presence.

There is so much still to be learned about the human mind and psyche, about known and unknown natural energies, and how they can all interact. These can result in phenomena such as poltergeists, teleportation, spontaneous human combustion, and others, which are not yet an accepted part of the prevailing world-view. Fear surrounds their outbreaks, and this in turn often produces a reaction which seeks to reject these rare phenomena, and people will even go so far as to claim that the phenomena do not exist, that the events are all explicable in mundane terms, and that hoax or misinterpretation is the true cause of the observed events.

Apart from these 'paranormal' phenomena whose existence

is still disputed, there are a number of natural phenomena whose existence is generally accepted but which are still not properly explained, such as ball lightning, will-o'-the-wisps, and other phenomena detailed in Chapters 23 and 24. In between these two extremes of rejection and acceptance lie the grey areas of phenomena which are accepted by some but rejected by others – sky falls, frogs and toads in rocks, big cats and other non-native animals, lake and sea monsters. The reality of all the mysteries in this book is difficult to demonstrate to those who have closed their minds to the 'impossible'. So many of the events are experienced by one lone witness and leave no trace of their happening. Such a witness invariably finds his veracity questioned, often even his sanity. He is no better off if he shows a photograph to 'prove' his experience. *Any* photograph of a strange phenomenon could have been faked. It probably wasn't – but it could have been. All the photographs in this book which show mysteries actually happening have been criticized and rejected by some 'expert' or other, and we cannot personally vouch for them as we were not present when they were taken. Only the photographer knows the truth – and even he may have been the victim of a hoax.

We expect that some readers of this book will conclude that it's all nonsense – that we are deluded, that the witnesses were deluded, that mysteries do not and cannot exist. But if you are one of the thousands who have experienced a mystery at first hand, you will be more receptive to other people's accounts, and will appreciate the problems they faced when they tried to tell other people about their experiences. As for ourselves, we have tried to remain totally open-minded towards mysteries and strange phenomena. We note everything, accept nothing unreservedly; but we do agree with Hamlet when he said, 'There are more things in heaven and earth, Horatio, than are dreamt of in your philosophy . . .'

Chronological List of Strange Events

More details of the events in this list can be found by looking under the relevant county in the Gazetteer which follows. The Gazetteer entry will also indicate whether an event is described in greater detail in an earlier chapter.

1885

23 February – John Lee became 'The man they couldn't hang', Exeter, Devon

23 July – moving electrified patches of light seen, Lothian Region

date unknown – phantom black dog seen on Meon Hill, Warwickshire

1886

15 February – mysterious murder, Fenny Compton, Warwickshire

8 July – fall of snails near Redruth, Cornwall

summer – sea monster seen in Loch Duich, Highland Region

1887

May–September – poltergeist at mill near Appleby, Cumbria

July – teleportation of woman, Swansea, West Glamorgan

30 July – sea monster seen off Shuna, Strathclyde Region

November–December – poltergeist at Bramford, Suffolk

date unknown – roaring noise heard, Somerset

1888

19 February – possible case of spontaneous human combustion, Aberdeen, Grampian Region

22 July – rain from a clear sky, Stevenage, Hertfordshire

31 August–9 November – 'Jack the Ripper' murdered five women in the East End of London

date unknown – strange creature seen in Loch Ness, Highland Region

1890

May – will-o'-the-wisp seen, Island of Luing, Strathclyde Region

1891

26 September and 1 October – will-o'-the-wisp seen at Crowborough, East Sussex

5 December – ghost photographed at Combermere Hall, Cheshire

date unknown – Professor Norman Collie heard footsteps on Ben MacDhui, Grampian Region

1892

7 May – ghost man seen in country
lane near St Boswells, Borders
Region
30 June – fall of frogs,
Birmingham, West Midlands
3 July – ball lightning seen,
Liverpool, Merseyside
3 October – sea monster seen off
Broughty Ferry, Tayside Region

1893

late May or early June – monster
seen beside Loch Duvat on
Eriskay, Western Isles
26 July – ball lightning seen,
Epping, Essex
September – sea monster seen in
Loch Alsh, Highland Region
date unknown – ghost cat seen,
Eccleshall, Staffordshire

1894

11 April – ball lightning seen near
Dunstable, Bedfordshire
August – fall of jellyfish, Bath,
Avon
13 December – start of poltergeist
outbreak, Durweston, Dorset

1895

January – sea monster seen at
Bernera on Lewis, Western
Isles
6 February – snow fell from a clear
sky, Surrey
7 February – sea monster seen off
the Butt of Lewis, Western Isles
summer – monster seen in Loch
Morar, Highland Region
18 December – ball lightning killed
a man, Devon

date unknown – parakeet caught in
farmyard, Ardgay, Highland
Region
date unknown – monster seen in
Loch Ness, Highland Region

1896

5 November – mock sun seen over
Wales

1897

26 April–8 May – poltergeist
outbreak at Tick Fen,
Cambridgeshire
20 July – ball lightning entered
house, Suffolk
August – 110-pound ice block
found in field, Stirling, Central
Region
date unknown – couple saw
phantom black dog near Diss,
Norfolk
date unknown – image of Dean
Vaughan seen on wall of Llandaff
Cathedral, South Glamorgan
date unknown – child saw pixie
near Shaugh Bridge on Dartmoor,
Devon

1899

November – winged cat,
Wiveliscombe, Somerset
10 December – blue flashes and
explosions in cave in the Manifold
valley, Staffordshire

1900

early February – ghost of
policeman seen near
Sunningdale, Berkshire
1 April – fall of dried beech leaves,
Wallingford, Oxfordshire
20 July – toad found in skull buried

269

under church, North Moreton, Oxfordshire

mid-December – disappearance of three men from Eilean Mor lighthouse, Western Isles

date unknown – man saw mermaid, Sandwood, Highland Region

this year – winged cat, Leeds, West Yorkshire

1901

March – mysterious stabbing of blind woman, Cambridge

28 May – ball lightning inside house, Liverpool, Merseyside

summer – boy saw UFO and entities, Bournebrook, West Midlands

1902

5 June – flames erupted from mudflat, Blundellsands, Merseyside

1903

December – monster seen in Loch Ness, Highland Region

1904

13 April – exploding fireball seen in Essex

15 April – darkness in daytime, Wimbledon, Greater London

c.July–mid-September – poltergeist outbreak, Up Holland, Lancashire

16 December – possible case of spontaneous human combustion, Falkirk, Central Region

29 December – wolf killed at Cumwhinton, Cumbria

date unknown – poltergeist outbreak, Coedkernew, Gwent

1905

January – possible case of spontaneous human combustion, Binbrook, Lincolnshire

25–6 February – possible case of spontaneous human combustion, Butlock's Heath, Hampshire

1 March – jackal killed near Sevenoaks, Kent

4 March – mystery fires at house in Derby

April – start of poltergeist outbreak, Tackley, Oxfordshire

2 September – large black winged object flew over Froncysyllte, Clwyd

October – mystery animal killing sheep, Great Badminton, Gloucestershire

date unknown – toad found in oak tree, Pulham St Mary, Norfolk

this year – strange lights seen during religious revival, between Barmouth and Harlech, Gwynedd

1906

8 February – huge ball of light seen, Barsham, Suffolk

3 March – sentry shot at ghost at Windsor Castle, Berkshire

13 May – ball lightning seen at Morchard Bishop, Devon

May – teleportation of horse, Lamberhurst, Kent

August – sea-serpent seen off Land's End, Cornwall

dates unknown – two cases of toads found in rock, Broseley, Shropshire

1907

5 April – ghost seen in Highworth church, Wiltshire

date unknown – drowned man later turned up alive, Greater London

1908

22 March – possible case of spontaneous human combustion, Whitley Bay, Tyne and Wear

2 July – ice fell from clear sky, Braemar, Grampian Region

date unknown – phosphorescent tree found in wood at Wishaw, Strathclyde Region

1909

23 March – airship seen over Peterborough, Cambridgeshire

13 May – encounter with landed airship and occupants, Ham Common, Greater London

18 May – C. Lethbridge saw airship and two men on Caerphilly Mountain, Mid Glamorgan

1910

date unknown – live toad found in lump of coal, Leicestershire

1911

24, 25, 29 April – soldiers mysteriously injured, Colchester, Essex

24 June – masses of insect eggs in jelly fell from sky, Eton, Buckinghamshire

September – Loch Ness Monster seen on land, Highland Region

date unknown – sea serpent seen off Westward Ho!, Devon

date unknown – Little People seen, Isle of Man

1912

late May – ghost of old lady seen by cyclists, Paddock Wood, Kent

5 July – sea serpent seen off Prawle Point, Devon

July – sea monster seen off Kessingland, Suffolk

summer – fall of frogs, Oswestry, Shropshire

1914

July – monster seen in Loch Ness, Highland Region

24 October – reflected coastal panorama seen at Mawnan, Cornwall

1915

summer and autumn – floating lights seen over Dartmoor, Devon

November – ghostly horse-drawn vehicle seen, Sunbury-on-Thames, Surrey

1917

July – first photograph of 'Cottingley fairies' taken, Cottingley, West Yorkshire

summer – sea monster seen in Loch Brittle, Isle of Skye, Highland Region

late October–November – poltergeist outbreak, Cheriton, Kent

1918

24 August – fall of sand-eels, Hendon, Sunderland, Tyne and Wear

271

1919

6 April – possible case of spontaneous human combustion, Dartford, Kent

May – live toad found in coal, Netherseal, Derbyshire

June – wheat grew where none was sown, Sturton/Stowe area, Lincolnshire

8 August–8 September – falls of liquids in rectory, Swanton Novers, Norfolk

August – wheat grew where none was sown, Ormskirk, Lancashire

August – sea monster seen off Hoy, Orkney

dates unknown – two deserted schooners found in the English Channel, off Kent and Cornwall

1920

9–14 August – showers of stones on house, South Woodford, Greater London

1921

May – fish found in new pond, Newick, East Sussex

17 August – fall of tiny frogs, Southgate, Greater London

17 August – pea-sized ball lightning seen indoors, Eastbourne, East Sussex

dates unknown – several mysterious road accidents near Postbridge, Devon

1922

summer – possible case of spontaneous human combustion, Sydenham, Greater London

9 September – lifeboatmen saw 'aeroplane' fall into sea, Barmouth, Gwynedd

18 December – ball lightning, Salisbury, Wiltshire

winter 1922/23 – phantom shining eyes seen, Horncastle, Lincolnshire

1923

April – Loch Ness Monster seen on land, Highland Region

10 May – hump of Loch Ness Monster seen, Highland Region

9 July – lightning made 'keranograph' on floor, Mincing Lane, London

August – sea serpent seen in Thames estuary, off Essex

date unknown – man killed by ball lightning, Grimsby, Humberside

date unknown – Dean Liddell's image appeared on wall, Christ Church, Oxford

date unknown – poltergeist outbreak, Penkaet Castle, Haddington, Lothian Region

this year – low-level lights seen, Burton Dassett, Warwickshire

1924

March – mysterious death of woman, Batley, West Yorkshire

summer – woman saw 'hairy hands' at caravan window, near Postbridge, Devon

date unknown – ghosts of prehistoric horse and rider seen on Bottlebush Down, Dorset

this year – low-level lights seen, Burton Dassett, Warwickshire

1925

October – mystery animal

slaughtered sheep around Edale,
Derbyshire
date unknown – man found
woman's leg at Stanford Rivers,
Essex

1926

October – phantom house seen at
Bradfield St George, Suffolk
date unknown – phantom cat seen
near Hambleton, Lancashire

1927

January – lynx trapped in
Inverness-shire, Highland
Region
date unknown – sentry saw ghost
at Windsor Castle, Berkshire
date unknown – phantom black dog
seen near Ramsey, Isle of Man

1928

January – poltergeist outbreak,
Battersea, Greater London
date unknown – ghost of living
woman seen at Northwood,
Shropshire

1929

August – hump of Loch Ness
Monster seen, Highland Region
29 December – rain from a clear
sky, Grayshott, Hampshire
date unknown – children saw tiny
plane with tiny pilot, Hertford

1930

June – sea monster seen north of
the Norfolk coast
14 July – undulating humps of
Loch Ness Monster seen,

Highland Region
date unknown – girl saw black dog
pass through wire fence, near
Upper Booth, Derbyshire
date unknown – black dog seen near
Buxton Lamas church, Norfolk

1931

early January – rain from a clear
sky, Grayshott, Hampshire
June – sea monster seen off
Thorpeness, Suffolk
date unknown – man cycling at
night saw over twenty phantom
dogs, near Barton, North
Yorkshire
date unknown – start of haunting
by mongoose Gef, Cashen's Gap,
Isle of Man

1932

7 February – hump of Loch Ness
Monster seen, Highland Region
February – crocodile seen in River
Ness, Highland Region
February–April – ghost of Samuel
Bull seen regularly, Ramsbury,
Wiltshire
summer – monster seen in Loch
Shiel, Highland Region
November – ghosts seen on
Marston Moor battlefield,
North Yorkshire
date unknown – ghost seen in
Peterborough Museum,
Cambridgeshire

1933

3 January – rain from a clear sky,
Grayshott, Hampshire
7 January – false dawn, near
Shaftesbury, Dorset
February – visions of the Virgin

Mary reported at Middleton, Suffolk

14 April – the Mackay sighting of the Loch Ness Monster (Highland Region) from the new road, widely publicized and followed by many more sightings throughout the year

22 July – Loch Ness Monster seen on land, Highland Region

early August – Loch Ness Monster seen on land, Highland Region

December – Loch Ness Monster seen on land, Highland Region

date unknown – sentry saw headless ghost of Anne Boleyn at the Tower of London

date unknown – winged cat kept at zoo, Oxford

1934

4 or 5 January – Loch Ness Monster seen on land, Highland Region

February – Loch Ness Monster seen on land, Highland Region

28 February – sea monster seen on land at Filey Brig, North Yorkshire

spring – mysterious murder of John Dawson, Bashall Eaves, Lancashire

5 June – Loch Ness Monster seen on land, Highland Region

date unknown – ghost of Oscar Wilde seen at Magdalen College, Oxford

date unknown – large ghost dog seen at Blyborough, Lincolnshire

throughout year – many sightings of the Loch Ness Monster, Highland Region

1935

20 January – rain from a clear sky, Benson, Oxfordshire

summer – monster seen in Loch Ness, Highland Region

date unknown – publishing executive saw phantom soldiers, near Holwell, Hertfordshire

1936

June – monster seen in River Ness, moving downriver towards the sea, Highland Region

5 August – sea monster seen off Eccles, Norfolk

August – sea monster seen off Mundesley, Norfolk

August – children saw phantom soldiers, Aberdeen, Grampian Region

19 September – photograph taken of the Brown Lady of Raynham Hall, Norfolk

October – monster seen in Loch Ness, Highland Region

November – verger saw ghost inside Highworth church, Wiltshire

this year – family cursed by Egyptian bone, Edinburgh, Lothian Region

1937

throughout year – several sightings of the Loch Ness Monster, Highland Region

1938

March – phantom landscape seen, Mansands near Dartmouth, Devon

27 August – possible case of spontaneous human combustion, Chelmsford, Essex

19 September – man found dead in

mysterious circumstances, Ben Avon, Grampian Region

21 October – sea monster seen off Southwold, Suffolk

autumn – man saw phantom black dog, Ditchingham, Suffolk

date unknown – ghostly light seen at hut on Barvas moor, Isle of Lewis, Western Isles

throughout year – several sightings of Loch Ness Monster, Highland Region

1939

16 June – frog fall, Trowbridge, Wiltshire

June – monster seen in Loch Ness, Highland Region

early July – sea serpent seen in the Firth of Forth off West Wemyss, Fife Region

November – phantom manor house seen, Start, Devon

November – UFO seen near Brockworth, Gloucestershire

date unknown – black dog seen near Blackmoor Gate, north Devon

date unknown – ghostly Roman soldiers seen, York, North Yorkshire

date unknown – water trickled night and day from tree, West Harling, Norfolk

this year – winged cat lived in Attercliffe, Sheffield, South Yorkshire

1940

5 May – monster seen in Loch Ness, Highland Region

10 November – ball lightning in Coventry, West Midlands

winter – man saw headless ghost

cyclist, Kingsthorpe, Northampton

date unknown – 'monster' shot near Bembridge, Isle of Wight

date unknown – children saw little man in toy car, Kilkhampton, Cornwall

1941

date unknown – phantom car seen near Sligachan, Isle of Skye, Highland Region

1942

June – fall of clods of earth and grass, Ruislip, Greater London

late summer – man abducted into UFO, near Newbiggin-by-the-Sea, Northumberland

1943

May – monster seen in Loch Ness, Highland Region

October – man heard, saw and shot at the 'Big Grey Man of Ben MacDhui', Grampian Region

19 November – possible case of spontaneous human combustion, Aldingbourne, West Sussex

24 December – black dog seen near Bewdley, Hereford and Worcester

1944

April – monster seen in Loch Ness, Highland Region

August – fall of frogs near Whittington Barracks, Staffordshire

October – poltergeist outbreak at Scrapfaggot Green, Great Leighs, Essex

Modern Mysteries of Britain

1945

14 February – mysterious death of farm-worker Charles Walton on Meon Hill, Warwickshire

May – monster seen in Loch Ness, Highland Region

late May – man encountered the 'Big Grey Man of Ben MacDhui', Grampian Region

early August – sea monster seen off Hilston, Humberside

date unknown – phantom tinker encampment seen near Castle Douglas, Dumfries and Galloway Region

1946

date unknown – ghostly Roman soldiers seen in York, North Yorkshire

1947

January – large black cat or dog seen at Chilham, Kent

spring – start of poltergeist outbreak, Tain, Highland Region

9 July – ball lightning seen, Kirkcudbrightshire, Dumfries and Galloway Region

17 August – ball lightning seen, Cornwall

August – strange disappearance of two men, Filey, North Yorkshire

date unknown – fisherman saw mermaid on Muck, Highland Region

date unknown – phantom horse seen on battlefield, near Kineton, Warwickshire

date unknown – monster seen in Loch Morar, Highland Region

throughout year – several sightings of the Loch Ness Monster, Highland Region

1948

30 July – monster seen in Loch Morar, Highland Region

December – monster seen in Loch Ness, Highland Region

1949

spring – ball lightning seen, Loch Duntelchaig, Highland Region

1 May – mirage of coastal scene, Hunstanton, Norfolk

5 July – two sea monsters seen off east Looe, Cornwall

August – phantom nun seen at Borley, Essex

date unknown – monster seen in Loch Ness, Highland Region

1950

3 January – woman saw phantom battle, Letham, Tayside Region

summer – sea-serpent seen off Cliftonville, Kent

November – ice lumps fell on farmland, one killed a sheep, North Molton, Devon

30 November – fall of ice block, Hampstead Norris, Berkshire

26 December – ice mass smashed on to road, Dunbarton, Strathclyde Region

throughout year – several sightings of the Loch Ness Monster, Highland Region

1951

28 January – hand impression seen on vestry door, Langenhoe, Essex

November – tall 'ghost' in breeches seen, Garston, Merseyside

date unknown – hump of monster seen in Loch Ness, Highland Region

1952

28 April – monster seen in Loch Ness, Highland Region

August–October – poltergeist outbreak, Runcorn, Cheshire

December – teleportation of mystic W. T. Pole, somewhere in Sussex

date unknown – phantom nun seen by several people, Princethorpe, Warwickshire

date unknown – family saw phantom lake, New Forest, Hampshire

date unknown – man saw landed UFO and spoke to occupants, near Castlemartin, Dyfed

1953

late June – cyclist saw ghostly horse and rider, Hickleton, South Yorkshire

August – ghostly phenomena experienced at Ardachie Lodge near Loch Ness, Highland Region

August – sea monster seen in the Firth of Clyde, Strathclyde Region

September, October, November and December – ghost seen monthly in York Museum Library, North Yorkshire

10 December – monster seen in Loch Ness, Highland Region

date unknown – workman saw ghostly Roman soldiers, York, North Yorkshire

1954

18 February – man saw UFO and spoke to a 'spaceman', near Lossiemouth, Grampian Region

13 May – man abducted into flying saucer, near Burnaston, Derbyshire

12 June – shower of frogs, Sutton Park, West Midlands

21 July – sea monster seen in Loch Linnhe, Highland Region

summer – girl saw UFO with entities, Kingston upon Hull, Humberside

summer – couple saw phantom landscape and people, Wotton, Surrey

September – woman received mystery blow to head, Bridlington, Humberside

21 October – woman and children saw UFO with entities, Ranton, Staffordshire

throughout year – several sightings of the Loch Ness Monster, Highland Region

1955

5 February – rain fell from a clear sky, Wrexham, Clwyd

15 February – snow fell from a clear sky, Wrexham, Clwyd

16 August – small entity in black seen in Bradford, West Yorkshire

summer – family tormented by poltergeist or haunting, Birmingham, West Midlands

10 October – plaster Madonna wept, Walker, Newcastle upon Tyne, Tyne and Wear

date unknown – black dog seen at Aston Dingle, Powys/Shropshire border

throughout year – several sightings of the Loch Ness Monster, Highland Region

1956

February – teleportation of knife, Brockworth, Gloucestershire

July – hump of monster seen in Loch Ness, Highland Region

13 August – UFO seen by pilots and on radar, Suffolk

September – fall of pennies and halfpennies, Hanham, Avon

October – people in car saw ghost standing in road, Mildenhall, Wiltshire

November – workmen saw ghost in mansion near Newton Stewart, Dumfries and Galloway Region

November – two men twice saw phantom kilted Highlanders, Cuillin Mountains, Isle of Skye, Highland Region

November – man contacted by UFO entity, Shefford, Bedfordshire

date unknown – phantom lorry seen near Stow, Borders Region

date unknown – ghost photographed in Eastry church, Kent

1957

15 June – two monsters seen in Loch Ness, Highland Region

August–November – poltergeist outbreak at Tydd St Mary, Lincolnshire

7 September – James Cooke travelled in flying saucer, Runcorn, Cheshire

October – ghostly couple crossed road in front of lorry, Gretna Green, Dumfries and Galloway Region

18 November – woman visited by UFO entity, Aston, West Midlands

1958

29 January – possible case of spontaneous human combustion, Hammersmith, Greater London

spring – monster seen in Loch Ness, Highland Region

September – monster seen in Loch Morar, Highland Region

date unknown – ghost of man seen at Arundel Castle, West Sussex

dates unknown – lorry-driver picked up phantom hitch-hiker several times, around Wellington on A38, Somerset

1959

26 June – two tall men with long blond hair disappeared, Whitefield, Greater Manchester

13 September – sea monster seen off Soay, Highland Region

autumn – black dog seen at Uplyme, on Devon/Dorset border

November – James Cooke travelled in flying saucer, Frodsham, Cheshire

winter – small entity with large head pushed car, Brocton, Staffordshire

1960

28 February – Loch Ness Monster seen on land, Highland Region

mid-March – elephant found in

trawler net, off Flamborough Head, Humberside

15 July – monster seen in Loch Lochy, Highland Region

November – phantom battle seen, near Otterburn, Northumberland

late November – poltergeist outbreak, Sauchie, Central Region

throughout year – several sightings of the Loch Ness Monster, Highland Region

1961

early May – 'abominable snowman' seen, Bilsington, Kent

27 July – monster seen in Loch Urabhal, Isle of Lewis, Western Isles

1962

9 February – UFO seen near Ivinghoe, Buckinghamshire

February – sea monster seen on shore at Helensburgh, Strathclyde Region

11 March – large unidentified lizard found in East Dulwich, Greater London

August – monster seen in Loch Ness, Highland Region

date unknown – little green man seen on the Berkshire Downs

date unknown – phantom horse and cart seen, Milton Combe, Devon

throughout year – 'Surrey puma' seen regularly, Surrey

1963

18 July – big cat seen at Shooter's Hill, Greater London

28 July – hooded men seen by motorists, Caterham, Surrey

August – sightings of the Loch Ness Monster, Highland Region

late August – sea monster seen off New Quay, Dyfed

6 November – ball lightning seen indoors, Nottingham

16 November – bat-winged 'man' seen, Sandling Park, Kent

date unknown – ghost of priest seen in mill, Standish, Greater Manchester

throughout year – 'Surrey puma' seen regularly, Surrey

1964

19 February – big cat seen at East Runton, Norfolk

spring – series of UFO close encounters began, Little Lever, Greater Manchester

May – figure in 'spacesuit' appeared on photograph, Solway Firth, Cumbria

2 June – children saw Little People, Gateshead, Tyne and Wear

early June – sea monster seen in the Sound of Jura, Strathclyde Region

22 June – monster seen in Loch Linnhe, Highland Region

July – phantom Daimler seen near Modbury, Devon

August – monster seen in Loch Morar, Highland Region

summer – little green men seen, Liverpool, Merseyside

12 November – big cat seen at Stoke Poges, Buckinghamshire

throughout year – many sightings of big cats in Surrey and Hampshire

throughout year – many sightings of the Loch Ness Monster, Highland Region

1965

4 February – big cat seen near
 Ashurst, Hampshire
24 April – man saw flying saucer
 and occupants, Scoriton, Devon
10 August – bright light fastened
 itself to lorry windscreen, near
 Warminster, Wiltshire
14 September – UFO seen at
 Langenhoe, Essex
30 September – possible sea
 monster seen on the A85 east of
 Perth, Tayside Region
this year – helmeted entity
 appeared several times to
 housewife, Bristol, Avon
throughout year – several sightings
 of the Loch Ness Monster,
 Highland Region

1966

1 January – disappearance of Alex
 Cleghorn, Glasgow,
 Strathclyde Region
May–July – crucifix shed tears,
 Walthamstow, Greater London
July – disappearance and
 reappearance of sleeping girl,
 Chatham, Kent
early August – alligator found in
 Leicester
August – ball lightning seen, Crail,
 Fife Region
1 September – start of poltergeist
 outbreak, Pontefract, West
 Yorkshire
mid-October – sea monster seen off
 Chapel St Leonards, Lincolnshire
autumn – tall hairy entity seen at
 Wollaton, Nottinghamshire
late December – dog scared to
 death by ghosts, Chipping,
 Lancashire
throughout year – many sightings

of the Loch Ness Monster,
 Highland Region

1967

28 January – children saw 'little
 blue man', Studham Common,
 Bedfordshire
March – John Fagan miraculously
 cured of cancer, Glasgow,
 Strathclyde Region
16 July – monster seen in Loch
 Linnhe, Highland Region
July – ghost seen at paper-mill,
 Greenfield, Greater Manchester
5 August – UFO seen near Capel
 Curig, Gwynedd
November – ghost seen at power
 station, Nottingham
dates unknown – sightings of
 phantom Daimler, near
 Modbury, Devon
throughout year – many sightings
 of the Loch Ness Monster,
 Highland Region

1968

18 August – ice fall, Sevenoaks,
 Kent
27 August – monster seen in Loch
 Morar, Highland Region
summer – woman saw humanoid
 with animal features, near
 Stratford-upon-Avon,
 Warwickshire
24 October – couple saw ghostly
 policeman, Birmingham, West
 Midlands
autumn – ghost in boiler suit
 vanished before witness,
 Kingston upon Hull,
 Humberside
early December – bent pennies fell
 on Ramsgate, Kent
date unknown – ghost of Tudor

lady seen at Rycote Chapel,
Milton Common, Oxfordshire
date unknown – ghosts seen on
Marston Moor battlefield,
North Yorkshire
throughout year – many sightings
of the Loch Ness Monster,
Highland Region

1969

4 January – phantom landscape and
people seen around
Havenstreet, Isle of Wight
22 or 23 February – ice block
crashed through van roof,
Bracknell, Berkshire
8 April – disappearance of April
Fabb, Metton, Norfolk
April – mysterious lift activity in
Palace Hotel, Southport,
Merseyside
May – house bombarded by bricks
etc., New Moston, Greater
Manchester
June – strange animal seen near
Witheridge, Devon
8 July – monster seen in Loch
Morar, Highland Region
11 and 16 August – monster seen
in Loch Morar, Highland
Region
summer – fall of frogs, Penn,
Buckinghamshire
October – 5-inch luminous flying
object seen, Bournemouth,
Dorset
date unknown – 'soot' in park
identified as fungus from New
Zealand, Cranford, Greater
London
throughout year – several sightings
of the Loch Ness Monster,
Highland Region

1970

5 February – monster seen in Loch
Morar, Highland Region
June – crocodile seen in River Ouse
at Little Barford, Bedfordshire
16 August – ice fall, Isleworth,
Greater London
date unknown – black dog seen in
cottage, Hoy, Orkney

1971

3 April – monster seen in Loch
Morar, Highland Region
spring to autumn – hyena often
seen on farm at Nutley, East
Sussex
15 July – policeman saw big cat,
Chiswell Green, Hertfordshire
August – phantom policeman seen
in Liverpool, Merseyside
September – two tall entities seen
in field, Oulton, Staffordshire

1972

23 January – ice fall, Shirley,
Surrey
February – 'Hexham heads'
unearthed, to be followed by a
werewolf sighting, Hexham,
Northumberland
19 April – coastguard saw black dog
which vanished, Gorleston,
Norfolk
14 June – sightings of big cat, near
Polegate, East Sussex
July – man saw ghostly
re-enactment of suicide at
Dalmarnock Road Bridge,
Glasgow, Strathclyde Region
August – wild boars seen in
Hampshire
September – ghost monk seen in
hotel, Great Missenden,
Buckinghamshire

September – monster seen in Loch
Lomond, Strathclyde Region

September – big cat seen at
Woodlands, Hampshire

8 October – huge UFO seen at
Cairo Mill, Oldham, Greater
Manchester

12 November – young children saw
ghost of murdered woman,
Collyhurst, Greater Manchester

November – ghost seen in factory
kitchen, Luton, Bedfordshire

winter – black dog seen inside
farmhouse on Dartmoor, Devon

date unknown – 'Hexham heads'
provoked werewolf sighting at
Southampton, Hampshire

1973

4 January – van collided with ghost,
Debenham, Suffolk

2 April – fall of ice block,
Manchester

early May – tall entity with 'hut'
talks to young children, near
Sandown Airport, Isle of Wight

May – female ghost stepped into
path of teacher's car, near
Llanidloes, Powys

early 1973 – young boy saw ghost,
Dagenham, Greater London

early 1973 – black dog seen at
Woodbridge, Suffolk

August – a rare tropical fish found
at Southend, Essex

22 September – fall of ice chunk,
Wombwell, South Yorkshire

16 October – woman claimed to
have been abducted into UFO,
near Milverton, Somerset

October – stones thrown at house
with no clues to culprit, Croydon,
Greater London

October – ghostly lady in white
seen in Royal Circus Hotel,
Edinburgh, Lothian Region

October – ghost seen in castle
dungeon, Winchester, Hampshire

date unknown – vicar saw phantom
monk, Stoke, Devon

date unknown – ghosts seen on
Marston Moor battlefield,
North Yorkshire

date unknown – man experienced
timeslip, Great Yarmouth,
Norfolk

1974

3 January – mysterious death of
woman, Blackpool, Lancashire

23 January – unexplained
explosion, near Llandrillo, Clwyd

February – humanoid entities seen
near power station, Bedford

25 March – fall of ice, Pinner,
Greater London

7 April – Tasmanian marsupial
wolf seen at Bournemouth,
Dorset

15 April – rushing noise heard,
Prescelly Hills, Dyfed

April – house bombarded with
stones, Swallowfield, Berkshire

April – smoking tree, East Cowes,
Isle of Wight

April – strange animal seen in
Delamere Forest, Cheshire

27 May – murder of girl echoes
similar murder 157 years before,
Erdington, Birmingham, West
Midlands

8 June – ball lightning seen in
bedroom, Wallsend, Tyne and
Wear

June – big cat seen on road by
several drivers, Beith, Strathclyde
Region

13 July – disappearance of road
accident victim, near Chatham,
Kent

10 August – ice fell through house
roof, Scunthorpe, Humberside

15 August – ball lightning seen on mountain in Glencoe, Highland Region

4 October – bright light deposited grey powder on car, Bala Lake, Gwynedd

13 October – 'star' or manned vehicle seen in glen below Ben Nevis, Highland Region

27 October – family abducted into UFO, Aveley, Essex

autumn – sound of marching army heard at Dunblane, Central Region

early December – falls of eggs, Wokingham, Berkshire

date unknown – policeman saw ghost cyclist, Robertsbridge, East Sussex

date unknown – phantom white hound seen at Beccles, Suffolk

1975

15 January – lion cubs seen at Langham, Norfolk

24 January – ice-fall, Fulham Road, London

February – van driver saw ghost which vanished, Birmingham, West Midlands

February – bear seen on Skipwith Common near Riccall, North Yorkshire

2 March – sea monster seen on shore at Barmouth, Gwynedd

March – puma sightings around Horsham, West Sussex

April – big cat seen, Willenhall, West Midlands

April – thousands of stone heaps found in field, near Chipping Sodbury, Avon

26 May – man found dying in mysterious circumstances, Nayland, Suffolk

10 July – tall, silver-suited entity seen, Ewloe, Clwyd

29 July – crocodile seen by River Stour, Sandwich, Kent

8 August – ball lightning in kitchen, Warley, West Midlands

August – baby alligator found at Stevenage, Hertfordshire

summer – butterfly found in sealed gas meter, Sheffield, South Yorkshire

September – phantom Daimler seen near Modbury, Devon

September – first sighting of Morgawr, sea monster, off Falmouth, Cornwall

30 September – couple saw monster in Loch Lochy, Highland Region

*c.*21 October – notecase fell on to Lynne Connolly's head, Kingston upon Hull, Humberside

19 December – 6-foot ice chunk fell near Thorpe Constantine, Staffordshire

date unknown – motorist saw ghostly lady cyclist near Coombe Abbey, Warwickshire

date unknown – ghostly nun seen by actors at the Theatre Royal, York, North Yorkshire

date unknown – ghostly woman seen by Abbey Tower at St Andrews, Fife Region

date unknown – mysterious death of unidentified man, West Botley flyover, Oxfordshire

1976

4 January – phantom monk seen in grounds of Hardwick Hall, Derbyshire

19 January – boy found dying in strange circumstances, Euston Road underpass, London

23 January – girl had UFO close encounter, Bolton, Greater Manchester

1 February – phantom hedges seen, Southwold, Suffolk

15 February – mystery bang over Bangor and Anglesey, Gwynedd

February – man found dead in mysterious circumstances, Dartmoor, Devon

March – wild boar killed near Nairn, Highland Region

17 April – 'Owlman' seen at Mawnan, Cornwall

11 May – woman saw UFO and silver entity, Leigh, Greater Manchester

15 May – ice smashed through house roofs, Reading, Berkshire

May – large black cat seen at Pitsea, Essex

12 June – bear seen at Leighton Buzzard, Bedfordshire

3 July – 'Owlman' seen at Mawnan, Cornwall

July – girl saw landed UFO and entity, Oakenholt, Clwyd

29 July, 1 August – sightings of lion around Tollerton, Nottinghamshire

6 August – mystery explosion, Berwyn Mountains, Clwyd

9 August – big cat with tufted ears seen at Glenfarg, Tayside Region

9 August – lion seen at Thorganby, North Yorkshire

mid-August – image of Christ appeared on henhouse wall, St Ives, Dorset

late August – children saw UFO and silver entity, North Reddish, Greater Manchester

August – monkey seen in Blyton/Northorpe area, Lincolnshire

3 September – two women saw landed UFO and entities, Fencehouses, Tyne and Wear

4 September – big cat seen, Nuneaton, Warwickshire

20 September – big cat seen, Skegness, Lincolnshire

22 September – sentry saw statue come to life at Windsor Castle, Berkshire

23 October – lioness seen in Upton, Cheshire

October – phantom car seen, Seaford, East Sussex

autumn – two flying men seen one night at Baddeley Green, Staffordshire

14 November and 30 December – man and woman saw UFO entity and were later abducted into a UFO, near Winchester, Hampshire

November – UFO seen at Marteg near Rhayader, Powys

November – raccoon found near Daventry, Northamptonshire

date unknown – phantom coach and horses seen, Ealing Common, Greater London

date unknown – man and dog saw ghostly woman at Beachy Head, East Sussex

date unknown – motorist ran into ghost on two occasions, Willingdon, East Sussex

1977

2 January – fall of ice through roof, Enfield, Greater London

31 January – M. Lindsay photographed Loch Morar monster, Highland Region

January – poltergeist outbreak, Handsworth, Birmingham, West Midlands

January and February – sightings of big black cat, North Berwick area, Lothian Region

early February – brightly-lit 'box-car' seen in road at Coldstream, Borders Region

early 1977 – 9-foot entity seen in garden, Huyton, Merseyside

9 March – huge UFO seen at Nelson, Lancashire

13 March – fall of hazelnuts, Bristol, Avon

11 April – boy saw humanoid entity, Herbrandston, Dyfed

21 May – Anthony Shiels photographed Loch Ness Monster, Highland Region

May – big cat seen at Leckwith, South Glamorgan

6 June – UFO encounter near Barnard Castle, Durham

8 June – giant ball lightning seen, Fishguard, Dyfed

18 June – children saw strange people with helmets, Cricklade, Wiltshire

29 June – ice smashed through garage roof, Epsom, Surrey

mid-year – egg-thrower struck in Abingdon, Oxfordshire

28 July – 8-foot white-robed figure seen beside Clowbridge Reservoir, Lancashire

July–September – garden walls attacked, Peckham, Greater London

8 August – fall of hay and grass with attached roots and soil, Poole, Dorset

10 August – policeman saw three dancing figures who disappeared, East Hull, Humberside

31 August – start of poltergeist outbreak, Enfield, Greater London

17 September – hazy green UFO seen from 5 feet away, Newmill, Cornwall

14 November – huge UFO seen at Partington, Greater Manchester

18 November – children at school saw UFO, Wawne, Humberside

26 November – 'message from outer space' broadcast on Southern TV, Berkshire and Hampshire

29 November – figure appeared in front of car and disappeared when struck, near Swinton, Borders Region

November – UFO witness visited by 'Man in Black', Haverhill, Suffolk

10 December – tall entity in white suit seen at Shotton, Clwyd

12 December – UFO seen by children, Clifton Campville, Staffordshire

21 December – unexplained explosions, Cornwall

25 December – cross seen in the sky, Whitstable, Kent

December – UFO seen at Tittensor, Staffordshire

late 1977 – start of food-throwing at bungalows, Castleton, Derbyshire

dates unknown – reports of a phantom hitch-hiker, Nunney, Somerset

date unknown – visitor saw phantom monks at Beaulieu Abbey, Hampshire

1978

1 January – unexplained explosions, Cornwall

6 January – couple saw phantom white dog, near Exford, Somerset

18 January – boy saw UFO and entities, Anlaby, Humberside

27 January – UFO entities captured cow in cage, Frodsham, Cheshire

January – big cat seen in the Bickerton Hills, Cheshire

6 February – dog burnt in possible case of spontaneous combustion, Jarrow, Tyne and Wear

17 March – Ken Edwards saw tall silver entity, Risley, Cheshire

March – dead crocodile found in Caerphilly, Mid Glamorgan

mid-April – kangaroo or wallaby seen at Hockcliffe, Bedfordshire

April – big cat seen near Rochford, Essex

c.4 June – 'Owlman' seen at Mawnan, Cornwall

19 June – family claimed to have been abducted by UFO, near Faringdon, Oxfordshire

23 June – fall of white substance which disappeared overnight, Cambridge

2 August – 'Owlman' seen at Mawnan, Cornwall

19 August – Genette Tate disappeared, Aylesbeare, Devon

September – visitor to church saw ghost which vanished, Westham, East Sussex

23 October – large low-level UFO seen by many witnesses, Leicestershire

October – ghostly recording of mining disaster, Whiteheath, Birmingham, West Midlands

October – aircraft instruments went haywire off Bournemouth, Dorset

12 November – possible case of spontaneous human combustion, Reading, Berkshire

date unknown – ghost which faded away seen in Deadman's Cove, Cornwall

date unknown – ghost of old man seen in Gladstone Pottery Museum, Stoke-on-Trent, Staffordshire

date unknown – big cat seen in Margam Forest, West Glamorgan

1979

4 January – woman saw UFO entities indoors, Rowley Regis, West Midlands

25 January – possible case of spontaneous human combustion, Hutton-le-Hole, North Yorkshire

January – large black cat seen in Faversham area, Kent

early February – large black cat seen at Kilry near Alyth, Tayside Region

12 February (and other times) – falls of mustard and cress seeds, peas and beans, Southampton, Hampshire

22 February – two girls saw UFO land in snow, Meanwood, West Yorkshire

22 March – helmeted, silver-suited entity seen on Isle of Sheppey, Kent

March – driver saw phantom road, Sevenoaks, Kent

24 April – ball lightning seen in kitchen, Hatcliffe, Humberside

early June – bear seen at Thetford, Norfolk

14 June – two motorists hit phantom woman, Sevenoaks, Kent

June – fall of rocks or clinker, Llangollen, Clwyd

June – fall of tiny frogs and spawn, Bedford

30 June or 1 July – large black cat seen near Eastbourne, East Sussex

July – strange animal, possibly a

monkey or bear, seen near
Claverton, Avon

August – big cat seen in Ayr,
Strathclyde Region

3 September – woman saw UFO
entities indoors, Gateshead,
Tyne and Wear

early September – monkeys seen at
Exton, Leicestershire, and
Stamford, Lincolnshire

10 September – big cat seen in
Tilgate Forest, West Sussex

23 September – children saw Little
People, Wollaton Park,
Nottingham

4 October – entity seen drilling hole
in garden, Handsworth,
Sheffield, South Yorkshire

12 October – man gave lift to
phantom hitch-hiker,
Stanbridge, Bedfordshire

October – monster seen in Lake
Bala, Gwynedd

early November – big cat seen at
Muie, Highland Region

9 November – man had close
encounter with large object,
Livingston, Lothian Region

3 December – ball lightning seen
indoors, Fleetwood, Lancashire

11 December – pilot paced by
UFO, Bolton, Greater
Manchester

December – wild boar seen around
Basildon, Essex

late 1979 – start of poltergeist
outbreak, Reading, Berkshire

date unknown – phantom
Wellington bomber seen, Towy
valley, Dyfed

1980

6 January – possible case of
spontaneous human combustion,
Ebbw Vale, Gwent

13 March – man burnt by heat from
UFO, Haselor, Warwickshire

7 or 8 April – fall of dried peas,
Tonna, West Glamorgan

14 April – ice smashed through
roof, Lyndhurst, Hampshire

16 May – crocodile seen crossing
M55 motorway, Preston,
Lancashire

21/22 June – stone chippings fell on
houses at Peterlee, Durham

28 July – ice smashed through roof,
Leamington Spa, Warwickshire

July – big cat seen,
Wolverhampton, West Midlands

August – cat-like animal seen in the
Handforth area of Cheshire

28 September – two roofs smashed
by falling ice, Plymouth,
Devon

29 September – lynx seen,
Churchstoke, Powys

11 October – block of ice fell on
Romford golf course, Greater
London

23 October – mystery animal
thought to be inside farm barn,
Llangurig, Powys

29 October – puma captured at
Cannich, Highland Region

23 November – ghostly old man
seen on the A12 near Hopton,
Norfolk

23 November and 3 December –
big black cat seen at Long
Marston, Warwickshire

25 November – big cat seen at
Cwmbelan, Powys

28 November – policeman
abducted into UFO,
Todmorden, West Yorkshire

November – possible case of
spontaneous human
combustion, Darlington,
Durham

4 December – possible case of
spontaneous human

combustion, Lockwood near Huddersfield, West Yorkshire

10 December – large ice-ball fell on Kings Norton, Birmingham, West Midlands

16 December – ice smashed through roof, West Kirby, Merseyside

late December – possible UFO landing at air base in Rendlesham Forest, Suffolk

1981

6 January – fall of ice lump, Truro, Cornwall

February – ball lightning seen indoors, Warminster, Wiltshire

February – sightings of big black cat around Tedburn St Mary, Devon

28 February – multi-coloured entity seen, Prees Heath, Shropshire

22 March – mystery burning of mop, Halesowen, West Midlands

March – big cat seen, Perton, Staffordshire

3 May – possible case of spontaneous human combustion, Wath upon Dearne, South Yorkshire

17 May – ball lightning seen indoors, Norfolk

28 May – fall of coins, Reddish churchyard, Greater Manchester

10 June – big cat seen, Leckwith, South Glamorgan

24 June – ice block smashed through roof, Anerley, Greater London

June – sightings of lion in Luton area, Bedfordshire

June – big black cat seen, Ysbyty Ystwyth, Dyfed

16 July – three young women claimed to have been abducted aboard a UFO, near Uppington, Shropshire

10 September – girl burned by light from UFO, Plymouth, Devon

28 September – fall of ice, Yateley, Hampshire

2 November – ghostly old man seen on the A12 near Hopton, Norfolk

November – big cat seen, Whitby, North Yorkshire

November – big grey and black striped cat seen, Tonmawr, West Glamorgan

27 December – bear seen on Hackney Marshes, Greater London

throughout year – stones thrown at houses in Ward End, Birmingham, West Midlands

1982

23 January – huge UFO seen at Rochdale, Greater Manchester

5 April – calf-size black animal seen on farm at Lydford, Devon

April – dead man found kneeling with head in the sand, Woolacombe, Devon

April – dead elephant found in the sea off Aberdeen, Grampian Region

29 May – big cat seen, Billericay, Essex

25 July – ice fall, Northampton

July – 'black panther' seen at Eaton Bray, Bedfordshire

12 and 25 August – big cat seen, Fobbing, Essex

early autumn – timeslip

experienced in Covent Garden, London

4 October – porcupine captured in Carshalton, Greater London

24 October – UFO seen near Carleton, North Yorkshire

23 December – cheetah seen, Brighton, East Sussex

late 1982 – locusts found at Hurstpierpoint, West Sussex

1983

January – metal debris fell on farmland, Llanilar, Dyfed

early February – big cat seen, Ilkeston, Derbyshire

13 February – red object fell from sky, Plymouth, Devon

February – first lamb kills attributable to the 'Exmoor Beast', near South Molton, Devon

early March – fall of beans, Topsham, Devon

22 March – rain of tiny shells, Dilhorne, Staffordshire

March – big cats seen around Morcombelake, Dorset

March – Arctic fox found at Saltaire, Bradford, West Yorkshire

April/May – big cat sightings in the Chilterns, Buckinghamshire

13 May – dog saved life of another dog, Barnsley, South Yorkshire

16 May – lioness seen at Cuffley, Hertfordshire

May – cheetah seen at Walton Heath, Surrey

5 June – dead crab fell from sky, Brighton, East Sussex

5 June – coke fell during thunderstorm, Bournemouth, Dorset

July – big cat-like animal seen at Earlston, Borders Region

12 August – ice fall, Bushey, Hertfordshire

12 August – man taken into UFO by entities, Aldershot, Hampshire

15 August and October – large black cat seen at Goffs Oak, Hertfordshire

27 August – fall of ice slab, Ampthill, Bedfordshire

30 August – ice fall, Hitchin, Hertfordshire

August – sightings of large ginger cat, Brechfa, Dyfed

mid-September – Loch Ness Monster photographed, Highland Region

September – marlin seen in River Leven, Cumbria

summer or autumn – big black cat shot at Dallas, Grampian Region

3 October – big black cat seen near Forden, Powys

24 October – raccoon caught in farmyard, Gellilydan, Gwynedd

4 and 11 November – big black cat seen, Horndon-on-the-Hill, Essex

November – ghost seen in pub, Manor, Sheffield, South Yorkshire

throughout year – big cat sightings, Devon

1984

January – white calf appeared in shed, Chillerton, Isle of Wight

early February – hermit crab fell on car, Bridlington, Humberside

27 March – disappearance of Revd P. R. M. Smith, St Helens, Merseyside

Easter – child's egg decorated with face of Christ seen to weep, Doncaster, South Yorkshire

22 April – UFO seen at Saltfleet, Lincolnshire

27/28 May – small fish found on roof, Newham, Greater London

May – dark-blue sphere fell on to farmland at Broughton, North Yorkshire

18 June – fall of winkles and starfish, Thirsk, North Yorkshire

19 June – ice fall, Exmouth, Devon

24 July – unidentified liquid fell from sky, Winton, Bournemouth, Dorset

July – strange wind, near Cheddar, Somerset

July – mystery animal killed chickens, Yelverton, Devon

3 August – monkey involved in car accident, near Devizes, Wiltshire

27 August – possible ball lightning seen near Edale, Derbyshire

August – big cat seen around Newton Abbot, Devon

August – big cat seen, Rossendale Valley, Lancashire

summer – balls of damp sand fell on Tuckton, Bournemouth, Dorset

mid-September – big black cat killed, Grantown-on-Spey, Highland Region

23 September – black glassy material fell on Swansea, West Glamorgan

September – tropical bat found at Exeter, Devon

23 October – ice fall, Leicester

27 October – 'Exmoor Beast' seen, at Brayford near South Molton, Devon

31 October – phantom black dog seen near Yeo Mill, Devon

8/9 November – fall of apples, Accrington, Lancashire

November – poltergeist outbreak at Ivybridge, Devon

early December – big cats seen in Stithians and Truro areas, Cornwall

7 December – huge cross around the moon seen at Bideford, Devon

8 December – bear reported at Heath-and-Reach, Bedfordshire

24 December – possible case of spontaneous human combustion, Newton Abbot, Devon

December – dog saved dog's life, Shipley, West Yorkshire

December – cat saved couple from fire, Halstead, Essex

date unknown – big cat sightings in Argyll, Strathclyde Region

throughout year – many sightings of big cats on the Isle of Wight

1985

28 January – possible case of spontaneous human combustion, Widnes, Cheshire

January – big cat seen at Achnamara, Argyll, Strathclyde Region

January – big cats seen around Stithians and St Austell, Cornwall

February – big cat seen at Dunlop, Strathclyde Region

March – ice fall, Chippenham, Wiltshire

March – 5,000 empty baked bean tins found on road between Penhow and Caerwent, Gwent

March – big black cat seen, Ardchronie Quarry, Sutherland, Highland Region

March – dog saved family and cat in house fire, Whitehaven, Cumbria

19 April – big cat seen, Barnham Common, Norfolk/Suffolk border

20 April – geese saved rabbit from stoat attack, Meriden, West Midlands

April – large black cat seen, Thetford, Norfolk

April – big cat seen around Elvedon and Honington, Suffolk

early May – big black cat shot, Advie, Highland Region

21 May – lynx-like animal seen at Bedhampton, Hampshire

25 May – possible case of spontaneous human combustion, Stepney Green, Greater London

May – dog found her way home off Dartmoor, Devon

May – dog fetched master home after burglary, Gulworthy, Devon

4 July – ice fall, Cadnam, Hampshire

30 August – big cat seen, Faversham, Kent

August – strange disappearance of two teenagers, Filey, North Yorkshire

summer – sightings of Morgawr, sea monster, off Falmouth, Cornwall

14 October – big black cat shot, Dallas, Grampian Region

November – big black cat seen at Westbury-on-Severn, Gloucestershire

County Gazetteer of Strange Events

ENGLAND

Avon

BATH   Thousands of small jellyfish fell during a thunderstorm; August 1894.

BRISTOL   Housewife was visited several times by tall, helmeted entity; 1965. Hundreds of 'fresh and sweet' hazelnuts fell from the sky; 13 March 1977 (see Ch.1).

NEAR CHIPPING SODBURY   Farmer found thousands of little stone heaps in his barley field; April 1975 (see Ch.24).

CLAVERTON   Several people saw 'The Beast of Brassknocker Hill', some describing it as a chimpanzee, or a baboon; it may have been a bear or polecat; July 1979.

HANHAM   Pennies and halfpennies fell around children; September 1956.

Bedfordshire

AMPTHILL   Slab of ice fell beside three-year-old girl and mother in garden; 27 August 1983.

BEDFORD   Man saw humanoid entities near power station; February 1974. Tiny frogs and spawn fell on a rainy day; June 1979 (see Ch.1).

NEAR DUNSTABLE   Ball lightning or fireball seen to fall from clouds during thunderstorm; it damaged a barn; 11 April 1894 (see Ch.10).

EATON BRAY   Large black cat, possibly a panther, seen in undergrowth; July 1982 (see Ch.11).

HEATH-AND-REACH   Brown bear seen by three people; 8 December 1984 (see Ch.9).

HOCKLIFFE   Kangaroo or wallaby seen in the fields; mid-April 1978 (see Ch.9).

LEIGHTON BUZZARD   Black bear seen and pawprints found; 12 June 1976 (see Ch.9).

LITTLE BARFORD   Four-foot crocodile seen in the River Ouse; June 1970 (see Ch.9).

LUTON   Canteen staff at Skefco ball-bearing factory saw ghost in kitchen; November 1972.

LUTON/TEBWORTH/TODDINGTON AREA   Several sightings of a lion; chiropodist had clear sighting in car headlights; June 1981 (see Ch.11).

SHEFFORD   John Whitworth claimed he had been contacted by a UFO entity; November 1956.

STANBRIDGE   Roy Fulton, driving

home at night, picked up a hitch-hiker who vanished from the van; 12 October 1979 (see Ch.16).

STUDHAM COMMON   Children playing on the common saw 'a little blue man with a tall hat and a beard' who disappeared; 28 January 1967 (see Ch.18).

Berkshire

BRACKNELL   Lump of ice crashed through roof of parked van; 22 or 23 February 1969.

THE DOWNS   Lost walkers were shown the right track by a 'small man in green'; 1962.

HAMPSTEAD NORRIS   Ice block 15 in. long, 7 in. wide, 4 in. thick, fell into garden; 30 November 1950.

MAIDENHEAD   Thousands of tiny frogs and tadpoles fell in violent storm; *c*.1910.

READING   Football-sized lumps of ice smashed through roofs of two houses; 15 May 1976. Mrs Lucy Gmiterek died of burns, a possible victim of spontaneous human combustion; 12 November 1978 (see Ch.21). Poltergeist outbreak in the Adams family, with furniture moved and broken, crockery smashed, and many other unpleasant events; late 1979–81 (see Ch.25).

BETWEEN SUNNINGDALE AND SOUTH ASCOT   Two ladies saw ghostly vanishing policeman; early February 1900.

SWALLOWFIELD   Home hit by stones at night for many weeks, but no culprit was caught; April 1974 (see Ch.25).

WINDSOR CASTLE   Sentries on duty at night have seen ghosts, for example on 3 March 1906, in 1927 and on 22 September 1976.

WOKINGHAM   Eggs fell on a school on several occasions; early December 1974 (see Ch.1).

WIDESPREAD   Southern TV viewers heard an announcement supposedly from outer space, which drowned out the 5 p.m. news broadcast; 26 November 1977 (see Ch.20).

Buckinghamshire

CHILTERNS   Six sightings of big cat at Stokenchurch, Chinnor, Sydenham, and Halton; 16 April–7 May 1983.

ETON   Masses of pea-sized jelly containing insect eggs found on pavements, tombstones, etc.; probably fell in rain; 24 June 1911.

GREAT MISSENDEN   Handyman saw ghostly monk in Little Abbey Hotel; September 1972.

NEAR IVINGHOE   UFO at least 40 feet wide seen by car driver as it hovered over road ahead; 9 February 1962.

PENN   Hundreds of thumbnail-sized black frogs fell in a rainstorm; summer 1969.

STOKE POGES   Big cat seen by two policemen near memorial to poet Thomas Gray; 12 November 1964.

TINGEWICK   Photograph of garden tea-party showed ghost dog; *c*.1916 (see Ch.17).

Cambridgeshire

CAMBRIDGE   Blind 72-year-old

Lavinia Farrar stabbed to death in mysterious circumstances; March 1901 (see Ch.6). A variety of ghostly phenomena experienced at Abbey House over many years; 1903–at least 1980. White, gloy-like, cellular substance, football-sized, glided down during rainstorm and settled on lawn 'like a jelly'; gone by next morning; 23 June 1978.

PETERBOROUGH   P.C. Kettle saw airship pass overhead; 23 March 1909 (see Ch.7). Ghost of young man seen in Museum and Art Gallery; 1932.

TICK FEN   Poltergeist outbreak; 26 April–8 May 1897.

to the planet Zomdic in a flying saucer; 7 September 1957; he also travelled to the planet Shebic from Frodsham in November 1959.

UPTON, CHESTER   Lioness seen, then disappeared again; none missing from Chester Zoo; 23 October 1976.

WARRINGTON   Haunting of former school experienced by shop staff; 1970s (see Ch.25).

WIDNES   Jacqueline Fitzsimon, 17-year-old cookery student, burst into flames at college, a possible victim of spontaneous human combustion; 28 January 1985 (see Ch.21).

Cheshire

BICKERTON HILLS   Two youths saw big cat clearly by moonlight; January 1978.

COMBERMERE HALL   Lord Combermere photographed in the library at the time of his burial; 5 December 1891 (see Ch.4).

DELAMERE FOREST   Strange animal seen, definitely not a fox yet having a tail like a fox's brush; April 1974.

FRODSHAM   Four men poaching by the River Weaver claimed to have seen a UFO with entities who trapped a cow in a cage; 27 January 1978 (see Ch.14).

HANDFORTH AREA   Sightings of a large black cat-like animal; August 1980 (see Ch.11).

RISLEY   Ken Edwards had close encounter with 7-foot silver entity; 17 March 1978 (see Ch.22).

RUNCORN   Poltergeist outbreak; August–October 1952. James Cooke claimed he took a journey

Cornwall

DEADMAN'S COVE, NEAR HUDDER DOWN   Ghost of man in black suit standing at water's edge seen by couple; as they spoke to him he faded away; 1978.

EAST LOOE   Writer on mysteries Harold T. Wilkins, with another witness, saw two sea monsters chasing fish up the creek; 5 July 1949 (see Ch.13).

FALMOUTH   During 1976 there were many sightings of a sea monster (nicknamed Morgawr, meaning sea-giant), and photographs were taken. The first sighting was in September 1975, and Morgawr reappeared several times during the summer of 1985 (see Ch.13).

KILKHAMPTON   Three young girls saw a 'little man in a tiny red car driving around in circles'; c.1940 (see Ch.18).

LAND'S END   Three people on liner rounding Land's End saw sea-serpent with 18 feet of its body visible; August 1906 (see Ch.13).

MAWNAN   Reflected panorama of coastal scene was visible in the clouds; 24 October 1914 (see Ch.23). Children saw 'the Owlman' over the church or in the woods nearby; 17 April, 3 July 1976, *c*.4 June, 2 August 1978 (see Ch.20).

NEWMILL   Couple saw hazy green UFO close to, and others saw UFOs in sky; 17 September 1977 (see Ch.7).

NEAR REDRUTH   Small land snails of a kind unknown in the district believed to have fallen in a thunderstorm; 8 July 1886.

ST MERRYN   Two girls saw a ship in the clouds, with Little People chattering and laughing and pointing; early years of this century (see Ch.18).

NORTH OF THE SCILLY ISLES   Abandoned schooner discovered; 1919 (see Ch.15).

STITHIANS/TRURO/ST AUSTELL   Numerous sightings of big cats during December 1984 and January 1985.

TRURO   Large ice lump with air bubbles fell on garden; 6 January 1981.

SOMEWHERE IN CORNWALL   Misty fireballs seen among trees; zigzag lightning flashed where they struck the trees; 17 August 1947.

WIDESPREAD   Unexplained explosions were heard throughout Cornwall, loud enough to shake buildings; 21 December 1977, 1 January 1978.

Cumbria

NEAR APPLEBY   At a mill on the Eden, poltergeist phenomena were experienced, with bangings, voices, stone-throwing and the movement of objects; May–September 1887 (see Ch.25).

CASTLERIGG STONE CIRCLE   Walkers returning to Keswick in the dark saw white lights moving in the stone circle; one came straight towards them, but went out as it drew near; Easter, pre-1919.

CUMWHINTON   Wolf 5 feet long found dead on railway line; 29 December 1904.

RIVER LEVEN NEAR ULVERSTON   6-foot marlin, a tropical fish, seen dying in the river – the first marlin recorded in our waters; September 1983.

NEAR SOLWAY FIRTH   Photograph of girl sitting in a field also showed what can be interpreted as a figure in a spacesuit; May 1964 (see Ch.17).

WHITEHAVEN   Pet labrador awakened family when their house was on fire, then went back inside to rescue the cat; March 1985 (see Ch.24).

Derbyshire

ALVASTON, DERBY   Children heard invisible horses passing close by them, with shouts and pistol-shots; late nineteenth century.

NEAR BURNASTON   Commander H. R. Penrose claimed that after a car crash he was abducted into a flying saucer and questioned; 13 May 1954.

CASTLETON   Food items were thrown at old people's bungalows over a two-year period, including black pudding, bread and eggs; 1977–8 (see Ch.25).

DERBY   Two fires broke out spontaneously at 75 Colville Street; a housemaid was accused of theft and arson but the latter charge was dropped because she was not in the house when the fires started; 4 March 1905.

NEAR EDALE   Ball of light passed through wire fence before climbing into sky; 27 August 1984 (see Ch.10). Large black mystery animal was slaughtering sheep at night and leaving the carcases dismembered and strewn about; October 1925.

HARDWICK HALL   Phantom monk seen in grounds on several occasions, including 4 January 1976.

ILKESTON   Man feeding his ducks found large black cat-like animal curled up in his orchard; early February 1983.

NETHERSEAL COLLIERY   Live toad found in coal 200 yards below ground; May 1919 (see Ch.3).

NEAR UPPER BOOTH   Girl saw black dog which passed through wire-mesh fence; 1930 (see Ch.5).

Devon

AYLESBEARE   Genette Tate disappeared without trace from a lane near her home; 19 August 1978 (see Ch.15).

BESIDE BARNSTAPLE–ILFRACOMBE ROAD   Twenty-three small live frogs found inside concrete block; some years before 1972 (see Ch.3).

BIDEFORD   Two postmen going to

work at 6 a.m. saw a huge cross in the sky, centred on the full moon. The beams of light forming the arms gradually faded after ten minutes; 7 December 1984.

NEAR BLACKMOOR GATE   Bus driver thought he had run into a black dog herding three sheep, but there were no animals to be found; 1939.

NEAR CHUDLEIGH KNIGHTON   Large black cat ran across road in front of motorcyclist who narrowly missed hitting it; other sightings of cats on Dartmoor; February 1983.

DARTMOOR   Several witnesses saw unexplained bright lights rise from the ground to 50 or 60 feet, move a short distance, then vanish; investigated by Military Intelligence as illicit signalling was suspected, but no spies appear to have been caught; summer and autumn 1915. Black dog's visit to farmhouse caused electrical failure, broken windows and a damaged roof; winter 1972. Unidentified man found dead in mysterious circumstances; February 1976 (see Ch.6). Border Collie lost on the moor found its way home, 30 miles including crossing roads and a motorway; May 1985 (see Ch.24).

EXETER   Three attempts were made to hang convicted murderer John Lee, and three times the trap failed to function; Lee was then given life imprisonment; 23 February 1885 (see Ch.20). Giant tropical fruit bat found clinging to car radiator; September 1984 (see Ch.9).

EXMOOR   'The Exmoor Beast'

created havoc on the north Devon/Somerset border beginning February 1983, killing 150–200 sheep and lambs between then and the end of June; many sightings of a large cat which proved impossible to corner and kill; sightings still being reported late in 1984.

EXMOUTH   Ice block smashed through bedroom ceiling; 19 June 1984 (see Ch. 1).

GULWORTHY   Jack Russell terrier ran 1½ miles to fetch its master from work after burglars raided the home; May 1985 (see Ch.24).

NEAR HAYTOR   Several individuals have seen a phantom cottage in a wood; c.1960 and later (see Ch.12).

IVYBRIDGE   Poltergeist outbreak in council house – creaking, tapping, musty smells, screaming, and smoky forms; November 1984 (see Ch.25).

LYDFORD   Farmer saw strange animal, calf-size and black but not a dog, among the sheep and lambs at night; 5 April 1982.

MANSANDS NEAR DARTMOUTH Man out walking saw a phantom landscape at the cliff edge; March 1938 (see Ch.12).

MILTON COMBE   Man in car saw phantom horse and cart which faded away; 1962 (see Ch.12).

BETWEEN MODBURY AND GARA BRIDGE   Several people have encountered a ghostly Daimler car on this narrow road; July 1964, 1967, September 1975 (see Ch.12).

MORCHARD BISHOP   Dark ball lightning shot out sparks of fire; 13 May 1906 (see Ch.10).

NEWTON ABBOT AREA   Big cat seen at Mile End and East Orwell; August 1984.

NEWTON ABBOT   Christine Middlehurst received serious burns in mysterious circumstances, a possible case of spontaneous human combustion; 24 December 1984 (see Ch.21).

NEAR NORTH MOLTON   A sheep killed by chunk of ice which fell from sky; November 1950 (see Ch.1).

OKEHAMPTON   Pony-sized black dog jumped out of castle grounds and glared at woman, child and donkey; c.1910.

NEAR OKEHAMPTON   Porcupines living wild, and breeding; early 1970s (see Ch.9).

PLYMOUTH   Falling ice chunks smashed through the roofs of a house and bungalow, just missing children in bedroom; 28 September 1980. Denise Bishop was burned on the hand by a light beam from a UFO; 10 September 1981 (see Ch.6). 'Red fiery circular object' dropped from sky, then shot up again; 13 February 1983 (see Chs 7 and 10).

POSTBRIDGE   Several unexplained accidents on road into Postbridge, and one motorcyclist said his hands were gripped by two rough and hairy hands; 1921; a woman staying in a caravan nearby also saw the hands at the window; 1924 (see Ch.20).

PRAWLE POINT   Sea captain and two others saw 20-foot sea-serpent; 5 July 1912 (see Ch.13).

SCORITON   E. A. Bryant claimed to have seen a flying saucer at close quarters and spoken to its occupants; 24 April 1965.

NEAR SHAUGH BRIDGE, DARTMOOR Child saw a pixie with a little pointed hat; 1897 (see Ch.18).

START Two ladies saw a phantom manor house; November 1939 (see Ch.12).

STOKE Vicar saw phantom monk who vanished in churchyard; 1973.

TEDBURN ST MARY AREA Sightings of big black cat; lorry-driver saw it twice in his headlights; children saw it prowling through woods and it chased off two dogs; February 1981.

TOPSHAM Fall of small pink beans or seeds, fresh not dried, in back garden; early March 1983.

UPLYME The legendary ghost of the Black Dog Inn seen by three holiday-makers – the black dog floated across the lane on the Devon/Dorset border from hedge to hedge in front of them; autumn 1959.

WARREN HOUSE INN, DARTMOOR Black dog ran alongside man on pony before vanishing; c.1924.

WASHFIELD Black dog seen by lad on road at Worth; he kicked at it and nearly fell over as it vanished. Dog seen by another man soon after; c.1887.

WESTWARD HO! 60–90-foot sea monster with brownish-grey scaly body seen; 1911.

NEAR WITHERIDGE Colonel Haines watched for three minutes an animal he could not identify: calf-sized, pug nose, large head, black eyes, brown in colour, three black spots on hindquarters, ridge of 2-inch hair along spine, long legs, long ropy tail; June 1969.

WOOLACOMBE Dead man found kneeling on beach with head buried in the sand; April 1982 (see Ch.6).

YEALMPTON Vicar and wife saw a deep hole in the church path, which had disappeared when they returned with planks to cover it; late 1940s (see Ch.20).

NEAR YEO MILL Driver saw tall black dog with green eyes that disappeared as he looked; 31 October 1984.

YELVERTON Mystery animal thought to be responsible for slaughter of hundreds of chickens; July 1984.

SOMEWHERE IN DEVON A fireball (ball lightning?) was seen travelling against the wind and tearing up the ground for 100 yards; it also killed a man; 18 December 1895.

Dorset

BOTTLEBUSH DOWN Archaeologist saw ghostly horse and rider, possibly from 3,000 years ago; 1924 (see Ch.8).

BOURNEMOUTH 'One day we had a violent thunderstorm. Having no shelter, I was wet to the skin in a few minutes, and saw small yellow frogs, about the size of a florin or half-crown, dashed on the ground all around me . . . Thousands were impaled on the furze bushes on the common close by, and days afterwards the stench from the decomposing bodies was very noticeable'; c.1891. Glowing object 5 inches across, shaped like a jellyfish, seen by three people before it flew out to sea; October 1969 (see Ch.10).

BOURNEMOUTH, POOLE AND CHRISTCHURCH Many pieces of

coke (some over 2 in. wide) fell over a wide area during thunderstorm; 5 June 1983.

OFF BOURNEMOUTH   25 miles out over the Channel, an aircraft's instruments went haywire; October 1978 (see Ch.20).

BRANKSOME, BOURNEMOUTH   Woman saw strange animal she later identified as a Tasmanian marsupial wolf; 7 April 1974.

DURWESTON   Poltergeist outbreak, with objects moving unnaturally slowly; 13 December 1894–c.March 1895 (see Ch.25).

FISHPOND BOTTOM   Inexplicable illness experienced by inhabitants and attributed to presence of electricity pylons; 1970s.

MORCOMBELAKE   Sightings of 'cats the size of sheepdogs' on National Trust land; also sightings in 1981; March 1983.

POOLE   Rain shower followed by fall of hay, grass, and clumps of grass with roots and soil, seen to be coming from rain cloud overhead; 8 August 1977 (see Ch.1).

ST IVES   The head and shoulders of a crucified Christ could be seen on a hen-house wall; mid-August 1976 (see Ch.17).

NEAR SHAFTESBURY   Traveller saw 'false dawn' at 5 a.m.; the light disappeared after twenty minutes and it was dark again; 7 January 1933 (see Ch.23).

TUCKTON, BOURNEMOUTH   Little balls of damp sand fell on numerous occasions; summer 1984.

WINTON, BOURNEMOUTH   Sheet of off-white or dove-grey liquid fell from sky on to traffic; no aircraft seen; 24 July 1984.

Durham

NEAR BARNARD CASTLE   Motorcyclist saw UFO which gave off heat and drained power from his engine; 6 June 1977.

DARLINGTON   19-year-old Vicky Gilmour burst into flames at a disco, a possible case of spontaneous human combustion; November 1980 (see Ch.21).

PETERLEE   Houses showered with stone chippings overnight; 21/ 22 June 1980 (see Chs 1 and 25).

Essex

ALPHAMSTONE   Greyhound-like creature seen inside dog-proof chicken-run; ran out through netting which was undamaged; late 1940s (see Ch.5).

NEAR AVELEY   Couple travelling by car lost three hours, and later discovered under hypnosis that they had been abducted into a UFO; 27 October 1974.

BASILDON   Wild boar known to be living in scrubland; dug up gardens and was seen grazing with horses; December 1979, January 1980 (see Ch.9).

BILLERICAY   Two sightings of big cat, thought to be a lioness; 29 May 1982 (see Ch.11).

BORLEY   Borley Rectory was dubbed 'the most haunted house in England' by psychic investigator Harry Price following reports of a variety of phenomena over many years: ghosts, voices, scratchings and other sounds, poltergeist phenomena – in fact anything you care to name seems to have happened there. It was built in 1863 and destroyed by fire in 1939. Great controversy followed Price's writings on Borley Rectory, and doubts were voiced as to whether the house was haunted at all. However, other people independent of Price saw ghosts and experienced other phenomena around the rectory site and the church. For example, Dr Margaret Abernethy, passing in her car, clearly saw a nun in the overgrown rectory entrance; she appeared to be a normal person, and smiled. The doctor decided to offer her a lift to the convent three miles away, so she stopped and backed up, but there was no nun to be seen, although the doctor searched for her; August 1949.

CHELMSFORD   22-year-old Phyllis Newcombe burst into flames at a dance, a possible victim of spontaneous human combustion; 27 August 1938 (see Ch.21).

COLCHESTER   On three separate nights, soldiers were 'struck senseless by an unseen assailant'; 24–29 April 1911 (see Ch.6).

EPPING   Ball lightning burst inside a house; 26 July 1893.

FOBBING   Two sightings of large sandy cat-like animal; 12, 25 August 1982 (see Ch.11).

NEAR HADLEIGH   Imposing Georgian house seen which later could not be located, and therefore was probably phantom; c.1946 (see Ch.12).

HALSTEAD   Cat woke owner and alerted him to a house-fire; December 1984 (see Ch.24).

HORNDON-ON-THE-HILL   Three sightings of a black cat-like animal, two on farmland and one in town; 4 and 11 November 1983.

LANGENHOE   Rector saw several ghosts and experienced poltergeist phenomena in church; 1937–1950s. In the haunted church, the white impression of a woman's hand was seen on the vestry door; 28 January 1951. Motorcyclist physically affected by close presence of UFO; 14 September 1965 (see Ch.7).

PITSEA   Large black cat seen; May 1976.

ROCHFORD/HAWKWELL AREA   Two sightings of a big cat, but police and tracker dogs found nothing; April 1978.

SCRAPFAGGOT GREEN, GREAT LEIGHS   Poltergeist outbreak following the moving of a large stone said to mark a witch's burial-place; October 1944.

SOUTHEND   A rare tropical fish found alive in the water under Southend Pier; August 1973.

STANFORD RIVERS   Motorcyclist found woman's leg inside laced boot and stocking; 1925.

THAMES ESTUARY   Two seamen saw the neck and head of a sea-serpent 8–10 feet high; August 1923.

SOMEWHERE IN ESSEX   During thunderstorm, fireball descended and exploded, 'casting darts' in all directions; 13 April 1904 (see Ch.10).

Gloucestershire

BROCKWORTH   Grey, bell-shaped UFO seen hovering above field; November 1939 (see Ch.7). Workman who had forgotten to pack a knife in his lunchbox suddenly saw a brand-new knife at his feet; February 1956 (see Ch.15).

GREAT BADMINTON Mystery animal was killing sheep, sucking the blood and leaving the flesh untouched; October 1905.

WESTBURY-ON-SEVERN Farmers were hunting a large black cat, 'four times the size of a domestic cat', which they feared would attack their livestock; November 1985.

Greater London

ADELPHI THEATRE, STRAND Many sightings of a male ghost, possibly actor William Terriss.

ANERLEY Ice block smashed 2-foot hole in house roof; 24 June 1981.

BATTERSEA Flows of copper coins and chunks of coal in a house – poltergeist?; January 1928.

CARSHALTON Policeman captured runaway porcupine in a dustbin; 4 October 1982.

CHISWICK HOUSE Ghostly smell of eggs and bacon experienced at irregular intervals; ghost researcher Andrew Green smelled it in the early 1970s.

COVENT GARDEN Woman experienced timeslip when she saw a man running towards her and the incident was then immediately repeated; early autumn 1982 (see Ch.20).

CRANFORD Layer of 'soot' in a park is identified as spores of a black fungus parasitic on grasses but found only in New Zealand; source unknown; 1969.

CROYDON Many large stones thrown at a house in Allen Road, but police could find no trace of the culprit; October 1973 (see Ch.25).

DAGENHAM Three-year-old boy regularly saw ghost he called 'The Bloke'; early 1973.

EALING COMMON On old coaching route, phantom coach and horses seen, which vanished as they neared the main traffic flow on Uxbridge Road; 1976 (see Ch.12).

EAST DULWICH Lizard-like animal 3 ft. long found killed by traffic; 11 March 1962 (see Ch.9).

EAST END 'Jack the Ripper', whose identity is still unknown though the subject of much speculation, murdered five women from 31 August to 9 November 1888 (see Ch.6).

ENFIELD Large piece of ice smashed through house roof and ceiling; 2 January 1977.
Poltergeist outbreak in council house – objects thrown, children levitated, furniture moved, stones thrown – beginning 31 August 1977, ending 1979 (see Ch.25).

EUSTON ROAD UNDERPASS 15-year-old Peter Watts found dying in unusual circumstances; 19 January 1976 (see Ch.6).

FULHAM Ice block, weighing 50–65 lb., fell on a block of flats and sent debris crashing into the street below; 24 January 1975.

GREENWICH Lighterman John Gobbett was found dead in the Thames and the body was identified by his wife and others. He had several distinguishing features: a long scar on his leg, which had been broken and badly mended; a scar on his nose; and a birthmark. After burial, Mrs Gobbett received a letter saying her husband was coming home, and he arrived the next day; *c*.1904. Compare the 1907 'death' of Albert Steer (Ch.6).

HACKNEY MARSHES Children saw a bear and found pawprints; 27 December 1981 (see Ch.9).

HAM COMMON Two men claimed to have seen a landed airship and spoken to the two men travelling in it; 13 May 1909.

HAMMERSMITH 69-year-old widow found dead, a possible victim of spontaneous human combustion; 29 January 1958.

HAMPTON COURT PALACE Many ghosts have been seen in the palace and grounds, the most famous being Catherine Howard who haunts the 'Haunted Gallery'.

HER MAJESTY'S THEATRE, HAYMARKET Ghost sometimes seen, perhaps of former manager John Buckstone.

HOUNSLOW Many tiny frogs fell during a storm; *c*.1910.

ISLEWORTH Lump of ice crashed through conservatory roof; 16 August 1970.

MINCING LANE During a storm, the lightning made a photograph or 'keranograph' of a waste-paper basket on the office floor; 9/10 July 1923 (see Ch.17).

NEWHAM Several small fish (flounders and smelts) found on roof, others reported nearby, but none actually seen to fall; 27/28 May 1984.

NORTH KENSINGTON Many witnesses claimed to have seen a ghost double-decker bus which had even caused motorists to have fatal accidents as they swerved to avoid it; early and mid-1930s (see Ch.12).

PECKHAM Someone was attacking garden walls, and between July and September 1977 had damaged or destroyed twenty-five.

PINNER Ice cube 18 in. square smashed into car bonnet, narrowly missing Mrs N. Wildsmith cleaning the car; ice yellow-brown in colour; 25 March 1974.

ROMFORD Block of ice at least 2 ft square fell on golf course from clear sky, leaving hole in ground; 11 October 1980 (see Ch.1).

RUISLIP Clumps of grass, roots and earth floated slowly down from clouds; June 1942 (see Ch.1).

SHOOTER'S HILL Lorry-driver David Back's sighting of a big cat with long legs and long pointed tail in south-east London led to a big-game hunt covering 850 acres and involving 126 policemen with 21 dogs; large footprints found, but no cat; sighting 18 July 1963.

SOUTHGATE After heavy shower, road swarmed with tiny frogs half-inch long; 17 August 1921.

SOUTH WOODFORD Showers of small stones fell on a house in Grove Road, but police found no clues; 9–14 August 1920 (see Ch.25).

STEPNEY GREEN Young man was suddenly engulfed in flames, a possible victim of spontaneous human combustion, except that he survived; 25 May 1985 (see Ch. 21).

SYDENHAM 68-year-old Euphemia Johnson was burned to death in her room, a possible victim of spontaneous human combustion; summer 1922 (see Ch.21).

RIVER THAMES NEAR CHELSEA
BRIDGE Drowned man
identified as Albert Steer, who
two months later turned up
alive; 1907 (see Ch.6).

THEATRE ROYAL, DRURY LANE
Several different ghosts,
including that of Dan Leno, seen
by many witnesses over the
years.

TOWER OF LONDON Many ghosts
have been seen here, including
that of Anne Boleyn whose
headless ghost was seen by a
sentry in 1933; she has also been
seen inside the Chapel of St
Peter ad Vincula where she is
buried. Also seen in recent
decades are Catherine Howard
and Lady Jane Grey.

WALTHAMSTOW Alfred Bolton's
crucifix shed tears on many
occasions; May–June 1966 (see
Ch.2).

WIMBLEDON During daytime, it
became dark for ten minutes;
there was no storm or smoke to
cause it; 15 April 1904 (see
Ch.23).

Greater Manchester

BOLTON Teenage girl saw UFO
close to, and later became ill;
other strange events occurred;
23 January 1976. Pilot flying
Cessna saw white UFO, then two
others; 11 December 1979 (see
Ch.7).

COLLYHURST Mother and two
young children saw ghost of
murdered woman in their flat,
the last occasion being 12
November 1972.

GREENFIELD Two workers at
paper-mill saw ghost on jetty
where an electrician had

drowned; July 1967.

LEIGH Woman saw silvery sphere
and entity in silver suit; 11 May
1976.

LITTLE LEVER Woman saw UFO
entities in her bedroom;
beginning spring 1964.

MANCHESTER Ice block *c*.4½ lb.
fell in Burton Road and was
collected and analysed by
scientist; 2 April 1973 (see
Ch.1).

NEW MOSTON Council house
bombarded with bricks, stones
and milk bottles, no culprit
found; May 1969 (see Ch.25).

NORTH REDDISH Children saw
UFO and entity in silver
one-piece suit, who scooped up
soil in a shovel and placed it in a
bag; late August 1976 (see
Ch.14).

OLDHAM Huge UFO,
saucer-shaped with a dome,
hovered over Cairo Mill; 8
October 1972 (see Ch.7).

PARTINGTON Huge UFO glided
silently overhead, seen by several
people; 14 November 1977.

REDDISH Fall of many coins in
churchyard; 28 May 1981.

ROCHDALE Huge UFO with many
coloured lights moved slowly
overhead; 23 January 1982.

STANDISH Mill-worker saw
floating ghost of local rector who
had died in 1938; 1963.

TRAFFORD PARK Winged cat made
its home in builder's yard; date
unknown, pre-1975 (see Ch.24).

WHITEFIELD Man saw two 6-ft
men who disappeared; 26 June
1959 (see Ch.22).

Hampshire

ALDERSHOT Albert Burtoo,

fishing in canal late at night, was taken by entities into landed UFO, and then turned out because he was too old for their purpose; 12 August 1983.

NEAR ASHURST 'Leopard like' animal jumped out of bushes in front of girl cycling home; 4 February 1965. Many other New Forest sightings of big cats in the mid-1960s and early 1970s.

BEAULIEU ABBEY The sound of chanting has been heard, and phantom monks seen, by visitors including Christine Little in 1977.

BEDHAMPTON Lynx-like animal with black tufted ears seen in field; 21 May 1985.

BURITON Several sightings of a ghostly friar at various locations in recent years.

BUTLOCK'S HEATH Mr and Mrs John Kiley were burned to death in their home, possible victims of spontaneous human combustion; 25/26 February 1905 (see Ch.21).

CADNAM Ice block crashed through a kitchen ceiling; 4 July 1985.

EWSHOT/CRONDALL AREA Big cat made periodic appearances on Bushylease Farm, seen and heard by farm manager, also its footprints and claw marks on tree trunks; 1962–4.

GRAYSHOTT Three observations of drizzle falling from a cloudless sky; 29 December 1929, early January 1931, 3 January 1933 (see Ch.23).

HOOK, ODIHAM, HARTLEY WINTNEY AREA Several witnesses saw wild boars; one was captured, another shot; August–September 1972 (see Ch.9).

LYNDHURST Bucket-sized lump of ice smashed through house roof and ceiling; 14 April 1980.

NEW FOREST, NEAR BEAULIEU ABBEY Family on holiday came across lake with a boulder in which a sword was embedded; afterwards unable to find the place again; 1952 (see Ch.12).

ROMSEY Alleged UFO landing at Broadlands, the Mountbatten home; witness saw entity in blue overalls; mid- to late 1950s.

SOUTHAMPTON Half-man half-beast appeared at the home of Dr Anne Ross who was examining the 'Hexham heads'; 1972 (see Ch.22). Falls of millions of mustard and cress seeds, also beans and peas; 12 February 1979 and other times (see Ch.1).

WINCHESTER Prisoner from Winchester jail cleaning out dungeons at the castle saw ghost disappear through wall 2 feet thick; October 1973.

NEAR WINCHESTER Joyce Bowles and Ted Pratt together claimed two UFO encounters, the first when a UFO entity looked at them inside their car, the second when they were abducted into a UFO; Mrs Bowles had a third encounter, when she was given a message; 14 November 1976, 30 December 1976, March 1977.

WOODLANDS Three young brothers and their Alsatian dog saw a big cat, possibly a puma, and their mother found large pawprints in mud; September 1972.

YATELEY Block of ice made 3-in. dent in lawn: 'It was uncanny. I heard a noise and saw this object coming down at a terrific speed. It plunged through the trees and smashed into the ground' (Joan Brazier); 28 September 1981.

WIDESPREAD Southern TV viewers heard an announcement supposedly from outer space, which drowned out the 5 p.m. news broadcast; 26 November 1977 (see Ch.20).

Hereford and Worcester

NEAR BEWDLEY Man walking at night near Tickenhill House saw phantom black dog with glowing eyes; 24 December 1943.

BREDON Child taking afternoon nap saw enormous black dog in bedroom, with glowing red eyes; *c*.1942.

Hertfordshire

BUSHEY Falling ice chunk just missed girl in garden; 12 August 1983.

CHISWELL GREEN Policeman saw '2 ft high, grey cat' at Plaistow Farm; 15 July 1971.

CUFFLEY Lioness seen by three witnesses including policeman; 16 May 1983.

GOFFS OAK Several sightings of a large black cat; 15 August, October and unknown dates, 1983.

HERTFORD Two children in the garden saw tiny biplane with a tiny pilot; 1929 (see Ch.18).

HITCHIN Falling ice block demolished part of garage roof; 30 August 1983.

NEAR HOLWELL Publishing executive saw ghostly soldiers sitting round blazing fires; 1935.

STEVENAGE An unusual rain, like 'a shower of luminous particles', fell from a cloudless sky; 22 July 1888 (see Ch.23). Baby alligator found at road junction; August 1975 (see Ch.9).

Humberside

ANLABY Boy saw UFO land on school's flat roof; three entities climbed out and walked around; 18 January 1978.

BRIDLINGTON Woman on clifftop received mystery blow to head; September 1954 (see Ch.6). 12-oz. hermit crab fell through car windscreen (possibly dropped by seagull?); early February 1984.

EASINGTON Woman on beach saw sea monster, green, with a flat head, protruding eyes and a long flat mouth; shortly after World War II (see Ch.13).

OFF FLAMBOROUGH HEAD Trawler nets burst by elephant which got away (alive or dead, not known); mid-March 1960.

GRIMSBY Ball of fire during thunderstorm exploded on chimney stack which collapsed and killed man standing beneath; 1923.

HATCLIFFE During thunderstorm, ball lightning hovered in kitchen for three seconds before vanishing without causing damage or injury; 24 April 1979.

HILSTON Baylis family saw a sea monster with several humps; early August 1945 (see Ch.13).

KINGSTON UPON HULL Girl saw UFO with two entities looking out of windows at her; summer 1954. John Scarah saw man in boiler suit late at night in the

street, who stared at him and then
vanished; autumn 1968. Small
silver notecase marked with
Lithuanian name fell on to
Lynne Connolly's head; *c.*21
October 1975 (see Ch.1). Police
constable on early morning
patrol saw three figures dancing
in a field, who disappeared as he
approached; 10 August 1977.

SCUNTHORPE Lump of ice over a
foot long smashed through
house roof and ceiling; 10
August 1974.

WAWNE About twenty children at
primary school saw silver UFO;
18 November 1977.

Isle of Man

CASHEN'S GAP Gef, the talking
mongoose, haunted a remote
house for several years; 1931–5
(see Ch.25).

NEAR RAMSEY Man met phantom
black dog with fiery eyes; 1927
(see Ch.5).

SOMEWHERE ON THE ISLE OF MAN
Man saw Little People dressed in
red, drilling like soldiers; 1911
(see Ch.18).

Isle of Wight

NEAR BEMBRIDGE Strange animal
shot: it had a head like a large
fox, a shaggy mane, body almost
hairless, large paws; 1940.

CHILLERTON Farmer discovered a
white bull calf among the
Hereford calves in his shed;
January 1984 (see Ch.15).

EAST COWES Smoke billowed out
of old tree trunk, no apparent
cause; April 1974 (see Ch.24).

AROUND HAVENSTREET Couple
driving at night saw phantom

landscape with figures, possibly
soldiers; 4 January 1969.

NEAR SANDOWN AIRPORT Girl and
boy met 7-ft entity who showed
them inside his 'hut'; early May
1973 (see Ch.22).

WIDESPREAD Many sightings of
big cats during the period
1979–85. 1985 sightings at
Merstone, Brighstone Down,
Ningwood, Cowes, Littleton
Down, Ryde area.

Kent

BILSINGTON Two schoolgirls saw
creature like 'the abominable
snowman'; early May 1961 (see
Ch.22).

BLUE BELL HILL NEAR CHATHAM
Many reports of a phantom
hitch-hiker being seen on the
hill. Maurice Goodenough hit a
young girl who later
disappeared; 13 July 1974 (see
Ch.16).

CHATHAM Four-year-old girl
disappeared from her bed,
reappearing there twenty
minutes later; July 1966 (see
Ch.15).

CHERITON, FOLKESTONE
Poltergeist outbreak; late
October–November 1917.

CHILHAM Large black cat or dog
seen near ancient mound; January
1947 (see Ch.5).

CLIFTONVILLE Two witnesses saw
sea monster with horse's ears;
summer 1950.

DARTFORD Author J. Temple
Thurston found dead in his
home, a possible victim of
spontaneous human combustion;
6 April 1919 (see Ch.21).

EASTRY Ghost appeared on

photograph of church interior; 1956 (see Ch.4).

FAVERSHAM   Sandy-coloured big cat with long thin tail seen in garden; 30 August 1985.

FAVERSHAM AREA   Several sightings of a large black cat; January 1979.

GOODWIN SANDS   Abandoned schooner discovered; 1919 (see Ch.15).

ISLE OF SHEPPEY   Driver saw helmeted silver-suited figure loping down bank at night; 22 March 1979 (see Ch.22).

LAMBERHURST   A horse missing from its stall was found in the adjoining hay room, but the doorway was too narrow to release it; May 1906 (see Ch.15).

PADDOCK WOOD   Two cyclists saw ghost of old lady cross the road ahead of them and vanish into the hedge; late May 1912.

RAMSGATE   Forty or fifty pennies fell during fifteen minutes one day early in November 1968.

SANDLING PARK, HYTHE   Four young people saw bright 'star' above the woods, which then landed, and they saw a black, human-sized, but headless figure with bat's wings coming across the field towards them; 16 November 1963.

SANDWICH   Yachtsman saw crocodile basking on bank of River Stour; 29 July 1975 (see Ch.9).

SEVENOAKS   Huge chunks of ice smashed roof, fell into garden, and dented car; 18 August 1968. Driver thought he had hit a woman crossing the road, but there was no body to be found; 14 June 1979 (see Ch.4).

SEVENOAKS BYPASS   Woman driving along dual carriageway at night saw phantom road; this phenomenon may have been partly responsible for inexplicable fatal crashes here in 1977–9; March 1979 (see Ch.12).

BETWEEN TONBRIDGE AND SEVENOAKS   After mysterious attacks on sheep, gamekeeper killed a jackal; 1 March 1905 (see Ch.9).

WHITSTABLE   Just before 7 a.m., Alice Camburn saw 'a large black cloud with a distinct crucifixion-like cross in . . . the centre'. It was white and seemed to be illuminated; it was seen for twenty minutes; 25 December 1977.

Lancashire

ACCRINGTON   Fall of at least 300 apples (Bramley and Cox) on gardens in East Crescent overnight; residents woken by 'thundering noises on the roof'; the fall continued for an hour or more; 8/9 November 1984.

BASHALL EAVES   John Dawson murdered by hand-made bullet, and his ghost haunts the spot; spring 1934 (see Ch.6).

BLACKPOOL   Dorothy Smith died in unusual circumstances; 3 January 1974.

CHIPPING   Woman, daughter and two dogs saw three ghosts; one dog was terror-stricken and died a week later; late December 1966 (see Ch.4).

CLOWBRIDGE RESERVOIR, DUNNOCKSHAWE   8-ft figure dressed in white briefly seen before vanishing; 28 July 1977 (see Ch.22).

FLEETWOOD   During

thunderstorm, two witnesses saw spiked ball lightning floating indoors before disappearing with a crack or pop; 3 December 1979 (see Ch.10).

FOULRIDGE   Many sightings of a ghostly little man with a bleeding severed arm at a farm near Lake Burwain; late 1950s.

NEAR HAMBLETON   Phantom black cat, the 'Pigtail Cat', recorded many times over 200 years, seen by Mr and Mrs Pennington who noted it left no footprints in the soft snow; 1926.

NELSON   Huge black UFO with mass of coloured lights seen by two men; 9 March 1977 (see Ch.7).

ORMSKIRK   In a field where the previous year's wheat crop died in a drought, a fine crop of wheat grew; August 1919 (see Ch.24).

PRESTON   Three motorists reported seeing a 6-ft crocodile crossing M55 motorway; 16 May 1980 (see Ch.9).

ROSSENDALE VALLEY   'Mountain lion' seen, sheep killed and cow attacked; August 1984.

UP HOLLAND   Poltergeist outbreak; *c.*July–mid-September 1904.

Leicestershire

EXTON   Several monkeys seen, said to be raiding dustbins and greenhouses; early September 1979.

LEICESTER   Alligator found in garden in Westleigh Avenue; early August 1966 (see Ch.9). Ice block smashed through bungalow roof leaving 10-ft hole and wrecking kitchen; 23 October 1984.

SOMEWHERE IN LEICESTERSHIRE Live toad found in lump of coal; 1910 (see Ch.3).

WIDESPREAD   Large triangular UFO moved north-north-west through the county and was seen by many witnesses; 23 October 1978 (see Ch.7).

Lincolnshire

BINBROOK   Poltergeist activity at a farm was followed by a possible case of spontaneous human combustion, when a servant girl received severe burns; January 1905 (see Ch.21).

BLYBOROUGH   Irishman working on potato harvest was followed by large ghost dog along road by fishpond, known to be haunted by black dog; 1934.

BLYTON/NORTHORPE AREA   Three sightings of a monkey 2 ft tall; August 1976.

CHAPEL ST LEONARDS   Man and wife saw humped sea monster; mid-October 1966 (see Ch.13).

HORNCASTLE   Man delivering milk on a winter evening saw 'two great bright shining eyes' in the centre of the path ahead of him. He stood and watched until the eyes were suddenly 'just blotted out'. He later found the spot was reputedly haunted, and a workmate claimed to have seen the eyes too; winter 1922–3.

SALTFLEET   UFO with coloured lights directed light beam on to witnesses; 22 April 1984 (see Ch.7).

SKEGNESS   Police surgeon and police constable watched sandy-coloured cat 5 ft long, after several sightings in the grounds of a convalescent home; September 1976.

STAMFORD Monkeys seen swinging through trees; early September 1979.

STURTON/STOWE AREA A field left fallow sprouted a fine crop of wheat; June 1919 (see Ch.24).

TRUSTHORPE Schoolboy saw sea monster with huge snake-like body; summer 1937 or 1938 (see Ch.13).

TYDD ST MARY Poltergeist outbreak at Hannath Hall: thumps and raps, footsteps and groans; August–November 1957 (see Ch.25).

WEST ASHBY Baker's roundsman saw phantom cyclist who startled his horse; late 1920s (see Ch.4).

Merseyside

BLUNDELLSANDS Flames burst out of mudflat with a strong smell of sulphur; 5 June 1902 (see Ch.23).

GARSTON Man working in ship-breaking yard saw tall figure with brush of hair and dressed in breeches; November 1951 (see Ch.22).

HUYTON Several people saw 9-ft entity in garden; early 1977 (see Ch.22).

LIVERPOOL Ball lightning fell into a lake and sent up a column of water 60 ft high; 3 July 1892. During thunderstorm, three lots of ball lightning flew into kitchen, causing no damage; 28 May 1901 (see Ch.10). Children saw little green men throwing stones and clods of earth; summer 1964 (see Ch.18). Ghostly policeman, killed in an air raid, appeared on his regular

beat in Lawrence Gardens; August 1971.

ST HELENS Revd P. R. M. Smith disappeared without trace; 27 March 1984 (see Ch.15).

SOUTHPORT When Palace Hotel, Birkdale, was being demolished, the lift moved when power was cut off; April 1969 (see Ch.25).

WEST KIRBY Football-sized chunk of ice smashed through house roof and ceiling, showering 90-year-old Mary Nickson with plaster and ice; 16 December 1980.

Norfolk

BARNHAM COMMON Big cat seen in woods; 19 April 1985.

BUXTON LAMAS Man tried to pat black dog he saw near the church, but it disappeared; his brother died at this time; 1930 (see Ch.5).

NEAR DISS Couple sitting on stile saw black dog briefly before it vanished; 1897.

DITCHINGHAM Man walking home at night saw black dog which vanished as it drew level with him; autumn 1938 (see Ch.5).

EAST RUNTON Big cat seen on railway embankment; 19 February 1964.

ECCLES Six witnesses saw sea monster 'skimming the surface of the water in a wormlike movement' in the evening; three others had seen a similar sight in the afternoon; 5 August 1936 (see Ch.13).

GORLESTON Coastguard saw black dog which vanished as it ran along beach; 19 April 1972 (see Ch.5).

GREAT YARMOUTH   Coin-collector visited shop to buy envelopes to hold coins. The shop was old-fashioned and the staff wore period costume. When he returned a week later, the shop was entirely different and the staff denied stocking the envelopes. The ones he had were dated to the 1920s – did he slip back in time? 1973.

HOLME HALE   Couple found themselves in the centre of a battle that they could hear but not see; date unknown (see Ch.8).

HOPTON   Several sightings of a ghostly old man on the A12, witnesses including Frank Colby on 23 November 1980 and Andrew Cutajar on 2 November 1981 (see Ch.4).

HUNSTANTON   People looking out to sea saw a mirage of the beach with people and objects reflected; 1 May 1949 (see Ch.23).

LANGHAM   Two lion cubs seen playing on council tip; 15 January 1975.

METTON   April Fabb disappeared somewhere along the lane to Roughton, leaving her bicycle behind; 8 April 1969 (see Ch.15).

MUNDESLEY   Four witnesses watched long-necked sea monster with five humps travelling fast through the water; August 1936 (see Ch.13).

PULHAM ST MARY   Live toad found embedded inside oak tree; 1905 (see Ch.3).

RAYNHAM HALL   The Brown Lady, a ghost seen on many occasions, was photographed walking downstairs; 19 September 1936 (see Ch.17).

STOCKTON   Farm-workers saw tiny frogs swarming on haystack after rain shower; *c*.1912.

SWANTON NOVERS   Paraffin, petrol, methylated spirits, sandalwood oil and water fell from rectory walls and ceilings; 8 August–8 September 1919 (see Ch.25).

THETFORD   Motorists on the A1066 at Snare Hill reported seeing a bear; early June 1979 (see Ch.9). Large black cat with red eyes seen in woods; April 1985.

NEAR THURTON   Black dog leapt out at man on bike, then vanished through brick wall; November 1944 or 1945.

WEST HARLING   Constant clear water trickled night and day from an old birch tree; 1939 (see Ch.24).

NORTH OF THE NORFOLK COAST   Steward on coaster saw sea monster with long neck for two minutes until it sank gently; June 1930.

SOMEWHERE IN NORFOLK   Tennis ball-sized ball lightning with four sharp points appeared inside a house; 17 May 1981.

Northamptonshire

CORBY   Woman claimed that three UFO entities spoke to her in her flat; June, early 1950s.

NEAR DAVENTRY   Raccoon found; November 1976 (see Ch.9).

KINGSTHORPE   George Dobbs saw phantom cyclist in car accident; winter 1940.

NORTHAMPTON   Chunk of ice fell into garden; 25 July 1982.

Northumberland

HEXHAM   Discovery of small stone heads followed by reports of half-animal half-man 6 ft tall; February 1972 (see Ch.22).

NEWBIGGIN-BY-THE-SEA   Albert Lancashire claimed to have been abducted into a UFO and given a medical examination; late summer 1942.

NEAR OTTERBURN   At the site of the Battle of Otterburn (1388), a woman and her taxi-driver saw ragged soldiers who faded away; November 1960 (see Ch.8).

Nottinghamshire

NOTTINGHAM   Man in bedroom saw egg-shaped ball of light which spread into sheet of greenish, then greyish, light before vanishing with a bang; 6 November 1963. Employees saw ghost of workman in North Wilford Power Station; November 1967.

SUTTON-IN-ASHFIELD   Winged cat exhibited at carnival; 1950s (see Ch.24).

TOLLERTON/NORMANTON ON THE WOLDS   Two milkmen saw a lion on 29 July; intensive police search drew a blank; on 1 August Dr John Chisholm, deputy coroner for the county, saw the lion in his garden; after a week the search was called off; July/August 1976.

WOLLATON   Youths encountered 6-ft hairy entity holding red glowing rods; autumn 1966 (see Ch.22).

WOLLATON PARK   Four children saw about 60 Little People with long white beards driving tiny cars and laughing; 23 September 1979 (see Ch.18).

Oxfordshire

ABINGDON   Eggs thrown at cars and people; mid-1977.

BENSON   Drizzle fell from a sunny, cloudless sky; 20 January 1935 (see Ch.23).

NEAR FARINGDON   Family travelling by car claimed to have been taken aboard a spaceship, where they met the Janos people and learned about their life and home; 19 June 1978.

MILTON COMMON   Custodian of Rycote Chapel saw ghost of lady in Tudor costume which vanished beneath tree; 1968.

NORTH MORETON   Toad found in skull buried 6 ft deep in church; 20 July 1900 (see Ch.3).

OXFORD   An image of the head of Dean Liddell appeared on a wall in Christ Church Cathedral; early 1920s (see Ch.17). Oscar Wilde's ghost seen in his old rooms at Magdalen College; 1934. Winged cat on show at the old Oxford Zoo; 1930s (see Ch.24).

TACKLEY   Poltergeist outbreak lasting almost three years, including all kinds of noises like footsteps, doors closing, etc., and a man's ghost was seen; April 1905–February 1908.

WALLINGFORD   For twenty minutes, many dried beech leaves fell from a great height; no beech trees within at least two miles; 1 April 1900.

WEST BOTLEY FLYOVER   Unidentified man found dead,

in possession of rare drugs; 1975 (see Ch.6).

Shropshire

BROSELEY   Toads found in rock on two occasions; 1906 (see Ch.3).

NORTHWOOD   Ghost of local woman, who was still alive, seen several times; 1928.

OSWESTRY   Fall of small frogs during heavy rainstorm; summer 1912.

PREES HEATH   Poachers saw multi-coloured floating entity; 28 February 1981.

NEAR UPPINGTON   Three women travelling by car saw a UFO; later under hypnosis they claimed to have been abducted and examined by entities; 16 July 1981.

Somerset

NEAR CHEDDAR   In mild weather, with no wind, a woman's washing was strewn over the garden and had obviously been ripped with considerable force from the dryer; July 1984 (see Ch.23).

NEAR EXFORD   Couple saw large white dog with red eyes, which presaged a death; 6 January 1978 (see Ch.5).

EXMOOR   'The Exmoor Beast' killed many sheep and lambs on the Somerset/Devon border during 1983; further sightings during 1984.

NEAR MILVERTON   Woman in car saw UFO, and claimed she was taken aboard, examined, then raped; 16 October 1973.

NUNNEY   Reports of a phantom hitch-hiker on the road to Frome; 1977.

SOUTH CADBURY   Woman visitor saw a phantom old house in a field, and two people dressed in period costume; late 1940s (see Ch.12).

WELLINGTON AREA   Several witnesses reported seeing a phantom hitch-hiker on the A38, including lorry-driver Harold Unsworth who picked him up more than once in 1958 (see Ch.16).

WIVELISCOMBE   Winged cat; November 1899 (see Ch.24).

SOMEWHERE IN SOMERSET   A rushing then a roaring noise heard in calm weather; 1887 (see Ch.23).

Staffordshire

BADDELEY GREEN   Boy saw two small men fly past his bedroom window, dressed in white with crash-helmets; autumn 1976 (see Ch.22).

BROCTON   Small entity with large head enclosed in a bowl pushed car uphill with ease; winter 1959–60 (see Ch.22).

CLIFTON CAMPVILLE   Four girls watched UFO with flashing lights; 12 December 1977 (see Ch.7).

DILHORNE   Rain of tiny shells; 22 March 1983.

LONGTON, STOKE-ON-TRENT   Ghost of old man seen in former pottery, now Gladstone Pottery Museum; 1978.

MANIFOLD VALLEY   Blue flashes seen and explosions heard at Old Hannah's Cave; late 1890s (see Ch.23).

OULTON   Two tall entities walking like astronauts on the moon seen in field; September 1971 (see Ch.22).

PERTON   Dark brown big cat about 4 ft long seen exploring partly built house; March 1981 (see Ch.11).

RANTON   Woman and children saw UFO hovering over their cottage, the two occupants gazing down at them; 21 October 1954 (see Ch.14).

THORPE CONSTANTINE   Chunk of ice 6 ft in diameter narrowly missed Eric Cooper; it whizzed past him and broke into three, the largest piece making a foot-deep hole on landing; 19 December 1975.

TITTENSOR   Glowing white UFO, travelling low over lane, seen clearly by witness; December 1977 (see Ch.7).

WALFORD NEAR ECCLESHALL   Student saw a phantom cat in the house where he was staying, and learned that the occupants saw it regularly; 1893.

A51 OPPOSITE WHITTINGTON BARRACKS   After rain-shower, road covered with frogs which jumped into gutter; August 1944.

Suffolk

ALDEBURGH   Woman saw flying platform with about twelve men standing on it; middle of World War I, *c*.1916/17 (see Ch.7).

BARSHAM   During thunderstorm, huge circle of light seen above tree; church damaged; 8 February 1906 (see Ch.10).

BECCLES   Woman in cemetery saw large white hound which faded away; 1974.

RAF BENTWATERS AND USAF LAKENHEATH   UFO showed up on radar screens and was seen by pilots; 13 August 1956.

BRADFIELD ST GEORGE   Two witnesses out walking saw phantom house, though they only discovered it was unreal when they walked the same way a few months later and found the house was missing; October 1926 (see Ch.12).

BRAMFORD   Poltergeist outbreak; November–December 1887.

DEBENHAM   Van collided with ghost in cloak and tall hat, then driver saw it running along grass verge; 4 January 1973.

ELVEDON/HONINGTON AREA   Sightings of big cat; pheasants killed; no cats missing from zoos or wildlife parks; April 1985.

HAVERHILL   'Man in Black' visited UFO witness; November 1977.

KESSINGLAND   Rider Haggard's two daughters saw a sea monster travelling very fast parallel with the shore; July 1912 (see Ch.13).

MIDDLETON   Visions of the Virgin Mary seen by rector; February 1933 (see Ch.2).

NAYLAND   Mysterious death of Sebastian Salaman, possibly murdered; 26 May 1975 (see Ch.6).

RENDLESHAM FOREST   Rumours of possible UFO landing in or close to US air base, the truth proving impossible to ascertain, though some blame lightships and stars; see Butler, Randles and Street, *Sky Crash*; late December 1980.

SOUTHWOLD   Two fishermen laying nets saw sea monster with large head, travelling very fast; 21 October 1938 (see Ch.13).

Man saw two phantom hedges near his home; 1 February 1976 (see Ch.12).

THORPENESS   Three women watched humped sea monster moving parallel to the shore at great speed; June 1931 (see Ch.13).

WETHERINGSETT   Shower of small frogs, yellow or dull green; *c*.1900.

WOODBRIDGE   Black dog ran alongside motorcyclist at 30 m.p.h.; early 1973.

SOMEWHERE IN SUFFOLK   During thunderstorm, egg-sized ball lightning entered house and exploded upstairs, causing damage to wallpaper and plaster; 20 July 1897 (see Ch.10).

Surrey

CATERHAM   Eight running men wearing black cowls seen by motorists; 28 July 1963 (see Ch.22).

EPSOM   Ice block smashed through garage roof; 29 June 1977.

SHIRLEY   Ice block 4 ft square made hole 2 ft deep in garden; 23 January 1972.

SUNBURY-ON-THAMES   Colonel Leland and his driver clearly saw phantom horse-drawn vehicle; November 1915 (see Ch.12).

WALTON HEATH   A large spotted cat, possibly a cheetah, ran across the road 25 yards ahead of witness; May 1983.

WEYBRIDGE   Ghosts seen and other phenomena experienced at the old Brooklands Racetrack; 1970s.

WOTTON   After visiting church, couple strayed into non-existent landscape and saw ghostly figures; summer 1954 (see Ch.20).

SOMEWHERE IN SURREY   At 9 a.m. light snow fell from a cloudless sky; 6 February 1895 (see Ch.23).

WIDESPREAD   Many sightings of the so-called 'Surrey puma' during the early 1960s; for the period September 1962 to August 1964 the Godalming police logged 362 sightings in their daybook; sightings have continued to the present day.

East Sussex

BEACHY HEAD   Ghosts seen here, and some people experience a compulsion to suicide. Woman in grey seen by man and dog in 1976, and again near cliff edge in 1978 (see Ch.4).

BRIGHTON   Cheetah seen lying on grassy bank; 23 December 1982 (see Ch.11). Large spider crab 25 cm across, dead and lacking two legs and a claw, dropped out of a storm cloud, followed by hailstones; 5 June 1983.

CROWBOROUGH   Nocturnal light or will-o'-the-wisp seen on several occasions, including 26 September, 1 October 1891.

EASTBOURNE   Pea-sized ball lightning came indoors and 'went out with a spitting sound' when it touched the tablecloth; 17 August 1921 (see Ch.10).

NEAR EASTBOURNE   Man walking on South Downs east of Eastbourne saw black cat-like animal 'the size of a small pony' which crossed his path 10 yards away; 30 June or 1 July 1979.

JEVINGTON AREA   Sightings of

large grey wolf-like animals; dates vague: pre-1957 and pre-World War II.

LEWES Workmen in quarry found mummified toad inside flint nodule; *c*.1900 (see Ch.3).

NEWICK Six months after pond was cleaned out and refilled, it was full of tench; May 1921 (see Ch.24).

NUTLEY Farmer had many sightings of a hyena on his farm; spring to autumn 1971 (see Ch.9).

OFFHAM HILL, LEWES Sounds of battle sometimes heard in late May on the anniversary of a battle when 3,000 men died (see Ch.8).

NEAR POLEGATE Two sightings of big cat which could run up to 35 m.p.h.; 14 June 1972.

ROBERTSBRIDGE Policeman saw ghost cyclist, said to have been killed in an accident ten years before; 1974.

SEAFORD Two people saw phantom car which vanished through sea wall; October 1976 (see Ch.12).

WESTHAM 'Man' walking down church path vanished when Michael Stone spoke to him; September 1978.

WILLINGDON Motorist collided with ghostly woman in grey at same place on two occasions; 1976, 1977 (see Ch.4).

West Sussex

ALDINGBOURNE Mrs Madge Knight suffered burning while in bed, a possible victim of spontaneous human combustion; 19 November 1943 (see Ch.21).

ARUNDEL CASTLE Young employee saw ghostly man in corridor; 1958.

HORSHAM AREA Big cat sightings; March 1975.

HURSTPIERPOINT Thirty sluggish locusts found in shrubbery; late 1982.

TILGATE FOREST Dark coloured big cat with small head, pointed ears and long tail seen by couple walking in forest; 10 September 1979.

Tyne and Wear

FENCEHOUSES Two women saw landed UFO with two entities close by, and one witness actually touched the UFO; 3 September 1976.

GATESHEAD Several children in the area saw Little People, one group were on top of a haystack and seemed to be digging, another dwarf was seen riding a cow; 2 June 1964 (see Ch.18). After several strange experiences, a woman saw tiny UFO entities indoors; 3 September 1979.

HENDON, SUNDERLAND Allotment holders observed ten-minute fall of several hundred dead sand-eels during a heavy thunderstorm; 24 August 1918 (see Ch.1).

JARROW Young golden retriever's belly was in flames – a possible case of spontaneous combustion?; 6 February 1978 (see Ch.21).

WALKER, NEWCASTLE-UPON-TYNE Theresa Taylor's plaster Madonna was seen to weep; 10 October 1955 (see Ch.2).

WALLSEND Orange sphere (ball

lightning?) hovered in bedroom before disappearing through ceiling; 8 June 1974.

WHITLEY BAY   Wilhelmina Dewar found burned to death in bed, a possible victim of spontaneous human combustion; 22 March 1908 (see Ch.21).

Warwickshire

BERMUDA VILLAGE AREA OF NUNEATON   Puma-like animal seen, but police search unsuccessful; 4 September 1976.

BURTON DASSETT   Many people saw low-level, bright, moving lights over the hills; 1923, 1924 (see Ch.23).

NEAR COOMBE ABBEY   Bud Booker saw lady on old-style bicycle who vanished as he overtook her; 1975.

FENNY COMPTON   Policeman William Hine was murdered and thrown into the canal by persons unknown for reasons unknown; robbery was not the motive; 15 February 1886.

HASELEY   Man saw ghostly woman in white by churchyard on three occasions; another time his mother saw her; late 1970s.

HASELOR   Car driver burnt by heat from cigar-shaped UFO; 13 March 1980 (see Ch.6).

NEAR KINETON   Phantom horse seen near communal graves on Edgehill battlefield; 1947 and 1950s (see Ch.8).

RUGBY–COVENTRY ROAD (A45) AT KNIGHTLOW HILL   Many drivers reported seeing a phantom lorry; after a bad crash, it was seen by a local police constable; 1950s (see Ch.12).

LEAMINGTON SPA   Chunk of ice holed house roof and ceiling; 28 July 1980.

LONG MARSTON   Two sightings of big cat, jet black, as big as a fox, and with a long bushy tail; 23 November, 3 December 1980 (see Ch.11).

MEON HILL, LOWER QUINTON   Ploughboy Charles Walton saw black dog on nine successive nights; 1885. Sixty years later, Charles Walton, now a farm-worker, was killed by a pitchfork in a still unsolved murder with overtones of black magic; 14 February 1945 (see Ch.6).

PRINCETHORPE   Walter Barlow saw ghosts of nun and priest struggling with soldiers; others saw phantom nun in the area; 1952 (see Ch.4).

NEAR STRATFORD-UPON-AVON   Woman saw malevolent fur-covered humanoid creature with pointed ears and a long muzzle; summer 1968.

West Midlands

ASTON   Cynthia Appleton claimed to have had several visits from spacemen, who spoke to her; first two visits 18 November 1957, 7 January 1958 (see Ch.14).

BIRMINGHAM   Pells family of Coxwell Road tormented by poltergeist-like phenomena; child saw ghostly white dog; summer 1955. Van driver nearing Hodge Hill Common almost ran into man, who then vanished; 1 February 1975.

NEAR BIRMINGHAM   Fall of little frogs, almost white; 30 June 1892.

BOURNEBROOK   Boy saw landed

UFO from which emerged two small entities; summer 1901 (see Ch.14).

CHADWICK END   Police officers twice saw several phantom nuns walking along road; mid-1960s.

COVENTRY   Blue-green ball lightning 2 ft across seen in garden; it moved away about a quarter of a mile and exploded, damaging public house; 10 November 1940 (see Ch.10).

ERDINGTON, BIRMINGHAM   Murder of 20-year-old Barbara Forrest has strange similarities to another murder 157 years earlier; 27 May 1974.

HALESOWEN   Blazing mop discovered in broom cupboard, a possible case of spontaneous combustion; 22 March 1981 (see Ch.21).

HANDSWORTH, BIRMINGHAM   Couple walking in Grove Lane saw bearded policeman carrying lantern who faded till only his trousers could be seen; 24 October 1968. Poltergeist outbreak – furniture moving, lights going on and off; late 1976–early 1977 (see Ch.25).

KINGS NORTON, BIRMINGHAM   Lump of ice weighing 1 lb 6 oz fell into garden; 9/10 December 1980 (see Ch.23).

MERIDEN   Flock of geese saved rabbit which was being chased by a stoat; 20 April 1985 (see Ch.24).

ROWLEY REGIS   Jean Hingley saw three tiny entities with wings flying into her living-room, where they sat and talked with her before taking off in a UFO from her lawn; 4 January 1979.

SUTTON PARK, SUTTON COLDFIELD   Thousands of tiny frogs showered on to umbrellas during rainstorm; 12 June 1954.

WARD END, BIRMINGHAM   Stones were thrown at houses in Thornton Road over several years, with no clues to the culprit despite intensive police work; beginning about 1979 (see Ch.25).

WARLEY   During thunderstorm, ball lightning appeared in kitchen; witness was injured when she touched it; 8 August 1975 (see Ch.10).

WHITEHEATH, BIRMINGHAM   Music tape picked up sounds which have been interpreted as a ghostly recording of an old mining disaster; October 1978 (see Ch.20).

WILLENHALL   Big black cat with bright red eyes seen; April 1975.

WOLVERHAMPTON AREA   Big brown cat seen in field by teacher, then seen by zoo officials, but police search was unsuccessful; July 1980 (see Ch.11).

Wiltshire

CHIPPENHAM   Block of pink ice crashed through roof; March 1985.

CRICKLADE   Children saw strange people in red and yellow one-piece suits with air tanks on their backs, running about very quickly; 18 June 1977.

NEAR DEVIZES   Male rhesus monkey injured in car accident at Black Dog crossroads; 3 August 1984.

HIGHWORTH   Four teenagers saw ghostly man with blank face inside church, 5 April 1907; verger saw white-robed ghost in church,

November 1936; there have been other reports.

MILDENHALL Four people in car saw man standing in road who vanished as they looked at him; October 1956.

RAMSBURY Samuel Bull's ghost appeared regularly to his family over two months; February–April 1932 (see Ch.4).

SALISBURY AREA Two-hour display of ball lightning hovering or darting about the sky among ordinary lightning; 18 December 1922.

NEAR SWINDON Girl cycling in a storm sought shelter at cottage she later discovered was derelict; 1930s (see Ch.20).

TROWBRIDGE Hundreds of tiny frogs seen to fall around the swimming pool in a heavy rain-shower; 16 June 1939.

WARMINSTER Marble-sized ball lightning entered kitchen and landed on electric ring where it burned fiercely; February 1981 (see Ch.10).

NEAR WARMINSTER Vibrating red light fastened itself to lorry windscreen before flying away; 10 August 1965 (see Ch.10).

North Yorkshire

NEAR BARTON Man cycling late at night saw over twenty large dogs running silently along the road; 1931 (see Ch.5).

BROUGHTON Farmer saw large sphere fall from sky; it had a chemical smell and began to melt; May 1984.

CARLETON MOOR Man and wife saw two 7-ft entities with waxy faces and pointed chins, who vanished; around 1982 (see Ch.22).

NEAR CARLETON Three witnesses including a policeman watched a low-flying, slow-moving UFO, possibly two UFOs; 24 October 1982.

FILEY BEACH Two men sailing in 10-foot boat disappeared without trace; August 1947. Two teenage sisters in an inflatable dinghy disappeared without trace; August 1985.

FILEY BRIG Coastguard saw sea monster 30 feet long on the shore; it moved into the sea when he threw stones at it; 28 February 1934 (see Ch.13).

HUTTON-LE-HOLE Mrs Lily Smith found dead of burns, a possible victim of spontaneous human combustion; 25 January 1979 (see Ch.21).

MARSTON MOOR Sightings of ghosts in period costume, possibly connected with the Civil War battle of 1644; November 1932, 1968, 1973 (see Ch.8).

NEWBY, NEAR RIPON The vicar, the Revd K. F. Lord, took photographs of the church interior, and on one a strange ghostly figure appeared; early 1960s (see Ch.17).

SKIPWITH COMMON, NEAR RICCALL Sightings of a strange animal, standing on hind legs and possibly a bear; February 1975 (see Ch.9).

THIRSK At least 30 miles from the sea, a fall of winkles (some alive) and starfish during a heavy thunderstorm; 18 June 1984.

THORGANBY Man saw big cat which he thought was a lion; it

sat with its paw raised as he walked past; 9 August 1976.

WENSLEYDALE   Cyclist saw woman in long dark dress who he later discovered to have been a ghost; 1920s.

RIVER WHARFE AREA   Wife disappeared from her family on the moors, and then reappeared; date unknown (see Ch.15).

WHITBY   Big cat seen attacking a cat; also a resident's gate was chewed away by a large animal; November 1981 (see Ch.11).

YORK   Harry Martindale, working in the cellar of the Treasurer's House, saw ghostly Roman soldiers marching past along former Roman road; 1953 (with earlier sightings by other people in 1939 and 1946) (see Ch.8). Ghost appeared at monthly intervals in museum library, searching among the books; September–December 1953 (see Ch.4). A ghostly nun has been often seen at the Theatre Royal, built on the site of the old St Leonard's Hospital founded in the twelfth century. Actors saw her twice during a rehearsal in 1975.

South Yorkshire

ATTERCLIFFE, SHEFFIELD   Winged cat; 1939 (see Ch.24).

BARNSLEY   Chihuahua knocked down by car thought to be dead and was buried in garden; family's terrier dug it up and it was found to be still alive; 13 May 1983 (see Ch.24).

DONCASTER   Child's egg decorated with Christ's face was seen to weep; Easter 1984 (see Ch.2).

HANDSWORTH, SHEFFIELD   Boy

saw 7-ft silver figure drilling a hole in the garden; 4 October 1979 (see Ch.22).

HICKLETON   Author Terence W. Whitaker saw ghostly horse and rider, in cape and tricorn hat, which vanished about 50 yards from him; June 1953.

MANOR, SHEFFIELD   Landlord Jack Wright and family saw ghost in Manor Castle pub; November 1983.

SHEFFIELD   Butterfly found inside gas meter, though there is no way it could have got there; summer 1975 (see Ch.15).

WATH UPON DEARNE   Woman burst into flames when lighting a cigarette, a possible case of spontaneous human combustion; 3 May 1981 (see Ch.21).

WOMBWELL   Chunk of ice smashed through bungalow roof; 6 lb. piece and hand-sized fragments found; 22 September 1973.

West Yorkshire

BATLEY   Death of Martha Senior in mysterious circumstances; March 1924.

BRADFORD   Lorry driver and son saw small entity in black, moving jerkily, near their home; 16 August 1955 (see Ch.22).

COTTINGLEY   Two girls claimed to have photographed fairies on several occasions from July 1917 to August 1920; over sixty years later a hoax was admitted, but the original stimulus may have been genuine fairy sightings (see Ch.18).

LEEDS   Winged cat, born in a Leeds workhouse, was on show

in a fairground; 1900 (see Ch.24).

LOCKWOOD, NEAR HUDDERSFIELD Mrs Frances Kenworthy died of burns, a possible victim of spontaneous human combustion; 4 December 1980 (see Ch.21).

MEANWOOD Two girls out sledging watched grey, egg-shaped object land in the snow; 22 February 1979 (see Ch.14).

PONTEFRACT Poltergeist outbreak in council house – water on the floor, objects moving, hooded ghost; 1 September 1966–1969 (see Ch.25).

SALTAIRE, BRADFORD Man walking beside River Aire saw white-coated animal which fought with his dog and was killed; later identified as Arctic fox; March 1983 (see Ch.9).

SHIPLEY Old dog who fell into hole was saved from death by its Alsatian friend who jumped in and kept it warm overnight till help arrived; December 1984 (see Ch.24).

TODMORDEN Zigmund Adamski found dead on coal tip with no sign of how he got there; 11 June 1980 (see Ch.6). PC Alan Godfrey saw landed UFO and later realized there had been a jump in time; under hypnotic regression he revealed he had been abducted into the UFO; 28 November 1980 (see Ch.14).

WALES

Clwyd

BERWYN MOUNTAINS Mysterious explosion, preceded by aerial lights but no trace of any meteoritic impact found; 23 January 1974. A similar explosion with lights was reported on 6 August 1976 (see Ch.20).

EWLOE Couple in car briefly saw tall entity in silver suit; 10 July 1975 (see Ch.22).

FRONCYSYLLTE Black object with short wings and four legs, looking like a pig, flew over at 20 m.p.h., about two miles high; 2 September 1905.

LLANGOLLEN About ten pieces of rock 'like hard-burned clinker' fell on house roof; June 1979.

OAKENHOLT Gaynor Sunderland saw a landed UFO and entity in July 1976 and thereafter had many strange UFO-linked experiences.

SHOTTON Man and dog saw tall entity in white padded suit in field at midnight; 10 December 1977 (see Ch.22).

WREXHAM Rain, and on a second occasion snow, fell from a cloudless sky; 5, 15 February 1955 (see Ch.23).

Dyfed

BRECHFA Several sightings of a large ginger cat which killed chickens and then killed a sheepdog tied up by the chicken run to protect them; August 1983.

NEAR CASTLEMARTIN Man saw UFO in sand dunes and spoke to its 'captain'; 1952 (see Ch.14).

FRANCIS WELL, CARMARTHEN Nocturnal light, or will-o'-the-wisp, seen a few days before a funeral following the same route; early twentieth century (see Ch. 23).

GARN FAWR MOUNTAIN, FISHGUARD   Bus-sized, yellow-green ball lightning seen floating down hillside; disappeared after three seconds; 8 June 1977 (see Ch.10).

HERBRANDSTON   Mark Marsden saw tall humanoid entity in a silvery suit; 11 April 1977; presumably connected with the large amount of UFO activity in the area during that year, some of which has been shown to be misidentification of mundane stimuli caused by UFO hysteria.

LLANILAR   Large quantity of metal debris of unknown origin fell on farmland; January 1983.

NEVERN   Yew tree in the churchyard 'bleeds'; 16,000 visitors in 1979 (see Ch.24).

NEW QUAY   Holidaymaker saw long-necked creature disturbing a seal colony; late August 1963 (see Ch.13).

PRESCELLY HILLS   Loud rushing noise heard, as if caused by a wind, but no sign of wind was seen; 15 April 1974 (see Ch.23).

TENBY CHURCH   Haunted by a priest; seen in the 1930s by lady working alone, and several times during 1960s and 1970s.

TOWY VALLEY BETWEEN LLANDEILO AND LLANDOVERY   Writer Martin Green twice saw phantom Wellington bomber flying down the valley; also seen by others; 1979 (see Ch.12).

YSBYTY YSTWYTH   Big black cat seen which was thought to have killed sheep and lambs; June 1981 (see Ch.11).

Mid Glamorgan

CAERPHILLY   Girl found 5-ft dead crocodile behind her home; March 1978 (see Ch.9).

CAERPHILLY MOUNTAIN   C. Lethbridge saw landed airship with two occupants, who left various items behind; 18 May 1909 (see Ch.7).

South Glamorgan

LECKWITH   Big cat, light brown in colour, seen on farmland and in woods; May 1977 and June 1981 (see Ch.11).

LLANDAFF   Image of Dean Vaughan, with initials DV, appeared on cathedral wall after his death; 1897 (see Ch.17).

West Glamorgan

ABERAVON   Three witnesses working in allotments saw the ghost of a man who was still alive, and at that moment at his mother's home two miles away; early years of this century.

DAN-Y-BRYN, TONNA   Hundreds of dried peas fell over several minutes; 7 or 8 April 1980.

MARGAM FOREST   Forester saw big cat with spots and stripes; 1978.

SWANSEA   Woman mysteriously transported (teleported?) over a wall; July 1887 (see Ch.15). Fragments of black glassy material fell in Norfolk Street, later identified as industrial refractory material and probably a by-product of smelting, but its arrival in the street is a mystery; 23 September 1984.

TONMAWR   Couple saw big grey and black striped cat with

bulldog-like muzzle which crossed road ahead of them; November 1981; sightings of cats by researcher Di Francis, and photographs were taken by her and Tonmawr resident Steve Joyce (see Ch.11).

Gwent

COEDKERNEW Poltergeist outbreak – objects and furniture moved, tricks played such as throwing butter at policeman; 1904 (see Ch.25).

EBBW VALE 73-year-old Henry Thomas burned to death at home, a possible victim of spontaneous human combustion; 6 January 1980 (see Ch.21).

BETWEEN PENHOW AND CAERWENT 5,000 empty baked bean tins without labels found along five miles of the A48 on three occasions early in 1985, origin unknown.

Gwynedd

ANGLESEY Winged cat living on farm; 1985 (see Ch.24).

BALA LAKE/LLYN TEGID Man driving past lake saw bright light flash over his car, leaving grey powder behind; 4 October 1974 (see Ch.7). Several reports made of strange animals in the lake, including one in October 1979 (see Ch.19).

BANGOR AND ANGLESEY Tremendous mystery bang shook property; 25 February 1976.

BARMOUTH Lifeboatmen on shore saw what they thought was an aeroplane fall into the sea; they searched the area but found

nothing, and no plane was missing; 9 September 1922. Six schoolgirls saw a 10-ft monster on the beach walking towards the sea; 2 March 1975 (see Ch.13).

NEAR CAPEL CURIG Travellers in car saw small UFO in mountain pass; 5 August 1967.

GELLILYDAN Raccoon spotted in farmyard by farmer's wife and caught by RSPCA officer; 24 October 1983 (see Ch.9).

ROMAN STEPS, NEAR HARLECH Redfern Thomas and his son saw a young girl who spoke in Welsh and then disappeared; *c*.1928 (see Ch.4).

TY CROES, ANGLESEY Boy in wood with aunt saw black dog which passed through fence and disappeared; 1976 or 1977.

WEST COAST BETWEEN BARMOUTH AND HARLECH Strange lights seen during religious revival, especially associated with preacher Mary Jones; 1905 (see Ch.2).

SOMEWHERE IN GWYNEDD Live frog found in solid rock in slate mine; *c*.1929 (see Ch.3).

Powys

ASTON DINGLE (on Powys/ Shropshire county boundary) Black dog haunts this spot, seen by Mr Williams in 1955.

CHURCHSTOKE District nurse saw a lynx; 29 September 1980 (see Ch.11).

CWMBELAN Grey cat-like animal seen moving in leaps and bounds across fields; paw prints identified as dog's; 25 November 1980 (see Ch.11).

NEAR FORDEN Black cat-like

animal seen; it spat at witness from a tree; police tracker dog drew a blank; 3 October 1983.

LLANGURIG   Farmer thought he had a big cat in his barn, but if so, it escaped, leaving only one enigmatic footprint; 23 October 1980 (see Ch.11).

NEAR LLANIDLOES   Female ghost stepped into the path of teacher's car; other witnesses had seen her in earlier years at the same spot near Red Bridge; May 1973 (see Ch.4).

MARTEG, NEAR RHAYADER   Lorry-driver saw UFO belching orange and red flame; November 1976.

SCOTLAND

Borders Region

COLDSTREAM   Couple in car followed brightly lit oblong 'box-car' which flew just above centre of road, before suddenly disappearing; early February 1977.

EARLSTON   Two sightings of big cat which growled like a lion; July 1983.

NEAR ST BOSWELLS   Tall man in black who faded away seen in road on several occasions, including 7 May 1892, late July 1892, 12 June 1893 (see Ch.4).

NEAR SWINTON   Tall, black, hooded figure appeared in front of car at night, and vanished when struck; 29 November 1977.

WATHERSTON HILL, NEAR STOW   Woman saw phantom lorry travelling across countryside; 1956 (see Ch.12).

Central Region

DUNBLANE   Man heard phantom army, possibly Roman, marching past; autumn 1974.

FALKIRK   Mrs Thomas Cochrane burned to death in her chair, a possible victim of spontaneous human combustion; 16 December 1904 (see Ch.21).

SAUCHIE   Poltergeist outbreak centred on young girl – movement of furniture, knockings, pinches; late November 1960–March 1961 (see Ch.25).

STIRLING   Block of ice weighing *c.*110 lb. found in field by shepherd after thunderstorm with hailstones; August 1897.

Dumfries and Galloway Region

NEAR CASTLE DOUGLAS   William MacJannett, cycling home late at night, saw phantom tinker encampment, with horse-drawn caravans and tinkers talking round a fire; next morning he found no trace of the camp at the site; 1945.

GRETNA GREEN   Lorry-driver saw couple crossing road arm-in-arm in front of his lorry, but when he stopped the accident 'victims' had vanished; October 1957.

NEAR NEWTON STEWART   Two workmen heard phantom carpet-sweeper and saw ghost of woman who vanished and then reappeared upstairs in a mansion on the Cairnsmore estate; November 1956.

PENPONT   Fall of oak leaves covering an area of one by two

323

miles, in an area lacking clumps of oaks; October 1889 or 1890.

SOMEWHERE IN
KIRKCUDBRIGHTSHIRE
Fireball seen running along electrical wire and then blasting a big oak tree to pieces; 9 July 1947.

Fife Region

CRAIL Ball lightning exploded by café and caused damage; August 1966 (see Ch.10).

ST ANDREWS Couple saw ghostly veiled woman in grey by the Abbey Tower; she vanished as they watched; 1975.

WEST WEMYSS Fishermen saw a sea monster; other sightings in the Firth of Forth; early July 1939 (see Ch.13).

Grampian Region

ABERDEEN 'Old soldier' found dead of burning, a possible victim of spontaneous human combustion; 19 February 1888 (see Ch.21). Children saw hundreds of soldiers, possibly ghosts, on a hilltop; August 1936.

OFF ABERDEENSHIRE COAST Fishermen found dead elephant floating in the North Sea 32 miles offshore; early April 1982.

BEN AVON, NEAR BRAEMAR Man found dead in strange circumstances on south face of mountain; 19 September 1938 (see Ch.6).

BEN MACDHUI Since the nineteenth century several people have heard the footsteps or seen the tall figure of 'the Big Grey Man of Ben MacDhui' (see Ch.22).

BRAEMAR Flat pieces of ice fell from clear sky with sun shining and thunder audible; 2 July 1908.

NEAR DALLAS Black cat as big as a dog shot by a gamekeeper as it approached pheasants. The body was frozen so that it could be examined and identified; 14 October 1985. There have been many sightings of big cats in this area, and another was shot in 1983 (see Ch.11).

NEAR LOSSIEMOUTH Cedric Allingham claimed to have met and spoken with a UFO occupant; 18 February 1954 (see Ch.14).

Highland Region

ADVIE Big black cat shot; early May 1985 (see Moray cat-killings in Ch.11).

LOCH ALSH Doctor and his wife saw a long-necked monster in a sea-loch, the neck as tall as the boat mast; September 1893 (see Ch.13).

ARDGAY Single parakeets caught in farmyard in 1895 and 1897.

BEN NEVIS 'Star' seen at night travelling slowly along the bottom of the glen; it hummed like an electricity generator and the policeman witness thought it was a manned vehicle, but not a recognizable plane or helicopter; 13 October 1974.

BRAHAN ROCK, DINGWALL Strange breathing noises heard at night around the cliff, over a long period of time (see Ch.23).

LOCH BRITTLE, ISLE OF SKYE Long-necked sea monster seen,

which submerged vertically; summer 1917 (see Ch.13).

CANNICH After many sightings of big cats in the area, a puma was caught in a trap by farmer Ted Noble; 29 October 1980; experts said it was tame and had lived in captivity. The sightings did not cease, and locals know that there is a breeding colony. Miss Janet Chisholm who lives in an isolated cottage sees them often, including cubs romping with the adults. In winter 1984–5 she reckoned there were twenty (see Ch.11).

DINGWALL AND INVERNESS AREAS Numerous sightings of big cats during 1970s and continuing to the present day.

LOCH DUICH Sea monster seen in sea-loch; summer 1886 (see Ch.13).

LOCH DUNTELCHAIG Large ball of light seen hanging in front of stationary car, then gradually faded away; spring 1949.

LOCH EIL Author 'B.B.' saw a monster – 'a large black shiny object which I can only compare with the blunt, blind head of an enormous worm . . . no face, or nose, no eyes' – which rose 3 ft out of the water and sank back; 17 October, year not known, though pre-1962.

GLENCOE Two men climbing on Bidean-nam-Bfan encountered ball lightning, and one was injured; 15 August 1974 (see Ch.10).

GRANTOWN-ON-SPEY Big black cat shot; mid-September 1984 (see Moray cat-killings in Ch.11).

SOMEWHERE IN INVERNESS-SHIRE Two large, yellow, fierce animals killed by a farmer; a third was

trapped and sent to London Zoo; identified as a lynx; January 1927.

LOCH LINNHE Monster seen in sea-loch, 1940s; another sighting on 21 July 1954 (see Ch.13) and in 1964 and 1967.

LOCH LOCHY Lake monster 30–40 ft long seen by Eric Robinson and nine other witnesses, 15 July 1960; monster with 15–20 ft of a black back visible, seen by Mr and Mrs Sargent, 30 September 1975.

LOCH MORAR Many sightings of a monster in the lake, from the late nineteenth century to the present day; many reports given in detail in E. M. Campbell *The Search for Morag* (see Ch.19).

ISLAND OF MUCK Children saw Little People in green on the shore; they also saw a tiny boat and were given miniature bread loaves to eat; *c*.1912 (see Ch.18). Fisherman saw a mermaid combing her hair; 1947 (see Ch.22).

MUIE Representative of many Scottish sightings of big cats: a company director saw 'a strange cat-like animal' in his headlights on the A839 late at night: 'It was about the size of a Labrador dog, dark in colour but with a distinctive cat's face . . . It was definitely a cat, but the size of a big dog'; early November 1979.

NEAR NAIRN Wild boar run over and killed on forestry road; March 1976 (see Ch.9).

LOCH NESS There have been hundreds of possible sightings of the Loch Ness Monster this century; also a few land sightings and some photographs (see Ch.19).

NEAR LOCH NESS   Dr and Mrs
McEwan and their housekeeper
and her husband experienced
ghostly phenomena, including
the ghost of a former owner of
the house, Ardachie Lodge;
August 1953.

RIVER NESS NEAR INVERNESS   Miss
K. MacDonald saw 'crocodile' 6–8
ft long with short neck and long
toothed jaws; February 1932.

ISLAND OF RHUM   Two old
fishermen saw a sea monster and
were so scared they made for the
shore; its neck was 30 ft long;
early years of this century (see
Ch.13).

SANDWOOD, SUTHERLAND
Alexander Gunn saw a mermaid;
1900 (see Ch.22).

LOCH SCAVAIG, ISLE OF SKYE
Fishermen saw the 20-ft neck or
tail of a sea monster rise out of
the water close to them; early
years of this century (see Ch.13).

LOCH SHIEL, MOIDART   Several
sightings of a monster have
been recorded, including one of
a head and neck and large
hump; summer 1932.

ISLE OF SKYE   Two men camping
in Harta Corrie, Cuillin
Mountains, on two nights saw
many kilted Highlanders,
possibly re-fighting a battle of
1395; November 1956 (see Ch.8).

NEAR SLIGACHAN, ISLE OF SKYE
Several sightings of a phantom car
travelling very fast; earliest
report 1941 (see Ch.12).

ISLAND OF SOAY   Two men
watched a sea monster with
turtle-like features for an hour;
13 September 1959 (see
Ch.13).

WIDESPREAD IN SUTHERLAND
Many big cat sightings, beginning

in 1975; a recent report told of a
3-ft black cat seen by two
policemen on the A9 at
Ardchronie Quarry; March 1985.

TAIN   Poltergeist outbreak in
rectory – footsteps, doors
opening, objects and furniture
moved; spring 1947–1948.

Lothian Region

DUNBAR   Sea monster seen; early
July 1939 (see Ch.13).

EDINBURGH   After a bone was
taken from an Egyptian tomb, the
family were haunted by ghosts
and poltergeists, and suffered
other misfortunes; 1936 (see
Ch.20). Porters in the Royal
Circus Hotel saw ghostly white
lady; October 1973.

LIVINGSTON   Robert Taylor saw
large dome-shaped object in forest
clearing; two spheres rolled
towards him and tore his trousers;
9 November 1979 (see Ch.14).

NORTH BERWICK AREA   Several
sightings of a big black cat during
September 1976 to summer
1977.

PENKAET CASTLE, NEAR
HADDINGTON   Poltergeist
outbreak lasting from 1923 to at
least 1947.

SOMEWHERE IN LOTHIAN REGION
Moving electrified patches of
light passed over witness causing
a weak electric shock; 23 July
1885.

Orkney Islands

ISLAND OF HOY   Lawyer on fishing
holiday saw a monster like a
huge seal or sea-lion with a long
neck; August 1919 (see Ch.13).
Man walking on cliffs in stormy

weather saw small 'wild men' dancing; World War II (see Ch.18). Black dog seen inside cottage by artist Barbara Myatt; 1970.

Strathclyde Region

ARGYLL Several sightings of big cats, around Kilmichael Forest, Knapdale, Lochgilphead, Craignish and Achnamara; 1984 and January 1985.

AYR Several big cat sightings, one witness being an RSPCA inspector who admitted it 'has all the characteristics of the puma family. Without doubt it is the largest cat I have come across . . . his body length is about four feet'; August 1979.

BEINN IME, GLEN CROE University lecturer climbing mountain met old man and talked to him; when he looked back the old man had gone, and there were no footprints in the snow other than his own; date unknown.

BEITH Several drivers saw big cat on road; a taxi had to stop because it was sitting in the road, and driver and passengers watched it in the headlights for five minutes, then they drove carefully round it. 'In doing so my car brushed against it and it growled.' No phantom that! June 1974.

DUNBARTON Ice mass fell on road and smashed; 112 lb. of ice collected; 26 December 1950.

DUNLOP Large black cat seen in hills by walker; February 1985.

FIRTH OF CLYDE Fishermen saw 30-ft sea monster; August 1953 (see Ch.13).

GLASGOW Mysterious disappearance of 19-year-old Alex Cleghorn, who was first-footing with his brothers; 1 January 1966 (see Ch.15). John Fagan miraculously cured of cancer after praying to the martyr John Ogilvie; March 1967 (see Ch.2). David Haggerty saw young man jump off Dalmarnock Road bridge over River Clyde, and then vanish; others have seen the same ghost; July 1972.

HELENSBURGH Man walking his dog saw a 30–40 ft sea monster on the beach and watched as it slithered into the water; February 1962 (see Ch.13).

ISLAND OF IONA Man watched phantom Viking invasion with fourteen longboats at the White Sands; others have seen it too (see Ch.8).

LOCH LOMOND Several people saw a monster with two humps at Duck Bay near Inchmurrin; September 1972.

ISLAND OF LUING Nocturnal light or will-o'-the-wisp was seen to vanish at a bridge which the following morning collapsed, causing the death by drowning of a man riding over it; May 1890 (see Ch.23).

SHUNA ISLAND Two naturalists becalmed off Shuna saw a many-humped sea monster; 30 July 1887 (see Ch.13).

SOUND OF JURA Two witnesses saw through a telescope a sea monster with a cow-like head; early June 1964 (see Ch.13).

WISHAW, NEAR GLASGOW Phosphorescent ash tree gave off enough light to read by; 1908 (see Ch.24).

Tayside Region

BROUGHTY FERRY Fishermen saw 40-ft sea monster with big round head; 3 October 1892 (see Ch.13).

GLENFARG Woman investigating the barking of her dog in the garden saw a large cat with orange eyes perched on the wall; it also had long pointed ears with tufts. It spat and snarled as she grabbed her terrified dog; 9 August 1976.

KILRY, NEAR ALYTH 'Large black cat-like creature' seen twice in snow-covered field; early February 1979.

LETHAM, NEAR BRECHIN Miss E. F. Smith saw the aftermath of the Battle of Nechtanesmere of AD 685, nearly 1,300 years later; 3 January 1950 (see Ch.8).

MONTROSE AIRFIELD Reports of ghostly pilots and aircraft seen by many people since World War I.

EAST OF PERTH Motorists travelling on the A85 at night saw what may have been a sea monster at the roadside; 30 September 1965 (see Ch.13).

Western Isles

LOCH DUVAT, ISLAND OF ERISKAY Man saw a 'water horse' beside the loch which terrified his horses when it screamed; late May or early June 1893 (see Ch.19).

FLANNAN ISLES Three men disappeared from Eilean Mor lighthouse; 15 December 1900 (see Ch.15).

ISLE OF LEWIS 60-ft sea monster like 'a huge hornless bull' seen at Bernera; January 1895 (see Ch.13). Minister saw sea monster with 'great staring eyes, like a bull's', off the Butt of Lewis; 7 February 1895 (see Ch.13). Two young poachers on Barvas moor at night saw ghostly light at turf shelter, but it was dark and empty when they entered. When they left, it became lit up again, but again was dark when they re-entered. A third time the light shone, and they heard ghostly music; 1938.

LOCH URABHAL, ISLE OF LEWIS Two fishermen saw a monster which appeared three times; 27 July 1961.

Bibliography

Abbott, G., *Ghosts of the Tower of London*, William Heinemann, 1980; David & Charles, 1986

Atkins, Meg Elizabeth, *Haunted Warwickshire*, Robert Hale, 1981

Bennett, Sir Ernest, *Apparitions and Haunted Houses: A Survey of Evidence*, Faber & Faber, 1939

Benwell, Gwen, and Arthur Waugh, *Sea Enchantress: The Tale of the Mermaid and Her Kin*, Hutchinson, 1961

Binns, Ronald, *The Loch Ness Mystery Solved*, Open Books Publishing, 1983; Star Books, 1984

Bord, Janet and Colin, *Alien Animals*, Granada Publishing, 1980; rev. edn, Panther Books, 1985

Bowen, Charles (ed.), *The Humanoids*, Neville Spearman, 1969

Brookesmith, Peter (ed.), *The Age of the UFO*, Orbis Publishing, 1985

—— *Ghosts*, Orbis Publishing, 1985

—— *Incredible Phenomena: Bizarre Events that Defy Science*, Orbis Publishing, 1985

—— (introduction by), *Creatures from Elsewhere: Weird Animals that No-one Can Explain*, Orbis Publishing, 1985

Brown, Theo, *Devon Ghosts*, Jarrold Colour Publications, 1982

Butler, Brenda, Jenny Randles and Dot Street, *Sky Crash: A Cosmic Conspiracy*, Neville Spearman, 1984; Granada paperback, 1986

Campbell, Elizabeth Montgomery, with David Solomon, *The Search for Morag*, Tom Stacey, 1972

Campbell, Steuart, *The Loch Ness Monster*, Aquarian Press, 1986

Corliss, William R. (compiler), *Handbook of Unusual Natural Phenomena*, The Sourcebook Project (PO Box 107, Glen Arm, MD 21057, USA), 1977

—— *Incredible Life: A Handbook of Biological Mysteries*, The Sourcebook Project, 1981

—— *Lightning, Auroras, Nocturnal Lights, and Related Luminous Phenomena: A Catalog of Geophysical Anomalies*, The Sourcebook Project, 1982

—— *Earthquakes, Tides, Unidentified Sounds and Related Phenomena: A Catalog of Geophysical Anomalies*, The Sourcebook Project, 1983

—— *Tornados, Dark Days, Anomalous Precipitation, and Related Weather Phenomena: A Catalog of Geophysical Anomalies*, The Sourcebook Project, 1983

—— *Rare Halos, Mirages, Anomalous Rainbows and Related Electromagnetic Phenomena: A Catalog of Geophysical Anomalies*, The Sourcebook Project, 1984

Costello, Peter, *In Search of Lake Monsters*, Garnstone Press, 1974; Panther Books, 1975

Devereux, Paul, *Earth Lights: Towards an Explanation of the UFO Enigma*, Turnstone Press, 1982

Dinsdale, Tim, *The Leviathans*, Routledge & Kegan Paul, 1966; Futura Publications, 1976

—— *Project Water Horse: The True Story of the Monster Quest at Loch Ness*, Routledge & Kegan Paul, 1975

—— *Loch Ness Monster*, Routledge & Kegan Paul, 1961, fourth edn 1982

Evans, Hilary, *The Evidence for UFOs*, Aquarian Press, 1983

—— *Visions, Apparitions, Alien Visitors*, Aquarian Press, 1984

—— (introduction by), *UFOs – Where Do They Come From?: Contemporary Theories on the Origin of the Phenomenon*, Orbis Publishing, 1985

Fairley, John, and Simon Welfare, *Arthur C. Clarke's World of Strange Powers*, Collins, 1984

Forman, Joan, *Haunted East Anglia*, Robert Hale, 1978

—— *The Haunted South*, Robert Hale, 1978

Fort, Charles, *The Book of the Damned* (1919), *New Lands* (1923), *Lo!* (1931), *Wild Talents* (1932), published together as *The Complete Books of Charles Fort*, Dover Publications, 1974

Francis, Di, *Cat Country: The Quest for the British Big Cat*, David & Charles, 1983

Gauld, Alan, and A. D. Cornell, *Poltergeists*, Routledge & Kegan Paul, 1979

Goss, Michael, *Poltergeists – An Annotated Bibliography*, Scarecrow, 1979

—— *The Evidence for Phantom Hitch-Hikers*, Aquarian Press, 1984

Gould, Rupert T., *The Loch Ness Monster and Others*, Geoffrey Bles, 1934; University Books, 1969

Green, Andrew, *Ghosts of Today*, Kaye & Ward, 1980

Green, Celia, and Charles McCreery, *Apparitions*, Hamish Hamilton, 1975

Harrison, Michael, *Fire from Heaven: A Study of Spontaneous Combustion in Human Beings*, Sidgwick & Jackson, 1976; rev. edn, Pan Books, 1977

Heuvelmans, Bernard, *In the Wake of the Sea-Serpents*, Rupert Hart-Davis, 1968

Hole, Christina, *Haunted England*, Batsford, 1940

Holiday, F. W., *The Great Orm of Loch Ness*, Faber & Faber, 1968

—— *The Dragon and the Disc*, Sidgwick & Jackson, 1973

—— and Colin Wilson, *The Goblin Universe*, Llewellyn Publications, 1987

Inglis, Brian, *The Paranormal: An Encyclopedia of Psychic Phenomena*, Granada Publishing, 1985

Ives, George (ed. Paul Sieveking), *Man Bites Man: The Scrapbook of an Edwardian Eccentric*, Jay Landesman, 1980; Penguin Books, 1981

Kingston, Jeremy, *Mysterious Happenings*, Aldus Books, 1979

McClure, Kevin, *The Evidence for Visions of the Virgin Mary*, Aquarian Press, 1983

McEwan, Graham J., *Mystery Animals of Britain and Ireland*, Robert Hale, 1986

MacGregor, Alasdair Alpin, *The Ghost Book: Strange Hauntings in Britain*, Robert Hale, 1955

—— *Phantom Footsteps*, Robert Hale, 1959

MacKenzie, Andrew, *Hauntings and Apparitions*, William Heinemann, 1982; Paladin Books, 1983

Mack, Lorrie (edited by), *The World of the Unexplained: Events and Phenomena that Defy Science*, Orbis Publishing, 1985

Mackal, Roy P., *The Monsters of Loch Ness*, Macdonald & Janes, 1976; Futura Publications, 1976

Michell, John, and Robert J. M. Rickard, *Phenomena: A Book of Wonders*, Thames & Hudson, 1977

—— *Living Wonders: Mysteries and Curiosities of the Animal World*, Thames & Hudson, 1982

Moss, Peter, *Ghosts Over Britain*, Elm Tree Books/Hamish Hamilton, 1977; Sphere Books, 1979

Paul, Philip, *Some Unseen Power: Diary of a Ghost-Hunter*, Robert Hale, 1985

Playfair, Guy Lyon, *This House is Haunted: An Investigation of the Enfield Poltergeist*, Souvenir Press, 1980

—— *The Haunted Pub Guide*, Harrap, 1985

Price, Harry, *Poltergeist Over England*, Country Life, 1945

—— and R. S. Lambert, *The Haunting of Cashen's Gap: A Modern 'Miracle' Investigated*, Methuen, 1936

Randles, Jenny, *UFO Study: A Handbook for Enthusiasts*, Robert Hale, 1981

—— *The Pennine UFO Mystery*, Granada Publishing, 1983

—— *UFO Reality: A Critical Look at the Physical Evidence*, Robert Hale, 1983

—— *Beyond Explanation?*, Robert Hale, 1985

Randles, Jenny, and Peter Warrington, *UFOs: A British Viewpoint*, Robert Hale, 1979

—— *Science and the UFOs*, Basil Blackwell, 1985

Randles, Jenny, and Paul Whetnall, *Alien Contact*, Neville Spearman, 1981

Rickard, Robert, and Richard Kelly, *Photographs of the Unknown*, New English Library, 1980

Rimmer, John, *The Evidence for Alien Abductions*, Aquarian Press, 1984

Rogo, D. Scott, *Miracles: A Parascientific Inquiry into Wondrous Phenomena*, The Dial Press, 1982

St Leger-Gordon, Ruth E., *The Witchcraft and Folklore of Dartmoor*, Robert Hale, 1965; EP Publishing, 1973

Smyth, Frank (introduction by), *Great Hauntings: The World's Most Fascinating and Best-Documented Phantoms*, Orbis Publishing, 1985

Story, Ronald D. (ed.), *The Encyclopedia of UFOs*, New English Library, 1980

Thurston, Herbert, *Ghosts and Poltergeists*, Burns Oates & Washbourne, 1953

Underwood, Peter, *A Gazetteer of British Ghosts*, Souvenir Press, 1971; rev. edn, Pan Books, 1973

—— *A Gazetteer of Scottish and Irish Ghosts*, Souvenir Press, 1973

—— *Ghosts in Wales*, Christopher Davies, 1978

—— *This Haunted Isle*, Harrap, 1984; Javelin Books, 1986

Vallee, Jacques, *Passport to Magonia: From Folklore to Flying Saucers*, Henry Regnery Company, 1969; Neville Spearman, 1970 (omitting the long and vital appendix 'A Century of UFO Landings')

Welfare, Simon, and John Fairley, *Arthur C. Clarke's Mysterious World*, Collins, 1980

Whitaker, Terence W., *Lancashire's Ghosts and Legends*, Robert Hale, 1980; Granada paperback, 1982

—— *Yorkshire's Ghosts and Legends*, Granada paperback, 1983

Whyte, Constance, *More Than a Legend: The Story of the Loch Ness Monster*, Hamish Hamilton, 1957

Wilkins, Harold T., *Mysteries: Solved and Unsolved*, Odhams Press, 1959

Wilson, Colin (introduction by), *Westcountry Mysteries*, Bossiney Books, 1985

Witchell, Nicholas, *The Loch Ness Story*, Terence Dalton, 1974; Corgi Books, 1982

Magazines containing items on strange phenomena in Britain

Exploring the Supernatural A monthly magazine which began publication in 1986, covering all strange phenomena. Subscription address: Aceville Ltd, 89 East Hill, Colchester, Essex CO1 2QN.

Fate A long-standing monthly magazine now into its thirty-eighth volume, covering mysteries around the world, including some British material. Subscription address: 170 Future Way, Marion, Ohio 43302, USA.

Fortean Times The foremost journal of strange phenomena, published quarterly. It began publication in 1973 as *The News*, changing to

Fortean Times at issue 16. Subscription address: 96 Mansfield Road, London NW3 2HX.

The Unexplained   This was a very successful partwork of the early 1980s, published by Orbis who have also published in book form several compilations of articles from the partwork; see under Brookesmith, Evans, Mack and Smyth for several titles relevant to this book.

The Unknown   A monthly magazine which began publication in 1985, covering strange phenomena of all kinds world-wide, but with a bias towards British material. Subscription address: Subscription Department, 'The Unknown', 1 Clarendon Road, Croydon, Surrey, CR0 3SJ.

Organisations in Britain dealing with strange phenomena

Association for the Scientific Study of Anomalous Phenomena (ASSAP)   Established in 1981, ASSAP investigates and studies all types of mysteries, holds meetings and training programmes, and publishes *ASSAP News*. Address: 56 Telemann Square, London SE3 9YS.

British UFO Research Association (BUFORA)   Founded in 1964, BUFORA's chief aim is to encourage and conduct unbiased scientific research into UFOs throughout Britain. They hold lectures and publish *BUFORA Bulletin* and *The Journal of Transient Aerial Phenomena*. Address: 16 Southway, Burgess Hill, Sussex, RH15 9ST.

Notes

See Bibliography for publication details of those books not fully described here.

1. Celestial garbage

1. Corliss, *Tornados*, X35, p.68.
2. Corliss, *Tornados*, X56, p.69
3. *Bedfordshire Times*, 27 July 1979, and correspondence between Mrs McWilliam and *Fortean Times*, noted in *Fortean Times* 35, pp.41–2.
4. Corliss, *Tornados*, X18, p.80.
5. Bristol *Evening Post*, 14 March 1977, noted in *Fortean Times* 26, pp.48–9; Welfare & Fairley, *Arthur C. Clarke's Mysterious World*, pp.35–6.
6. Corliss, *Tornados*, X7, p.63.
7. *Fortean Times* 28, p.16.
8. *Daily Express*, 9 August 1977, quoted in *Fortean Times* 26, p.50.
9. Michell & Rickard, *Living Wonders*, p.88.
10. Michell & Rickard, *Living Wonders*, p.88.
11. *Hartlepool Mail*, 25 June 1980, noted in *Fortean Times* 35, p.43.
12. Investigated by Anthony J. Bell; see his article in *Fortean Times* 20, pp.16–17.
13. London *Evening News*, 9 November 1950, noted in Michell & Rickard, *Phenomena*, p.17.
14. *Evening Echo* (Essex), 19 October 1980, quoted in *Fortean Times* 34, pp.33–4.
15. *Fortean Times* 13, pp.9–10 based on a report by Dr Griffiths in the *Meteorological Magazine*, September 1975, pp.253ff. Also see Welfare & Fairley, *Arthur C. Clarke's Mysterious World*, pp.42–3.
16. p.40.

2. A weeping Madonna and other religious phenomena

1. Quoted in McClure, *The Evidence for Visions of the Virgin Mary*, p.111.
2. Published 1984 by Fowler Wright Books, Leominster, Herefordshire.
3. All described in detail in McClure, *The Evidence for Visions of the Virgin Mary*.
4. Details taken from the Abbey Chronicle for 1880, and quoted in McClure, pp.118–20.
5. *News Chronicle*, 27 February 1933, reprinted in *Lantern* 37, p.9.
6. Full details of this and other

similar cases can be found in Rogo, *Miracles.*

7. All three examples are illustrated in Michell & Rickard, *Phenomena,* pp.20–1.

8. Michell & Rickard, *Phenomena,* p.21.

9. *Earthquest News* 13, p.29.

10. Father Herbert Thurston SJ, *The Physical Phenomena of Mysticism* (Burns Oates & Washbourne, 1952), pp.92–5.

11. Rogo, *Miracles,* pp.267–71.

12. Revd A. T. Fryer, 'Psychological Aspects of the Welsh Revival: 1904–5' in *Proceedings* of the Society for Psychical Research, Part LI, vol. xix, December 1905, pp.148–9; also quoted in Kevin and Sue McClure, *Stars, and Rumours of Stars* (privately published booklet, no date).

13. Paul Devereux, Paul McCartney and Don Robins, 'Earth Lights', *Anomaly* 1, pp.10–18.

3. *Toad (and frog) in the hole*

1. These figures are taken from the records of Bob Skinner, who has made a speciality of research into 'toad in the hole' reports.

2. Michell & Rickard, *Living Wonders,* p.97. This book also contains a comprehensive description of the phenomenon worldwide.

3. *Nature Notes,* the journal of the Selborne Society, vol.xi (1900), quoted in Michell &

Rickard, *Living Wonders,* p.98.

4. Name of newspaper unknown, report reproduced in Ives, *Man Bites Man,* p.69.

5. Both reports from *The Countryside* (2 June 1906), vol.3, no.55, p.51 and (30 June 1906), vol.3, no.59, p.109.

6. Information from Bob Skinner's records.

7. 'Toads and Frogs in Stones', *Nature* (1910) no.83, pp.406–7.

8. A contemporary *News Chronicle* report, quoted in Gerald L. Wood, *Guinness Book of Animal Facts and Feats* (Guinness Superlatives, 1972 edn), pp.206–7.

9. Quoted in F. J. North, D.Cc., FGS, 'Toads in Stone: A Popular Fallacy', *The Welsh Outlook* (March 1929), p.91.

10. *Animals* (April 1972), p.178, reprinted in *Fortean Times* 36, pp.18–19.

11. *New Zealand Herald,* 9 December 1982, reproduced in *UFO Newsclipping Service/ Forteana News* 164, p.18.

12. *Hartlepool Free Press,* 15 April 1865, reported in Paul Screeton, 'The Enigma of Entombed Toads', *Fortean Times* 39, p.36.

13. Michell & Rickard, *Living Wonders,* p.98.

14. Michell & Rickard, *Living Wonders,* pp.98–9.

15. Los Angeles *Times,* 20 June 1954, noted in Michell & Rickard, *Living Wonders,* p.102.

16. *Vaasa,* 17 November 1969, noted in *Fortean Times* 36, p.19.

17. Reported in Michell & Rickard, *Phenomena*, p.71.

4. *Ghostly people*

1. Bennett, *Apparitions and Haunted Houses*, p.273.
2. Atkins, *Haunted Warwickshire*, pp.131–2.
3. Report in *The County Times and Express* (Mid-Wales), 2 June 1973.
4. Report in *The County Times and Express* (Mid-Wales), 14 July 1973.
5. Reported fully by Ivan Bunn in *Lantern*, 35, 36.
6. Green, *Ghosts of Today*, pp.95–6.
7. Green, *Ghosts of Today*, p.36.
8. Whitaker, *Lancashire's Ghosts and Legends*, pp.22–4.
9. Personal correspondence with Redfern Thomas, July 1973.
10. Bennett, *Apparitions and Haunted Houses*, pp.62–73; MacKenzie, *Hauntings and Apparitions*, pp.171–5 (Heinemann edn).
11. Green, *Ghosts of Today*, p.34.
12. Nigel Watson, 'Notes on Lincolnshire Ghost Phenomena', *Fortean Times* 6, p.18.
13. Moss, *Ghosts Over Britain*, pp.104–7.

5. *Phantom black dogs*

1. McGregor, *The Ghost Book*, pp.66–7.
2. McGregor, *The Ghost Book*, pp.162–3.
3. *Eastern Daily Press*, 27 April 1972.
4. Personal correspondence, March 1981.

5. Katharine Briggs, *A Dictionary of Fairies* (Allen Lane, 1976), p.301.
6. Ivan Bunn, 'Black Shuck', *Lantern* 18, p.4.
7. Personal correspondence, February 1983.
8. Personal correspondence, October 1983.
9. Personal correspondence, June 1981.
10. D. A. MacManus, *The Middle Kingdom* (Max Parrish, 1959), pp.67–8.
11. Personal correspondence, January 1983.

6. *Mysterious deaths and injuries*

1. Whitaker, *Lancashire's Ghosts and Legends*, pp.95–6.
2. Published by John Long Ltd, 1968.
3. Three articles by Francis King in *The Unexplained*, issues 131, 132, 133, present the thinking behind some of the suggested identifications, and there are also three recent books on the murders: Daniel Farson, *Jack the Ripper* (Michael Joseph, 1972), Stephen Knight, *Jack the Ripper – the final solution* (Panther Books, 1981), Donald Rumbelow, *The Complete Jack the Ripper* (Star, 1981).
4. *Cambridge Daily News*, 16 March 1901, reported in Fort, *The Complete Books*, p.916.
5. *Sunday Express*, 8 June 1975, noted in *Fortean Times* 13, p.17.
6. Fenton Bresler, 'How did

Peter meet his death so far from home?', *Sunday Express*, 7 April 1985.

7. Jenny Randles, 'Death of a Famous Name', *The Unexplained* 151, pp.3010–13, and 'Shock, Horror, UFO Drama', *The Unexplained* 153, pp.3058–60; also see Randles, *The Pennine UFO Mystery*, pp.15–20, 22–6.

8. *Sunday Post*, 18 July 1976, noted in *Fortean Times* 21, p.12.

9. *Sunday Express*, 3 July 1977; on 10 March 1978 the police confirmed to Paul Pinn that they had not identified the corpse – see 'Fortean Follow-ups', *Fortean Times* 40, p.38.

10. Paul Begg, 'Out of Thin Air', *The Unexplained* 72, p.1421.

11. North Devon *Journal-Herald*, 22 April 1982, noted in *Fortean Times* 39, p.24.

12. A 1907 press report from Ives, *Man Bites Man*, p.132. A similar tale reported a few years earlier (*c*.1904) concerning the misidentification of the corpse of lighterman John Gobbett of Greenwich (Greater London), and other similar cases elsewhere in the world, make us wonder if this might not be an 'urban legend' . . . but maybe not. The Gobbett case was reported in *Letter from London c*.1904, reprinted in *Farnham Herald*, 6 July 1984, and noted in *Fortean Times* 45, p.6.

13. *Daily Express*, 8 September 1954, noted in *Fortean Times* 13, p.15.

14. *Lloyds Daily News*, 30 April 1911, reported in Fort, *The Complete Books*, pp.858–9.

15. Tony Green, 'Witness Burned by a Passing UFO', *Flying Saucer Review*, vol.26, no.5, p.32.

16. Robert Boyd, 'Burned by a UFO's Laser Beam?', *Flying Saucer Review*, vol.28, no.3, pp.15–19.

7. *Unidentified flying objects*

1. Nigel Watson, 'The British Scareship Invasion', *The Unexplained* 96, pp.1910–13, and 'Who Sent the Scareships?', *The Unexplained* 97, pp.1938–40.

2. 'The Aldeburgh Platform', *Flying Saucer Review*, vol.15, no.1, pp.23–4.

3. Jenny Randles, 'Bell-like UFO from W.W.2', *The Probe Report*, vol.3, no.4.

4. Ron Sargeant and Jenny Randles, 'Aircraft in Encounters over Bolton', *Flying Saucer Review*, vol.26, no.1, pp.19–21.

5. Randles & Warrington, *UFOs: A British Viewpoint*, pp.108–10.

6. Martin Keatman, 'Down on a Staffordshire Farm', *Flying Saucer Review*, vol.24, no.3, p.29.

7. Martin Keatman and Stephen Banks, 'More Children and UFOs', *Flying Saucer Review*, vol.26, no.4, p.19.

8. Jenny Randles, 'The Saltfleet Encounter', *Northern UFO News*, 113, pp.10–11.

9. Terry Cox, 'Green Mist UFOs

at Newmill', *Flying Saucer Review,* vol.24, no.1, pp.28–30.

10. Randles & Warrington, *UFOs: A British Viewpoint,* p.118.

11. Charles Bowen, 'Two Electrifying Experiences', *The Unexplained,* 45, pp.898–9.

12. *Liverpool Echo,* 11 October 1974, noted in *Fortean Times* 9, p.10.

13. Eric Morris, 'Two UFO Sightings', *BUFORA Bulletin* 18, pp.9–10.

14. Jenny Randles, 'The Case of the Silent Vulcan', *Northern UFO News* 101, pp.14–15.

8. *Phantom soldiers, armies and battles*

1. Atkins, *Haunted Warwickshire,* pp.73–6.

2. MacGregor, *Phantom Footsteps,* p.93.

3. Joan Forman, 'Old Soldiers Never Die', *The Unexplained* 68, p.1341.

4. MacGregor, *Phantom Footsteps,* pp.99–104.

5. Hole, *Haunted England,* pp.74–5.

6. Underwood, *A Gazetteer of Scottish and Irish Ghosts,* pp.122–3.

7. James F. McHarg, 'A Vision of the Aftermath of the Battle of Nechtanesmere AD 685', *Journal* of the Society for Psychical Research, vol.49, no.778, pp.938–48, reported at length in MacKenzie, *Hauntings and Apparitions,* pp.161–9.

8. 'York Man Saw Ghost Story Come to Life Before His Eyes', *Palm Beach Post-Times* (Florida, USA), 24 April 1977.

9. Moss, *Ghosts Over Britain,* pp.80–2.

10. Green, *Ghosts of Today,* p.45.

11. Joan Forman, 'Ghosts on the March', *The Unexplained* 70, pp.1390–1.

12. Bennett, *Apparitions and Haunted Houses,* pp.284–7.

13. Green, *Ghosts of Today,* p.176.

14. Michell & Rickard, *Phenomena,* pp.94–5.

15. Michell & Rickard, *Phenomena,* pp.66–7; MacGregor, *Phantom Footsteps,* pp.105–6.

16. This summary of the report comes from *Fortean Times* 28, pp.14–15, with the permission of the editor.

9. *Out-of-place animals roaming the countryside*

1. *Shropshire Star,* 3 October 1984.

2. The last two examples taken from Peter Roberts, 'Aliens Among Us', *Fortean Times* 19, pp.18–20.

3. Michell & Rickard, *Living Wonders,* p.59.

4. *Sunday Express,* 25 November 1984, noted in *Fortean Times* 43, p.13.

5. London *Evening Standard,* 20 April 1978, noted in *Fortean Times* 28, p.50.

6. *Daily Mail,* 4 August 1975, noted in *Fortean Times* 19, p.10.

7. An article by Rosemarie Wittman in the *Sunday Times*, 22 July 1973, reprinted in *Fortean Times* 8, p.17.
8. *Sunday Mirror*, 21 November 1976, noted in *Fortean Times* 19, p.11.
9. *The Cambrian News*, 28 October 1983.
10. *Sunday Express*, 30 October 1983.
11. *Aldershot (Midweek) News*, 8 August, 15 August, 18 August, 8 September 1972, noted in *Fortean Times* 19, p.9, and Michell & Rickard, *Living Wonders*, p.58.
12. *Daily Telegraph*, 16 March 1976, noted in Michell & Rickard, *Living Wonders*, p.58.
13. Michell & Rickard, *Living Wonders*, p.59.
14. *Yorkshire Evening Press*, 13, 14, 17 February 1975, noted in *Fortean Times* 9, p.16.
15. *Fortean Times* 37, p.44.
16. *Beds & Bucks Observer*, 11 December 1984.
17. *Fortean Times* 30, p.11.
18. Robert Rickard, 'The Hackney Horror' and 'Headless in Hackney', *Fortean Times* 37, pp.45–6.
19. All crocodilian reports from Michell & Rickard, *Living Wonders*, p.56.
20. *Sunday Express*, 18 May 1980.
21. Quotations from *Farm and Home*, 16 March 1905, noted in Fort, *The Complete Books*, pp.666–7.
22. Reported in Michell & Rickard, *Living Wonders*, pp.55–6.
23. *Sunday Express*, 6 March 1983.

10. *Ball lightning: mysterious exploding spheres*

1. G., 'Thunderbolt', *English Mechanic* 74, p.15 (1901), quoted in Corliss, *Lightning*, GLB4 X2.
2. A.P. Chattock, 'Globular Lightning Discharge', *Nature* 109, p.106 (1922), and 'Ball Lightning', *Meteorological Magazine* 57, p.46 (1922), quoted in Corliss, *Lightning*, GLB6 X1.
3. *Sunday Express*, 22 February 1981.
4. E. Hill, 'Globular Lightning', *Nature* 56, p.293 (1897), quoted in Corliss, *Lightning*, GLB1 X8.
5. Welfare & Fairley, *Arthur C. Clarke's Mysterious World*, pp.207–8.
6. Worthington G. Smith, 'Fireball', *Nature* 49, p.577 (1894), quoted in Corliss, *Lightning*, GLB1 X7.
7. E. Matts, 'A Fire-Ball?', *Weather* 19, p.228 (1964), quoted in Corliss, *Lightning*, GLB14 X2.
8. 'Lightning at Barsham, Suffolk, February 8, 1906', Royal Meteorological Society, *Quarterly Journal* 32, p.170 (1906), quoted in Corliss, *Lightning*, GLB7 X2.
9. Ian Jones, 'Giant Ball Lightning', *Journal of Meteorology* 2, p.271 (1977), quoted in Corliss, *Lightning*, GLB7 X4.
10. Mark Stenhoff, 'Ball Lightning', *Nature* 260, p.596 (1976), and 'Woman Burned by Ball Lightning', *New*

Scientist 70, p.128 (1976), quoted in Corliss, *Lightning*, GLB10 X9.

11. *Sunday Express*, 18 August 1974, noted in *Fortean Times* 7, p.15.

12. Michael W. Rowe, 'Another Unusual Ball Lightning Incident', *Journal of Meteorology* 9, p.135 (1984), noted in *Science Frontiers* 36, p.3.

13. *English Mechanic* 79, p.453 (1904), quoted in Corliss, *Lightning*, GLB9 X3.

14. G., S.E.L., 'Fireball', *Symons's Meteorological Magazine* 41, p.191 (1906), quoted in Corliss, *Lightning*, GLB11 X2.

15. Report and quotation from Arthur Shuttlewood, *The Warminster Mystery* (Neville Spearman, 1967), pp.59–61.

16. Bournemouth *Evening Echo*, 22 October 1969, noted in *Fortean Times* 9, p.14.

17. *BUFORA Bulletin* 18, p.9.

18. *Northern UFO News* 112, p.11.

11. *Alien big cats or an unknown native species?*

1. Francis, *Cat Country*, pp.20–4; Bob Rickard, 'Scottish Puma – Saga or Farce?', *Fortean Times* 34, pp.24–5; *The Scotsman*, 7 February 1985.

2. Extract from a letter from Mike Williams to Janet and Colin Bord dated 4 December 1980.

3. *Stockport Advertiser*, 4 September 1980, noted in *Northern Earth Mysteries* 9.

4. These events were widely reported in the press, including the local papers *County Times & Express* and *Shropshire Star*.

5. *Gloucestershire Echo*, 4 December, and Bristol *Evening Post*, 10 December 1980, noted in *Fortean Times* 34, p.22.

6. *Shropshire Star*, 17 March 1981, and Birmingham *Evening Mail*, 20 March 1981.

7. *Luton Herald*, 11, 18, 25 June 1981.

8. Francis, *Cat Country*, p.85.

9. *Shropshire Star*, 15 June; *County Times & Express* (Mid-Wales), 16 June 1981.

10. Francis, *Cat Country*, p.85.

11. *Sunday Express*, 8 November 1981.

12. Bord, *Alien Animals*, p.65.

13. *Evening Echo*, 1 June 1982, noted in *Earthquest News* 5, p.7.

14. *Dunstable Evening Post*, 15 July 1982.

15. Andy Collins, 'The Fobbing Puma and Other Essex Felines', *Earthquest News* 5, pp.2–5.

16. Brighton *Evening Argus*, 24 December 1982, noted in *Fortean Times* 40, p.52.

17. Francis, *Cat Country*, p.114.

18. A fuller report on the Moray cats was published in *Fortean Times* 45, pp.10–12.

12. *Ghostly houses and vehicles*

1. The first-hand accounts are quoted in full in Bennett, *Apparitions and Haunted*

Houses, pp.363–6; see also G.W. Lambert, 'Phantom Scenery', *Journal* of the Society for Psychical Research, vol.42, no.721, p.346, and 'The Phantom House of Bradfield', *Lantern* 24, pp.2–3.

2. G.W. Lambert, 'Phantom Scenery', *Journal* of the Society for Psychical Research, vol.42, no.721, pp.346–7.
3. Hole, *Haunted England*, pp.57–8.
4. Brown, *Devon Ghosts*, pp.124–6.
5. St Leger-Gordon, *The Witchcraft and Folklore of Dartmoor*, pp.100–1.
6. *Journal* of the Society for Psychical Research, vol.34, p.74.
7. 1969 press report reproduced in Michell & Rickard, *Phenomena*, p.51.
8. *Halesworth Times & Southwold Mercury*, 6 February 1976, noted in *Lantern* 13, pp.8–9.
9. *Sunday Express*, 1 April 1979.
10. Bennett, *Apparitions and Haunted Houses*, pp.366–8.
11. *Western Morning News*, 2 January 1971, noted in Brown, *Devon Ghosts*, p.94.
12. Green, *Ghosts of Today*, p.111.
13. 1934 press report in Ives, *Man Bites Man*, p.101; see also Frank Smyth, 'Ghosts without souls?', *The Unexplained* 28, p.550.
14. Atkins, *Haunted Warwickshire*, pp.136–9.
15. MacGregor, *Phantom Footsteps*, p.116.
16. Underwood, *A Gazetteer of*

Scottish and Irish Ghosts, pp.173–4.
17. Brown, *Devon Ghosts*, p.95; Green, *Ghosts of Today*, p.24.
18. *Daily Mirror*, 22 October 1976, noted in *Fortean Times* 24, p.14.
19. Frank Smyth, 'Ghosts of the air', *The Unexplained* 125, p.2500.

13. *Morgawr and other sea monsters*

1. Heuvelmans, *In the Wake of the Sea-Serpents*, pp.337–8.
2. All information from Heuvelmans, *In the Wake of the Sea-Serpents*.
3. Fuller report in our *Alien Animals*, pp.32–4 (hardback edn).
4. *Fortean Times* 11, p.22, quoting a report in *Nature*, vol.27 (1883).
5. Dinsdale, *The Leviathans*, pp.181–3.
6. Heuvelmans, p.495.
7. *Scottish Daily Mail*, 3 February 1962, noted in Dinsdale, *The Leviathans*, p.167.
8. Heuvelmans, pp.529–31.
9. Heuvelmans, pp.290–2.
10. Dinsdale, *The Leviathans*, p.233.
11. Dinsdale, *The Leviathans*, p.69.
12. Quoted in Heuvelmans, pp.340–1; Dinsdale, *The Leviathans*, pp.236–7; Gould, *The Loch Ness Monster*, pp.217–18.
13. Heuvelmans, p.580.
14. Heuvelmans, p.371.
15. Heuvelmans, pp.400, 371.
16. Heuvelmans, pp.497–502;

Dinsdale, *The Leviathans*, pp.73–4.

17. Heuvelmans, p.362.
18. Heuvelmans, pp.402–4.
19. Heuvelmans, pp.336–7.
20. F.W. Holiday, 'The Monster of the A85', *Flying Saucer Review*, vol.19, no.2, pp.24–5.
21. Heuvelmans, p.460.
22. Report in *Daily Telegraph*, 1 March 1934, quoted in Heuvelmans, p.456.
23. Heuvelmans, pp.407–8.
24. Heuvelmans, p.459.
25. Heuvelmans, p.495.
26. Heuvelmans, p.458.
27. Heuvelmans, p.536.
28. Heuvelmans, p.435.
29. Dinsdale, *The Leviathans*, pp.106–8.
30. Heuvelmans, p.457.
31. Heuvelmans, p.388.
32. Heuvelmans, pp.435–6.
33. Heuvelmans, p.458; Ives, *Man Bites Man*, p.71.
34. Heuvelmans, pp.408, 495.
35. Heuvelmans, p.388.
36. Heuvelmans, p.358.
37. Wilkins, *Mysteries: Solved and Unsolved*, p.199.
38. From A. Mawnan-Peller, *Morgawr*, noted in *Fortean Times* 19, p.14.
39. *Falmouth Packet*, 5 March 1976.
40. *Falmouth Packet*, 26 July 1985.

14. *UFO close encounters: landings, entities and abductions*

1. Randles, *The Pennine UFO Mystery*, pp.58–60.
2. Steuart Campbell, 'Close Encounter at Livingston', BUFORA Case History No. 1,

British UFO Research Association, 1982.
3. Gavin Gibbons, *The Coming of the Space Ships* (Neville Spearman, 1956), pp.64–75.
4. Jenny Randles and Paul Whetnall, 'Four Young Men and a UFO', *Flying Saucer Review*, vol.26, no.3, pp.5–7.
5. David Rees, ' "Floating" Entity at Reddish', *Flying Saucer Review*, vol.25, no.2, pp.29–31.
6. Jenny Randles and Philip Barnet, 'Humanoids Encountered in 1901?', *Flying Saucer Review*, vol.24, no.5, pp.28–9.
7. Letter to UFO researcher Lucius Farish, reprinted in *UFO Newsclipping Service* 140, p.12.
8. Robert Chapman, *Unidentified Flying Objects* (Arthur Barker, 1969; Mayflower paperback, 1970), p.117 (paperback edn).
9. Bowen, *The Humanoids*, pp.17–18.

15. *Mysterious disappearances – and sometimes reappearances*

1. J.-O. Bovin *et al.*, 'Imaging of Atomic Clouds Outside the Surfaces of Gold Crystals by Electron Microscopy', *Nature* 317, p.47 (1985), noted in *Science Frontiers* 42, p.4.
2. Kingston, *Mysterious Happenings*, pp.53–7.
3. Press cutting reproduced in Ives, *Man Bites Man*, p.133.
4. *Scottish Daily Press*, 27 December 1971, noted in

Michell & Rickard, *Phenomena*, p.99.

5. 'Vanishing Children', *Fortean Times* 9, p.6.

6. Jillian Powell, 'Genette Tate', in Wilson, *Westcountry Mysteries*, pp.34–47. See also two books by Genette's father, John Tate: *Genette is Missing* (1982) and *Genette, Where is She Now?* (1985).

7. *Sunday Express*, 29 May 1984, and letter to the authors from Merseyside Police dated 21 November 1984.

8. *Cambrian Daily Leader*, 7 July 1887, noted in Fort, *The Complete Books*, p.694.

9. Quoted in Michell & Rickard, *Phenomena*, p.102.

10. Quoted in *Fortean Times* 9, p.8.

11. 'A hitch in time', *The Unexplained* 70.

12. Harold T. Wilkins, *Strange Mysteries of Time and Space* (1958), noted in Michell & Rickard, *Phenomena*, p.107.

13. *Daily Mail*, 28 May 1906, noted in Fort, *The Complete Books*, pp.915–16.

14. *The Countryman*, vol.81, no.2, pp.175–6.

15. *Morgan Sports Car Club Magazine* (August 1977), noted in Michell & Rickard, *Living Wonders*, pp.100–1.

16. *Sunday Express*, 5 February 1984, and letter from Derek Steedman to the authors dated 17 November 1984.

16. *Phantom hitch-hikers*

1. All described in Jan Harold Brunvand's book *The Vanishing Hitchhiker: American Urban Legends and Their Meanings* (W. W. Norton, 1981).

2. Michael Goss interviewed Roy Fulton, and full details are given in Chapter 5 of his book *The Evidence for Phantom Hitch-Hikers*.

3. Goss, pp.83–6; Moss, *Ghosts Over Britain*, pp.147–8.

4. Goss, pp.111–14, and see the whole of Chapter 6 for discussion of the ghosts of Blue Bell Hill.

17. *Mysterious images*

1. MacGregor, *Phantom Footsteps*, pp.170–1.

2. Hole, *Haunted England*, pp.67–8.

3. pp.54–5.

4. *Meteorological Magazine* 58, p.166 (1923), quoted in Corliss, *Handbook of Unusual Natural Phenomena*, p.101.

5. Thames & Hudson, 1979.

6. Rogo, *Miracles*, p.125; see also Michell & Rickard, *Phenomena*, pp.58–9 for this and other examples.

7. Rogo, *Miracles*, pp.123–5.

8. The photograph is reproduced in Michell, *Simulacra*, p.92.

18. *The Little People*

1. Ralph Whitlock, *The Folklore of Devon* (Batsford, 1977), pp.33–4, quoting the account from *The Transactions* of the Devonshire Association.

2. Jerome Clark & Loren Coleman, *The Unidentified* (Warner Paperback Library, 1975), p.25.

3. *Folklore, Myths and Legends*

of Britain (Reader's Digest Association, 1973), p.121.

4. Ernest W. Marwick, *The Folklore of Orkney and Shetland* (Batsford, 1975), p.38.

5. Compiled from press reports and the report in *Fortean Times* 31, p.42.

6. Letters from Mrs Marina Fry dated 9 and 20 February 1973.

7. Gordon Creighton, 'A Weird Case from the Past', *Flying Saucer Review*, vol.16, no.4, p.30.

8. Witness's name and address on file; details from private correspondence drawn to our attention by Joan Amos.

9. Alasdair Alpin MacGregor, *The Peat-Fire Flame* (The Ettrick Press, 1937), pp.26–8.

10. R. H. B. Winder, 'The Little Blue Man on Studham Common', *Flying Saucer Review*, vol.13, no.4, pp.3–4.

11. Clark & Coleman, *The Unidentified*, pp.24–5.

19. *The Loch Ness Monster and other lake creatures*

1. Campbell, *The Search for Morag*, p.135.

2. *Sunday Express*, 14 October 1979; *Shropshire Star*, 17 October 1979.

3. An account of the netting attempt is given in Holiday, *The Dragon and the Disc*.

4. Mackal, *The Monsters of Loch Ness*, p.240, observation no.109.

5. Mackal, observation no.200.

6. Dinsdale, *The Leviathans*, pp.65–6.

7. Mackal, p.262.

8. F. W. Holiday, 'The Monster of the A85', *Flying Saucer Review*, vol.19, no.2, p.25.

9. Letter to F. W. Holiday dated 16 December 1936, reproduced in Dinsdale, *The Leviathans*, pp.66–7.

10. Based on Roy Mackal's impressions given in *The Monsters of Loch Ness*, pp.263, 264.

11. Whyte, *More Than a Legend*, p.74.

12. Whyte, *More Than a Legend*, p.81.

13. Mackal, p.262.

14. Mackal, p.264.

15. Campbell, *The Search for Morag*, p.117.

16. Campbell, *The Search for Morag*, p.136.

17. Campbell & Hall, *Strange Things* (Routledge & Kegan Paul, 1968), p.300.

20. *An assortment of mysteries – including some possible illusions*

1. *Sunday Express*, 18 June 1972.

2. *Sunday Express*, 30 November 1975.

3. *Sunday Express*, 8 August 1976.

4. *Sunday Express*, 19 September 1982.

5. *The News* (Aldershot), 27 July 1984, reproduced in *UFO Newsclipping Service* 181, p.18.

6. Letter in *Fortean Times* 29, p.54.

7. Two good sources of further information are Corliss, *Earthquakes*, section GSH5,

'Unidentified Humming Sounds', pp.178–9, and Steve Wilson, 'Mystery of People Who Hear the Hum', *New Scientist*, 13 December 1979.

8. 'Natural Explosion Phenomena', *Scientific American* 113, p.3 (1915), quoted in Corliss, *Earthquakes* X2, p.144.

9. William Porter, 'Rumblings from Arthur's Table', *Fortean Times* 5, pp.10–13.

10. Letters in *The Unexplained* 18, 36.

11. Ian Mrzyglod, 'As round as saucers', *The Unexplained* 121, pp.2418–20.

12. Bob Rickard, 'Alien Corn', *Fortean Times* 40, pp.27–30.

13. Full transcription published in *Viewpoint Aquarius* 66.

14. 'Broadcasting Below the Belt', *Studio Sound*, August 1978.

15. *Hello World* (Autumn 1978), p.4, noted in Bob Rickard, 'QE2's Mystery Message', *Fortean Times* 28, pp.13–14.

16. *Sunday People*, 8 October 1978, noted in *Fortean Times* 28, p.15.

17. Jim Miles, 'The British Triangle', *Fate* 358, p.89.

18. Marc Cramer explains how the Indian Rope Trick was performed in his article 'The rise and fall of the rope trick', *The Unexplained* 56, pp.1101–5; see also Harry Price, *Confessions of a Ghost-Hunter* (Putnam, 1936), ch.21.

19. Brown, *Devon Ghosts*, pp.15–17; see also Frank Smyth, 'Third Time Lucky', *The Unexplained* 123, pp.2446–9.

20. Theo Brown, *Tales of a Dartmoor Village*, West Country Folklore No.7 (The Toucan Press, St Peter Port, Guernsey, 1973), pp.26–8; Brown, *Devon Ghosts*, pp.95–9.

21. Underwood, *A Gazetteer of Scottish and Irish Ghosts*, pp.73–8.

22. Brown, *Devon Ghosts*, pp.24–6.

23. Bord, *Alien Animals*, pp.135–7, 141 (hardback edn).

24. Letter in *The Unexplained* 125.

25. Kathleen Wiltshire, *Ghosts and Legends of the Wiltshire Countryside* (1973), noted in Michell & Rickard, *Phenomena*, p.50.

26. Mary Rose Barrington, 'A Slip in Time and Place', *Fate* 427, pp.88–94.

27. 'A Hitch in Time', *The Unexplained* 70, back cover.

21. *Spontaneous human combustion*

1. *British Medical Journal*, 21 April 1888.

2. *Daily News*, 17 December 1904, noted in Fort, *The Complete Books*, p.656.

3. *Louth and North Lincolnshire News*, 28 January 1905, quoted in Fort, *The Complete Books*, pp.663–4.

4. *Hampshire Advertiser*, 4 March 1905, noted in Harrison, *Fire From Heaven*, pp.49–50.

5. Reports in *Blyth News*, noted in Fort, *The Complete Books*, pp.929–30.

6. *Dartford Chronicle*, 7 April 1919, noted in Fort, *The Complete Books*, pp.911–13.
7. Harrison, *Fire From Heaven*, p.76.
8. Harrison, pp.103–5.
9. Harrison, p.102; Bob Rickard, 'Mysteries of the Human Bonfire', *The Unexplained* 5, p.86.
10. *Newcastle Journal*, 7 February 1978, noted in *Fortean Times* 27, p.14.
11. *Reading Chronicle*, 14, 17 November 1978, noted in *Fortean Times* 38, p.33.
12. *Yorkshire Evening Press*, 15 February 1979, noted in *Fortean Times* 35, p.11.
13. *South Wales Argus*, 8 February 1980, noted in *Fortean Times* 35, p.10. John Heymer reported his impressions on BBC 'Newsnight', 13 January 1986, quoted in *Fortean Times* 46, p.8. See also his fuller report in Forum, *New Scientist*, 15 May 1986, pp.70–1.
14. *News of the World*, 16 November 1980, noted in *Fortean Times* 35, pp.11–12.
15. *Huddersfield Examiner*, 5 December 1980, noted in *Fortean Times* 35, p.12.
16. Wolverhampton *Express & Star*, 23 March 1981, noted in *Fortean Times* 38, p.33.
17. *Daily Star*, 4 May 1981, noted in *Fortean Times* 35, p.12.
18. *Western Morning News*, Exeter *Express & Star, Daily Star*, all 27 December 1984.
19. Peter A. Hough and Jenny Randles, 'A Case of Spontaneous Human Confusion', *The Unknown* (December 1985), pp.46–51, and (January 1986), pp.24–29; see also *Fortean Times* 44, pp.21–2.
20. London *Standard*, 31 May 1985; *National Enquirer*, 23 July 1985; noted in *Fortean Times* 46, p.24.
21. *Doctor*, 5 September 1985.
22. Bob Rickard, 'Mysteries of the human bonfire', *The Unexplained* 5, pp.84–7; see also his 'Ashes to Ashes', *The Unexplained* 2, pp.24–7, and 'A strange unnatural fire', *The Unexplained* 3, pp.46–9.

22. *Beings from another world?*

1. Intcat 592 & 593 in *MUFOB New Series* 7, p.8.
2. Wilfrid Daniels, 'A Staffordshire Creature Report', *Flying Saucer Review*, vol.13, no.3, p.19.
3. Investigated by Martin Keatman with Tony Pace and reported in *Northern UFO News* 66, p.6.
4. Investigated by Andy Collins and Martin Keatman and reported in *Northern UFO News* 82, p.6.
5. Investigated by Brian Fishwick and reported in *Northern UFO News* 60, p.6.
6. Investigated by David Clark and reported in *Northern Ufology* 73, p.4.
7. Investigated by Ron Sargeant and reported in *Northern UFO News* 41, pp.4–5.
8. *BUFORA Journal*, vol.8, no.5, p.2.
9. Jenny Randles and Paul Whetnall, 'Entity Encounter

at Risley', *Flying Saucer Review*, vol.24, no.2, pp.16–20; Jenny Randles, 'Aftermath of an Encounter', *Northern UFO News* 109, pp.10–11.

10. Investigated by Stephen Banks and Martin Keatman and reported in *Northern UFO News* 82, pp.5–6.

11. 'Sandown Spaceman or Golf-links Ghost?', *BUFORA Journal*, vol.6, no.5, pp.10–12.

12. Gay Mosley, 'UFOs: Local History – and the "Kingdom of the Elves" ', *BUFORA Journal*, vol.5, no.2, p.12.

13. Intcat 892 in *Magonia* 1, p.9.

14. *Caterham Times*, 2 August 1963, noted in *Flying Saucer Review*, vol.9, no.5, p.20.

15. *Northern UFO News* 43, p.5.

16. *Quest*, vol.3, no.2, p.13.

17. Both cases from Affleck Gray, *The Big Grey Man of Ben MacDhui* (Impulse Books, Aberdeen, 1970).

18. Aquarian Press, 1984.

19. *Sunday Telegraph*, 14 May 1961.

20. Frank Earp, 'Of Boggarts and Things', *Northern Earth Mysteries* 11, pp.7–11.

21. BBC-TV 'Nationwide' interview, 20 February 1976, reported in *Fortean Times* 15, p.5; see also Paul Screeton, 'Curse of the Hexham Heads', *The Unexplained* 117, pp.2326–9, and *Tales of the Hexham Heads* (Outlaw Press, 5 Egton Drive, Seaton Carew, Hartlepool, Cleveland, TS25 2AT).

22. Alexander Carmichael, *Carmina Gadelica* (1900), reported in Benwell & Waugh, *Sea Enchantress*, p.117.

23. Both cases from Benwell & Waugh, p.261.

23. *Mysteries above and below*

1. *Journal of Meteorology* 6, p.46; *Birmingham Evening Mail*, 10 December 1980, noted in *Fortean Times* 34, p.34.

2. See also 'Giant Hailstones' in Corliss, *Tornados*, section GWP5.

3. J. P. Maclear, 'Snow from a Cloudless Sky', *Symons's Monthly Meteorological Magazine* 30, p.27 (1895), quoted in Corliss, *Tornados* X10, p.86.

4. S. E. Ashmore in *Meteorological Magazine* 70, p.116 (1935), quoted in Corliss, *Handbook of Unusual Natural Phenomena*, pp.287–8.

5. J. S. Dines in *Meteorological Magazine* 70, p.16 (1935), quoted in Corliss, *Handbook*, p.287.

6. S. E. Ashmore, 'Precipitation with a Clear Sky', *Meteorological Magazine* 84, p.156 (1955), quoted in Corliss, *Tornados* X16, X17, p.86.

7. Samuel Jones, 'Rain from a Cloudless Sky ("Serein") at Stevenage, July 22nd, 1888', Royal Meteorological Society, *Quarterly Journal* 15, p.123 (1889), quoted in Corliss, *Tornados* X8, p.86.

8. Corliss, *Tornados*, section GWP1.

9. See Corliss, *Tornados*, section GWD; the Wimbledon case was X45 on p.33, from Stanley Single, 'The Remarkable Darkness of April 15th', *Symons's Monthly Meteorological Magazine* 39, p.69 (1904).

10. J. H. Cumming, *Meteorological Magazine* 71, pp.189–90 (1936), quoted in Corliss, *Handbook*, pp.33–4.

11. Corliss, *Lightning*, see p.53, 'False Dawn'.

12. H. Percy Horton, 'Mirage on the Cornish Coast', Royal Meteorological Society, *Quarterly Journal* 41, p.71 (1915), quoted in Corliss, *Rare Halos* X4, p.156.

13. S. Szczyrbac, 'May-day Mirage', *Weather* 4, p.234 (1949), quoted in Corliss, *Rare Halos* X3, p.150.

14. 'Mock-Suns close to the Sun and Lateral Mirage', *Weather* 22, p.260 (1967), noted in Corliss, *Rare Halos* X1, p.78.

15. 'Curious Noise – Earthquake?', *English Mechanic* 45, p.372 (1887), quoted in Corliss, *Earthquakes* X3, p.164.

16. Letter from Judith Eagle in *Country Life*, 9 May 1974, noted in Corliss, *Earthquakes* X3, pp.177–8.

17. *Sunday Express*, 8 July 1984, noted in *Fortean Times* 43, p.22.

18. Underwood, *A Gazetteer of Scottish and Irish Ghosts*, p.62.

19. Colin Pounder, 'Speculations on Natural Explosions at Old Hannah's Cave, Staffordshire, England', National Speleological Society *Bulletin* 44, pp.11–14, reproduced in *Pursuit*, vol.15, no.4, pp.157–60.

20. L. de Sibour, 'The Existence of Luminous Birds', *Knowledge* 10, pp.321–2 (1913), quoted in Corliss, *Incredible Life*, pp.349–52. There is also a good account of the evidence for luminous owls in David Clarke & Granville Oldroyd, *Spooklights* (1985), pp.10–18.

21. A. A. Mills, 'Will-o'-the-wisp', *Chemistry in Britain* 16, pp.69–72.

22. H. T. Dixon, 'Flames from Mud on a Sea-Shore', *Nature* 66, p.151 (1902), quoted in Corliss, *Lightning* X36, p.172.

23. *Birmingham Gazette*, 20 February 1923, reproduced in full in David Clarke & Granville Oldroyd, *Spooklights* (1985), pp.29–31; this publication gives a very full account of the lights in the Burton Dassett hills.

24. MacGregor, *The Ghost Book*, pp.208–9.

25. MacGregor, *The Ghost Book*, pp.218–19.

26. Hilary Evans, 'BOLs', *Probe Report*, vol.3, no.1, pp.6–18; Hilary Evans, 'Seeing the Lights', *Fate* 427, pp.82–7, and 428, pp.87–92. The quotation is from issue 427, p.82.

24. *Mysteries of nature*

1. *Fortean Times* 1, pp.7–8.

2. Michell & Rickard, *Living Wonders*, p.119.

3. *Fortean Times* 1, p.3.
4. Press report reproduced in Ives, *Man Bites Man*, p.39.
5. Michell & Rickard, *Living Wonders*, p.119.
6. Michell & Rickard, *Living Wonders*, p.120.
7. *Manchester Evening News*, 23 December 1975.
8. For some further examples from other parts of the world, see 'Cats with Wings' in Michell & Rickard, *Living Wonders*, pp.118–20.
9. Ives, *Man Bites Man*, p.66.
10. Ives, *Man Bites Man*, p.66.
11. 'The Legend of the Rain Tree', *Scientific American* 105, p.244 (1911), quoted in Corliss, *Incredible Life*, pp.805–6.
12. *Sunday Express*, 28 April 1974, noted in *Fortean Times* 35, p.38.
13. 'Gas in the Cavities of Trees', *Scientific American* 109, p.207 (1913), quoted in Corliss, *Incredible Life*, pp.784–5.
14. *Sunday Express*, 7 October 1979, noted in *Fortean Times* 43, p.42.
15. Press reports noted in Fort, *The Complete Books*, p.596.
16. *Daily Mail*, 6 October 1921, noted in Fort, *The Complete Books*, pp.594–5.
17. *Sunday Express*, 4 May 1975, noted in Michell & Rickard, *Phenomena*, p.87.
18. pp.121–4.
19. Press reports summarised in *Fortean Times* 40, p.13, and *Pursuit*, vol.16, no.3, p.134.
20. *Sunday Express*, 23 December 1984.
21. *Sunday Express*, 30 December 1984.
22. *Sunday Express*, 31 March 1985.
23. Letter in *The Guardian*, 4 May 1985.
24. *Sunday Express*, 21 July 1985.
25. *Shropshire Star*, 16 May 1985.
26. *Sunday Express*, 19 May 1985.

25. *Poltergeists*

1. Press report reproduced in Ives, *Man Bites Man*, p.97.
2. Gauld & Cornell, *Poltergeists*, p.109.
3. Colin Wilson, 'Black Monk's Reign of Terror', *The Unexplained* 150, pp.2986–9; see also his book *Poltergeist!*
4. Thurston, *Ghosts and Poltergeists*, pp.187–8.
5. Gauld & Cornell, *Poltergeists*, pp.215–16.
6. Colin Wilson, 'Black Monk's Reign of Terror', *The Unexplained* 150, p.2986.
7. Letters from Stan Evans dated 27 November and 10 December 1984.
8. Fort, *The Complete Books*, pp.577–8; Michell & Rickard, *Phenomena*, p.23.
9. Compiled from press reports quoted in *Fortean Times* 12, p.21.
10. *Sunday Express*, 20 February 1977, noted in *Fortean Times* 21, p.4.
11. *Western Morning News*, 22 November 1984, noted in *Fortean Times* 43, p.16.
12. Enid Anthony, 'A Smashing English Poltergeist', *Fate* 411, pp.68–73.
13. pp.312–18.
14. Gauld & Cornell, *Poltergeists*, pp.79–83.
15. Also see Melvin Harris, 'The

Mongoose that Talked' and 'Lost for Words', *The Unexplained* 97, pp.1921–5, and 98, pp.1946–9, from which the quotation is taken.

16. Price, *Poltergeist over England*, pp.204–12.

17. Fort, *The Complete Books*, p.938.

18. Press reports noted in *Fortean Times* 6, p.9.

19. London *Evening Standard*, 20 October 1973, noted in *Fortean Times* 6, p.10.

20. Noted in *Fortean Times* 6, p.9.

21. Illustrated in the plates in Playfair, *This House is Haunted*.

22. *Hartlepool Mail*, 25 June 1980, noted in *Fortean Times* 35, p.43.

23. *Shropshire Star*, 15 December 1981; Fairley & Welfare, *Arthur C. Clarke's World of Strange Powers*, pp.31–2.

24. *Sunday Express*, 3 December 1978, and *The Guardian*, 11 November 1978, noted in *Fortean Times* 28, p.17, under the heading 'Dinner's on the House!'

Index

Index

Index

Index

Index

Index

Index

Index

Mysteries of the universe – revealed

Charles Berlitz		
Without a Trace	£1.50	☐
The Mystery of Atlantis	£1.50	☐
The Bermuda Triangle (illustrated)	£2.50	☐
Doomsday: 1999	£1.50	☐
Henry C Roberts		
The Complete Prophecies of Nostradamus	£2.50	☐
Jenny Randles		
The Pennine UFO Mystery (illustrated)	£1.50	☐
Colin Wilson		
Mysteries	£5.95	☐
Starseekers	£1.95	☐
The Occult	£4.95	☐
Graham Philips and Martin Keatman		
The Green Stone (illustrated)	£2.50	☐
B Butler and others		
Sky Crash: A Cosmic Conspiracy (illustrated)	£2.95	☐

To order direct from the publisher just tick the titles you want
and fill in the order form.   **GF3681**

The best in occult and astrology – now available in Grafton Books

Harrison Ainsworth
Lancashire Witches   £2.50 ☐

Colin Wilson
The Occult   £4.95 ☐
Mysteries   £5.95 ☐
Starseekers   £1.95 ☐

Michael Bentine
The Door Marked Summer   £1.95 ☐

Terence Whitaker
Lancashire's Ghosts and Legends (illustrated)   £1.50 ☐
Yorkshire's Ghosts and Legends (illustrated)   £1.50 ☐

Erica Jong
Witches   £5.95 ☐

Henry C Roberts (Editor and translator)
The Complete Prophecies of Nostradamus   £2.50 ☐

Stearn Robinson and Tom Corbett
The Dreamer's Dictionary   £2.95 ☐

Doris Collins
A Woman of Spirit   £2.50 ☐

Graham Philips and Martin Keatman
The Green Stone (illustrated)   £2.50 ☐

To order direct from the publisher just tick the titles you want
and fill in the order form.   **GOA182**

All these books are available at your local bookshop or newsagent, or can be ordered direct from the publisher.

To order direct from the publishers just tick the titles you want and fill in the form below.

Name _____

Address _____

Send to:
Grafton Cash Sales
PO Box 11, Falmouth, Cornwall TR10 9EN.

Please enclose remittance to the value of the cover price plus:

UK 60p for the first book, 25p for the second book plus 15p per copy for each additional book ordered to a maximum charge of £1.90.

BFPO 60p for the first book, 25p for the second book plus 15p per copy for the next 7 books, thereafter 9p per book.

Overseas including Eire £1.25 for the first book, 75p for second book and 28p for each additional book.